The Long Road to Annapolis

The Long Road to
Annapolis

The Founding of the Naval Academy
and the Emerging American Republic

WILLIAM P. LEEMAN

The University of North Carolina Press   Chapel Hill

Library of Congress Cataloging-in-Publication Data
Leeman, William P.
The long road to Annapolis : the founding of the Naval Academy and the emerging American republic / William P. Leeman.
p. cm.
Includes bibliographical references and index.
ISBN 978-0-8078-3383-4 (cloth : alk. paper)
1. United States Naval Academy—History—19th century. 2. Military education—Social aspects—United States—History—19th century. 3. United States. Navy—Officers—Training of—History—19th century. 4. Political culture—United States—History—19th century. 5. Nationalism—United States—History—19th century. 6. Democracy and education—United States—History—19th century. I. Title.
V415.L1L44 2010
359.0071'173—dc22   2009044822

14 13 12 11 10   5 4 3 2 1

To my parents,

BARBARA E. LEEMAN

and

WILLIAM H. LEEMAN III

CONTENTS

TABLES AND ILLUSTRATIONS

Tables

Illustrations

ACKNOWLEDGMENTS

I have enjoyed a long history with the subject matter of this book and over the years, I have benefited immensely from the encouragement, advice, guidance, and support offered by my family and my professors as well as by various scholars. I am grateful to them all. I first learned about the naval academy debate as an undergraduate while researching and writing about historian George Bancroft's tenure as secretary of the navy under President James K. Polk. The topic continued to fascinate me and eventually became the subject of extensive research during my graduate school years at Boston University. At BU, my adviser, Nina Silber, made numerous contributions to my professional development as a historian and to the study that formed the basis for this book. She has a unique ability to ask exactly the right questions, which enabled me to look at the naval academy debate in new ways. Three other professors—Jill Lepore, Julian Zelizer, and Andrew Bacevich—read an early version of the manuscript and raised insightful questions that challenged me to improve the book's main arguments concerning American nationalism, the politics of the early republic, and military education and professionalism, respectively. William Fowler, of Northeastern University, agreed to read an early draft of the manuscript before he had even met me; his expertise and enthusiasm for early American naval history contributed a great deal to this book and to my development as a historian. I could not have asked for better role models for outstanding scholarship than these five historians.

Four excellent scholars of American naval history provided valuable advice, encouragement, and constructive criticism. Peter Karsten and James C. Bradford read the entire manuscript, offered several helpful suggestions for improvement, and saved me from making a few errors of fact or interpretation. Christopher McKee also read the entire manuscript and offered an in-depth critique of my work, using his unmatched knowledge of the social history of the early American navy to help me improve my book in matters great and small. I benefited from a conversation about naval education and the early history of the U.S. Naval Academy with Craig Symonds, professor of history emeritus, during one of my research trips to Annapolis. Three of my former undergraduate professors also deserve recognition. The late Robert Deasy, my undergraduate adviser, directed my research project on

George Bancroft's tenure as secretary of the navy, which ultimately led to this book. His infectious enthusiasm for history and his genuine kindness influenced the lives of thousands of students over the course of a remarkable fifty-two-year career. James McGovern and Joseph Cammarano have encouraged my scholarly endeavors since I was an undergraduate; each has had a major influence on my development as a historian and a professor. I am also grateful to Steven Kenny, one of my former history teachers, for his encouragement during my graduate school years and beyond.

I was very fortunate to receive generous financial support for this project from the Naval Historical Center, the Boston University Humanities Foundation, and the Boston University Department of History. In the summer of 2004, I was selected to participate in the West Point Summer Seminar in Military History at the U.S. Military Academy. In addition to imparting a great deal about West Point and the military history of the Western world, the seminar provided a generous stipend, much of which I used to cover research expenses.

I thank the staffs of the following libraries and museums for their professionalism and their contributions to this book: the Special Collections and Archives Department, Nimitz Library, U.S. Naval Academy; the Special Collections and Archives Division, U.S. Military Academy Library; the National Archives; the Manuscript Division of the Library of Congress; the Massachusetts Historical Society; the Hagley Museum and Library; the Department of Rare Books and Special Collections, Princeton University Library; the Rare Book, Manuscript, and Special Collections Library, Duke University; the Special Collections Research Center, Earl Gregg Swem Library, College of William and Mary; the Historical Society of Pennsylvania; the Samuel Eliot Morison Memorial Library, USS *Constitution* Museum; the U.S. Naval History and Heritage Command; the U.S. Naval Academy Museum; and the Anne S. K. Brown Military Collection, Brown University Library. The American Memory project at the Library of Congress deserves particular mention for three outstanding online collections that made my research considerably easier: "The George Washington Papers at the Library of Congress, 1741–1799"; "The Thomas Jefferson Papers"; and "A Century of Lawmaking for a New Nation: U.S. Congressional Documents and Debates, 1774–1875."

It has been a pleasure to work with the staff at the University of North Carolina Press. My editor, Charles Grench, has done an excellent job guiding this first-time author through the process of publishing a book. I also thank Katy O'Brien, Tema Larter, and Ron Maner for their enthusiasm, helpfulness, and professionalism, as well as for answering my numerous questions about publishing procedures. Stevie Champion did a superb job copyediting the manuscript.

Finally, I am grateful for the encouragement I have received from my family. My sister, Mary-Jeanne Leeman, provided technical assistance when my computer was less-than-cooperative. My parents, William and Barbara Leeman, sparked my interest in history when I was a young child through family vacations to various historical places and have always supported my decision to make a career out of teaching and writing about history. My mother has earned special recognition for reading every work of history I have ever written, from middle school, high school, college, and graduate school papers through the multiple drafts of this book.

The Long Road to Annapolis

Armed Ambassadors

Modesty was not one of George Bancroft's notable character traits. He possessed the intellectual superiority of a distinguished scholar and the self-assured swagger of an influential politician. In describing his role in creating the United States Naval Academy, Bancroft triumphantly declared: "As to the Naval School at Annapolis, I was its originator. It was my original conception, mine alone, and in every particular carried out by me."[1] Bancroft's proud statement might lead one to assume that the idea of establishing a naval academy in the United States did not surface until 1845, the year Bancroft became President James K. Polk's secretary of the navy. Although Bancroft's legacy as the Naval Academy's founder is secure (the massive midshipmen's dormitory is named in his honor), his assertion is not exactly accurate. The idea for a naval academy was not Bancroft's "original conception." As early as 1777, during the Revolutionary War, Captain John Paul Jones called for the establishment of small academies at American shipyards to educate the officers of the Continental navy. Although the Continental Congress never implemented Jones's recommendation, it began a national debate on the merits and the potential dangers of founding an academy to prepare young men for service as naval officers.

Since its formation in 1845, the U.S. Naval Academy has achieved a high level of prestige as a national military, educational, and cultural institution. Its students are among the best and the brightest the nation has to offer. The Yard, the academy's Annapolis campus, is one of the country's great landmarks, attracting approximately 1.5 million visitors each year. The entertainment industry has promoted an "All-American" image of the school, most recently in Hollywood's portrayal of the struggles of a blue-collar plebe in the 2006 feature film *Annapolis*. The annual Army-Navy football game pitting the Naval Academy's midshipmen against the cadets of the U.S. Military Academy at West Point is one of the classic rivalries in college sports. Naval Academy graduates have served as some of the country's most prominent leaders not only in war but also in government, diplomacy, science, engineering, and business. The academy's alumni include one president of the United States (Jimmy Carter), cabinet secretaries, senators, congressmen, governors, ambassadors, Nobel Prize winners, Medal of Honor recipients, and Rhodes Scholars. Since the Naval Academy opened its doors, instances of misconduct and academic dishonesty by midshipmen have attracted the attention of political leaders, the press, and the public precisely because such incidents do not conform to the institution's distinguished reputation. Historically, the Naval Academy has reflected American society, particularly in the struggles associated with the integration of African Americans and women into the Brigade of Midshipmen.[2] In many ways, the U.S. Naval Academy is a distinctly American institution. Yet, during the nation's formative period, many citizens considered a naval academy to be inherently un-American. A naval academy was unnecessary and, more importantly, they believed it would violate the principles that were supposed to define the new American republic.

Although several historians have studied the evolution of the Naval Academy since its establishment in 1845, none has placed the school's controversial origins within a broader historical framework.[3] This book examines the naval academy debate and the advancement of the American naval profession in the context of the nation's development as a republican society and a world maritime power during the seventy years after the American Revolution. The naval academy debate was, in essence, a debate about the character of the American republic and the role of the United States in international affairs. There was a direct connection between emerging American nationalism in the early republic and the naval officer corps. Nationalism is a kind of national consciousness—the ideals, attitudes, aspirations, prejudices, and fears of a people. It is an ideological and emotional process through which people perceive their nation and its principles. In the late eighteenth and early nineteenth centuries, Americans were in the process of forming their new nation by debating the political, economic, and social principles that would define the republic. The growth of the American nation depended on the U.S. Navy. The naval officers of the early republic were "armed ambassadors" who represented and defended the United States and its citizens on the high seas and in foreign lands. The professional and personal improvement of naval officers, as America's most visible citizens, became an important national issue since other nations would judge the United States and its republican character based on the merits of the naval officer corps.[4] By studying the idea of a naval academy and the debate it generated in the context of emerging American nationalism, this book aims to provide a more complete understanding of the evolution of the American naval profession as it relates to the political, social, and intellectual development of the early republic.

Nationalism is subjective and relative, not absolute; it often involves the people of one nation defining themselves against the people of other nations. In the first decades of the American republic, the nation against which citizens most often defined themselves was Great Britain. The purpose of the American Revolution had been twofold: first, to free the American colonies from British political control and, second, to separate America from the imperialism, militarism, and moral corruption that characterized Britain and, in a broader sense, all of Europe. The United States, in contrast to the Old World, would dedicate itself to sustaining a republic of liberty and virtue. That required not only the creation of a republican form of government, but also the formation of a republican social order that could support the virtuous citizenry necessary to preserve the republic. Common devotion to the principles of representative government and individual liberty did not mean that all Americans viewed their nation in the same way. Citizens could take pride in their revolutionary heritage without agreeing on the Revolution's political and social legacy. Different conceptions of the American nation and its principles provided the basis for conflicts over policy issues such as public finance, national security, foreign relations, commerce, federal authority, states' rights, executive power, education, and westward expansion. Differences of opinion concerning the nation's development and its republican character ultimately led to the rise of political parties, each with its own vision for America's future.[5]

National security was one of the most controversial issues in the early republic. Debates concerning the structure and organization of the defense establishment were, at their most basic level, disagreements about the country's national character. Would the United States remain a simple agrarian republic defended by amateur militia soldiers and part-time sailors, or would it become an industrial and commercial empire like Britain and employ a professional army and navy to defend its territory and its interests abroad? Studying a society's attitudes toward military institutions can yield unique insight into its social and cultural values since every military organization is a product of the society that creates it. Historically, American attitudes toward the military have appeared contradictory. This was especially true during the early national period. On the one hand, Americans seemed to celebrate all things military. They referred to their fellow citizens by military titles usually gained through membership in a local militia company. They elected former generals like George Washington, Andrew Jackson, and William Henry Harrison to the presidency. They took great pride in battlefield victories such as Saratoga, Yorktown, and New Orleans. American works of history, literature, and art often emphasized the military aspects of the young nation's history. Pride in the country's military accomplishments and its military heroes became the central component of American patriotism. As David Curtis Skaggs has pointed out, the military was "one of the few citadels of nationalistic patriotism" at a time when state and sectional loyalties often overshadowed allegiance to the nation. The connection between patriotism and the military was only natural in a country that had gained its independence during a war and revered a general as its greatest citizen. The United States was, in Marcus Cunliffe's words, "a nation fashioned on the battlefield no less than in the council chamber." At the same time, Americans were deeply suspicious of military professionals, a consequence of their negative experience with the highly trained British army and navy during the colonial and revolutionary periods. A professional and aristocratic military officer corps was one of the hallmarks of the European monarchies and seemed un-American. Although U.S. political leaders reluctantly accepted, in the early national period, the necessity of maintaining a permanent army and navy, they took steps to ensure that the country's military institutions never grew to be as extensive or as powerful as those in Europe, which, in the minds of most Americans, bred political corruption, moral degeneracy, and social class distinctions.[6]

For early national Americans, the best way to prevent the rise of a powerful, European-style military establishment was to rely on the militia. The citizen soldier—the reluctant warrior who left his family and his livelihood to defend his country—became an almost mythical ideal in the United States. The minutemen of Lexington and Concord and the frontier riflemen of New Orleans demonstrated that Americans were natural warriors who did not need special military education or training. As Alexis de Tocqueville has observed, "No kind of greatness is more pleasing to the imagination of a democratic people than military greatness, a greatness of vivid and sudden luster, obtained without toil, by nothing but the risk of life."[7] Willingness to defend one's nation was one of the requirements of citizenship in a republic. If a nation had virtuous citizens, it did not need a large, professional military. "What do we want with such a navy as Great Britain has?" asked Pennsylvania congressman Joseph Fornance. "It would cost hundreds of millions to build it and keep it in repair, murder and plunder to sustain it, and millions every year to man and equip it. What do we want with such an army as France and Russia have? It, too, would cost millions to support it, and might be used by some popular and aspiring chieftain to promote his own ambitious designs."[8] The military establishments of Europe wielded great power because of their foundation in the nobility and their close relationship with the monarch. If the American experiment in republicanism was to succeed, the nation could not allow the creation of a military aristocracy.

Although the need for an informed citizenry has been a fundamental tenet of the American republic since its inception, this educational ideal did not apply to the military. Most Americans believed that military education was unnecessary given Americans' natural military prowess. Military education would also represent a direct threat to the stability and survival of the republic by creating an elite military aristocracy that inevitably involved the country in wars or, even worse, launched a military coup against the civil government. European military academies confirmed the potential dangers associated with such institutions. By the late eighteenth century, Prussia, Russia, France, Britain, and the Netherlands all operated academies that imparted technical knowledge of military science and usually had close ties to the nobility and the monarchy. Kings took a special interest in their military academies and the development of military officers because maintaining and expanding royal power depended on the effectiveness of the crown's military might.[9] Having just overthrown the rule of King George III, Americans were understandably wary of establishing institutions that, in Europe, served the interests of the monarchy and the aristocracy.

During the early national period, then, Americans preferred to depend on citizen soldiers who served in local militia companies while pursuing a civilian occupation and on citizen sailors who alternated between the merchant marine and the navy. The minimal military education and training an officer needed could be acquired through an informal apprenticeship: drilling with a militia company; serving with an army unit in the field or, for naval officers, on a ship at sea; observing superior officers; discussing military or naval affairs with fellow officers; and reading books on military and naval history, strategy and tactics, and discipline and organization. With the establishment of West Point in 1802, the U.S. Army began the transition to an institutional form of military education that employed an academic approach to officer development.[10] It would take another forty-three years for the U.S. Navy to make that same transition.

The commercial and territorial expansion of the republic and the spirit of nationalism that pervaded American society after the War of 1812 ultimately called for a naval academy. The late eighteenth and early nineteenth centuries represented the formative period in the maturation of the United States. James Fenimore Cooper, in his popular history of the American navy, compared this stage in the country's development to the physical and mental growth of a human being: "As in a single life, man passes through the several stages of his physical and moral existence, from infancy to age, so will the American of the present generation, witness the advance of his country, from the feebleness, doubts and caution of a state of conscious weakness, to the healthfulness and vigour of strength." Postrevolutionary Americans had a naive and uncertain conception of their new nation. Although the revolutionary generation had devised a set of political and social principles, it was the responsibility of future generations to transform these abstract principles into a workable government and social order. America's military forces, as defenders of the republic and its citizens, were crucial to the process of national development. Several threats to America's security, both foreign and domestic, during the early national period suggested that the United States would be a short-lived experiment in republicanism. Shays's Rebellion and the danger of internal disorder, the threat to American commerce posed by the Barbary corsairs, the Quasi-War with France, and the War of 1812 all put the new nation's survival at risk.[11]

During the uncertainty of the late eighteenth and early nineteenth centuries, the United States required naval officers who could defend the republic and its commerce. Because of the slow nature of communications, these officers had a great deal of discretion in carrying out their mission to protect the United States and its interests abroad. With the country's actual survival at stake, the navy required enterprising officers who were expert seamen and tenacious warriors. The on-the-job method of educating midshipmen on board ships at sea, derived from the British system of officer development, instilled discipline, obedience, initiative, professional knowledge, and leadership skills. According to the common wisdom of the time, classroom studies on shore could not produce skilled combat leaders. The navy needed to expose midshipmen to the harsh, unforgiving, and dangerous nature of life at sea as soon as possible. In addition to developing its own midshipmen, the early U.S. Navy recruited seasoned mariners from the merchant marine to serve as officers, though this practice essentially ended with the close of the Quasi-War in 1800. The vast majority of commanding officers who served in the War of 1812 had begun their naval careers as midshipmen.[12] Judging by the navy's impressive performance in the Quasi-War, the Barbary Wars, and the War of 1812, the initial system of officer development, which was entirely practical in nature, was effective and produced the country's earliest naval heroes. Furthermore, educating midshipmen informally on board ships at sea conformed to the predominant attitude of Americans at the time, particularly the fear of a standing military establishment and the idea that the United States should remain a simple agrarian republic with a minimal naval force. National political leaders believed that this was the best way to ensure that America avoided the imperialism, militarism, and aristocracy of Europe.

Despite the navy's early success, however, events after the War of 1812 indicated the need for a different system of education, one that would better prepare future naval officers for their noncombat responsibilities. As the nation developed in the first half of the nineteenth century, both as a society and as a participant in world affairs, the navy's role changed and altered the country's predominant attitude toward the officer corps. In a sense, the United States and its navy outgrew the traditional educational methods used since the late eighteenth century. As American interests spread to new areas of the world, the navy took on an important role in U.S. economic development by expanding commerce through scientific exploration and diplomacy. In this new role, naval officers had to do more than just fight battles. To keep pace with the European maritime powers, the U.S. Navy reluctantly made advancements in steam power. Commanding a ship at sea gradually became less of an art and more of a science. The expanded responsibilities of naval officers and the specific expertise needed to carry them out led to the development of a professional identity that was distinct from the merchant marine and suggested the need for an academic background in the sciences, steam engineering, international law, and modern languages. Led by a group of progressive, reform-minded officers, the naval officer corps sought greater professionalism through education.

With its political independence secure after the War of 1812, America could turn its full attention to national progress—defined broadly as republican government, economic prosperity, territorial expansion, scientific advancement, and moral improvement. The concept of progress was nothing new; it had been part of the national character since the Revolution. But not every American interpreted progress or improvement in the same way. Different concepts of national progress, often rooted in social class, formed the basis for political partisanship and influenced policy debates, including the naval academy debate. The navy's expanded role in national life took place in the context of the gradual emergence, beginning in the 1830s and 1840s, of the American middle class. The middle class, which produced the majority of U.S. naval officers, had a profound impact on the burgeoning naval reform movement by spreading a culture of intellectual, professional, and moral improvement throughout American society. This middle-class reform culture stressed the importance of formal education as a means of self-improvement and character development; it also encouraged the pursuit of leisure activities that were morally uplifting. Reformers emphasized the creation of "crucibles of character"—institutions intended to foster middle-class moral values and to create an environment conducive to the development of good character. The ultimate goal of middle-class reformers was to help people, especially young men, liberate themselves from the burden of immoral behavior.[13] Because a military academy was in many ways the ultimate "crucible of character," the middle class embraced formal military education as an important institution in American society.

American expansion required naval officers who possessed greater knowledge, a higher degree of professionalism, strong moral character, and cultural refinement, all of which suggested the need for an academic course of studies for midshipmen. U.S. naval officers had to be able to compete with their aristocratic British peers professionally and socially if the United States was to secure access to lucrative new markets in Asia, the Pacific, and Latin America. But recognition of the need for a naval academy occurred gradually and inconsistently among naval officers, politicians, and ordinary citizens. Disagreements in Congress about the naval academy issue and about West Point were the principal factors that delayed the establishment of a naval academy. But by the late 1830s and early 1840s, the naval academy movement had gained momentum. Although some traditionalists still opposed the idea, it had become clear to many Americans that educating midshipmen at sea was no longer adequate given that naval officers now wore many hats in the service of their country: those of warrior, diplomat, explorer, and technician. In 1843 the *National Intelligencer* lamented, "We have not the means provided now for making even a decent belles lettres scholar in the Navy." The fact that a prominent national newspaper would criticize the lack of academic attainments among U.S. naval officers demonstrated that the country's image of the ideal naval officer had changed significantly since the period before the War of 1812. Americans felt the need to prove to the rest of the world, particularly Europe, that a republic could turn out virtuous and talented citizens. The success of the United States depended on producing an American "noble man," a gentleman of intelligence, culture, and professional distinction. Achieving this ideal was even more important for naval officers, who sailed all over the world and, other than State Department officials, were the primary representatives of the United States abroad. Other nations would form their opinion of the American republic based on the quality of its naval officers. As the *Army and Navy Chronicle* declared, American naval ships were "emblems of liberty" to the rest of the world. Thus in many ways the officers who sailed under the stars and stripes were symbols of the American republic.[14]

The U.S. Naval Academy was established to produce the model American naval officer—an educated gentleman who possessed strong moral character and a high degree of military professionalism. Although seamanship and navigation skills were still necessary, character development took on greater importance because of the navy's increasingly poor public image in the antebellum period. The infamous *Somers* affair of 1842, in which a midshipman and two crew members were hanged for mutiny on board a navy training ship, was the most public demonstration that the navy needed reform. Even though the traditional education conducted at sea had produced skilled combat leaders who won battles, the system had become obsolete in the decades after the War of 1812, particularly as it related to character development. The nature of their duties meant that naval officers were frequently the public face of the American republic. If the rest of the world was going to respect the United States as a nation of progress, one characterized by commercial wealth, scientific and technological achievements, and moral superiority, American naval officers had to exhibit professional, intellectual, and moral excellence.

A naval academy seemed to be the best way to address the navy's and the country's needs. By the mid-nineteenth century, professional military officers had gained status and respect in the United States mostly because of West Point's influence. As Thomas J. Fleming has observed, "The U.S. Military Academy was an uneasy compromise between young America's suspicion of a standing army and the nation's obvious need for soldiers skilled in the art and science of war." Even in the 1830s and early 1840s, when Jacksonian Democrats subjected the Military Academy to withering criticism, competition for cadet appointments was keen as many young men throughout the country dreamed of wearing the gray uniform of a West Point cadet. Most Americans in the late eighteenth and early nineteenth centuries did not see the need for anything more than basic military training—that is, the acquisition of practical military skills. That attitude began to change with West Point's post–War of 1812 renaissance under superintendent Sylvanus Thayer. Thayer and others argued that military officers required more than just practical training; they needed the intellectual and moral benefits of higher education. Military officers had to acquire knowledge of the arts and sciences and learn how to apply that knowledge to warfare. They had to be soldiers and, to a degree, scholars.[15]

West Point was the educational model for the U.S. Naval Academy and not just in the curriculum's emphasis on scientific and technical subjects. West Point demonstrated that the "military virtues," the character traits military officers must possess, could be developed in a military academy environment. Honor, courage, discipline, professionalism, and patriotism defined military officership in nineteenth-century America just as they still do today.[16] Before the War of 1812, most naval officers and political leaders believed that the best way, really the only way, to develop these character traits was through service at sea. Only a warship could provide the professional and social environment necessary to integrate middle-class young men into the naval culture of that period. But after the War of 1812, an increasing number of Americans, both within and outside the U.S. Navy, gradually realized that midshipmen could more readily develop the requisite qualities if educated in a more controlled learning environment that was both academic and military.

The central question that this study seeks to answer is why it took so long for the United States, a maritime nation, to establish an institution for the education of its naval officers—sixty-eight years after John Paul Jones first recommended one and forty-three years after the founding of West Point to educate army officers. The most important force acting on the naval academy debate was American nationalism or, more specifically, Americans' competing concepts of their nation, often rooted in class identity and expressed through partisan politics. Support for or opposition to a naval academy derived from one's concept of America's character at home and its proper activities abroad. As the United States developed as a republican society and a world maritime power, the ideals and attitudes of its people toward the navy changed; ultimately, the citizenry accepted professional officers who received their preparatory education at a naval academy. The academy's purpose was to create a naval meritocracy that could compete with Britain's naval aristocracy in war, commercial expansion, exploration, and diplomacy. Americans sought to prove to the world that a republic could produce not only virtuous citizens, but also distinguished officers and gentlemen of the highest professional and moral caliber.

The Maddest Idea in the World

Rumor had it that he once flogged a sailor to death on a voyage across the Atlantic. He arrived in America under an assumed identity, a fugitive from justice, after killing a mutinous sailor on the Caribbean island of Tobago. At first glance, John Paul Jones might seem to be an unlikely advocate of naval professionalism. Americans best remember him as the daring sea captain of the Revolutionary War who, according to legend, defiantly shouted "I have not yet begun to fight!" during his famous battle against the HMS *Serapis* in 1779. To his enemy, Jones was little more than a glorified pirate who raided the British coast and brought a distant colonial war to the front doorsteps of British civilians.[1] While John Paul Jones was indeed a swashbuckling naval adventurer, he was also a "complete naval officer." Undeniably a great combat leader, Jones was also a student of the naval science of his time, a self-taught expert on navigation, tactics, and naval architecture.[2]

He was born John Paul Jr., on July 6, 1747, in a small cottage on the grounds of the Arbigland estate in Scotland, where his father was the gardener and his mother was the housekeeper for the lord of the estate. Arbigland was waterfront property, and young John soon became fascinated with the sea and ships. As a boy, he would assemble his friends in small rowboats, form them as a fleet, and bark orders as if he were an admiral waging a naval battle. But the water was not merely a source of wonder and recreation; Jones looked to the sea as a means of improving his station in life. He often dreamed of becoming an officer in the Royal Navy, but his family's lack of political connections made that impossible. Jones had to settle for the next best thing, and, at the age of thirteen, he left home to become an apprentice seaman on a merchant ship sailing out of the port of Whitehaven, England. Years later, during America's war for independence, Captain Jones would raid that same port.[3]

After spending four years learning seamanship, navigation, and ship-handling, Jones worked briefly in the slave trade. The stench, filth, and inhumanity of the slave ships were unpleasant enough to make him return to the merchant marine. At the age of twenty-one, Jones became master of a merchant ship involved in the West Indies trade. Within the merchant marine community he quickly became known as a "dandy skipper" because of his gentlemanly appearance. He displayed refined manners, dressed neatly, read the classics of literature, and wrote well. Jones's constant goal was self-improvement, and he felt a maritime career provided excellent opportunities for personal advancement. There was always something new to learn, something new to see, and something more to achieve.[4]

Despite his genteel bearing, Jones was a strict, even brutal, disciplinarian. On a voyage from Britain to Tobago in late 1769 and early 1770, Jones ordered the ship's carpenter flogged for disobedience and incompetence. When the ship arrived at its island destination, the carpenter filed charges against Jones for excessive brutality. A vice-admiralty court dismissed the charges, ruling that the sailor's disobedience and inattention to duty warranted the punishment. The court also believed that the sailor's wounds were superficial. Unfortunately for Jones, the sailor died en route to London on board another ship. The sailor's father blamed Jones for the death, and, on Jones's return to Britain, had him arrested for murder. After making bail, Jones returned to Tobago to retrieve evidence that would exonerate him. He brought back statements from the vice-admiralty court that had acquitted him and from the captain of the ship on which the sailor had died. It turned out that the cause of death was a fever the sailor had contracted at sea. Although this testimony cleared Jones of the murder charge, the rumor that he had flogged a sailor to death continued to circulate within the merchant marine community.[5]

Jones's colorful past also included an incident that he once described to Benjamin Franklin as "the greatest misfortune of my life." This event occurred in 1773 while he was master of the merchant ship *Betsy*. In October of that year, his ship was in port at Tobago in need of repairs. The delay caused by the time in port ruined Jones's cargo of butter. He decided to spend what currency he had in hand on a new cargo for the return voyage to Britain. This left him without enough money to pay his crew an advance on their wages. On returning to the ship, Jones informed the men that they would be paid when the ship arrived in Britain. This news was not well received, and one of the sailors, who had been troublesome on the voyage to Tobago, incited the crew to mutiny. As the insurgents were about to leave the ship, Jones brandished his sword in the hope that they would lose their nerve and back down. The show of force did not work, and the ringleader went after Jones with a club. Just as he was about to strike Jones in the head, Jones ran him through with the sword and killed him. Convinced that a vice-admiralty court would clear him of any wrongdoing in putting down an attempted mutiny, Jones went ashore and turned himself in to the local authorities. He was told there was no vice-admiralty court in session at the time, so he would have to stand trial in a regular court. Because the man he killed was a Tobago native, the locals were unlikely to exonerate Jones. He thus abandoned the *Betsy* and all of his property (except for £50 cash), fled by horseback across the island, and boarded a ship leaving Tobago.[6]

A friend of Jones suggested that he secretly travel to America for a fresh start. The idea was appealing. Ever since visiting Virginia as an apprentice seaman in 1761, Jones had dreamed of earning sufficient funds as a sea captain to return there and enjoy the life of an aristocratic planter. After the Tobago incident, his first step was to change his name, first to "John Jones" and then to "John Paul Jones." He lived in Virginia for a time, but by September 1775, he was in Philadelphia looking for a job. Fortunately for Jones, he ended up in the right place at the right time. Five months earlier the first shots of the American Revolution had been fired on the village green in Lexington, Massachusetts. The maritime character of the American colonies made it inevitable that the Revolutionary War would also be waged at sea. The prospect of taking on the powerful Royal Navy prompted Samuel Chase, a Maryland delegate to the Continental Congress, to argue: "It is the maddest Idea in the World to think of building an American Fleet!" Yet Congress did exactly that on October 13, 1775, when it passed resolutions creating the Continental navy. Through the influence of North Carolina delegate Joseph Hewes, Jones's friend and a member of the Marine Committee of the Continental Congress, Jones received an officer's commission in the fledgling American navy on December 7.[7]

John Adams once described John Paul Jones as "the most ambitious and intriguing Officer in the American Navy. [He] has Art, and Secrecy, and aspires very high." Adams went on to explain that "Excentricities and Irregularities are to be expected from him—they are in his Character, they are visible in his Eyes. His Voice is soft and still and small, his Eye has keenness, and Wildness and Softness in it." Despite his reputation as a fierce warrior, Jones was by no means physically imposing. Only five feet, five inches tall, he had hazel eyes, high cheekbones, and a slender nose. His chestnut hair was always neatly arranged and tied in the back. A sign of the eccentricity Adams alluded to, Jones wore his own variation of the prescribed Continental navy officer's uniform—a dark blue coat with white lapels, gold epaulets, gold buttons, a white waistcoat, white breeches and stockings, and a sword. His uniform resembled that of a Royal Navy captain, and Jones wore it to give himself a sense of "martial equivalency" with the enemy. According to one subordinate, Jones had "a visage fierce and warlike." Yet the piercing look of a born fighter was balanced by "the appearance of great application to study."[8]

Jones was as comfortable sipping tea and chatting in a Paris salon as he was shouting orders on the deck of a ship. He wrote poetry and could discuss the classics with the most learned of polite society. Abigail Adams provided the best description of this side of Jones's personality:

> From the intrepid character he justly supported in the American Navy, I expected to have seen a rough, stout, warlike Roman—instead of that I should sooner think of wrapping him up in cotton wool, and putting him in my pocket, than sending him to contend with cannon-balls. He is small of stature, well proportioned, soft in his speech, easy in his address, polite in his manners, vastly civil, understands all the etiquette of a lady's toilette as perfectly as he does the mast, sails and rigging of his ship. Under all this appearance of softness he is bold, enterprising, ambitious and active.

In Jones's mind, an officer should by definition be a gentleman. Despite the outward appearance of confidence, Jones had an inferiority complex. His humble origins and his previous experience as a merchant mariner rather than a naval officer made him insecure. He tried to compensate with polished manners, social sophistication, and a personality characterized by egotism and vanity. Thirsty for glory and public recognition, he was always striving for more attention, more acclaim, and more respect. He was extremely jealous of his personal honor and had a violent temper.[9]

Jones's personal insecurity was one of the factors that led to his crusade for greater professionalism in the Continental navy. Jones believed education was the key to gentility and professionalism. His own formal studies at the local parish school in Kirkbean, Scotland, had ended at age thirteen when he became an apprentice seaman. However, Jones put a great deal of effort into self-education, mostly by reading the classics. He loved books and pored over them for hours so he could converse with knowledgeable gentlemen. Overall, his endeavors for self-improvement were very successful. Evan Thomas, one of his biographers, states that Jones's letters "are far more literate than those of his contemporary sea captains and not unworthy of the lawyers and merchants who went to Philadelphia as delegates to the Continental Congress." Jones, like all naval captains of his era, was a mentor to the teenage boys preparing for a naval career by serving as midshipmen, a rank that had originated in the Royal Navy. The British first used the term "midshipman" to describe men or boys stationed amidships for the purpose of relaying orders and messages fore and aft. By the late eighteenth century the word had evolved into a rank for apprentice officers in the Royal Navy, and this was how the American navy would use the term. Since learning manners was an important part of every gentleman's education, Jones tutored his midshipmen in etiquette by inviting them to dine with him periodically. He believed it was his duty to make sure that his midshipmen became refined gentlemen during their naval apprenticeship. The midshipmen at Jones's table were required to dress in their finest clothes and to behave accordingly or risk their captain's wrath.[10]

In addition to being a gentleman, a naval officer had to be a competent sailor with expert knowledge of the practical and theoretical aspects of his profession. In Jones's opinion, "a Captain of the Navy ought to be a man of Strong and well connected Sense with a tolerable Education [,] a Gentleman as well as a Seaman both in Theory and Practice, for, want of learning and rude Ungentle Manners are by no means the Characteristick of an Officer." Elaborating on this theme in a letter to the Marine Committee of the Continental Congress, Jones asserted that "none other than a Gentleman, as well as a Seaman both in Theory and in Practise is qualified to support the Character of a Commission Officer in the Navy, nor is any Man fit to command a Ship of War, who is not also capable of communicating his Ideas on Paper in Language that becomes his Rank." To make certain that only educated gentlemen received officer commissions, Jones recommended the establishment of naval academies "at each dockyard, under proper Masters whoe's duty it should be to Instruct the Officers of the Fleet, when in Port in the Principles, and Application of the Mathematicks, drawing, Fencing, and other manly Arts and Accomplishments." Providing such instruction would ensure that the navy was "Officered by Gentlemen and Men of Sense, instead of Men of no Education, with limited Capacities, whom nature never intended for a Rank superior to that of Boatswain."[11]

Although Jones's recommendations would have improved the American navy, the Continental Congress largely ignored them. Near the end of the Revolutionary War, Jones complained that "I have continually Suggested what has occured to me as most likely to promot [the navy's] honor and render it servicable to our Cause; but my Voice has been like a cry in the Desert."[12] Despite the Congress's disinterest in naval affairs, Jones was determined to continue his own professional development. In November 1782 he petitioned the Continental Congress for the opportunity to observe the French navy, which he described as "the best military school in the world." There he would be able to "acquire very important knowledge about conducting large-scale military operations." Congress approved his request in early December, and Jones reported to the *Triomphant*, the flagship of the admiral Marquis de Vaudreuil. From December 1782 to May 1783, Jones sailed with the French fleet in the West Indies and "received much usefull Instruction" by observing the French ships practicing naval tactics, talking with French officers, and reading books on naval warfare. He hoped one day to use the knowledge he gained on the voyage as the commander of an American fleet. Jones returned to the United States with numerous ideas about how to make the American navy more professional and more effective.[13]

Jones articulated many of his ideas for improving the Continental navy in an early draft of a letter to Robert Morris in October 1783. Morris, a wealthy financier, was serving as the Continental government's superintendent of finance and agent of marine (the navy's administrator). "It is the Work of many years study and experience to acquire the high degree of Science, necessary for a great Sea Officer," Jones explained. Instruction was necessary both at sea and on shore. Jones envisioned a fleet of American frigates, each with a school on board to instruct off-duty officers in mathematics and mechanics. These schools afloat would be complemented by naval academies, located at each shipyard, where officers would learn "every Art and Science that is necessary to form the character of a great Sea Officer." Learning by observation was also a key component of Jones's plan for naval education. He suggested sending a frigate to Europe to "display our Flag" in foreign ports and to observe the organization and operations of the European naval powers. "In time of Peace," Jones cautioned, "it is necessary to prepare, and be always prepared for War by Sea." Although he had put a great deal of thought into his recommendations, Jones omitted most of them, including his plan for naval education, from the final draft of his letter to Morris. Jones probably realized that Congress would ignore his suggestions.[14] Given the pitiful state of the Continental navy by 1783, he was undoubtedly correct.

"In looking over the long list of vessels belonging to the United States taken and destroyed, and recollecting the whole history of the rise and progress of our navy," John Adams lamented, "it is very difficult to avoid tears." Commiserating with Jones in 1782, Adams had declared: "Nothing gives me So much Surprise, or so much regret, as the Inattention of our Country men to their Navy."[15] By 1782, only two frigates remained in commission. The rest of the American fleet had been lost at sea, captured or destroyed by the British, or sold by the Continental Congress. Perhaps most illustrative of the decline of the Continental navy was the *America*, Jones's new command and the only ship of the line built for the American navy. In what must have been a devastating blow to Jones's ego and his professional ambitions, Congress presented the *America* to the French government as a gift in recognition of the important role France had played in the winning of

American independence. Congress sold the last Continental navy ship, the frigate *Alliance*, for $26,000 at auction in Philadelphia in August 1785.[16]

John Paul Jones's dream of commanding a great American fleet was dead. He had envisioned the United States becoming a first-rate naval power with a large fleet of ships of the line and frigates cruising the world's oceans, proudly flying the American flag as they protected the new republic's interests abroad. A highly professional corps of officers and gentlemen would lead this great American navy. In Jones's mind, it was his destiny to command the U.S. Navy as its first admiral. Sadly for Jones, others did not share his vision of a powerful fleet that could challenge British supremacy on the high seas. Despite Jones's efforts to educate his adopted country about the necessity of a professional naval force for a newly independent maritime nation, the American people, basking in their revolutionary victory, saw no need for such an expensive, aristocratic, and, worse, autocratic institution. Professional navies were the instruments of kings and queens who ruled colonies around the globe and plundered the shipping of their enemies. The United States was going to be different—an agrarian republic that shunned the trappings of Europe's militaristic empires. Unwilling to wait for his fellow Americans to heed his message, Jones left the United States in search of personal glory and an admiral's uniform.

CHAPTER 1

Defending the New Republic

The United States emerged from the Revolutionary War as a sovereign nation, at least on paper. Independence brought the promise and the expectation of self-determination as well as the reality that America no longer enjoyed the protection of the British Empire on land or at sea. Despite threats to their security on several fronts, the victory over the British had given many Americans a sense of complacency and there was little perception of urgency when it came to military preparedness. Despite the initial apathy, however, the new nation would soon realize that preserving independence required a system of national defense. Because of their traditional suspicion and fear of standing military establishments, the American people had only reluctantly accepted the need for an army and a navy during the war. After achieving independence, one of the crucial issues facing the United States was how to create a peacetime system of national defense that conformed to the republican principles of the American Revolution. In the decades following the Revolution, the American people attempted to forge a distinctive military tradition that would preserve the new republic they had secured through war.

Freedom from British rule did not mean that America was free of war. When Americans looked at the eighteenth-century world in which they lived, it seemed almost inevitable that their country would be involved in another war at some point in the future. The European monarchies, with their standing armies and commercial rivalries, were natural aggressors and frequent combatants. In the minds of U.S. leaders, Europe's wars ultimately led to the degradation of the European people. Monarchs started wars to expand their realms geographically and to secure greater control of international commerce. These wars were fought at great public expense by aristocratic officers leading armies and navies composed largely of the dregs of society. Americans made it their goal to avoid the militarism, corruption, aristocracy, and degradation that characterized Europe by limiting contact with the European powers and by adhering to the revolutionary principles of liberty, virtue, and republicanism. The United States would serve as a model for the rest of Western society by demonstrating the superiority of a republican government, an economy based on free trade and individual enterprise, and a society without hereditary distinctions.[1]

The Military Legacy of the American Revolution

The key to avoiding Europe's fate was to steer clear of one of the great symbols of eighteenth-century Europe—a professional military force. The eighteenth century witnessed the rise of military professionalism in Europe. The leading nations used their vast administrative and financial resources to form and maintain large permanent armies and navies. As the century progressed, military science—especially artillery and military engineering—became more complex and required that officers become educated professionals. European monarchs used their standing armies not only to fight wars with foreign powers but also to maintain law and order at home, put down domestic rebellions, and enforce the payment of taxes within the realm. They operated navies to protect commerce and maintain overseas empires.[2]

Americans looked upon military professionals with suspicion and fear. This mindset had its origins in British history, particularly the radical Whig tradition that emerged in the seventeenth century during the English Civil War and the Glorious Revolution. The American colonists adapted the political and social ideas of the radical Whig writers to their own situation in the late eighteenth century. As an opposition group, the English Whigs saw themselves as the guardians of liberty and warned of the dangers of increased political power in the hands of the king's ministers. According to the Whigs, one of the most dangerous instruments of executive power was the standing army, which represented a direct threat to liberty. Standing armies could violate the individual rights of the people; they were especially perilous if they did not remain under the direct control of civil authority.[3] Americans were very receptive to these warnings. It was, after all, the highly trained British military that had harassed American colonists, violated their rights, and disrupted colonial trade in the years leading up to the Revolutionary War.

Despite the Continental army's prominent role in winning independence, mutual distrust marred the relationship between the officer corps and the civilian population. Many credited the victory not to the army per se but to the revolutionary virtue of the American people as a whole, personified in the ideal of the citizen soldier. To many Americans, the army's officers, with the exception of George Washington, did not conform to revolutionary ideals and seemed more European than American. They were too professionalized and seemed more interested in personal glory, status, and privilege than in personal sacrifice. Americans' worst fears were confirmed in 1783, when a group of Continental army officers formed a veterans organization known as the Society of the Cincinnati. Its members, who included Continental naval officers, wore special badges and passed their membership on to their eldest sons, making the organization hereditary. Many Americans viewed the society as an attempt to create a European-style hereditary aristocracy in America. Benjamin Franklin commented that American officers had been overly impressed with the medals and military decorations worn by foreign officers during the war and wanted their own status symbols.[4] The American Revolution had created an atmosphere in which any kind of artificial social distinction was seen as inappropriate, undemocratic, even dangerous. The Society of the Cincinnati was the epitome of this kind of social distinction. Its purpose seemed to be the creation of an elite social class with special privileges—a military aristocracy—such as existed in Britain, where men of the upper classes often wore military uniforms to distinguish themselves from the rest of society.[5]

There were good reasons for Americans to oppose such an elite. As the British example demonstrated, military aristocrats welcomed war as an adventure, an opportunity for fame and glory, and a chance to put their patriotism on display. Americans also feared a military aristocracy because of the influence it could wield over the civil government. In Britain, large numbers of militia, army, and navy officers served as members of Parliament, giving the legislature a distinctly military character and military aristocrats a great deal of power in government.[6] For Americans in the immediate post-Revolution era, independence did not just mean freedom from British authority; it also meant avoiding the moral and political corruption that characterized Europe in general and Britain in particular. American fear of a standing, professional military establishment was not limited to the threat of military dictatorship. Political corruption resulting from military patronage, military contracts, and frequent wars was a much more likely danger to the republic.[7]

Despite its victory over the British, the United States was by no means secure in 1783. The continued presence of the British, along with the Spanish and the Indians, along the American frontier meant that some form of national defense was necessary. But any such provision had to conform to America's republican principles. An important question facing American leaders was whether liberty and military proficiency were compatible. Many people considered the militia to be the safest guardian of the republic, yet militia troops had been mostly unreliable and ineffective during the war. With the lackluster performance of the militia in mind, some Americans argued for a professional military establishment. Others asserted that maintaining a standing military force in peacetime was incompatible with the principles of the Revolution and would eventually lead to moral and political corruption, which would destroy the republic. For Americans of this persuasion, only the militia could defend the nation without threatening liberty. Virtue and sacrifice motivated citizen soldiers; a desire for glory and privilege drove professional soldiers.[8]

In early April 1783, the Continental Congress appointed a special committee to devise a peacetime plan for the nation's defense. The committee, chaired by Alexander Hamilton, was charged with developing a system that conformed to republican principles. Having served as George Washington's aide-de-camp during much of the Revolutionary War, Hamilton now turned to his mentor for advice on how to form a national military establishment that would "conciliate security with economy and with the principles of our governments."[9] Washington, in turn, asked for the opinions of some of his senior Continental army officers and others—among them, Baron von Steuben (inspector general), Henry Knox (chief of artillery), Timothy Pickering (quartermaster general), and New York governor George Clinton.

The military needs of the United States after the war included defending the frontier and the coast with forts and garrisons, guarding arsenals, maintaining internal order, developing a munitions manufacturing capability, and creating some system of military education. In the opinion of Washington and his advisers, the militia was incapable of performing all of these functions. Part-time soldiers could not be expected to garrison a remote frontier fort, or keep order among their neighbors, or devote the necessary time to the study of military science. Washington and his advisers also knew, however, that a large regular army would be unacceptable to the vast majority of the American people for ideological and financial reasons. Therefore, improving the militia became central to their plan for a peacetime system of national defense. Militia reform, in theory, would ensure greater uniformity in training, equipment, and organization and produce a more effective fighting force. Washington prepared his "Sentiments on a Peace Establishment" and submitted it to Hamilton in early May. The plan called for four elements: a small regular army to garrison frontier forts and guard arsenals, a "well-organized" militia, federal arsenals, and military academies. Washington briefly mentioned the need for a navy but did not elaborate because he felt that naval affairs were beyond his expertise.[10]

Although the military academies were the most controversial component of Washington's plan, the idea was nothing new. By the late eighteenth century, European powers such as Britain, France, and Prussia had established academies to create a loyal, efficient, and professional military force. Military education was particularly important for officers specializing in artillery and engineering, both of which had become much more scientific and complex over the course of the eighteenth century. In Europe, officer candidates received instruction in military science, mathematics, natural sciences, geography, drawing, the classics, and modern languages. During the Revolutionary War, many American officers, including Washington and Knox, had been impressed with the military knowledge and skill of the foreign officers who had studied at European military academies.[11]

Henry Knox had attempted to open a military academy during the war. A self-taught soldier who had been a bookseller in Boston before the Revolution, Knox read numerous books on the military art and discussed military affairs with the British army officers who patronized his shop. Knox's only military experience prior to the war was service as a lieutenant in the Boston Grenadier Corps, a local militia company. Early in the war, Knox complained that many of his fellow officers were "a parcel of ignorant, stupid men, who might make tolerable soldiers, but bad officers."[12] To correct his colleagues' deficiencies, Knox called for the establishment of a military academy modeled after the British academy at Woolwich. In this endeavor, he had a congressional patron in John Adams. In May and June 1776, the two men exchanged correspondence regarding the Continental army's need for books on military science. Their mutual interest in this subject naturally led to a discussion of military education. Knox and Adams agreed that the United States needed institutions "for promoting every art, manufacture, and science, which is necessary for the support of an independent State. We must, for the future, stand upon our own legs, or fall."[13]

In Adams's opinion, a military academy was vital to America's cause because the Continental army "was a scene of Indiscipline, Insubordination, and Confusion." To be effective, officers needed both courage and education. Americans had the courage but were "deficient in reading." In fact, Adams said, he "had read as much on the military Art and much more of the History of War" than most of the American officers. Although Congress appointed a committee to study the issue, it took no further action, and military education during the war was limited to Knox's occasional lectures on artillery and tactics.[14]

When Washington and his advisers considered the advisability of setting up military academies in 1783, there was some disagreement. Timothy Pickering and George Clinton opposed the idea. Pickering wondered how such a school would attract students. Without a large standing army, few young men would be interested in studying the military art as a profession. The small number wishing to do so could attend one of the military academies in Europe. Moreover, Pickering pointed out, the arts and sciences—the foundation of military science—were, or soon would be, available at American colleges. If the Continental government decided that a military academy was necessary, he would favor a small academy for artillerists and engineers, to be attached to the fortifications at West Point, New York. Clinton advocated what was essentially an early form of ROTC. He recommended funding a military professorship at one civilian college in each state. Students would be required to complete a certain number of military science courses and earn their degree in order to receive an officer's commission.[15]

Not surprisingly, Henry Knox and Baron von Steuben supported the establishment of military academies in the United States. For Knox, the nation's very survival was at stake: "Causes of war will happen, and we shall not long retain our existence, without being possessed of the means to exert ourselves to the greatest effect. A perfect knowledge of the principles of war by land and sea is absolutely incumbent on a people, circumstanced as we are and determined to be free and independent." To preserve its independence, Knox argued, the United States should organize separate military and naval academies. For the military branch, he recommended a three-year curriculum emphasizing artillery and engineering. Students would pay tuition, while the government would provide their clothing, room, and board at public expense. Von Steuben, a product of the highly trained and professional Prussian army, agreed that military academies were vital to the security of the United States. He advocated a comprehensive three-year course of study in mathematics, history, geography, law, natural and experimental philosophy (physics), rhetoric, literature, architecture, French, fencing, music, and dancing. Admission would be limited to fourteen- and fifteen-year-old boys who had completed a grammar school education that included arithmetic.[16]

In his plan for a peacetime military establishment, Washington stated that a military academy "would be highly expedient." However, he realized that the financial situation of the United States at the end of the war meant that there were limited resources available for military education. He therefore suggested the halfway measure of offering instruction for young men at a convenient army post. Some provision for schooling in artillery and engineering was absolutely necessary unless, in Washington's words, "we intend to let the Science become extinct, and to depend entirely upon the Foreigners for their friendly aid." His implication was clear: America could never be truly independent if it continued to rely on foreign officers for its defense.[17]

After receiving Washington's plan, Alexander Hamilton drafted one of his own. Hamilton's plan made the regular army, not the militia, the primary defense organization for the United States and gave Congress ultimate control over the administration and operation of all U.S. military forces. It was Hamilton's plan that Congress received in June 1783. Hamilton disagreed with Washington's recommendation concerning military instruction, maintaining that such schooling was not worth the expense and that officers could best learn the military art by serving in the field.[18] A few days after Hamilton submitted his report, a group of disgruntled soldiers marched into Philadelphia to demand back payment from Congress for their service during the war. Faced with a horde of angry soldiers, the lawmakers fled to Princeton, New Jersey. This incident followed the more famous Newburgh conspiracy of March 1783, an aborted attempt by Continental army officers to force Congress to address their grievances. These events reinforced the notion that a regular army in peacetime was dangerous. By January 1784, Congress had reduced the American army to approximately six hundred soldiers whose duties consisted of guarding the federal arsenal in Springfield, Massachusetts, and providing a garrison for the fortifications at West Point.[19]

Any military institutions established in the United States had to conform to its republican character, which meant that a standing army and navy were simply not an option in the minds of many Americans. After all, the country had just fought a long and costly war to rid itself of such organizations. Because of this attitude, America's military capability was practically nonexistent during the Confederation period. The miniscule army suffered from the lack of manpower and financial support. There was no American navy. Many states were concerned only with their own security and did not consider the defense needs of the nation as a whole. A maritime state like Rhode Island was more interested in establishing a naval force to protect itself than in providing frontier defense measures for upstate New York. During the Revolutionary War, the union of the states had remained intact only by the necessity of defeating a common enemy. With peace, however, there was little to keep the states together. The result was an inefficient and highly decentralized government, especially when it came to military affairs.[20]

Perhaps the best indication of America's military weakness was Shays's Rebellion, an uprising of disgruntled farmers in western Massachusetts in 1786. When the local militia was unable to put down the revolt, volunteers financed by Boston-area merchants were sent to restore the peace. The incident demonstrated Congress's inability to maintain order within the United States, to say nothing of its ability to defend the nation against foreign invasion if that were to occur. In George Washington's opinion, Shays's Rebellion proved that something more had to be done to ensure the country's security: "What stronger evidence can be given of the want of energy in our governments than these disorders? If there exists not a power to check them, what security has a man for life, liberty, or property?"[21]

At the Constitutional Convention of 1787, the framers intended to correct the obvious weaknesses of the Confederation government, including national defense. The new Constitution gave Congress the power to declare war, "raise and support Armies," "provide and maintain a Navy," and "make Rules for the Government and Regulation of the land and naval Forces" of the United States; it made the president commander in chief of the army and navy. The new administrative structure placed military authority firmly with the federal government rather than with the states. The states could not maintain armies or warships in peacetime or engage in warfare without the approval of Congress.[22] With the ratification of the Constitution, the United States finally had a theoretical framework for creating a more effective system of national security. It was the responsibility of the first president, George Washington, and his administration to put that theoretical framework into practice.

The Birth of the U.S. Navy

The issue of national defense was a divisive one, with two rival camps taking form during Washington's first term. The first camp, which later became known as the Federalist Party, included many former Continental army officers, most notably Alexander Hamilton (who was serving as secretary of the treasury) and Henry Knox (the secretary of war). This group favored the creation of a professional military establishment to defend against foreign powers and to maintain internal order. Their personal experiences during the Revolutionary War had convinced them that only professional soldiers could safeguard the republic. The second camp, led by Secretary of State Thomas Jefferson and Representative James Madison, ultimately formed the Democratic-Republican Party. With the image of the British military a recent memory, this group argued that a professional military force was a threat to liberty and that the militia, under the control of the state governments, was the only safe means of national defense.[23] In his political writings, Madison declared that those who sought to create a professional military establishment wrongly believed "that government can be carried on only by the pageantry of rank, the influence of money and emoluments, and the terror of military force."[24] The presence of professional soldiers would spawn a propensity for war, which would greatly increase the power of the executive and corrupt the republic. Wars required an army, military contracts, and new government offices, all of which would be under the executive's control.[25] The debate over the type of defense establishment the United States should develop was just one of the issues that fueled the growing spirit of partisanship during Washington's presidency.

Initially, naval affairs were not a priority in Washington's administration. The Indian threat on the frontier meant that the army, by necessity, received more attention. Furthermore, despite the fact that the Constitution had given Congress the power to maintain a navy and made the president its commander in chief, no American naval force existed. Washington himself gave little thought to naval matters. "As our people have a natural genius for Naval affairs and as our Materials for Navigation are ample," he reasoned, "if we give due encouragement to the fisheries and the carrying trade, we shall possess such a nursery of Seamen and such skill in maratime [sic] operations as to enable us to create a Navy almost in a moment." What this first president envisioned for America's maritime defense was essentially a naval militia. In time of war, the government could organize a navy composed of sailors from the merchant and fishing fleets. This view reflected the prevalent attitude among politicians at the time that there was no real difference between the naval and merchant services; they were both part of a single maritime profession.[26] In early 1790 the House of Representatives received a petition from a group of former Continental navy officers requesting the half pay and land bounty given to Continental army officers as compensation for their service during the war. According to Representative Theodore Sedgwick of Massachusetts, the naval officers were not entitled to the same compensation as their army counterparts because they were essentially "continuing in that business to which they had been educated." In contrast, army officers had had to abandon their usual professions to serve in the military and had therefore made the greater sacrifice for their country. Based on this rationale, Congress rejected the naval officers' petition.[27]

Also in early 1790, Secretary of War Knox submitted a plan to Congress for creating a national defense organization that was appropriate for a republic. His plan called for a national militia, a small corps of artillerists and engineers, and a legion of regular army soldiers to comprise a frontier constabulary force and to guard federal arsenals. Knox believed it was necessary "for the great body of the people to possess a competent knowledge of the military art." To accomplish this goal, Knox revived his idea of organizing military academies, which would not only provide military knowledge but also foster patriotism. He also recommended universal military training for able-bodied men between the ages of eighteen and sixty.[28]

Because American seaports and commerce were vital to national interests and needed protection by some kind of naval force, Knox proposed the creation of a register of fit seamen who could be called upon to man armed ships in times of national emergency. The sailors enrolled in this register would be exempt from militia service on land. Although Knox had recommended the establishment of military and naval academies in 1783, he no longer saw the need for a naval academy by 1790. Soldiers required "a degree of discipline, which cannot be learned without much time and labor." Serving on merchant ships "differs but little from the service required on board of armed ships; therefore, the education for war . . . will be obtained [in the merchant service] without any expense to the State." But other policy issues, such as Hamilton's public finance plan, took precedence, and Congress virtually ignored Knox's defense plan. In May 1792, however, the lawmakers did exempt seamen from militia duty on land.[29]

There was a great deal of instability in the Western world during America's formative period. The outbreak of war in Europe in February 1793 forced the United States to take a more active interest in naval affairs. Commerce was the key to U.S. economic development, and free trade with all nations was a basic tenet of the new republic. Given the great demand for American agricultural products in war-torn Europe, the United States traded with both Britain and France, the main combatants. The British and French navies began intercepting all ships bound for the enemy's ports, and U.S. merchant ships soon fell victim to European transgressions at sea. Although many Americans had hoped the Atlantic Ocean would insulate them from European conflicts, the nation's burgeoning commerce quickly became a target for the British and the French. With only two brief periods of temporary peace, war would rage in Europe until 1815. This sustained warfare helped to fuel U.S. economic growth, with exports soaring from $19 million in 1791 to $49 million in 1807. But by interfering with America's maritime commerce, the British and the French challenged its national sovereignty and threatened its economic prosperity. Both European powers were dictating where the United States could and could not engage in commerce, essentially reducing America to colonial status.[30]

Americans also faced a renewed threat from the Barbary States of North Africa, which included Morocco, Algiers, Tunis, and Tripoli. Barbary corsairs attacked any merchant ship flying the flag of a country that did not pay annual subsidies (often referred to at the time as "tribute") to their state. The North Africans believed these attacks were justified for two reasons. First, the Barbary States had formally declared war on any nation that did not pay the subsidies, which made their attacks on enemy shipping legal. And second, the North Africans, who were Muslims, targeted ships operated by Christians, whom they considered infidels. Since handing over the tribute was easier and more cost effective than waging a sustained naval war against the corsairs, Britain and most other European powers paid off the Barbary States. The American colonies had enjoyed the protection provided by the British payments, but after 1783, U.S. ships became fair game for Barbary corsairs in the Mediterranean. Initially, Algiers posed the biggest problem. Its corsairs had been a threat to American shipping since July 1785, when Algiers declared war on the United States and began attacking U.S. merchant ships in the Mediterranean and the Atlantic.[31]

These actions had prompted some politicians, especially John Jay and Thomas Jefferson, to call for the rebirth of the American navy to meet the Barbary threat. Jay and Jefferson argued that it was unbecoming of the United States, as a sovereign nation, to pay subsidies to Algiers or to negotiate a treaty with it. Giving in to seagoing criminals would not only be a national embarrassment; it also would invite further violations of America's rights on the high seas. Congress did not agree that the Barbary threat in the mid-1780s warranted the creation of a navy and instead favored negotiations with Algiers as the best way to halt the attacks. The problem was resolved when Portugal, whose ships had also fallen victim to the corsairs, blockaded Algiers and prevented further raids.[32] The Barbary threat returned in 1793, when Britain negotiated a settlement between Portugal and Algiers. Britain hoped to gain the Portuguese navy's assistance against the French. The end of the blockade set the corsairs loose to attack American ships, which prompted President Washington to recommend that Congress devise a plan for countering this renewed threat. On January 2, 1794, the House of Representatives passed a resolution to form "a naval force, adequate to the protection of the commerce of the United States against the Algerine corsairs."[33]

Although Congress had decided that the country should have a naval force, there was disagreement regarding the type of navy it needed. Navalists were those politicians who believed the navy should be strong enough to ensure some influence abroad, one that would deter aggression and require other nations to respect the sovereignty of the United States. Alexander Hamilton had clearly articulated the navalist argument years earlier during the debate over the Constitution. Even if an American navy did not match the fleets operated by the European naval powers, it could still be a factor when used in conjunction with one of the competing European powers. America could become "the arbiter of Europe," influencing the balance of power according to U.S. interests. Antinavalists argued that the American navy should remain a small, defensive force used only to protect merchant ships and patrol harbors and the coast. They feared that a large, offensive navy would entangle the United States in European affairs and possibly provoke a war. At the root of the debate was a fundamental disagreement over the proper role of the United States in world affairs. Navalists had a more activist vision, looking to Britain and its naval power as a model to emulate. Antinavalists asserted that, to preserve its independence and the liberty of its people, the United States should remain disengaged from world affairs as much as possible. They viewed the British example as something to be avoided at all costs.[34]

On March 7, 1794, a bill to create a navy was introduced in the House of Representatives. The measure, which sparked a heated debate in Congress, authorized the construction of four 44-gun frigates and two 36-gun frigates. Representative William B. Giles of Virginia spoke for many antinavalists when he declared that the bill had a larger purpose than simply protecting American commerce from the Barbary corsairs. He claimed that the proponents of the bill wanted to build the foundation for a permanent naval establishment. In Giles's opinion, the number of ships called for was inadequate to subdue the Barbary corsairs, whose warlike nature, large number of "fighting men," and extensive naval experience would overwhelm a small U.S. fleet. Paying subsidies was a more cost-effective solution to the problem. "A navy is the most expensive of all means of defence, and the tyranny of Governments consists in the expensiveness of their machinery," Giles observed. A navy cost large amounts of money to build, operate, and maintain; moreover, it would require an administrative bureaucracy and higher taxes. The European naval powers were a case in point. According to Giles, it was the expenses of the French navy and the resulting need for higher tax revenue that ultimately led to the French Revolution. As for the British, "The extensiveness of the [British] Government is the true ground of the oppression of the people. The King, the Nobility, the Priesthood, the Army, and, above all, the Navy."[35]

Over the antinavalist objections, Congress passed the naval bill and Washington signed it into law on March 27, 1794. The legislation authorized the construction of the six frigates and listed the number of officers and seamen required to man them. To allay antinavalist fears about a permanent naval establishment, the law provided that the naval act would be nullified in the event that the United States achieved peace with Algiers.[36] The U.S. Navy was born, albeit on a less-than-permanent basis.

One of the six men chosen in 1794 as a captain in the revived American navy was Thomas Truxtun, the only newly appointed officer who had not served in the Continental navy. Orphaned at age ten, Truxtun became an apprentice sailor on a merchant ship when he was twelve years old. He served on privateers during the Revolutionary War and rose to command his own ship. After the war, Truxtun was heavily involved in the China trade and formed a business association with financier Robert Morris.[37] Despite the fact that Truxtun's previous maritime experience was in the merchant service and on privateers, he became an early advocate of naval professionalism. In 1794 he published an instructional manual on navigation and nautical science for young and inexperienced sailors, particularly navy midshipmen. Truxtun believed it was the duty of all midshipmen to master not only practical seamanship, but also scientific subjects such as astronomy, geometry, and mechanics. To fail to carry out this duty was, in Truxtun's words, "a heinous Crime indeed."[38] According to Truxtun, those chosen to serve as officers should be "young men of principle, good education, high sense of honor, manly deportment, prudence, and of respectable connections." Midshipmen should study their profession in detail, be obedient to their superior officers, "act with humanity," and avoid distracting vices like drinking and gambling. It was crucial for the United States to promote the professional development of its naval officers. "The ships cannot manuvre [sic] themselves," Truxtun pointed out to Secretary of War James McHenry, "nor will the best of soldiers answer as substitutes for seamen. . . . If we are to have a Navy, we must make officers to manage that Navy." To give young officers practical experience at sea, Truxtun said, the United States must maintain a navy in peacetime.[39]

Truxtun's vision for a permanent navy seemed to be in danger when the United States reached a settlement with Algiers in September 1795. Although the frigates were under construction, the main reason for their existence was gone. Congress had authorized the creation of a navy specifically to meet the threat posed by Algiers, not to form a permanent fleet. American relations with Britain also improved after the Jay Treaty of 1794. For the time being, then, U.S. shipping was safe. Nevertheless, Washington hoped that work on the frigates would continue. In March 1796 he recommended that Congress allow for the completion of at least some of the frigates despite the clause of the 1794 naval act that called for a halt to the project in the event of peace. Besides his belief that the ships were an important component of national defense, the president feared that ending construction would have negative domestic consequences, including the "dissipation of workmen."[40]

Washington's recommendation revived the congressional debate over U.S. naval policy. Navalists wished that construction be continued on at least half of the frigates. Representative William L. Smith of South Carolina believed all six ships should be completed. Once at sea, the ships would perform an important defense function while also serving "as a kind of Naval Academy, in teaching our youths intended for the sea service naval tactics." Representative Samuel Smith of Maryland pointed out that Congress had already taken steps to protect the agricultural interests of Americans by enlarging the army to defend the frontier. Citizens engaged in maritime pursuits deserved to have their interests protected as well. New York congressman John Williams disagreed. The government should stop construction on the frigates, he argued, since the Revolutionary War had proved that privateers were more effective than a navy. They were also much cheaper. A standing navy would require an administrative apparatus, which would expand the size of the federal government and invite corruption. For Representative Albert Gallatin of Pennsylvania, the navy's financial cost was most disturbing. The cost of completing the ships, outfitting them, manning them, and maintaining them would be astronomical. In the end, in April 1796, Congress compromised: the frigates *Constitution*, *Constellation*, and *United States* would be finished but work on the other three ships (*Congress*, *President*, and *Chesapeake*) would cease.[41]

The Quasi-War

In *The Federalist*, Alexander Hamilton wrote that a country's "rights of neutrality will only be respected when they are defended by an adequate power. A nation, despicable by its weakness, forfeits even the privilege of being neutral."[42] Hamilton's words were prophetic. By the late 1790s, America's relationship with France had severely deteriorated. Since their successful alliance during the Revolutionary War, the Jay Treaty between the United States and Britain, American neutrality in the wars of the French Revolution, and other matters had driven a wedge between the former allies. In 1797 French ships seized over three hundred U.S. merchant ships. The new American president, John Adams, attempted to resolve the situation by sending three envoys to restore diplomatic relations with France and nego-tiate a peace agreement. In the notorious xyz affair, agents of the French government informed the U.S. envoys that their mission would succeed only if the agents received a substantial bribe. The Americans promptly refused these terms. On learning of the incident, the Federalists in Congress were outraged and published documents on the affair. This evidence of French perfidy infuriated the American public, sparked a war fever, and prompted the U.S. government to abrogate its treaties with France, including the Treaty of Alliance from 1778.[43]

In response to the rising tensions with France, the Federalists pushed legislation through Congress to build up the American military. Funds were appropriated for the fitting out of the three vessels finished in 1797, the completion of the frigates *Congress*, *President*, and *Chesapeake*, and the pur-chase of sixteen smaller ships. The lawmakers also authorized U.S. ships to attack French ships in the Caribbean and the Atlantic. Other preparations for war included measures for coastal and harbor defense, the purchase of munitions, and appropriations to build foundries. There were also plans to expand the army from approximately 3,000 to 14,000 men.[44] Although Congress authorized him to increase the size of the army, President Adams believed that a naval buildup was more important—for two reasons. The first was practical: France was attacking American ships at sea. The second reason was Adams's personal preference for the navy. Writing to the Boston Marine Society in 1798, he declared: "Floating Batteries and wooden walls have been my favorite System of warfare and Defence for this Country."[45]

The frigate *United States* was launched in May 1797, and the *Constel-lation* and the *Constitution* soon followed in September and October, re-spectively. By the summer of 1798, the U.S. Navy was prowling the seas in search of French ships. The involvement of the navy in an undeclared war at sea and the growing size of the fleet seemed to indicate the need for a separate department for naval administration; since its establishment in 1794, the navy had been part of the War Department. Another motivation for a separate navy department concerned Secretary of War James McHenry. McHenry, who had served as a surgeon in the Continental army during the Revolutionary War, was a holdover from Washington's cabinet. Although he was popular with his peers, there were questions about his administrative competence. Even his close friend Alexander Hamilton once commented, "My friend, McHenry, is wholly insufficient for his place." Adams also had doubts about McHenry's abilities, especially when it came to naval affairs. This was problematic since the Quasi-War, as the conflict with France came to be known, was being fought entirely at sea.[46]

Although some lawmakers objected to the creation of a separate naval department, the wartime atmosphere in the United States was conducive to military reform. On April 30, 1798, Adams signed legislation creating the Department of the Navy and a new cabinet-level position, secretary of the navy, to head it. On July 11 the new department expanded when Congress revived the U.S. Marine Corps for service in the Quasi-War. Infantrymen who fought at sea or on land, marines performed several important functions when attached to naval vessels—among them, serving as sentries, the ship's police force, sharpshooters, members of boarding parties, and honor guards. By escorting American merchant ships and engaging French privateers, the U.S. Navy had effectively nullified the French threat in American coastal waters and the Caribbean by mid-1799. The overall success of these naval operations combined with the most famous victory of the war— Captain Thomas Truxtun's defeat of the French frigate *L'Insurgente* while in command of the frigate *Constellation*—gave Americans a sense of national pride. In 1800 the United States and France negotiated a peace settlement that ended the Quasi-War. By then, the U.S. Navy owned over thirty ships and employed thousands of men.[47]

The wartime enlargement of the army and navy did not sit well with the Republican Party. Although concerned with the expense of a large military establishment, its members worried more about the militaristic direction of the United States under Federalist leadership. Republicans tended to see the army and navy "not from a military point of view, but from a political, philosophical, and even moral, viewpoint."[48] In their minds, the Adams administration used the Quasi-War as an excuse to expand the army and navy as well as to extend the power of the executive branch in relation to Congress and the states. As the *Philadelphia Aurora* explained, "This has been the policy of all Aristocratic governments, to procure an armed force under pretext of some existing differences with other powers, when the true object was to provide some lucrative and honourable places for the 'well born,' and to have that force in readiness to quell their own people in case of opposition to oppressive measures." Many Republicans believed, correctly, that Hamilton was the force behind the Federalist military program, and they feared that he was attempting to transform the United States into a militaristic empire based on the British model.[49]

A key component of Hamilton's plan was to establish a national military academy, an institution that caused a great deal of apprehension on the part of Republicans. The issue had been raised during Washington's presidency and, not surprisingly, had been one of the points of disagreement between the emerging Federalist and Republican parties. In a November 1793 meeting, Washington and his cabinet reviewed topics that should be covered in the president's annual message to Congress. At the time, the United States was facing the Indian threat on the frontier as well as threats at sea from Britain, France, and the Barbary States. Among the topics discussed by the cabinet was a plan to fortify the Atlantic coast, particularly America's principal seaports. Henry Knox pointed out that no U.S. military officers possessed the engineering knowledge needed to build such fortifications. To address this deficiency, Knox recommended the establishment of a military academy.[50]

Thomas Jefferson opposed the idea because, he stated, the Constitution did not give the federal government the power to do so. Although Washington believed a military academy would be beneficial, he decided to avoid the issue for the time being, not wanting "to bring on anything which might generate heat and ill humor." At another cabinet meeting a week later, the military academy proposal surfaced again, with Knox, Hamilton, and Attorney General Edmund Randolph all supporting it. Jefferson renewed his objection on constitutional grounds. Because of the benefit the nation would derive from such an institution, however, Washington elected to put the idea before Congress and let it decide whether a military academy was constitutional.[51] "However pacific the general policy of a nation may be," he asserted in his last annual message to Congress, "it ought never to be without an adequate stock of military knowledge for emergencies." It was unrealistic to assume the United States did not need military science: "Whatever argument may be drawn from particular examples superficially viewed, a thorough examination of the subject will evince that the art of war is at once comprehensive and complicated, that it demands much previous study, and that the possession of it in its most improved and perfect state is always of great moment to the security of a nation."[52] Although Washington was unable to convince Congress of the importance of military education, the Quasi-War and the subsequent expansion of the army and navy gave the matter greater urgency.

Alexander Hamilton was the architect of American military preparations during the Quasi-War. Born into obscurity on an island in the West Indies, Hamilton came to America to receive his education. A student at King's College (present-day Columbia University) in New York City when the Revolutionary War began, he became an officer in the Continental army and spent most of the war serving as George Washington's aide-de-camp. Having witnessed firsthand the ineffectiveness of the Continental Congress, especially regarding military affairs, Hamilton became a staunch nationalist after the war and played a major role in securing the ratification of the Constitution.

After serving as secretary of the treasury from 1789 to 1795, he practiced law in New York until the Quasi-War broke out. As the crisis with France heated up, President Adams called George Washington out of retirement to serve as the commanding general of the expanded army. At Washington's request, Adams reluctantly appointed Hamilton inspector general of the army with the rank of major general. Officially, Hamilton was Washington's second in command; in reality, the former president was merely a figurehead. It was Hamilton who handled officer appointments, recruitment, finance, supply, organization, military law, and strategy.[53]

Hamilton considered a military academy to be of vital importance to the United States, listing the establishment of "an academy for naval & military instruction" as a measure that should be enacted "*without delay*." He viewed it as a necessary national institution, not a temporary wartime measure.[54] To meet this need, Hamilton devised a plan for a comprehensive national military academy that would educate officers for both the army and the navy. The academy would consist of five schools: the Fundamental School, the School of Engineers and Artillerists, the School of Cavalry, the School of Infantry, and the School of the Navy. Students would begin their studies at the Fundamental School, which would provide basic instruction in mathematics, natural philosophy (physics), mechanics, geography, surveying, drawing, and the principles of tactics. After completing two years at the Fundamental School, the students would move on to one of the four advanced schools. Future artillery officers and engineers would enter a two-year program focusing on natural philosophy, gunnery, fortifications, chemistry, mineralogy, munitions manufacturing, and civil engineering. Future cavalry officers would spend a year studying cavalry tactics and practicing riding and swordsmanship. Infantry officers would complete a year of infantry training and instruction in tactics. Young men destined for the navy would undertake a two-year study of navigation, astronomy, and naval architecture. Army and navy officers would form the academy's administration. As for the site of the proposed school, Hamilton recommended it be located on "navigable water" (to benefit the naval students) near a foundry that produced cannons and small arms. After completing his plan, Hamilton sought Washington's opinion of it. Writing from his Mount Vernon estate two days before his death, Washington endorsed the proposal: "The Establishment of an Institution of this kind, upon a respectable and extensive basis, has ever been considered by me as an Object of primary importance to this Country."[55]

In January 1800 John Adams submitted to Congress a report, written by Secretary of War McHenry, on a proposal for a military academy that was nearly identical to Hamilton's plan. Using an argument first made by

Hamilton, McHenry stated that since the principles of the United States "are opposed to the maintenance of a large military force, it is important that as much perfection as possible be given to that which may at any time exist." A nation could not reject military institutions and remain safe. Weakness would "attract injuries and enemies" and would ultimately result in "national degradation." "To avoid great evils," McHenry declared, following Hamilton's wording almost exactly, "we must either have a respectable force always ready for service, or the means of preparing such a force with certainty and expedition." Drawing on a maritime analogy for emphasis, McHenry maintained that a "corps of well-instructed officers and troops are to a country, what *anchors* are to a ship driven by a tempest towards a rocky shore."[56]

Elaborating on the School of the Navy, McHenry recommended that its director be a naval officer and report to the secretary of the navy. He also suggested that its students be required to participate in training cruises "under skilful officers" to practice seamanship, navigation, piloting, rigging, and gunnery. McHenry indicated that the plan for the military academy was based on the organization and course of studies of European military academies, especially those in France, and pointed out that "our late venerated President" had supported it. Realizing that funding might be an obstacle, McHenry assured Congress that the academy would entail only "a moderate expense."[57]

By the end of January, McHenry had dropped the infantry, cavalry, and naval schools from his proposal, leaving only the Fundamental School and the School of Artillerists and Engineers. The reason was economy. Undoubtedly, the fact that the navy was no longer under his jurisdiction as secretary of war influenced his action as well. Although willing to reduce the size of the military academy, McHenry still believed that instruction in artillery and engineering was vital. Artillery officers and engineers were responsible for fortifying harbors and the frontier. Engineers also served an important civil function by building roads, bridges, and canals. Warfare was subject to "mechanical, geometrical, moral, and physical rules" that required "profound study." "Is it possible," McHenry asked rhetorically, "for an officer of militia to obtain a competent knowledge of these things in the short space his usual avocations will permit him to devote to their acquisition?" In addition, he questioned whether officers with knowledge of military science could effectively instruct militia troops given the limited amount of time then devoted to militia training.[58] Despite McHenry's emphasis on the importance of a military academy, he had little hope that Congress would authorize its establishment. The reason, in his opinion, was that some people in the government (he was almost certainly referring to Adams) favored the navy at the expense of the army. In April 1800 the House of Representatives voted to postpone consideration of the military academy proposal; it was "unnecessary business" that did not have to be enacted before the close of the first session of the Sixth Congress.[59]

Although the lawmakers were not interested in establishing a military academy, Adams and his new secretary of war, Samuel Dexter, pressed for some form of military education based on legislation already enacted by Congress. A law from July 1798 authorized the president to appoint four teachers to instruct army artillery officers and engineers. Dexter recommended forming a school for cadets serving in the U.S. Army Corps of Artillerists and Engineers by hiring four teachers and providing the necessary books and instruments. He also mentioned a request from the secretary of the navy to admit midshipmen to the school.[60] Adams supported Dexter's plan and indicated that he would appoint the full number of cadets authorized by law and would hire instructors. Moreover, the president agreed that the admission of midshipmen to the school would be beneficial to the navy. Midshipmen acquired all of their education and training at sea. Adams hoped to improve this system by sending midshipmen to the proposed military school when they were on shore and by providing a better means of education at sea through the establishment of "a school on board every frigate." Adams had a special interest in the midshipmen, once confiding to Secretary of the Navy Benjamin Stoddert that he wished he had a son or grandson of the appropriate age to receive a midshipman's appointment. To upgrade the professional knowledge of naval personnel, Adams asked Stoddert to prepare a list of books, written in English, French, Spanish, and Dutch, on naval architecture, navigation, gunnery, hydraulics, hydrostatics, mathematics, and naval biography. The purchase of these books represented the beginning of the Navy Department Library, which still exists today.[61]

John Adams considered his efforts on behalf of the navy, especially his creation of the Navy Department, to be among his greatest achievements in public service: "The counsel which Themistocles gave to Athens . . . I have always given and shall continue to give to my countrymen, that as the great questions of commerce and power between nations and empires must be decided by a military marine, and war and peace are determined at sea, all reasonable encouragement should be given to the navy. The trident of Neptune is the sceptre of the world."[62] Adams's interest in naval affairs began during the Revolutionary War, when he drafted a set of rules and regulations for the Continental navy. Another more personal experience during the war reinforced this interest. From February to April 1778, Adams sailed across the Atlantic on board the frigate *Boston*. He was traveling to France to assist Benjamin Franklin in negotiating a treaty with the French. Although Adams arrived in Paris too late to participate in the negotiations, which Franklin had already completed, the voyage proved to be a defining moment in Adams's life. During his journey, he experienced several adventures at sea, most notably a battle with an armed British merchant ship. Consumed by a desire for martial glory, Adams grabbed a musket and joined the Continental marines during the battle.[63]

The month and a half spent at sea was a learning experience for Adams, who took it upon himself to become familiar with everything about the ship, its operation, and its crew. Unfortunately for the *Boston*'s captain, Samuel Tucker, Adams was not overly impressed with what he saw and was not shy about saying so. He disapproved of the "general relaxation of order and discipline" on the ship. The crew's habit of profanity was also disturbing to Adams, especially since his ten-year-old son, John Quincy, had accompanied him on the mission to France. Of even greater concern was the sailors' lack of proficiency in gunnery and the disgusting, unsanitary conditions on board, which Adams knew contributed to the spread of disease. The fact that he had written the naval regulations certainly made him more aware that the *Boston*'s crew was failing to live up to the ideals he had set forth for the American navy. To correct the deficiencies he observed, Adams was constantly advising Captain Tucker on matters of discipline and cleanliness. Tucker did try to improve the situation on board in accordance with Adams's suggestions, which was fortunate since the ship "would have bred the Plague" if the crew had not made more of an effort at sanitation.[64]

Adams's adventure at sea had convinced him of the need for formal naval education. "Our Captain was an able Seaman, and . . . a brave, active and vigilant Officer," Adams recalled, "but he had no great Erudition." He went on to list the small number of books in the captain's library, which included a dictionary, a novel, a book on Paraguay, and a couple of other titles. "More Science than this is required in a Naval Officer," Adams concluded. Education would produce more professional naval officers and strengthen discipline, morality, and efficiency within the navy.[65]

Adams was unable to establish educational institutions for the army and navy during his presidency. With the end of the Quasi-War in 1800, the urgent need for military and naval preparations subsided, and the army was reduced to its pre-1798 manpower level. The size of the navy was also cut. A naval act, signed into law on March 3, 1801, authorized the president to sell off all naval vessels except for thirteen frigates. Of the frigates retained, only six would be deployed on active service; the other seven ships were to remain in port. The officer corps was trimmed to 9 captains, 36 lieutenants, and 150 midshipmen with the provision that officers would only receive half pay when not actually at sea. Adams realized that peace with France and his loss to Thomas Jefferson in the presidential election of 1800 meant reductions in the size of the U.S. Navy. By selling off the ships that were no longer needed, Adams hoped to ensure that the core of the American fleet—the frigates—would remain intact, giving the United States a permanent peacetime navy.[66]

The Federalist military program, first envisioned in 1783, included a regular army, a navy, munitions foundries, arsenals, coastal fortifications, frontier fortifications, and a military academy. By the time John Adams left office in March 1801, the Federalists had succeeded in implementing their entire military agenda, with the exception of a military academy. The Federalists had used such crises as the Indian threat on the frontier, the Barbary menace at sea, and the Quasi-War with France to justify the creation of a national military establishment.[67] One of the ironies of American history is that it was the Federalists' greatest rival, Thomas Jefferson, who completed their unfinished military program.

Thomas Jefferson, Commander in Chief

Thomas Jefferson liked to think of his electoral victory as the "Revolution of 1800," a second American Revolution. This time the rebellion was against the Federalists, who, like the British, supported a strong central government, rule by the elite, professional military establishments, and an economy based on maritime commerce. Under the Federalists, American trade had steadily increased. The Republicans disapproved of this commercial emphasis partly because such an economic policy favored wealthy merchants over farmers. Of even greater concern was the fact that America's commercial activities had resulted in collisions at sea with the British, the French, and the Barbary corsairs, which ultimately led to the creation of a standing navy. In January 1800 Jefferson complained that America was "running navigation mad, and commerce mad, and navy mad, which is worst of all."[68] The commercial and military orientation of the Federalists was dangerous because it provided the necessary preconditions for war. Interference with American commerce by foreign powers presented a cause for war. The standing military and naval forces created by the Federalists offered the means to fight wars.

Because of its frequent wars, Britain maintained extensive military and naval forces, which cost a great deal of money, increased the national debt, and required the citizenry to bear a heavy tax burden. The Republicans feared that the same thing was happening in America because of the Federalists' policies. Permanent military and naval establishments, combined with increased taxes and a national debt, bred political corruption and undermined the liberty of the people. To Thomas Jefferson and the Republicans, Federalist policies were transforming the country into a European-style power state. The United States was supposed to be a different kind of nation—a simple, agrarian republic. Jefferson's goal as president was to restore the principles of the American Revolution by undoing the damage the Federalists had done to the infant republic.[69]

While praising the militia as the foundation of America's national defense, President Jefferson acknowledged the need for regular forces in time of war. He ordered reductions in the size of the army and the navy, but he did not eliminate the military and naval establishments created by the Federalists. The new president feared the effects of war and a permanent military on American society; he thus favored peaceful economic coercion over military force as an instrument of foreign policy. But Jefferson was also a pragmatist who understood that in an imperfect world, war was an inevitable part of national life. If peaceful coercion failed, military force was the only option. It was necessary, therefore, to be prepared for war.[70]

Jefferson demonstrated his willingness to use military force when necessary by ordering successive naval squadrons to the Mediterranean to deal with the continued threat to American shipping posed by the Barbary States. The enemy this time was Tripoli, whose ruler, the bashaw, had declared in 1800 that he was increasing the subsidy payments required to exempt U.S. shipping from attacks in the Mediterranean. The bashaw also threatened to declare war if the United States did not comply. Jefferson responded by ordering, in succession, squadrons under Commodores Richard Dale, Richard Morris, Edward Preble, Samuel Barron, and John Rodgers to the Mediterranean to protect American commerce and convince the bashaw, by a show of force, to back down on his demands. Although the United States suffered the humiliation of the frigate *Philadelphia*'s capture by the Tripolitans after the ship ran aground, overall the war against Tripoli was a major success for the navy. America's sustained show of force persuaded the bashaw to stop attacking U.S. merchant ships without demanding an increase in the amount of the annual subsidy payment.[71]

Jefferson realized that military education was a necessary component of any nation's preparation for war. On March 16, 1802, he signed into law an act setting up a peacetime military establishment for the United States. Reducing the size of the army by roughly one thousand men, the act stipulated that the peacetime army would consist of two infantry regiments, one artillery regiment, and the Corps of Engineers. The most important and lasting provision of the act was Section 27, which stipulated that "the said corps [of engineers] when so organized, shall be stationed at West Point, in the State of New York, and shall constitute a military academy."[72] Located on the strategically important Hudson River, West Point had been a crucial American fortification during the Revolutionary War. It was most famous for having been the site of Benedict Arnold's betrayal of the American cause in 1780. After receiving command of West Point, Arnold conspired with the British to hand the fortification over to His Majesty's forces. Fortunately for the United States, the plot was discovered and West Point never fell into enemy hands. Since the end of the war, West Point had been home to a small garrison and the Corps of Artillerists and Engineers.[73]

At first glance, Jefferson's action would seem to contradict his previous views on military education. He had strongly opposed the creation of a military academy in 1793, arguing that the Constitution did not give the federal government the power to establish such an institution. In January 1800, while discussing his own plans for a new university in Virginia, Jefferson dismissed the national military academy plan submitted by McHenry as being devoted to branches of study "now valued in Europe, but useless to us for ages to come."[74] Yet Jefferson's founding of the U.S. Military Academy, when examined within the proper context, was not contradictory. The academy established in 1802 was nothing like the institution Hamilton and McHenry had envisioned. West Point was organized on a much smaller scale with instruction focused narrowly on mathematics. Furthermore, Jefferson's earlier opposition to a military academy was based more on partisan politics than actual opposition to the idea of military education. He would have opposed any plan, military or not, that originated with Alexander Hamilton.[75] Despite his earlier opposition to academy proposals in 1793 and 1800, Jefferson believed that military education was important to the nation's survival. In addition to the Military Academy at West Point, he favored military instruction at civilian colleges, once writing to James Monroe that the United States must "make military instruction a regular part of collegiate education. We can never be safe till this is done." Jefferson devoted his retirement years to establishing the University of Virginia at Charlottesville. In his plan for the university, Jefferson included military and naval science in the curriculum as well as military drill.[76]

Jefferson believed that scientific instruction was also useful to naval officers and that a scientific approach to warfare would enable the United States to maintain a smaller, but more effective, army and navy. Fascinated by the work of Robert Fulton, he thought inventions like Fulton's torpedo (mine) and "submarine boat" could be used against conventional naval forces and serve as an important component of harbor defense. Jefferson envisioned the formation of a corps of naval engineers to design and operate these weapons, noting that expertise in such devices would require "a course of training."[77] His interest in Fulton's naval inventions suggests that he viewed the principles governing warfare at sea to be just as scientific as those for warfare on land. As president, Jefferson endorsed two proposals that would have provided naval officers with scientific instruction.

Jefferson supported his friend Joel Barlow's 1806 plan for the establishment of a national institution for the advancement of knowledge. Formed around a central university in Washington, D.C., with several satellite campuses, the national institution would have its own printing presses, libraries, laboratories, botanical gardens, farmland, and a patent office. Barlow recommended moving the U.S. Military Academy from West Point to Washington, where it would become part of the national university along with a new naval academy. A bill based on his proposal was introduced in Congress but never enacted.[78]

Jefferson later backed the proposal of West Point superintendent Jonathan Williams to provide naval instruction as part of an expanded and reorganized U.S. Military Academy. In its early years, West Point was not much more than "a little Mathematical School."[79] It had no standard curriculum. Cadets received their officer commissions whenever the faculty decided they had mastered the material, be it in six months or several years. There were no admission requirements (other than being male). The few cadets who attended the academy were extremely varied in terms of age and educational background. One cadet was only ten years old, while a classmate was married and had a family. Some cadets were already college graduates; others had little formal education. Instruction at West Point was limited to mathematics and some basic science.[80]

Despite its poor state, Superintendent Williams had a broad vision for the Military Academy, one very similar to the institution envisioned by Alexander Hamilton almost a decade earlier. In March 1808 Williams submitted a report to Congress in which he laid out his plan for expanding and relocating the academy. In Williams's opinion, the school was not living up to its potential because the federal government had virtually ignored the academy since its establishment. "The Military Academy, as it now stands, is like a foundling," Williams complained, "barely existing among the mountains, and nurtured at a distance, out of sight, and almost unknown to its legitimate parents." He attributed the lack of interest in the school to its natural isolation at West Point and its geographic distance from the nation's capital. To correct this situation, Williams strongly hinted that the government should relocate the Military Academy to the Washington, D.C., area, where it could become "an honorable and interesting appendage to the national family."[81]

The superintendent also made several recommendations for improving instruction at the school. On the expanded faculty there should be professors of natural and experimental philosophy, mathematics (including navigation and nautical astronomy), engineering, architecture, chemistry and mineralogy, as well as a riding master and a master swordsman. Additional appropriations for buildings, a library, and scientific equipment were necessary. Williams also advised that the student body be enlarged to include not only army cadets but also navy midshipmen and any other young men who desired a military education. What Williams envisioned was a comprehensive national military university that would educate young men for service in the army, the navy, and the militia. Those students who did not plan to enter the army or navy would pay tuition to help finance the institution. These "citizen youth" attending the academy would be subject to military discipline and regulations but on graduation would return to civilian life and "would naturally become militia officers." This new, expanded academy, Williams explained, would make the army, the navy, and the militia more effective through the scientific study of warfare.[82]

In endorsing Williams's plan, Jefferson noted: "The scale on which the Military Academy at West Point was originally established is become too limited to furnish the number of well-instructed subjects in the different branches of artillery and engineering which the public service calls for." Relocating the Military Academy to the nation's capital would be beneficial for two reasons: It would place the institution "under the immediate eye of the Government," and it would "render its benefits common to the Naval Department."[83]

Williams's grand plan for a national military university never came to fruition. The vast majority of Republican senators and congressmen did not wish to adopt a proposal that would increase the power of the executive branch and require substantial appropriations. Once the new administration of James Madison came to office in 1809, there was an additional reason why Williams's plan failed to gain much support. Secretary of War William Eustis disapproved of professional military officers and had no interest in expanding the Military Academy. A native of Massachusetts, Eustis revered the minutemen of the Revolutionary War who fought the country's first battles at Lexington, Concord, and Bunker Hill. In Eustis's mind, the citizen soldier was the ideal defender of American freedom. Although he gave rhetorical support to Williams's plan, probably because he thought Madison was in favor of it, his actions toward West Point as secretary of war demonstrated his opposition to military education. Eustis reduced the size of the faculty, took away space from the academy by assigning other army units to West Point, and devised a plan that would have required West Point graduates to begin their army careers as enlisted soldiers instead of commissioned officers.[84]

Congress rejected both plans to provide scientific education for naval officers, and Jefferson was unwilling to spend any more of his political capital to pursue the matter further. Although he believed that scientific education would be useful to naval officers, there were logical reasons why he did not see it as being as necessary for the navy as it was for the army. First, Jefferson subscribed to the prevalent view that naval officers and merchant mariners did not possess separate professional identities but were instead members of a single maritime profession. Although formal naval education was desirable, the merchant service was a practical and acceptable alternative. Officers could acquire expertise in seamanship and navigation in the merchant service, at private expense, and, when needed, apply that knowledge to the operation of naval vessels. The nation's earliest naval heroes, including John Paul Jones, John Barry, Thomas Truxtun, and Edward Preble, all had extensive experience in the merchant marine. During peacetime, naval officers, especially midshipmen, were encouraged to take furloughs from the navy to serve on merchant ships. In addition to the financial benefits, the merchant marine provided excellent training in seamanship and navigation and offered greater opportunities for leadership, including a much quicker route to command of a ship. Time spent in the merchant service was particularly important for younger, less experienced officers. In a memorandum sent to midshipmen, Secretary of the Navy Robert Smith encouraged the young men to make good use of their time away from active duty by devoting themselves to professional improvement. The best way for midshipmen to develop their nautical skills and gain valuable experience was by sailing in the merchant service, which was sure to provide "great advantages" to the midshipmen and to the country as a whole.[85]

Jefferson's naval policy was the best evidence that he did not regard naval service as a distinct profession. In his book, *Notes on the State of Virginia*, he wrote that "the sea is the field on which we should meet a European enemy. On that element it is necessary we should possess some power. To aim at such a navy as the greater nations of Europe possess, would be a foolish and wicked waste of the energies of our countrymen." Any European naval power would be able to deploy only a small part of its fleet against the United States, which led Jefferson to conclude that "a small naval force . . . is sufficient for us, and a small one is necessary." Just as Jefferson's ideal peacetime military establishment would combine the militia with a small regular army specializing in artillery and engineering, his naval policy called for maintaining a balance between a small "regular navy" composed of frigates and a naval militia that would deploy small gunboats for coastal and harbor defense.[86]

Gunboats were shallow-draft vessels, forty to eighty feet long, armed with one or two guns. In the minds of many Republicans, they were the perfect means of maritime defense because they were inexpensive to build and maintain and performed a limited defensive role. Their small size made gunboats ideal for coastal and harbor defense since they could navigate easily in shallow water. When deployed with coastal fortifications and floating batteries, they seemed to represent a practical and cost-effective means of defense. Although each boat individually was small in size, the Republicans believed that a "mosquito fleet" of gunboats working together could be an effective weapon against an enemy's larger naval vessels. Jefferson's naval defense plan called for a fleet of two hundred gunboats stationed at strategic locations throughout the United States, including the Mississippi River, Savannah and Charleston harbors, Chesapeake Bay, the Delaware River, New York and southern New England, and Boston. In peacetime, the navy would deploy only a small number of gunboats, with the remainder stored in large dry dock facilities for future use.[87]

The gunboats would be manned by a national naval militia composed of all "free, able-bodied white male citizen[s]" from eighteen to forty-five years of age who made their living as seamen. Exempt from service in the land militia, these "citizen seamen" would be organized into companies under the command of officers appointed by the state governments to defend the harbors and seaports in their own districts. The naval militia officers would be required to provide training in artillery and gunboat maneuvering for the men in their respective companies every two months. The federal government could call the naval militia to active duty in response to a foreign invasion or a domestic insurrection.[88] Congress never enacted Jefferson's plan for a naval militia, arguing that it was inappropriate for the federal government to possess increased control over the militia, which was a state institution.[89] Because Jefferson favored a part-time naval militia as the country's primary means of maritime defense, it is understandable that he would view the merchant marine as an acceptable school for the professional development of naval officers.

A second reason why a naval academy seemed less important than a military academy was that the navy did not represent a direct threat to liberty and the republic the way the army did. The army and the navy Jefferson

inherited from the Adams administration were decidedly Federalist institutions. Republican opposition to the Quasi-War with France did not en-
dear the party to army and navy officers, many of whom voiced their anti-
Republican sentiments after Jefferson's election in 1800. Although Jefferson
did distrust Federalist naval officers, he was far more concerned about the
loyalty of the army's officer corps to his new Republican administration.
One way to overcome this problem was to purge the army of its Federalist
officers and replace them with men from Republican backgrounds. To serve
effectively, these Republican officers would have to receive proper military
education and training. This was Jefferson's goal in establishing West Point:
to educate Republican youth in military science. By producing Republican
officers, Jefferson could create a less dangerous, more democratic, and more
loyal army.[90] A navy was an inefficient and impractical instrument for a
would-be dictator bent on taking over the United States. It would be virtually impossible for naval forces to assume control of the country since inland
areas were not vulnerable to attack by ship. Moreover, because America
was a seafaring nation, heavily involved in maritime industries such as shipbuilding, fishing, and the merchant business, sailors were a familiar sight on
the streets of seaport cities and did not generate the suspicion and fear that
professional soldiers did. Jefferson himself acknowledged that navies were
not as dangerous as armies: "A naval force can never endanger our liberties,
nor occasion bloodshed; a land force would do both."[91] If a Federalist navy
posed less of a threat than a Federalist army, it was only logical for Jefferson
to focus on military rather than naval education.

A third factor influencing this issue was politics. The Republicans in
Congress during Jefferson's presidency opposed the navy on ideological
grounds, having absorbed the attitudes of antinavy writers like Tench Coxe.
Contrary to common belief, Coxe maintained that navies posed a danger to
liberty, as the Royal Navy had demonstrated during the American Revolution. Navies were expensive, and they were constantly provoking wars with
other nations. Moreover, the patronage associated with naval appointments
and contracts could lead to corruption.[92] Looking back on his presidency,
Jefferson recalled the antinavy sentiment in Congress. Referring specifically
to his plan to build a large dry dock to house the frigates not deployed at
sea, he stated that "the majority of the legislature was against any addition
to the navy."[93] A pragmatic politician, Jefferson realized that Congress was
unlikely to pass legislation creating a naval academy. He was therefore unwilling to use his political influence to achieve that goal: "There is a snail-
paced gait for the advance of new ideas on the general mind, under which we
must acquiesce. A forty years' experience of popular assemblies has taught

me, that you must give them time for every step you take. If too hard pushed, they balk, and the machine retrogrades." In the end, Jefferson decided that it was unwise to challenge Congress on a policy issue that, while desirable, was not absolutely necessary. Throughout his political career, Jefferson sought to avoid unnecessary confrontations with his colleagues. He was repelled by heated disagreements and tended to tailor his views to the particular constituency he was addressing in order to avoid any unpleasant encounters.[94] Given his character and personality, it is understandable that he would prefer to focus on policy areas in which he and the Republican-controlled Congress agreed.

One person who was disappointed, but not surprised, by Jefferson's failure to establish a naval academy was Thomas Truxtun. In an 1806 letter to Timothy Pickering, Truxtun lamented the lack of naval education available to midshipmen, especially when it came to the more theoretical aspects of the profession: "We have many good Seamen but very few tactitians among them, and this will be the case until a national marine academy is established on similar principles to those in the maritime countries of Europe. But such an institution is not likely to be created in our day, as we have no Naval Pride, and other projects to exhaust the Treasury, are not wanting in our all-wise Cabinet."[95] This was regrettable in Truxtun's opinion because many naval officers were "uninformed men, who mostly have an aversion to reading and studious application."[96]

By the end of Jefferson's presidency, the United States maintained standing military and naval forces. The Washington and Adams administrations had effectively used international crises such as the Barbary threat and the Quasi-War to create permanent military and naval establishments in a gradual manner. The only component of their military program that the Federalists were unable to achieve was the establishment of a military academy. Ironically, it was Thomas Jefferson who founded the U.S. Military Academy at West Point, the final component of the Federalists' military agenda, as a way to minimize Federalist influence within the army officer corps. Even though the army and navy had become permanent institutions, Americans were still reluctant to embrace military professionals and had not yet accepted the idea of formal military education for army and navy officers. Although the army operated an academy to educate and train its officers, that academy existed on a very limited scale and its survival was by no means certain. As for naval officers, they would continue to learn their profession in the only school provided for them by the federal government—a U.S. Navy ship.

CHAPTER 2

Learning the Ropes

A young man who accepted an appointment as a midshipman in the U.S. Navy of the early republic received his professional education at sea. Captain Charles Stewart spoke for many naval officers and politicians when he declared, "The best school for the instruction of youth in the [naval] profession is the deck of a ship." The navy's system of education was a combination of classroom instruction, practical training, active duty service, and professional socialization that ultimately provided naval officers with what David Curtis Skaggs has described as the "corpus of knowledge necessary for the daily survival of their ship and its crew."[1] The navy's leadership believed that service at sea during time of war was the most effective way of educating and training midshipmen. Defending U.S. commerce, and by extension America's sovereignty and rights as a neutral power, had resulted in the Quasi-War with France, conflicts with the Barbary States of North Africa, and the War of 1812, all of which provided ample opportunities for U.S. Navy midshipmen to learn their profession under the most challenging circumstances. There were two main benefits to the navy's "learn by doing" approach to education. First, it was cost effective, which endeared the system to a Congress that tended to place economy above all other considerations. Second, it developed officers who were capable mariners and effective combat leaders.

Despite the fact that the United States had won its political independence from Great Britain, there remained a strong British cultural inheritance within American society. This cultural heritage was especially visible in the U.S. Navy, which consciously modeled itself after the Royal Navy. American officers read books and journals written by British naval experts, and they observed the British fleet in action. Prior to the War of 1812, it was fairly common for American and British officers to socialize and discuss professional subjects during their encounters at sea or at various ports of call.[2] American naval education derived from the British system. In the Royal Navy, the most frequent path to an officer's commission was to begin one's career by direct appointment to a ship as a captain's servant. A smaller number of Royal Navy officers started by enlisting as seamen or joining the merchant marine. The least common track to a commission was through the Royal Naval Academy at Portsmouth, England, which the British government had established mainly for aristocratic young men selected for naval service by the Admiralty. These officer candidates spent three years studying mathematics, navigation, English, French, gunnery, naval architecture, and drawing at Portsmouth before going to sea. Academy students paid tuition and were required to have completed some previous classical education to qualify for admission. Both of these qualifications limited attendance, and the academy was never full. Within the British navy, having studied at the Royal Naval Academy was not regarded as an important qualification for a future naval officer. In fact, many senior officers considered time spent at Portsmouth to be more of a detriment, and there was a strong bias within the fleet against "Academy Boys." Seamanship was the most important skill needed by future naval officers, and midshipmen could only learn that at sea.[3]

The French, on the other hand, emphasized a more theoretical and scientific approach to the development of naval officers. Officer candidates studied mathematics, hydrography (oceanography), naval architecture, English, and Spanish at schools located at France's major naval ports, then went to sea to learn navigation and seamanship. Reforms in the 1780s led to the creation of a corps of *élèves de la marine*, who studied mathematics and other technical subjects at naval colleges before their practical training on board ship. Beginning in the era of the French Revolution, some naval officers, mostly naval architects and gunnery officers, studied at the famous École Polytechnique in Paris. During the Napoleonic period, officer candidates also attended naval academies at Brest and Toulon.[4]

In some ways, American attitudes toward the navy seem contradictory. The purpose of the Revolution was to separate the colonies from the morally corrupt and militaristic British Empire. Yet the U.S. Navy consciously looked to the Royal Navy as a professional model and adopted its system of naval education. This apparent inconsistency derives from the fact that, as a new nation, the United States was still in the process of forming its own identity. Americans' first concept of their country was that it was something different in the world—a working republic based on liberty and equality. At the same time, however, citizens had not entirely rejected the cultural traditions they inherited from the British. Once its leaders determined that the United States needed some kind of force to defend its interests on the high seas, it was only logical to look to the British as their model. The Royal Navy was universally acknowledged as the finest in the world. Although French officers possessed a greater theoretical knowledge of naval science, the British produced better combat officers who almost always defeated the French in battle. Because the British system was battle-tested and highly effective, American midshipmen received their professional education and training according to the British model.

"A Corps of Young Gentlemen"

Thomas Jefferson once characterized the U.S. Navy's midshipmen as "a corps of young gentlemen of the best characters & standing from different parts of the union who are destined for future commands in the navy. The state of midshipman is a kind of apprenticeship to the knolege [sic] necessary to qualify him for future command." As Jefferson pointed out, midshipmen were the future of the navy, the individuals who would one day command America's warships. Their selection and their professional development were matters of national importance. Secretary of the Navy Benjamin Stoddert described ideal candidates as "sprightly young men of good Education, good Character, and good connexions." Applicants who set their sights on a naval career had to undergo a highly subjective selection process. In general, they had to be the proper age; in good health, possessing energy, stamina, and courage; of good moral character and a respectable family background; and reasonably well educated. They also needed to exhibit a strong desire for glory.[5]

Ideally, the navy sought candidates between the ages of twelve and eighteen. The majority of young men (64.6 percent) who received appointments in the period before the War of 1812 fell into this category. However, some were older than eighteen (31.9 percent) and much fewer under twelve (3.5 percent). Boys under age twelve usually had connections to senior naval officers or high-ranking government officials. A somewhat ridiculous example was the appointment of the two-year-old child of a deceased naval officer. Louis Goldsborough, the son of the Navy Department's chief clerk, became a midshipman at the age of six. The average age of a midshipman at the time of his appointment was seventeen. Although many boys who entered the navy as midshipmen were very young by modern standards, they were considered old enough to begin a career in the late eighteenth and early nineteenth centuries. Apprenticeships in professions such as law or medicine often began around age sixteen.[6]

Other than age and physical health, the most important criteria for selection as a midshipman were U.S. citizenship (though there were a few exceptions), parental consent, respectability, the quality of an applicant's recommendations, and geography. Respectability carried a great deal of weight because the navy expected midshipmen, as future officers and gentlemen, to behave in a manner befitting their rank and status. Robert Smith, who served as secretary of the navy under Thomas Jefferson, observed: "The correct habits as well as the honorable and manly feelings of a gentleman are essentials in the character of an officer of the Navy of the United States."[7]

Exactly what constituted respectability was somewhat subjective. Generally, there were two considerations. The first was family background. Respectability could mean having a family member who fought on the patriot side during the Revolution (though some young men from loyalist families also received midshipman appointments) or who was a prominent government official—senator, congressman, cabinet secretary, governor, judge, customs collector, navy agent, postmaster, or military officer. Although Thomas Macdonough was an orphan by the time he entered the navy, his family connections virtually assured him a midshipman's appointment. His late father had been wounded in battle as a major in the Continental army; he later served as a colonel in the Delaware militia and as a member of the Delaware privy council (governor's cabinet). In addition, Thomas's older brother James was a midshipman on the frigate *Constellation* during the Quasi-War and was severely wounded in that ship's famous battle with the French frigate *L'Insurgente*. Although his naval career ended, James had impressed his commanding officer, Thomas Truxtun, and his first lieutenant (second in command), John Rodgers, both of whom became patrons of young Thomas Macdonough when he entered the navy. The application of a young man like Samuel Francis Du Pont was almost guaranteed an appointment. With family connections to former president Thomas Jefferson and President James Madison, young Samuel not only was accepted as a navy midshipman but also received an appointment to West Point. He chose the navy and entered the service in 1815. Applicants with ties to one of the "learned professions" (law, medicine, or the ministry), to maritime businessmen (merchants, shipbuilders, and insurance brokers), or to successful artisans or small businessmen were also considered respectable.[8]

The second way to establish one's respectability was to submit a letter of recommendation from a prominent person. Senators, congressmen, cabinet secretaries, governors, federal or state judges, senior naval officers, navy agents, or prominent merchants, lawyers, or ministers were the best options. Recommendations were important because a respectable family did not necessarily ensure acceptability. Discussing an applicant recommended by Roman Catholic bishop John Carroll of Baltimore, Secretary of the Navy Robert Smith stated that although the young man's estimable family background was clearly a plus, "unhappily the respectibility of the father does not always descend to his posterity." To be certain that the rank of midshipman remained "a respectable and honorable station," Smith declared, only "gentlemen of [the] most unexceptionable characters" should receive appointments. Although a recommendation from a prominent person was very important, it was crucial that the individual providing the testimonial know the applicant personally. It was Smith's view that letters from people who did not have that personal knowledge were useless, regardless of their prominence. Smith informed New York City mayor DeWitt Clinton that his recommendation of a young man was not valid since the mayor did not appear to have "personal knowledge" of the applicant.[9] There was some criticism of this selection process on the grounds that it bred favoritism. Young men with political connections who received appointments as midshipmen were, in the words of Massachusetts congressman Cyrus King, "mere children, of the favored few . . . who never were on board a ship of war, and have nothing of the seaman about them except the anchor on their buttons." King believed that such appointments should go to experienced sailors who had earned the privilege.[10]

Respectability did not necessarily mean financial security, and some young men embarked on naval careers in order to enjoy some degree of financial stability or even upward social mobility. Most midshipmen had middle-class backgrounds. While many did come from families that were comfortable financially, the families of other officer candidates, while respectable, were on the verge of financial ruin. For example, the finances of the Du Pont family were precarious when Samuel reached college age, and his father could not afford to send him to a civilian school. The military was an honorable profession with a steady income, which was the reason Samuel embarked on a naval career.[11]

Geography was also an important consideration in the selection process. Generally, the number of midshipmen appointed from each region of the country corresponded to the number of applications received from that region. Before and during the War of 1812, the middle Atlantic states (New York, New Jersey, Pennsylvania, Delaware, Maryland, Virginia, and the

District of Columbia) dominated the navy. Although this region contained 48.4 percent of the country's free white male population aged sixteen to twenty-five, it was home to 64.6 percent of the youths who entered the navy as midshipmen. Within the region, Maryland, Virginia, and the District of Columbia produced the most midshipmen. Interestingly, despite New England's maritime character, only 17.4 percent of midshipmen came from that region and only 12.6 percent were from the Deep South. The most reasonable explanation for the dominance of the Chesapeake area was its proximity to the nation's capital, which likely resulted in a closer association with the federal government and a prominent federal institution such as the navy. Young people from New England and the Deep South were more likely to embrace a state or sectional outlook than a national one. Not surprisingly, the major seaport cities—Philadelphia, New York City, Charleston, Baltimore, and Boston—turned out large numbers of midshipmen. Overall, the vast majority of midshipmen were from maritime areas such as the Atlantic coast, seaport cities, or inland towns on navigable rivers.[12]

Although previous experience at sea was not a requirement for a prospective midshipman, some of them had spent time on merchant ships before joining the navy. Less common were those who had served on navy ships as captain's clerks or enlisted seamen.[13] If previous sea experience was not necessary, some education was required. This was a change from the Revolutionary War, when schooling was not an important qualification for midshipmen in the Continental navy. Nathaniel Fanning, a midshipman under John Paul Jones, admitted that he possessed "barely a common education." The basic educational requirement for midshipmen in the early national period was completion of elementary school, which would have provided instruction in reading, spelling, grammar, penmanship, arithmetic, history, and geography. Most midshipmen had continued their studies on the secondary school level at Latin grammar schools or at academies, which taught Greek, Latin, literature, history, geography, and mathematics. A small minority had attended college, with even fewer having received a bachelor's degree. Among the exceptional midshipmen who had attended college was Robert F. Stockton, who completed three years of study at Princeton. William Lewis was perhaps the best-educated officer of the early navy, having earned a bachelor's degree from the College of William and Mary and studied medicine and law before becoming a midshipman in 1802. Whereas today almost all naval officers possess a college education, the navy of the early national period was not looking for scholars. The knowledge, skills, and temperament needed to flourish at an institution of higher learning were not necessarily the same characteristics that spelled success for a naval officer. Although many midshipmen had the intellectual ability to pursue a college education, they were better suited to a naval career. In this period, a college education was not necessary for most professions (the ministry being the main exception to this rule). The goal for a young man ready to begin a career was to find the right profession, then complete the level of education it required.[14]

There were several reasons why a young man from a respectable family would embark on a naval career. Many were motivated by a desire for a vigorous life (to escape the boredom of formal education or an unexciting job), a fascination with the sea and ships, an aspiration to see the world, a thirst for adventure and glory, ardent patriotism, a wish for independence from parental authority, or the hope of financial security. In the case of some youths, others had made the decision for them. Some parents relied on navy discipline to salvage their uncontrollable sons. The "typical midshipman" of the early national period, then, came from the coastal areas of Maryland or Virginia; his father, if still living, was a federal government official or maritime businessman; his family was middle class with good political connections; he had previously studied at a Latin school or academy; he had some experience at sea in the merchant service; he was seventeen years old at the time of his appointment; and he had joined the navy mostly for the stable income, the status that came with being an officer, and the adventure associated with life at sea.[15]

A New World

The successful aspirant officially accepted his appointment in a letter to the secretary of the navy and took the midshipman's oath. Some new officer candidates were directed to report to their first assignment immediately. Others did not receive orders for a month or even a year depending on the needs of the navy. When a midshipman finally did board his first ship, he entered a new world, one with its own language, customs, rules, and traditions.[16] He would have already purchased his uniform and other necessary items. The midshipman's dress uniform consisted of a blue wool jacket with brass buttons and a stiff standing collar, blue and white pants (worn according to the season), a white vest, a white shirt, a black cravat, a cocked hat, boots, a top coat for winter, and a sword. In addition to clothing, new candidates were required to obtain a quadrant and a copy of Nathaniel Bowditch's textbook on navigation ("the midshipman's Bible"). Matthew Fontaine Maury's purchases amounted to $200 — a hefty sum considering that midshipmen of the early national period made only $228 a year.[17]

Once on board, a new midshipman, or "green horn" in navy parlance, would need to adjust to a completely different lifestyle. U.S. Navy ships were extremely crowded. The frigate *United States*, for example, usually carried a complement of 430 men, including 23 officers, 357 enlisted seamen, and 50 marines.[18] Life on a navy ship was governed by one thing—rank, which "determines the apartment in which an officer sleeps, the position of his chair at the table when eating, his relative position on entering or leaving the ship, his place of promenade on deck, and the fashion and decorations of his clothes. The official worth of a man on board ship is read by his fellow officers from the buttons and gold bullion on his coat, and he is esteemed accordingly."[19] Midshipmen had a somewhat anomalous position within the ship's community. Although some navy men joked that midshipmen were senior only "to the ship's cat," this was not quite accurate. Midshipmen were senior to enlisted sailors, but they were not yet officers. Their unique situation created a great deal of camaraderie and solidarity among their peers.[20]

Among the officers, there were three distinct social classes. At the top of the social hierarchy was the captain, who lived in a cabin that was, by navy standards, spacious. He was the only person on board who enjoyed any measure of privacy. Under the captain were the lieutenants, the sailing master, the surgeon, the purser, the chaplain, and the marine lieutenant. These officers were social equals. They dined together in the wardroom and lived in small cabins adjacent to the wardroom. Below the officers came the midshipmen. They lived and ate in the steerage, a large single compartment located on the berth deck (the deck below the gun deck) between the wardroom and the crew's quarters. The steerage left much to be desired. One midshipman complained that "the apartment belonging to us is very confined and hot, very low, for I was obliged to stoop in it, and altogether quite disagreeable." Since the steerage was below the ship's waterline, it had little ventilation or light. The furnishings included a table, some stools for seating, and two water basins for washing. Wooden lockers for its occupants lined the bulkheads. The midshipmen slept in hammocks. Stiflingly hot in summer, the steerage was freezing in winter. To keep warm, the midshipmen would place a hot twenty-four-pound cannon ball in a bucket of sand and then stick their feet into the bucket. Unfortunately, the midshipmen were not the compartment's only residents—navy ships were crawling with rats and cockroaches.[21]

Midshipmen were often referred to as "the young gentlemen" and were expected to behave as such. A gentleman in the early republic was "a man who does not engage in any menial occupation or in manual labor for gain, and who lives by a certain code of behavior thought appropriate to his exalted status." Within the U.S. Navy, there was a strict social line separating commissioned officers, who were considered gentlemen, from enlisted seamen, who were not so regarded. Some warrant officers, such as chaplains, pursers, and sailing masters, also enjoyed the status of gentlemen. Boatswains, carpenters, gunners, and sailmakers, though technically warrant officers, could not claim the title because they performed manual labor. As future commissioned officers, midshipmen were required to develop behaviors that were appropriate to their future rank and status. Gentlemanly conduct was "a broad umbrella, embracing ethical conduct, internalized discipline, avoidance of indulgence or self-destructive excess, courteous and harmonious relationships with one's peers, manners, personal cleanliness, neatness in one's belongings and surroundings, refined personal interests, and the habit of associating with, and emulating . . . those of superior social standing." The navy expected midshipmen to behave like gentlemen at sea and on shore. Secretary of the Navy Paul Hamilton believed it was his job to ensure that they lived up to this ideal. He once told Captain Thomas Tingey, commandant of the Washington Navy Yard, to inform a group of midshipmen who had been spotted drinking and playing billiards at a local pub "that the eye of the Department is upon them—that such practices will not be permitted— that a perseverance in them will make it my duty to dismiss them—and I shall not fail to perform my duty on the occasion."[22]

Navy regulations were somewhat vague on exactly what midshipmen were supposed to do on board ship, as "No particular duties can be assigned to this class of officers." The regulations did require them to obey the orders of their superiors and keep a regular journal of the ship's operations and activities. The navy expected commanding officers to consider midshipmen "a class of officers, meriting in an especial degree, the fostering care of their government." Captains were to look after the education of their midshipmen, ensuring that they received proper instruction and became proficient in "those sciences appertaining to their department." Midshipmen, in turn, were to study naval tactics and acquire "a thorough and extensive knowledge of all the various duties to be performed on board of a ship of war."[23]

The navy expected captains to go beyond the regulations and look after the development of their midshipmen as gentlemen. Captains should not only serve as professional role models, but also as models of gentility. It was the duty of commanding officers to instruct their midshipmen in etiquette and protocol and to correct improper conduct. Midshipmen often received invitations to dine with the lieutenants in the wardroom or with the captain in his cabin. This practice introduced them to the social aspects of their profession and provided an opportunity for them to learn proper manners, which every officer should exhibit. Naval officers had frequent interaction with foreign dignitaries and military officers as well as high-ranking U.S. officials—

cabinet secretaries, senators, congressmen, ambassadors, generals, and possibly even the president. Captains who took their mentor role seriously used the time at dinner to discuss leadership, history, tactics, and current events with their midshipmen. One of these captains was Oliver Hazard Perry, who made sure his charges attended class, studied their lessons, and developed into true gentlemen. He personally taught his midshipmen correct manners and even provided dancing lessons for them. Perry's younger brother and fellow naval officer, Matthew Calbraith Perry, also put a great deal of effort into instructing the midshipmen under his command. While serving as first lieutenant on board the ship of the line *North Carolina*, Matthew wrote that it was the duty of all first lieutenants to show a "parental interest and regard for the improvement and welfare of the Midshipmen."[24]

The School of the Ship

The U.S. Navy believed that officers were born, not made. The purpose of naval education was to develop "attributes and aptitudes that were innate. . . . No amount of education could make a sea officer of someone whom Nature had never intended for that calling." Among the traits that midshipmen needed to develop were discipline, obedience, initiative, ambition, physical and moral courage, professional studiousness, gentlemanly conduct, leadership, and a strong sense of honor. To foster these attributes, the navy employed a multifaceted approach to education encompassing classroom instruction, seamanship training, professional socialization, and character development. In a sense, early naval education amounted to "directed doing."[25] It was common wisdom that the only place for the education and training of midshipmen was at sea, preferably on a frigate or a ship of the line. Serving on larger ships not only enabled the midshipmen to learn navigation, seamanship, gunnery, and tactics, but it also immersed them in the professional culture of the navy and offered role models in the captain and his lieutenants.[26]

Initially, navy chaplains were responsible for the classroom instruction of midshipmen at sea. Navy regulations required the chaplain to teach the young men writing, arithmetic, navigation, and any other subjects that would contribute to their professional development. In the early national period, then, the chaplain's role was more educational than spiritual. In fact, many chaplains were not ordained ministers. During the War of 1812 the navy began hiring civilian schoolmasters, who, over time, superseded the chaplains as the midshipmen's primary instructors. By 1841, navy regulations no longer included teaching among the chaplain's duties.[27]

Instruction combined lectures, question-and-answer sessions, and individual attention. For the most part, there were few written examinations. Mathematics was the most important subject because of its practical application to navigation. In addition, midshipmen usually received some instruction in foreign languages (especially French and Spanish), astronomy, and gunnery. Classes were usually held in a small, screened-off room on the gun deck. Some captains offered their cabin for use as a classroom. The younger midshipmen received orders from the captain to attend class. The captain often gave older midshipmen the choice of attending class or studying on their own. The schoolmaster was required to prepare a weekly report for the captain on the subjects taught, attendance, and general comments regarding each student's performance.[28]

Although the combination of classroom instruction and practical training at sea would seem to be an ideal system for producing naval officers, several problems arose. A warship was not the best learning environment because there were too many distractions on board. Members of the crew were frequently talking and shouting, making it difficult to find a quiet space for classes and study. Another problem was the varying quality of the instructors. Although most chaplains were educated men, one has to question their qualifications to teach navigation, which was their most important responsibility. Serious consequences could result if a midshipman failed to learn the correct way to navigate a vessel. Many chaplains saw their position merely as a stepping-stone to the more lucrative purser's position. Even chaplains who did not have loftier career ambitions had other duties to perform. In addition to their religious and teaching functions, chaplains often served as secretary to the captain of a ship or the commodore of a squadron. Civilian schoolmasters received just twenty-five dollars a month and only when the navy actively employed them at sea. Further, they often had to share quarters with their students. It was difficult for the navy to find qualified instructors who were willing to live the hard life at sea for so little compensation or prestige.[29]

Although their formal instruction focused on mathematics and navigation, midshipmen were expected to study other subjects on their own—then and throughout their entire career. The more scholarly midshipmen devoted much of their leisure time to broadening their knowledge by reading books on history, philosophy, law, geography, and naval science as well as classical literature. In a letter to a newly appointed midshipman, navy schoolmaster George Jones recommended that the young man purchase books about the history and geography of the region his ship would be visiting; he also suggested works on natural history and a copy of the Bible. Some midshipmen taught themselves foreign languages, while others studied mathematics in greater depth outside the classroom. Among the more studious midshipmen of the early republic were David G. Farragut, Samuel F. Du Pont, Robert F. Stockton, Matthew Fontaine Maury, and John A. Dahlgren. Although Stockton left Princeton before earning a degree, he continued to read books on history, philosophy, religion, ethics, and law.[30] Du Pont claimed that "all my leisure hours are occupied by reading & studying." Like many of his peers, Du Pont had access to his captain's personal library. It was common for senior naval officers to maintain personal libraries on board ship, and many captains opened their libraries to their junior officers and midshipmen. Captain (later Commodore) Edward Preble owned a library composed mainly of books on professional naval subjects, including seamanship, navigation, naval affairs, law, history, and travel narratives. He also owned a collection of American patriotic songs and enjoyed singing with his guests after dinner. Captain Oliver Hazard Perry amassed a fine library that included works of history, ancient and modern literature, dictionaries and encyclopedias, travel narratives (some of them on the Mediterranean region), and books on navigation, naval operations, and tactics. Captain George Read's wide-ranging library contained volumes covering navigation and seamanship; naval tactics and gunnery; American, maritime, and international law; English grammar and rhetoric; history, geography, and climates; religion and moral philosophy; and diplomacy.[31]

Some navy captains placed little importance on academic studies, believing midshipmen could learn everything they needed to know through observation and practical experience. In his instructions to the young charges under his command, Captain Alexander Murray indicated these priorities when it came to naval education: "You are to be inquisitive to learn all the art & mystery of Seamanship, to do this, you must attend to every thing that is going on onboard. . . . You must be constant in your attendance upon Deck in your respective Watches, & never by any means presume to sleep, on your Watch, and keep in motion, and take frequently the rounds of the Ship, to see that the Sailors do not Sleep." After performing these duties, midshipmen could then devote attention to their studies in navigation.[32]

Early naval education thus emphasized the learning that took place in "the salty school of firsthand experience." The number of midshipmen on a ship varied according to the vessel's size and mission; eleven were usually assigned to a frigate. Once on board, a new midshipman would have to learn the basics of navy life, such as becoming familiar with naval terminology, showing the proper respect to an officer, climbing the ship's rigging, and manning battle stations.[33] Perhaps the most crucial skill to be acquired was what Captain Isaac Chauncey called "the art of governing men"—that is, how to lead the enlisted sailors. A prerequisite for leading was earning the respect of those under one's command. To gain that respect, midshipmen had to master all aspects of seamanship including the duties assigned to enlisted sailors. According to Thomas Truxtun, "An ignorance in this practical knowledge will . . . necessarily be thought an unpardonable deficiency by those who are to follow his directions." The strictly hierarchical social order on a navy ship created a relationship between officers and enlisted seamen that might best be described as paternalistic. An officer was supposed to look after the welfare of his men and make sure they were healthy, clean, well fed, and well clothed. Officers were also responsible for instilling morality in their men by prohibiting profanity, gambling, drunkenness, and blasphemy. Enlisted sailors were required to obey and give deference to their officers and to the midshipmen. The navy did not permit midshipmen to fraternize with enlisted men. As gentlemen and future commissioned officers, midshipmen were in a class above the common sailor; as such, the navy required them to keep a certain social distance from the enlisted men. This would help the midshipmen develop command presence—an absolute necessity for future officers.[34]

Most captains required their midshipmen to be on deck eight hours a day. They reported to the captain at noon daily to chart the ship's course, determine the latitude and longitude of the ship's location, and calculate the distance to the ship's destination. They also had to maintain a journal of the vessel's operations and activities in preparation for one day keeping a ship's log. This journal, which was usually submitted to the captain for review twice a month, recorded such information as the ship's course and coordinates, weather data, sightings or contact with other ships, the number of crew members reported sick, shipboard punishments (the offender, the offense, and the number of lashes inflicted), training exercises, the taking on of supplies, and the arrival or departure of crew members and visitors. Some midshipmen also included descriptions of the places they visited and of animal and plant life they encountered. The journals might also include charts of ports and harbors drawn by by their own hand.[35]

Though Navy regulations did not specify their duties on board ship, midshipmen performed a variety of jobs, such as relaying orders, delivering messages, and assisting the lieutenants in supervising the enlisted sailors. Senior midshipmen were assigned more important tasks, such as standing watch at the forecastle, where they would assist the officer of the deck and were responsible for the forward sails. Less experienced midshipmen often supervised the sailors scrubbing the deck. Other duties included mustering the crew, drawing the daily liquor ration for the enlisted men, and assisting the lieutenants in leading gunnery divisions (a division operated eight to ten guns). One popular, but dangerous assignment was reefing the topsails, which required climbing the masts. This job earned midshipmen the nickname "reefers." When in port, midshipmen took charge of the ship's boats. It was standard procedure for them to take a boat ashore to obtain fresh water and supplies. This routine task could get exciting at any moment. Sailors sometimes attempted to desert the navy during these supply runs, and the midshipmen were responsible for stopping them. Midshipmen might also have to deal with unruly natives on shore. One of their least popular jobs was to go ashore at the end of liberty to round up any sailors who had failed to report back to the ship.[36]

The navy had no standardized system of education and training. Every captain and every chaplain or schoolmaster had his own ideas and expectations concerning the education of midshipmen. Therefore, each midshipman had a unique learning experience. Some midshipmen earned the opportunity to command a vessel—usually a gunboat or a captured prize. David Farragut was only twelve years old when given command of a captured British ship during the War of 1812. Midshipmen often served as acting lieutenants or sailing masters. On smaller vessels, they might stand watch as the officer of the deck. There were also opportunities on shore. Robert Stockton served as an aide to the secretary of the navy in Washington, D.C. In addition to their naval service, many midshipmen went on furlough in order to enter the merchant service, which provided additional opportunities for professional development and command at sea.[37]

Together with classroom instruction and practical training, naval education also offered the experience of life at sea. Midshipmen encountered a wide range of exciting adventures—visiting exotic ports, observing marine animals like sharks and whales up close, helping to rescue a shipmate who had fallen overboard, participating in naval traditions and ceremonies, and attending social functions. Among the less glamorous aspects of that exposure were coping with seasickness and being tossed around the ship during a storm. Serving on a warship was dangerous, with the possibility of death ever present. Battle, disease, accidents, and fatal duels were all part of navy life. Many young men witnessed death for the first time as midshipmen. During the War of 1812, David Farragut saw one crewmate disemboweled by cannon shot and another crewmate's leg blown off; he was himself spattered with a third crewmate's brain matter. Young Farragut was also a British prisoner of war for a short time. During his first cruise as a midshipman, Franklin Buchanan witnessed a failed effort to rescue a sailor who had fallen overboard. He also saw five seamen fall to their death after the mainmast

*Midshipman David G. Farragut (right) talking to a boatswain's mate during
the War of 1812. Farragut, who would go on to become the U.S. Navy's first admiral
during the Civil War, began his naval career as a midshipman at the age of nine.
Courtesy U.S. Naval Institute.*

split.[38] Learning to deal with the hardships of life at sea was a vital part of every midshipman's professional development.

By necessity, midshipmen found ways to cope with the stress of navy life. "Skylarking" was a general term used to describe various activities pursued by midshipmen in their off-duty hours. These activities included horseplay, wrestling, singing, making noise, or anything that helped midshipmen blow off steam. According to George Jones, skylarking often "got the better of Bowditch and study." Midshipmen were legendary practical jokers. In his memoir, navy schoolmaster E. C. Wines tells the story of one midshipman who returned to the steerage at the end of his watch to find a goat in his hammock. Tragically, some midshipmen were unable to deal with the strain of life at sea. Walter Winter of the frigate *John Adams* "lost his senses and became a lunatic," according to one of his fellow midshipmen. Winter neglected his duties, spoke incoherently, stopped eating, and ignored the "calls of nature." He ultimately suffered a nervous breakdown in 1803.[39]

In the opinion of Secretary of the Navy Robert Smith, a midshipman needed four or five years of experience on active duty to qualify for promotion to lieutenant. Before and during the War of 1812, four to six years of service was the norm. On average, a midshipman entering the navy during this period could expect to make captain in just under fifteen years. Stephen Decatur was an exception to the rule, rising from midshipman to captain in only six years as a reward for heroism. Decatur led the successful raid to destroy the captured frigate *Philadelphia* in Tripoli Harbor during the Barbary Wars. After the mission, Commodore Edward Preble wrote to President Jefferson recommending that Lieutenant Decatur receive an immediate promotion to captain; this would act "as a stimulus" to other officers by demonstrating that the government would reward bold and fearless conduct.[40]

Although midshipmen lived a hard life, there was never a shortage of applicants for the post. As one historian has pointed out, "The absolute desirability of naval appointments is in no way better documented than by the congressman who might one day be a vigorous critic of naval expenditures on the floor of the House, but on another could be found climbing the stairs to the secretary [of the navy]'s office to solicit a midshipman's appointment for his son."[41]

Learning under Fire

Service at sea during wartime represented the ultimate form of on-the-job training for midshipmen. When Thomas Jefferson deployed a naval squadron to the Mediterranean in 1801 to confront the Barbary corsairs, one of its missions was "the instruction of our young men so that when their more active services shall hereafter be required, they may be capable of defending the honor of their Country." In 1803 Secretary Smith reminded Commodore Edward Preble "that in all our Mediterranean expeditions the improvement of our officers is a favorite object." In the minds of most early nineteenth-century political and naval leaders, there was no better school for midshipmen and junior officers than a ship actively deployed in combat operations. Smith believed that war was a crucible that helped to identify young men unfit for a naval career: "If it should so happen that you should have . . . in any of the vessels of your squadron any midshipmen who are worthless, vicious, [or] dishonorable in their conduct, or in any respect obviously unworthy of the rank they hold in the Navy, or who are of such a torpid, sluggish disposition as in your opinion they evidently cannot be respectable or useful officers, all such midshipmen, it is my wish, ought to be sent home in the returning vessels."[42]

One of the great benefits of the navy's approach to education and training was the opportunity it provided midshipmen to learn their profession under the guidance of mentors who, in many cases, were the country's first naval heroes. Mentorship was crucial in the development of competent naval officers. Though he had a great deal of experience as a merchant mariner, including command of his own ship, John Rodgers lacked firsthand knowledge of the navy when he signed up during the Quasi-War. His first assignment was serving as first lieutenant on board the frigate *Constellation* under the command of Thomas Truxtun, who would become Rodgers's naval mentor. A strict disciplinarian, Truxtun issued an extensive set of rules and regulations to govern his command. The Truxtun system left an imprint on Rodgers, who modeled his own style of leadership and discipline after his mentor's. Rodgers believed one of his responsibilities as a commanding officer was to weed out those midshipmen and junior officers who were unfit for service, while recognizing and developing men who demonstrated the potential to become outstanding officers. Rodgers's approach to mentorship was not limited to instruction in seamanship and navigation; he also cultivated their patriotism and sense of honor. Among his celebrated protégés were Isaac Hull, Oliver Hazard Perry, David Porter, James Lawrence, Robert F. Stockton, and Matthew C. Perry.[43]

Edward Preble, commodore of the U.S. Navy's Mediterranean Squadron from 1803 to 1804, also took his officer development role seriously. Despite his notoriously abrasive personality, Preble was an excellent role model who earned the respect of his subordinates for his skill as a combat leader, his determination, his patriotism, his willingness to sacrifice for his country, his high standards of professionalism and morality, and his propensity to challenge subordinates by giving them important responsibilities. During their tour of duty in the Mediterranean, Preble's officers (including Stephen Decatur, Charles Stewart, Isaac Hull, James Lawrence, and Thomas Macdonough) experienced naval combat, commanded smaller ships or gunboats, and even conducted an early form of special warfare by destroying the captured *Philadelphia* in Tripoli Harbor. Looking back on his service in the Mediterranean, Thomas Macdonough described the Barbary Wars as a tremendous learning experience for him and for the navy. Macdonough, who served his naval apprenticeship under Edward Preble and Stephen Decatur, participated in Decatur's raid to destroy the *Philadelphia* and fought the Tripolitans in a gunboat battle in Tripoli Harbor. In the Mediterranean, Macdonough developed leadership skills that could be acquired only through experience. He learned the importance of planning, attention to detail, boldness, and leading by example. He also absorbed a great deal about naval strategy and tactics. He proved his bravery and tenacity to his superiors as well as to himself, which gave him confidence in his own abilities as a naval officer.[44]

If Decatur, Rodgers, and Preble were strong professional role models for their subordinates, other officers proved to be examples of what not to do as a naval commander. Most glaring was Richard Morris, Preble's predecessor as commodore of the Mediterranean Squadron. Morris acquired a reputation for being overly cautious in dealing with the threat posed by Tripoli's corsairs. His squadron neither engaged the Tripolitans nor enforced an effective blockade of the city. In short, Morris failed to demonstrate American naval power to the enemy. This failure resulted in low morale and the breakdown of discipline within his squadron. Another example was offered by Captain William Bainbridge. Although he was popular with his fellow officers and scored an impressive victory against the British during the War of 1812, Bainbridge was a questionable role model. A captain at age twenty-five, Bainbridge felt the need to prove his authority to the men under his command, becoming a petty tyrant in the process. He flogged his sailors excessively and sometimes struck them over the head with his sword. Not surprisingly, the men feared and despised him. Bainbridge also seemed to experience more than his fair share of mishaps at sea. During the Quasi-War, he became the first, and at the time the only, American captain to surrender his ship to the enemy. He later allowed the dey of Algiers to commandeer another ship under his command, the frigate *George Washington*, for the purpose of delivering the dey's tribute to the ruler of the Ottoman Empire. Bainbridge then suffered the worst disgrace of his career by running the *Philadelphia* aground off Tripoli. The Tripolitans captured the ship and imprisoned Bainbridge and his crew for almost two years.[45] Observing the superior leadership of men like Preble or Decatur or the inept leadership of men such as Morris or Bainbridge had a profound influence on junior officers and midshipmen, providing them with professional models to emulate or to avoid.

By all indications, the on-the-job education provided by the U.S. Navy produced a corps of highly competent officers during the early national period. The navy performed well in the Quasi-War with France and dealt effectively with the threat to American commerce posed by the Barbary States. During the War of 1812, the U.S. Navy distinguished itself in one-on-one naval duels with British warships and in larger engagements on Lake Erie and Lake Champlain. Despite this success, the War of 1812 acted as a catalyst for changing attitudes within the officer corps and among some politicians concerning the type of naval officer who would best serve the United States. After 1815, the emergent nation required naval officers who were more than just capable warriors. These changing views of the naval profession would eventually lead to a spirited debate among American political leaders regarding the best system of education for navy midshipmen.

CHAPTER 3

A West Point for the Navy?

The War of 1812 was a testing ground for U.S. Army and Navy officers. The army's performance was generally poor and an embarrassment to the nation in the eyes of many Americans. In a war that witnessed the ultimate national disgrace—the burning of the country's poorly defended capital at the hands of the British—the navy was the one bright spot. The victory of the frigate *Constitution*, nicknamed "Old Ironsides" for the way British cannonballs seemed to bounce off its hull, over the HMS *Guerrière* in August 1812 sparked an outpouring of national pride. "Don't give up the ship"—Captain James Lawrence's dying order to his men on board the frigate *Chesapeake*—became a rallying cry for the navy and the nation. Oliver Hazard Perry's victory in the Battle of Lake Erie in September 1813 and Thomas Macdonough's triumph on Lake Champlain a year later further fueled the public's adoration of the navy. Lake Erie and Lake Champlain took their places alongside Lexington and Concord, Bunker Hill, Saratoga, and Yorktown in the hearts of the American people. The performance of army and navy officers inevitably led to an examination of both services' system of officer education. West Point, founded ten years before the outbreak of the war, existed on a very limited scale; it had not yet produced enough officers to influence the army's performance in the war. West Point graduates, however, generally did better than their fellow officers who lacked formal military education. This fact led to a reappraisal of the importance of formal education for U.S. Army and Navy officers.

The Idea of a Naval Academy

The naval success of the United States, in one contemporary observer's words, "reflected the greatest honour upon the national character."[1] "Our Naval triumphs have astonished an admiring world . . . we have seen again and again the British Lion cowering beneath the American Eagle," proclaimed Virginia congressman Thomas Gholson with more than a touch of exaggeration. As Indiana congressman William Hendricks explained, "The navy of the United States, since the late war, has been the peculiar favourite of the nation. Previous to that war, the bravery and skill of our seamen . . . had not fully developed themselves to the American people. Until then, the people of the United States were opposed to an extensive or permanent [naval] establishment, and the naval armaments of former times were only intended for temporary purposes." Thomas Jefferson added his praise in a letter to John Adams: "I sincerely congratulate you on the success of our little navy; which must be more gratifying to you than to most men, as having been the early and constant advocate of wooden walls." Not wishing to portray himself for posterity as an enemy of the now popular navy, Jefferson added: "If I have differed with you on this ground, it was not on the principle, but the time."[2]

Despite the navy's success during the War of 1812 and its immense popularity with the public, there had been serious problems with the Navy Department's organization and its management of the war effort. Jefferson's emphasis on the use of gunboats had proved ineffective in wartime. The navy's administrative structure needed an overhaul, and there were questions concerning the adequacy of the professional education provided for naval officers. This situation prompted Secretary of the Navy William Jones to initiate reforms while the war was still going on. A veteran of the Revolutionary War, Jones had fought in the battles of Trenton and Princeton and served at sea on a privateer commanded by Thomas Truxtun. After the war, he became a merchant in his hometown of Philadelphia and served one term in the U.S. House of Representatives. He had previously turned down the navy secretaryship when Thomas Jefferson offered it to him in 1801. When James Madison asked him to take it during the War of 1812, Jones accepted out of duty. He was a strong supporter of the nation's second war against Britain and felt obligated to serve his country.[3]

Jones had an expansive but pragmatic vision for the U.S. Navy. In the short term, during the War of 1812, he called for reversing the Jeffersonian emphasis on gunboats and concentrating instead on acquiring fast-sailing sloops and brigs that were quicker to build than ships of the line and frigates but were still effective against British commerce. In the long term, Jones favored developing a fleet composed mainly of ships of the line and frigates that could protect the United States from invasion and prevent an enemy blockade. He believed an expanded navy deploying a fleet of more powerful ships would make a large-scale army unnecessary and would actually be a more cost-effective system of national defense than reliance on an extensive regular army. Jones was also a proponent of innovation in shipbuilding. He was an early advocate of steam power for naval vessels as well as standardization of ship design. Based on his experience leading the Navy Department in wartime, Jones argued that a major reorganization of the naval establishment was necessary. Specifically, he favored the creation of a board composed of senior naval officers and qualified civilians to assist the navy secretary with administrative tasks and advise him on naval affairs. Although American naval officers had fought well in the young nation's first conflicts at sea, Jones believed that the powerful navy he envisioned would require a higher level of professionalism and formal education within the officer corps. To meet this need, he called for the establishment of a naval academy.[4]

Jones submitted a comprehensive plan for the reorganization and reform of the Navy Department to Congress in November 1814. Its main features were the creation of a Board of Inspectors to assist the secretary in naval administration and the formation of a naval academy to instruct midshipmen in mathematics, the sciences, gunnery, naval architecture, and mechanical drawing—all of which were "necessary to the accomplishment of the naval officer."[5] Informal naval schools had been set up before and during the War of 1812 to provide basic instruction for the midshipmen who were not at sea. In 1802 navy secretary Robert Smith had ordered Robert Thompson, a navy chaplain, to organize a small school to teach mathematics and navigation at the Washington Navy Yard. Although attendance would be voluntary, Smith strongly urged midshipmen to take advantage of this educational opportunity. The school remained open until 1804, when Thompson went to sea. Thompson resumed teaching at the Washington Navy Yard in 1806 and, beginning in 1808, traveled to the New York and Norfolk navy yards to provide instruction for the midshipmen stationed there. After Thompson's death, Secretary of the Navy Paul Hamilton appointed Andrew Hunter, a Presbyterian minister and former professor of mathematics and astronomy at Princeton, as the navy's principal instructor in Washington. Beginning in 1811, Hunter operated an informal academy at the navy yard and offered classes in mathematics, navigation, and astronomy. The school closed in 1812 because the navy needed all of the midshipmen for sea duty. During the war, there was a small "mathematical school" for midshipmen and junior officers in upstate New York on the shores of Lake Ontario. The most unique arrangement for naval education was seen during the Barbary Wars, when the imprisoned midshipmen of the frigate *Philadelphia* used their period of confinement in Tripoli to further their studies. With the assistance of a Danish diplomat, the prisoners gained access to a collection of books, some of which probably came from their own ship's library. The *Philadelphia*'s officers started a school in the prison, instructing the captured midshipmen in mathematics, navigation, and naval tactics.[6] Secretary Jones hoped to build on these limited efforts by establishing an institution that more closely resembled West Point.

Representative William Reed, chairman of the House naval committee, wrote to several senior naval officers to ask their opinions of Jones's reform plan. Most of the replies focused on the proposed Board of Inspectors. Only three of the eight officers whose responses were printed in the *American State Papers* discussed the naval academy proposal. Captain Samuel Evans believed a naval academy "would unquestionably be productive[,] of great advantage to the service." Captain Thomas Tingey agreed, stating that an academy would "tend to preclude the probability of public ships and vessels falling under the management of incompetent [and] uninformed men." Captain Charles Stewart opposed the idea, believing time at sea in the merchant marine was a more valuable school for midshipmen than an academy on shore. The merchant service provided "the essential knowledge of seamanship, the properties of different species of vessels, an acquaintance and familiarity with coasts, countries, and nations; a knowledge of their marine, commerce, and fortresses; the genius of the people, and their language; which would be essential to them as officers, and important to the nation."[7] In the end, the only part of Jones's plan that Congress accepted was the creation of a Board of Navy Commissioners to assist the secretary with administrative matters such as procurement, finance, supply, shipbuilding, and the deployment of ships. The officer corps had acquitted itself well during the War of 1812, which meant that administrative reform took precedence over educational reform.[8]

Sylvanus Thayer and the West Point Renaissance

If the navy was riding high in the wake of the War of 1812, the army was experiencing a low point in its history. "Every American was proud to know that victories brilliant and decisive had been achieved by our naval heroes on the ocean and the lakes," proclaimed Representative William Gaston of North Carolina. Unfortunately, in Gaston's opinion and that of many Americans, the army's performance in battle left much to be desired.

The campaign against Canada, in particular, had been a disaster. Gaston was forced to conclude that America's "military character has been degraded." Incompetent officers were the norm, and militia units, necessary because of the vastly reduced size of the regular army in the years leading up to the war, were mostly ineffective and unreliable. Organizational, administrative, supply, and discipline problems plagued the army and hampered the war effort. Although Americans were fond of bragging about how they had won a great victory against the British for the second time, the reality was that the United States had merely survived the War of 1812.[9]

The military policies of Jefferson and Madison had left the United States unprepared for the war with Britain. A new breed of young Republicans, who burst onto the political scene just before the conflict began, understood this and became strong advocates of a more aggressive and professional approach to national defense. These Republicans, called "War Hawks" because of their strong support for war against Britain, were led by John C. Calhoun of South Carolina and Henry Clay of Kentucky. Over the course of the war, the new, nationalist Republicans would overshadow the older, Jeffersonian Republicans and move their party and the nation in a new direction. Republicans had traditionally feared war because it increased the national debt, raised taxes, and required standing military forces. New Republicans like Calhoun and Clay accepted, and in some cases even welcomed, war as a necessary part of national life and as a vehicle for policymaking. The War of 1812 produced a surge of nationalism in America, and in the postwar period the republic began to assert itself on the world stage as it never had before. Standing up to the British a second time, and living to tell the tale, had emboldened the United States. Economic development and military proficiency became the new hallmarks of the Democratic-Republican Party and the nation as a whole. Expanded commerce, increased manufacturing, a vigorous search for new economic opportunities overseas, and a system of internal improvements such as roads and canals would fuel unprecedented prosperity for the American people. This new, more aggressive approach to economic development meant that the United States would have to maintain stronger, more effective military and naval establishments that could better protect the nation and defend its interests abroad.[10]

The Federalist Party's opposition to the War of 1812 had killed any chance it had to remain a force in American politics. The decline of their opposition party led the Republicans to embrace some policies that were Federalist in origin, policies that increased the power of the federal government. With the Federalists finished as a viable political party, there was no longer any fear of monarchical or aristocratic elements taking over the republic. Since the nation was secure, there was no danger in adopting policies that expanded the government's role in fostering economic growth or increasing military professionalism.[11] Virginia congressman John Kerr articulated this perspective in a circular letter to his constituents:

> We now occupy an honorable and dignified attitude; we have established a national character; we have solved the interesting problem, and proved to the astonished world, that we are capable of self-government; that republican principles and policy can unite and sustain a great and magnanimous people amidst the most awful conflicts and difficulties; we have shown that we have the best materials for an army and navy that the god of nature ever formed, and that these materials can be brought into action.[12]

Although Kerr believed that America's citizen soldiers had ably defended the country against the British, other political leaders disagreed; they argued that the United States needed military professionals to protect itself against future enemies.

John C. Calhoun became a prominent spokesman for military preparedness and professionalism. A Yale graduate and lawyer, Calhoun had served in the South Carolina state legislature before his election to Congress in 1810. He held a seat in the U.S. House of Representatives from 1811 to 1817, when he became President James Monroe's secretary of war. The War of 1812 had proved that reliance on the militia for America's national security was a mistake. To Calhoun's way of thinking, it was vital for the United States to adopt a more professional approach to national defense by acquiring "military skill and means, combined with the tone of thinking and feeling necessary to their use." Calhoun was a realist who recognized that America's commercial interests inevitably led to collisions with Britain and France that could easily involve the nation in a European war. "The ambition of a single nation," he cautioned his fellow citizens, "can destroy the peace of the world."[13] For Calhoun, a professional military was the best means of defense in an uncertain and potentially dangerous world.

Postwar nationalism and the emergence of a new, more aggressive brand of Republicanism helped to spawn a renaissance at West Point. Under the leadership of superintendent Sylvanus Thayer, the U.S. Military Academy became a respected and prestigious national institution. Born in 1785 in Braintree, Massachusetts, Thayer had graduated first in his class from Dartmouth College in 1807. After entering West Point, he completed his studies in less than a year and was commissioned into the Corps of Engineers in 1808. He became an assistant professor of mathematics at West Point before serving in the War of 1812. Thayer saw the only combat of his military career in the ill-fated Canada campaign, an experience that convinced him of the need for highly trained, professional officers. After the war, Thayer spent two years studying the fortifications and military schools in France. The federal government funded the trip and authorized Thayer to purchase books, maps, and engineering models for West Point while he was abroad. Thayer returned to West Point as the new superintendent in 1817.[14]

Thayer was only thirty-two years old when he took over the Military Academy. Quiet and studious, he was a brilliant scholar who possessed expert knowledge of every subject taught at West Point. As superintendent, he made sure he was aware of everything that transpired there. He knew every cadet by name and was familiar with the young man's academic and military standing. A perfectionist by nature, Thayer demanded strict adherence to academy regulations and expected every cadet to meet his rigorous academic standards. Any student who failed to do so found himself standing on the academy's boat dock with a ticket home. Personally, Thayer was something of an enigma. He had a reputation for being cold, even ruthless; it seemed that the only emotion he possessed was resentment toward those officers and cadets who did not meet his high standards of intelligence, discipline, and professionalism. He had few friends, never married, and was not particularly close to his family. He made no effort to cultivate his popularity among the cadets or the faculty, and it does not appear that he was ever well liked. According to Cadet Robert E. Lee, a member of the Class of 1829, the cadets disliked Thayer because they thought he spied on them. Yet he did have their respect. West Point cadets of the early nineteenth century often gave private nicknames to the officers assigned to the academy staff. Thayer never had a nickname; he was always referred to as "the superintendent" or by his rank. There was, however, a softer side to Thayer. He was in many ways a father figure to the cadets, showing great concern for their general welfare. He was always compassionate when tragedy struck their families. And he closely followed their careers, usually with pride though sometimes with disapproval, as in the case of Cadet Jefferson Davis of the Class of 1828. Davis's poor grades and frequent visits to Benny Havens's tavern earned him the superintendent's scorn. Thayer viewed Davis as a poor excuse for an army officer and, later, as a less-than-impressive secretary of war.[15]

Thayer's goal at West Point was to create a learning environment that would produce his model American army officer—a disciplined gentleman of strong moral character and military bearing who applied his expert scientific knowledge to the conduct of warfare. The Thayer system had three major components: academics, which featured a prescribed, scientific cur-

Sylvanus Thayer, the "Father of the Military Academy," served as West Point's superintendent from 1817 to 1833. His academic and military reforms helped to transform West Point from a small mathematical school into a prestigious national institution. Portrait by Robert Weir in the West Point Museum. Photo courtesy Wisconsin Historical Society (Image #WHi-66183).

riculum and an instructional method that required daily recitations by all cadets; discipline and character development; and military training. Every aspect of the West Point experience, from the austere living conditions to mandatory attendance at chapel, served Thayer's ultimate purpose of turning out the ideal army officer. His philosophy of education derived from the French system of military and technical schooling that he had observed during his travels in Europe after the War of 1812. His views on curriculum, textbooks, organization, admission requirements, examinations, grading, faculty, and military training all originated in his observations of the École Polytechnique, France's premier military and engineering school. On becoming superintendent of West Point, Thayer immediately set out to put his educational philosophy into practice. He conducted examinations of all of the cadets, which led to the dismissal of twenty-one of them for academic deficiency. He then proceeded to reorganize and reform the academy. Unlike his predecessor, Alden Partridge, Thayer was willing to delegate authority. Although he closely monitored each cadet's academic performance by requiring weekly progress reports from the faculty, Thayer did not teach any classes. He created a new officer position—commandant of cadets—to supervise their discipline and military training. Thayer also appointed army lieutenants to serve as tactical officers. In addition to assisting the commandant with military instruction, the tactical officers lived in the cadet barracks in order to maintain discipline through constant supervision. To provide the cadets with leadership experience, Thayer organized the Corps of Cadets as a battalion. Cadets held officer positions within the battalion and its two companies on a rotational basis.[16]

Before Thayer took over, academy life had little structure. Cadets arrived at West Point at different times, had examinations at different times (if at all), and graduated at different times. Thayer transformed this haphazard system. He instituted general examinations in January and June, with graduation scheduled after the June examination. Much to the cadets' dismay, Thayer eliminated the annual summer vacation, believing it was

> not only unnecessary but highly injurious to the Cadets & to the Institution. The Cadets being supplied at the Academy with every thing necessary to them have no occasion to go home for supplies of cloathing [sic] & money as is the case with students at our Colleges. Accordingly I am well assured that much the greatest portion of the Cadets did not visit their homes during the last Vacation but flocked, as usual, to New-york & other cities there to indulge in dissipation & to contract disease, vices & debts. Many were there detained some months, either by disease or on account of debts, others were put in jail, & several of the young gentlemen I have not heard of since.

Thayer replaced the summer vacation with a military encampment to introduce the cadets to army life, including daily inspections, living in tents, parades, musket firing, and infantry and artillery drill. All cadets were required to report to West Point in June for the encampment. Their only vacation was in the summer after their second year at the academy; this was the only time they could leave West Point during their four years as a cadet. Thayer also issued a comprehensive set of rules and regulations governing life at the academy. Leaving the post without permission, drinking, card playing, cooking in the barracks, fighting, dueling, publishing articles about the academy, receiving money from home, wearing civilian clothes, holding unauthorized meetings, and forming social clubs were all prohibited.[17]

Thayer standardized the West Point curriculum as a four-year program emphasizing scientific and technical subjects such as mathematics, chemistry, natural philosophy, and military and civil engineering. The cadets also received instruction in drawing, English grammar and composition, French, geography, history, law, and ethics in addition to their military training. Each cadet's mastery of this curriculum was measured by Thayer's new system of ranking each cadet within his class according to academic and military performance. This merit roll was probably Thayer's most significant academic reform. He created the merit system to establish an objective and efficient method for assigning graduating cadets to a particular branch of the army and to foster some healthy competition within the corps. Cadets were graded in every aspect of their West Point experience—academics, conduct, and military training. Every cadet received a daily grade in each course based on the quality of his recitation. Although academic performance had the most weight, everything counted toward a cadet's ranking—how he performed during military drill, his personal behavior, the appearance of his uniform, the cleanliness of his barracks room. Cadets received demerits for violating the academy's rules and regulations. By the time graduation arrived, there was a vast amount of information available on each cadet. The merit roll helped to ensure that ability, not political connections or wealth, was the primary factor in the West Point experience and in each newly commissioned officer's branch assignment. Generally, only those cadets who graduated at the top of their class could become engineers. Those finishing in the upper half could become artillery officers, while those graduating in the bottom half usually served in the cavalry or the infantry.[18]

Because daily recitations could only work in small sections, Thayer increased the size of the faculty, using recent West Point graduates and some advanced cadets as assistant professors. Thayer and the faculty assigned cadets to course sections based on ability, enabling each cadet to pursue his studies at the appropriate learning pace. The academy library expanded by over one thousand books and five hundred maps and charts, most of which Thayer had purchased during his time in France. In 1818 two important organizations became part of West Point life: the Academic Board and the Board of Visitors. The Academic Board, chaired by the superintendent and composed of the principal professors at West Point, was responsible for the curriculum and for administering cadet examinations. The Board of Visitors consisted of distinguished gentlemen and scholars appointed each year from outside the academy. The visitors were responsible for supervising the June examination and for reporting on the state of the academy to the secretary of war. In addition to its academic and oversight functions, the board played a substantial public relations role when Thayer decided to use it to enhance West Point's reputation with the American people. The superintendent made sure to publish the board's reports, which were almost always favorable. Since they were prepared by the well-known and influential men who sat on the board, these reports helped to promote West Point as a prestigious national institution.[19]

West Point's image was a major concern for Thayer. As a consequence of its geographic isolation, many Americans had never seen a cadet and had no idea what went on at the academy. To increase the public's interest in and contact with the school, Thayer organized a series of annual cadet marches from 1819 to 1821 to cities and towns in the Northeast. The cadets' appearance and their marching skills undoubtedly impressed spectators, especially when compared to the less professional appearance and abilities of local militia companies. Despite their traditional suspicion of standing armies and military professionals, Americans remained fascinated by all things military, especially uniforms, infantry drill, and bands. During the marches, the Corps of Cadets visited such cities as Poughkeepsie, Albany, New York City, Philadelphia, Boston, Worcester, Springfield, Providence, New London, and New Haven. These demonstrations were discontinued after 1821 because Thayer felt they took too much time away from military training; he also feared that all of the social activities to which the cadets were invited would have a bad influence on them. By that point, the marches had served their purpose by gaining West Point a great deal of favorable press coverage.[20]

Although Thayer's reforms and public relations campaign greatly enhanced West Point's national reputation and prestige, some politicians became openly hostile to the academy. The most extreme opponent was Tennessee congressman Newton Cannon, who introduced a resolution in the House of Representatives to abolish West Point and sell the land to the highest bidder. In Cannon's opinion, its sole purpose was providing for "the gratuitous instruction of a privileged class of youth." New Hampshire congressman Josiah Butler agreed, denouncing the academy as a "sink of dissipation."[21]

There were two major reasons why some politicians opposed West Point. The first was that graduates received preferential treatment in the distribution of officer commissions. A reduction in the size of the army in 1821 meant that fewer commissions were available. Because Secretary of War Calhoun was a strong advocate of military education in general and West Point in particular, he favored academy graduates in the appointment of officers. In 1817 only 14.8 percent of army officers were West Point graduates. By 1830, however, graduates composed 63.8 percent of the army officer corps, and allegations of a West Point monopoly on officer commissions became more widespread. Opposition to the U.S. Military Academy also arose as a consequence of the transportation revolution in the United States. West Point was the nation's only school of engineering during this period, and the scientific and technical knowledge cadets acquired there had useful civilian applications. Given the technical curriculum, academy graduates were in high demand as civil engineers. Companies involved in building roads, canals, and bridges offered West Point graduates much higher salaries than the army could. Although graduates had to serve in the army for five years, the four years spent at the academy counted toward that number, meaning that graduates could resign from the army after only a year of service in the field. Increasing numbers of officers did exactly that to accept more lucrative positions with engineering companies, state governments, and civilian colleges. The academy's critics, such as Representative William Eustis (the former secretary of war), argued that "many young men have been sent to the academy for the purpose of receiving a general education, without the intention of engaging in military service." *Niles' Register* complained that West Point existed "to educate and fit for *private* life, the sons of the most wealthy or most influential persons in the United States."[22] Although these opponents failed to tarnish the academy's prestigious image in the 1820s, their criticisms gained strength during the 1830s.

West Point's rise to national prominence under Sylvanus Thayer played a significant role in reviving the naval academy debate. Another factor was the growing attitude within the naval community that the naval profession was distinct from the merchant service and required mastery of a different body of knowledge and skills. Although it continued to have close ties with the latter service, the naval officer corps had become "self-perpetuating" by the War of 1812 era, meaning that the navy developed its own officers rather than commissioning men directly from the merchant marine. Officers and midshipmen increasingly adopted the view that there was something inherently different about the naval profession, something that young men could not learn by sailing with the merchant marine. Midshipmen used this argument to oppose the promotion of sailing masters to the rank of lieutenant. A sailing master was an experienced seaman, usually hired from the merchant service, who was responsible for navigation, the sails and rigging, stores and supplies, and the logbook. In an 1815 petition to the Senate, midshipmen contended that the sailing masters' previous experience in the merchant marine did not qualify them for commissions as naval officers. Furthermore, many sailing masters accepted naval employment only on a temporary basis and returned to the merchant service when the opportunity presented itself. Midshipmen, in contrast, were "trained and educated from very early years" to be officers and devoted themselves to the public service as their only profession. The petition concluded by respectfully suggesting that the federal government offer a better system of naval education if it had doubts about their qualifications to be officers.[23] One could make the argument that the midshipmen were simply trying to eliminate their chief competition for promotion. Nevertheless, their reasoning illustrates the growing sense of professional identity within the naval officer community.

Commodore John Rodgers, president of the Board of Navy Commissioners, also believed that the navy was a higher calling than the merchant marine, one that required specialized knowledge and a unique set of skills. This sentiment might seem strange given the fact that Rodgers began his career in the merchant service and had commanded a merchant ship before reaching the age of twenty. Rodgers joined the navy in 1798 for service in the Quasi-War and soon became, in the minds of many, the model professional naval officer. Senator Thomas Hart Benton of Missouri once described him as "the complete impersonation of my idea of the perfect naval commander—person, mind, and manners." Writing in 1821, Rodgers asserted: "In the merchant service seamanship may, it is true, be learnt—but that only, and that constitutes but a very small part of the education of a navy officer." Only navy ships could provide a suitable environment for the professional development of midshipmen, although he also saw the need for naval education on shore. In an 1815 report of the Board of Navy Commissioners, Rodgers and fellow board member David Porter advocated the establishment of a naval college for midshipmen to supplement the instruction they received at sea. The report further recommended that the navy require midshipmen to pass an examination administered by the commissioners (or officers specially appointed for that purpose) that tested their professional knowledge.[24]

In 1819 the navy introduced a professional examination for promotion to lieutenant. Over the years this event was held in various locations, including New York, Baltimore, Washington, and even on deployed ships. The examining board usually consisted of a commodore, two captains, and a navy schoolmaster. Initially, midshipmen took the examination after seven years of service; the navy later changed the rule to five years. Any midshipman who failed, or "bilged," the exam twice was dismissed from the navy. Most midshipmen dreaded the test. One midshipman claimed that waiting to take it was worse than going into battle. The subject matter covered in the examination, which was oral and one or two hours in length, was limited to mathematics, navigation, and seamanship. The examining board usually required some chalkboard demonstrations of mathematical problems. Midshipmen generally considered the seamanship component to be the most difficult. It was common knowledge that to pass the navigation component, one need only memorize the formulas in Bowditch's *Navigator*. Samuel F. Du Pont described his exam on board the ship of the line *North Carolina* as "long, strict, and tedious beyond measure," but the end result was "glorious."[25] In 1827 the navy created the rank of "passed midshipman" to serve as a transition for midshipmen who had passed their exam but could not receive a promotion to lieutenant because there were no vacancies in that rank.

In 1820 the navy had implemented a second reform to eliminate midshipmen unfit for service as naval officers. The Navy Department began issuing acting midshipman appointments to young men entering the navy. Previously, new candidates received their midshipman's warrant immediately on their appointment. In other words, they were full-fledged midshipmen right from the start. After 1820, they were required to serve on probation for six months. If his service during this period was satisfactory, a candidate would receive his warrant and become a full midshipman; if not, he was dismissed from the navy.[26]

Despite the use of examinations to measure the professional competency of midshipmen and a probationary period to weed out the unfit, there were still politicians who called for the establishment of a naval academy. At the very least, they said, an academy would provide an appropriate environment for study. Although some midshipmen spent many hours studying for the examination, most of them resorted to last-minute cramming and hoped for the best. Among the academy advocates were former presidents John Adams and Thomas Jefferson. Writing to Jefferson in 1821, Adams commented that West Point had been "brought to a considerable degree of perfection" and asked, "Would not a similar establishment for the education of naval Officers be equally Usefull? The public Opinion of the nation seems now to be favourable to a Navy as the cheapest and safest Arm for our national defence. Is not this a favourable moment for proposing a naval Academy?" Jefferson agreed that "there should be a school of instruction for our navy"; he suggested that perhaps the U.S. Military Academy could serve the educational needs of both the army and the navy.[27]

Secretary of the Navy Smith Thompson gave some attention to the naval academy issue during his administration. A native of Dutchess County, New York, Thompson was a Princeton graduate and lawyer who was serving as chief justice of the New York State Supreme Court at the time of his appointment as secretary of the navy. Lacking any experience in naval affairs, Thompson's main qualification for the job apparently was his residence in New York (President Monroe needed someone to represent the middle states in his cabinet). Thompson's tenure at the Navy Department was unremarkable. In fact, his major claim to fame seems to have been that he spent more time away from Washington than any other navy secretary.[28]

In December 1822 Thompson did submit recommendations to Monroe for reorganizing the navy, including some much-needed reforms and the establishment of a naval academy. His proposal for the latter was less than forceful: "This is intended as a mere suggestion of a measure deserving consideration." One congressman advanced the idea that a school for naval instruction be attached to West Point, and the House Naval Affairs Committee issued a statement that there should be no reductions made in the number of midshipmen because they were "a class of officers to whom our future Navy must look for experience, discipline, and nautical science." But Congress failed to take any action concerning naval education.[29] Thompson never put much effort into making the system of naval instruction more effective. He found the administration of the Navy Department tedious and left much of the paperwork to the chief clerk and the Board of Navy Commissioners. For the most part, the department during Thompson's tenure was a ship without a captain.[30] What the navy needed was a secretary who understood that a naval academy was essential and, more importantly, who was willing to use his influence to push Congress toward its establishment.

Naval Education and National Improvement

In August 1823 Smith Thompson accepted President Monroe's appointment as an associate justice of the U.S. Supreme Court. Monroe chose Senator Samuel L. Southard of New Jersey to replace Thompson at the Navy Department. Born in 1787 into an ardent Jeffersonian Republican family, Southard was a Princeton graduate who had taught school and practiced law before entering politics. He served in the New Jersey legislature and sat on the New Jersey Supreme Court before his election to the U.S. Senate. Taking office in 1821, Southard soon became uncomfortable in the Senate. He disliked public speaking and was insecure around his colleagues, whom he considered his intellectual and oratorical superiors. Southard decided to do everything possible to earn an appointment to another federal office, preferably the cabinet or a seat on the highest court. Fortunately for Southard and his ambition, he quickly struck up a friendship with James Monroe. Southard became a frequent guest at official White House functions and often accompanied the president on walks around the capital. When a Supreme Court justice died in March 1823, Southard hoped that Monroe would offer him the vacant seat on the bench. Monroe chose Smith Thompson instead, but gave the Navy Department to Southard. A friend advised Southard, who had no previous experience in naval affairs, to "stick to your law and to politics, about which you know something; but let alone the navy, about which you know nothing." Nevertheless, Southard's ambition and energy more than made up for his lack of knowledge and experience in naval matters, and he embraced the opportunity to prove he could be a capable administrator.[31]

After taking office, Southard picked up where Thompson left off on the naval academy issue. In January 1824 he issued a report articulating his views on naval education. To produce competent naval officers, he believed, the United States had to educate and train midshipmen both at sea and on shore. While admitting that a "great portion of the science of the naval commanders can be acquired only on the ocean," Southard contended that the best place for the early education of midshipmen was at a naval academy. He reiterated this argument in a report to Congress in December, specifically alluding to West Point as evidence of the benefits associated with an academy education: "We have now the light of experience on this point in the army, and its salutary effects are very manifest. Instruction is not less necessary to the navy than to the army." Although Congress mostly ignored Southard's recommendation, his ideas did receive some favorable press. One newspaper observed that an academy would be "a radical improvement" for the navy by instilling in the midshipmen "proper habits, sentiments, and feelings" in addition to improving the intellect and discipline of the navy's future officers.[32]

Southard waited only a month before resuming his argument. Because of America's geographic location, the navy formed the front line of the nation's defense. The education of naval officers was, therefore, a vital national concern. Through scientific education, the service would become more efficient and more economical—a more effective naval force would allow the United States to maintain a smaller navy in peacetime. A naval academy would also improve discipline and reduce the number of courts-martial convened every year. In an academy, "moral principles are secured, good habits formed, subordination learned, honorable feelings encouraged and confirmed, skill acquired, science and discipline necessarily combined." Southard went on to explain that midshipmen

> are taken from the poor, who have not the means of a good education, as well as the rich, who have. They enter, from the nature of the duties, at so early an age, that they cannot be accomplished, nor even moderately accurate, scholars. They are constantly employed on ship board, or in our navy yards, where much advancement in learning cannot be expected. . . . The consequence necessarily is . . . that very many advance in age, and rise in grade, much less cultivated and informed than their own reputation and that of the country require.

The only solution to this problem was the establishment of a naval academy that would "combine literary with professional instruction." Education was even more necessary for a naval officer than for an army officer because the naval officer was the "representative of his country in every port to which he goes; and by him is that country, in a greater or less degree, estimated." Southard believed the navy could establish an adequate school at Governors Island, New York (the location of a U.S. Army post), at a cost of only ten thousand dollars.[33]

Southard pursued the establishment of a naval academy during a period of ardent nationalism in the United States. After successfully defending its territory and independence against the British in the War of 1812, America became more assertive in the international arena, seeking to extend its maritime commerce to new parts of the globe while also expanding territorially across the North American continent. President James Monroe and Secretary of State John Quincy Adams were the "primary architects of the nationalistic policies" of the postwar era. The Monroe Doctrine of 1823, devised by Adams and proclaimed by Monroe, has been described as America's "declaration of diplomatic independence." Monroe introduced the doctrine in response to the emergence of independent republics in Latin America. It stated that the United States would not tolerate further European colonization in the Western Hemisphere or European interference with independent nations in the hemisphere. In return, the United States pledged not to interfere in European affairs or with existing colonies in the New World. The Monroe Doctrine did not have a significant impact on American foreign policy before the Civil War. But it did make an important statement to the world that the United States was establishing its identity in international affairs and staking its claim as a power in the Western Hemisphere. Though the doctrine was directed at all of Europe, U.S. leaders were particularly concerned with Great Britain. Americans viewed the British as their principal rival and the most powerful obstacle to U.S. expansion. Britain was the world's strongest commercial and naval power and maintained a formidable presence in the Western Hemisphere through its colonies in the West Indies and its possession of Canada. Mutual animosity from the Revolutionary War and the War of 1812 became even more intense as a result of Anglo-American competition for markets in the Pacific, Asia, and Latin America as well as territory in North America, especially California, Texas, and Oregon. The United States wanted to expand commercially and territorially, while Britain wanted to prevent any American expansion that might threaten its own commercial dominance and its colonial possessions in the Western Hemisphere.[34]

This Anglo-American rivalry had important implications for U.S. naval education. As Southard pointed out, naval officers were representatives of the United States. Other nations would judge the republic based on their opinion of the American naval officers they encountered on the high seas and in seaports around the world. American naval officers had to compete with British naval officers in the discovery and acquisition of lucrative new markets. Because America lacked an aristocracy from which to draw its officers, Southard and others believed a naval academy was necessary to elevate American midshipmen, most of whom came from the middle class, to an intellectual and social level that rivaled their counterparts in the Royal Navy. British officers at this time comprised a decidedly elite corps. Although there had been some democratization of the Royal Navy during the Napoleonic Wars because of the great need for officers, the officer corps reversed its democratic turn after Napoleon's defeat and became even more aristocratic. Of the young men entering the Royal Navy as officers in the post-1815 period, 45.4 percent came from titled aristocracy (members of the House of Lords or baronets) and landed gentry. Another 54.2 percent hailed from elite or influential professional backgrounds (military, clergy, law, politics/civil service). The Royal Navy's elite character was even more apparent in the officer corps' highest ranks (admirals and captains). Although it was still possible for a young man from a nonelite background to receive a commission, he had little chance of rising above the rank of lieutenant or possibly commander. Almost every captain serving in the post-1815 era was the son of a high-ranking naval or army officer; titled aristocrat; or member of the landed gentry, Parliament, or high clergy.[35] Such an elite corps would surely impress foreign leaders. American naval officers had to match British professional, intellectual, and social sophistication if the United States had any hope of competing for new markets. In Southard's opinion, a naval academy was necessary to achieve that goal. Both the Senate and the House of Representatives referred the naval academy issue to committees for further consideration, but neither body took any action.[36]

When James Monroe's second term ended in March 1825, incoming president John Quincy Adams retained Southard as secretary of the navy. The fact that Southard had initially supported John C. Calhoun in the 1824 presidential campaign was not a problem for Adams. Southard and Adams got along well, agreed on most policy issues, and had served together in Monroe's cabinet. Adams was convinced that Southard's political experience and administrative ability would contribute a great deal to his administration, and Southard soon became one of Adams's most trusted advisers.[37]

John Quincy Adams articulated a broad vision for America's development as a nation. If one word described that vision, it was "improvement." He believed in federal government support for industry, transportation, commerce, education, and science. Federal power, to Adams's way of thinking, should not be limited to physical improvements such as roads and canals; it should include moral and intellectual improvement as well. During his presidency, he called for the establishment of a national university, a naval academy, national scientific endeavors, internal improvement projects, and economic development programs. In the new president's mind, the United States had developed to the point where aristocratic or militaristic influences no longer threatened the republic and liberty. Americans, therefore, had nothing to fear from a powerful and activist federal government.[38]

The ambitious and scholarly Adams envisioned the United States becoming a great empire, not one based on conquest but an "Empire of Learning and the Arts." He interpreted America's development as unfolding in three stages. The first stage was the "acquisition of the right of self-government" through the Declaration of Independence and the Revolutionary War. The second stage was the drafting and ratification of the Constitution, which solidified the union of the states in a national government. The final stage was "the adaptation of the powers, physical, moral, and intellectual, of this whole Union, to the improvement of its own condition."[39] This last stage was what Adams hoped to achieve during his presidency.

In his first annual message to Congress in December 1825, Adams declared that the federal government's primary responsibility was "the progressive improvement of the condition of the governed." Internal improvements such as roads and canals were certainly important, but knowledge was the foremost instrument of improvement for individuals and for society. Therefore, along with internal improvements, Adams affirmed the importance of "public institutions and seminaries of learning." However, merely having educational institutions was not enough. The United States had to take an active role in the acquisition and distribution of knowledge through scientific discovery, particularly in the fields of geography and astronomy. Because it benefited from the scientific endeavors of nations such as Britain, France, and Russia, America had an obligation to make its own contributions to human knowledge. Adams had a nationalist motivation for endorsing science. In recommending the establishment of a national astronomical observatory, Adams said it was an embarrassment that the United States did not have such an institution when Europe had constructed over a hundred "light-houses of the skies."[40]

In contrast to the traditional view that liberty meant less government and less involvement in the world, Adams proclaimed that "liberty is power" and that "the nation blessed with the largest portion of liberty must in proportion to its numbers be the most powerful nation upon earth." This great power should be used for the improvement of individuals and the entire nation; otherwise, the United States would confine itself to "perpetual inferiority."[41] This expansive vision for America was perhaps too expansive. In his diary, Adams admitted that his cabinet suggested he tone down his rhetoric before sending the message to Congress. Secretary of State Henry Clay thought the national university idea was unconstitutional and "entirely hopeless" as to its prospects in the House and Senate. Attorney General William Wirt said the internal improvements section of the message was "excessively bold" and made it seem like Adams was trying to expand federal power beyond acceptable limits. Despite these warnings, the president was determined to proceed with his "perilous experiment."[42]

Like his father, John Quincy Adams was a patron of the navy and viewed it as an important instrument of national progress. In his first annual message to Congress, John Quincy advocated the establishment of a naval academy along with his recommendations for internal improvements, a national university, an observatory, and scientific exploration. In his words, "The want of a naval school of instruction, corresponding to the Military Academy at West Point, for the formation of scientific and accomplished officers, is felt with daily increasing aggravation." Adams believed it was America's destiny to expand its influence beyond North America and to become "a great naval power." Naval reform, especially a naval academy, was necessary to achieve that goal.[43]

With the enthusiastic support of the commander in chief, Samuel Southard set out to transform the U.S. Navy. A reformer by nature, he embraced innovation, which included such measures as constructing dry docks for the repair and maintenance of navy ships; improving existing navy yards and building a new navy yard at Pensacola, Florida; creating a criminal code for the navy to help to standardize discipline; constructing additional naval hospitals and increasing the pay of medical personnel; reforming the promotion system, including the creation of flag rank (admirals); reorganizing the navy's system of recruiting seamen, with special emphasis on trying to attract men from the interior regions of the country; launching scientific expeditions and coastal surveys; and, lastly, establishing a naval academy.[44]

On January 20, 1826, New York representative Henry Storrs, chairman of the House Naval Affairs Committee, introduced a bill to organize a naval school. Southard had prepared the bill in consultation with the president. A day earlier, South Carolina's Robert Y. Hayne, chairman of the Senate Naval Affairs Committee, had introduced a similar bill in the Senate. The House bill gave the president the authority to select a suitable location for the school on public land the government already used for military purposes and gave the president the power to devise a set of regulations for its operation. The bill also authorized the president to appoint a navy captain to serve as commandant and to appoint a professor of natural and experimental philosophy, a professor of mathematics and navigation, a teacher of geography and history, a teacher of the French and Spanish languages, and a fencing master. The secretary of the navy was empowered to purchase any books and scientific equipment needed for the school. The Senate bill was slightly more general but similar in scope.[45] Neither house took immediate action on their respective bills.

The president's public support for a naval academy and the introduction of a bill to establish it in each house of Congress quickly resulted in petitions from seaport cities wishing to become the home of the proposed academy. The Maryland House of Delegates passed a resolution calling upon the state's senators and representatives in Congress to endorse the capital city of Annapolis as an excellent location. In February 1826 the citizens of New London, Connecticut, entered the competition. In their petition to Congress, they pointed out the advantages of their city. New London was a "remarkably healthy" location that offered all the benefits of a larger city without the "temptations to idleness and vice." It was a bustling seaport with a good harbor that provided easy access to the ocean for training cruises. Furthermore, the city had several sites that could accommodate the academy and presented no "rival institution" (civilian college). Finally, in an apparent appeal to the sympathies of the federal government, the Connecticut petition pointed out that New London had suffered a great deal during the Revolutionary War, the British having burned much of the city. A naval academy would be a welcome addition to the community and the local economy.[46]

In May 1826 the Senate prepared to address the bill to establish a naval academy. But North Carolina senator John Branch suggested that, since the congressional session was drawing to a close, the Senate should focus on the most important legislation before it. Because, he said, the academy bill was "problematical" and had little chance of passing during the current session, he moved to postpone consideration of the measure indefinitely. Senator Elias Kane of Illinois disagreed. Kane stated that the proposed naval academy was a subject of great importance and the Senate would take it up in the next session. Perhaps feeling that the proposal was losing steam in Congress, Adams again recommended the establishment of an academy in his second annual message. He reasoned that since the navy did not need any more ships, the money allocated for them could be spent on a naval academy and other naval improvement projects.[47]

On February 15, 1827, the naval academy proposal resurfaced in the Senate as part of the debate on a naval improvement bill.[48] Robert Hayne addressed his colleagues at length on why the bill was important. Though history remembers him most as a staunch states' rights southerner who debated the doctrine of nullification with Daniel Webster, Hayne was also a strong advocate of naval expansion and reform and a friend of Samuel Southard.[49] He argued that the navy, through its past successes, had proved itself to be the best means of national defense. Concerning "the great, the interesting question of the Naval Academy," Hayne emphatically supported its establishment. Education, in general, not only expanded the intellect but also improved moral character. This was as true for naval officers as it was for everyone else. "In former times," Hayne explained, "it was believed to be necessary, to complete the character of a Naval Officer, that he should be a profane swearer and a hard drinker; that he should be proud of his ignorance, despise books, and be distinguished by habits, manners, and language, different from the rest of the world." This was no longer the case. A naval academy would elevate America's middle-class midshipmen intellectually and morally, making them cultivated gentlemen, more efficient officers, and more effective representatives of the nation abroad. "The success of individuals as well as of nations," Hayne declared, "will be in exact proportion to their intellectual and moral strength."[50]

Hayne made it clear that he was not disparaging American naval officers. The naval heroes of the War of 1812 were "men of cultivated minds, elegant manners, and the noblest sentiments of honor—men who graced the drawing-room as well as the quarter-deck." Hayne admitted that these officers were mostly self-educated. But, he argued, that did not mean a naval academy would not benefit the country: "There is no mistake . . . greater or more common, than that which condemns education as useless, because eminent men have educated themselves." A naval academy would "give to all the young men in our Navy, the means of becoming Decaturs and Perrys."[51]

This academy plan called for an initial two-year period of study for young men entering the navy. Instruction would take place on shore at the proposed academy and at sea on a training ship that would conduct practice cruises along the coast. At the academy students would study naval science and other subjects intended, in Hayne's words, "to imbue their minds with a love of knowledge, to give them a taste for books, to encourage good habits and principles, to hold out proper examples for their imitation, and to convince them that their future standing in the service will be exactly proportioned to their professional acquirements, and intellectual and moral character." A naval academy would not only increase the professional skill and knowledge of the officer corps, but it would also eliminate "vice and ignorance" within the navy. After completing two years at the academy, midshipmen would serve for five or six years on active duty before undergoing examination for promotion. During that period, midshipmen would report to the naval academy whenever they were on shore and would devote themselves to self-improvement rather than surrendering to the various temptations of city life.[52]

The provisions for a naval academy represented by far the most controversial part of the bill and received the most attention during the lengthy deliberations that followed Hayne's opening remarks. The Senate debate turned into a political and personal showdown reflecting the bitter partisanship and animosity generated by the John Quincy Adams presidency. Senator Asher Robbins of Rhode Island argued in favor of the naval academy, believing such an institution was vital if the United States aimed to rely on the navy as its primary means of defense. "Genius is the gift of nature," Robbins explained, "but art is the gift of education. This is true of all the arts, . . . [and] is eminently true of the great art of war; and no less of its naval than of its military branch." The main question was whether the United States would depend on "education upon accident or . . . upon such as the country may provide" and have some control over. In Robbins's opinion, America needed a naval academy not to replace the education and training that took place at sea, but to supplement it—just as West Point had provided the army with skilled officers beyond what service in the field alone could have produced.[53]

Maine senator John Holmes questioned the need for a naval academy. In his opinion, a midshipman could learn the naval profession only at sea. He advocated improving the existing system of shipboard instruction rather than establishing an unnecessary institution of dubious benefit to the nation. Holmes viewed naval education in strictly practical terms; he did not give any attention to the development of character among the midshipmen. Holmes's colleague from Maine, John Chandler, also opposed a naval academy, arguing that it represented a vast and potentially ominous increase in executive power.[54]

Senator William Henry Harrison of Ohio refuted the opinions voiced by the Maine senators. Harrison, a former general, though admitting he had little knowledge of naval affairs, believed the navy was the foundation of America's national security and should have an academy to educate its officers. He agreed that midshipmen must learn navigation at sea but said there was a great deal of valuable information they could obtain at an academy. Maryland senator Samuel Smith supported Harrison's arguments by adding that the current instruction at sea was of poor quality, making a naval academy a vast improvement over the existing system. Army officers defended the nation at home, Smith pointed out, but naval officers spent most of their time abroad and had to understand subjects beyond naval science; for example, an ability to communicate in French and Spanish was crucial in conducting diplomacy. Smith knew of many midshipmen who had a sound, practical knowledge of naval science but lacked a theoretical understanding of mathematics and astronomy—both vital to navigation. As a result, otherwise promising officer candidates failed their examination for promotion. A naval academy could address this problem. Combining practical training at sea with instruction in mathematics, astronomy, and foreign languages on shore would produce officers who, when abroad, could "appear in any society, to the credit of themselves and their country."[55]

The next day, February 16, Senator William Smith of South Carolina led the opposition by moving to strike out the academy sections of the naval improvement bill. Although he supported the rest of the legislation, he would not vote for it if it included the naval academy provisions. Smith viewed West Point in a negative light and did not consider it an institution worthy of emulation by the navy. The U.S. Military Academy, founded on a limited scale as a school for army engineers, continued to grow in size and financial cost well out of proportion to what was appropriate in a republic. Furthermore, Smith did not think education made great generals. Specifically mentioning Julius Caesar, Joan of Arc, and Andrew Jackson, Smith argued that none of the great military leaders of history had attended a military academy. They learned to fight and lead men on the battlefield through experience. Smith then rhetorically asked Senator Harrison, who was seated nearby, if the former general's lack of military education had hampered his military campaigns in any way. In Smith's mind, "military talent would unfold itself, whenever an opportunity offered, without establishing nurseries for its cultivation."[56]

Turning his attention to the navy, Smith declared that the greatest naval heroes in history—including the Royal Navy's Lord Nelson (the hero of the Battle of Trafalgar and the most revered naval officer of the age) and American officers like Stephen Decatur, Oliver Hazard Perry, Thomas Macdonough, Isaac Hull, and William Bainbridge—all learned their profession at sea, in the "school of adversity," not "playing on shore" in an academy. Taking an obvious swipe at the scholarly and diplomatic attainments of John Quincy Adams, Smith asserted that an academy education might provide "accomplishments which would fit men to appear to advantage in the Courts of France and Spain," but it would not produce great warriors. Naval officers needed to learn how to fight battles; they could do without the social niceties practiced in the royal courts of Europe. "The Navy does not want a host of tender youths, carefully nursed and indulged in a quiet life," Smith claimed, using manhood as an argument against an academy education; "neither did it stand in need of a troop of silk stocking gentry to lead to battle our hardy seamen, who would look with contempt upon trifling or effeminate leaders." In Smith's view, the world itself was the best school for the education of naval officers. In alluding to manhood and masculinity, he introduced a new dimension to the naval academy debate. In the period after the American Revolution, gender notions became enmeshed with nationalism. Many Americans regarded European men as aristocratic, idle, and effeminate. Although it was important for American officers to behave as gentlemen, they should avoid European notions of masculinity and instead embrace "republican manhood." Whereas book learning, refinement, and effeminacy characterized European men, natural wisdom, courage, action, and manliness were the hallmarks of American manhood and should define U.S. military officers.[57]

After the opposing remarks by Senator Smith, William Henry Harrison again took the floor to defend the naval academy proposal and military education in general. As a military man himself, he was a firm believer in the value of military education. Ignorant men could not lead armies effectively. Although there were instances throughout history when uneducated men won military glory for themselves and their country, the victors usually came by those laurels by pure luck or against an enemy that was even more ignorant than they were. To ensure victory against a skilled opponent, the United States had to provide scientific education for its officers. According to Harrison, the best evidence of the importance of military education was Napoleon, who saw to it that his officers possessed expert knowledge of military science. Harrison refuted Smith's claim that America's naval heroes lacked formal education, stating that, although not schooled in a naval academy, the men in question had received fairly good educations prior to joining the navy. Many who entered the navy as midshipmen were not as fortunate and lacked preparatory education. It was the government's responsibility to provide a strong education for the young men it would one day entrust with the nation's defense.[58]

The senators continued to debate the merits and detriments of a naval academy, resorting to many of the same arguments repeatedly. Rejecting William Smith's reasoning that history had proved military education unnecessary, Hayne asked facetiously if Joan of Arc's military prowess meant that the United States should entrust its security to an army of women. He also pointed out that many generals who lacked military education themselves, such as Andrew Jackson and Winfield Scott, were strong supporters of West Point. The naval academy would not become "a place of amusement" as suggested by the senator from South Carolina; rather, like West Point, it would be a place of "laborious study and constant improvement." Senator Smith of Maryland argued that the lack of military science among American officers ultimately led to the loss of life. He pointed to the army's dismal performance in the War of 1812 as a consequence of the failure to provide military education. William Henry Harrison added his opinion that the nation's capital would not have fallen to the British during that conflict if there had been more American officers schooled in the military art. It should "be obvious to every unprejudiced mind," he concluded, that a naval academy was necessary.[59]

North Carolina senator Nathaniel Macon, who remained devoted to the agrarian republican principles of Jefferson and had not embraced the nationalist republicanism of the post-1815 era, opposed the creation of a naval academy. In his mind, it would be an unwarranted and dangerous expansion of executive power. Moreover, like his colleague William Smith of South Carolina, Macon believed that book learning did not win battles, whether on land or at sea. He pointed to Benjamin Franklin's achievements as evidence that formal education was unnecessary. For emphasis, Macon added: "The greatest fool I ever knew was the greatest classical scholar." Macon also feared that increasing the number of educated, professional military men would inevitably lead to war: "Can you expect to keep the country at peace, when it is full of soldiers? Don't you see that these men must have fighting to do, to keep them from doing mischief?"[60]

When the time came to vote on the amendment proposed by Senator Smith of South Carolina, which would have eliminated the provisions for a naval academy, the amendment was defeated by a vote of 24-22. On February 17, the Senate passed the naval improvement bill, including the naval academy sections, by a vote of 28-18.[61]

When the House of Representatives took up the naval improvement bill on March 1, 1827, New Hampshire congressman Nehemiah Eastman immediately moved to strike the provisions for a naval academy. Much of the reasoning used to oppose it during the Senate debates resurfaced in the House. In response, Representative John Weems of Maryland made an impassioned defense of the academy proposal. He pointed out that the school would certainly be located on the water to provide midshipmen with practical training in seamanship and navigation. In an effort to diffuse the argument that West Point was an elitist institution that catered to the sons of the wealthy and influential, Weems suggested that Congress reform the appointment system at West Point and the new naval academy (when in place) to make the admission process more equitable. Despite Weems's arguments, the House voted to amend the naval improvement bill by eliminating the provisions for a naval academy.[62]

The House sent the amended bill back to the Senate, which in a very close vote, 22-21, upheld the House amendment to remove the naval academy provisions. Partisan politics in the Senate involving the supporters of John Quincy Adams and those of Andrew Jackson was the root cause of the measure's defeat. Among the senators who stood behind Jackson, 70.8 percent voted to uphold the House amendment. Of those supporting Adams, 73.7 percent voted against it. There was little difference in voting when it came to factors such as the geographic section or educational background of the senators (see Appendix, Table 1). John Quincy Adams had given more attention to the naval academy issue than any other president. Its establishment was one of the main features of his legislative agenda for national improvement. This fact, more than actual hostility to the idea of a naval academy, explains the opposition of the Jacksonian senators.[63]

This kind of partisanship was not unique to the naval academy issue; it characterized the Adams presidency. The broad, nationalist vision of federal activism Adams articulated for the United States was not well received by his fellow Americans and caused a firestorm of protest in Congress. Adams let his idealism cloud his judgment and sense of reality, and he attempted too much too soon. Although his cabinet had advised him against overreaching, Adams was determined to forge ahead with his agenda because he wanted to secure his legacy as a forward-thinking statesman and man of vision. Many politicians were concerned that he was trying to expand his own power and the power of the federal government to unprecedented levels, giving the government authority over commerce, industry, science, and even the arts. Furthermore, Adams was extremely unpopular with the followers of Andrew Jackson because of his controversial election in 1824. Although Jackson had won the popular vote and received a plurality of electoral votes, he had failed to win a majority in the electoral college. The House of Representatives subsequently elected Adams to the presidency. Soon afterward, Adams appointed Speaker of the House Henry Clay as secretary of state, the traditional stepping-stone to the presidency at the time. Jackson supporters accused Adams of making a "corrupt bargain" with Clay in order to win the presidency.[64]

Adams was unprepared for the partisan politics he would face as president. He believed his administration was merely a continuation of the ideas put forth by his predecessor, James Monroe; he thought he would be able to pursue his agenda of economic development and scientific, intellectual, and moral improvements in an atmosphere of consensus. Instead, partisan strife plagued his administration from start to finish. Once Jackson's supporters gained control of Congress in the 1826 midterm elections, the White House had no hope of achieving its policy agenda. The antagonistic lawmakers defeated one policy initiative after another, preventing Adams from accomplishing anything close to his vision for the United States. Having spent most of his political career serving in appointed diplomatic positions (ambassador and secretary of state), he had little experience dealing with Congress on domestic issues. The fact that he had lost the popular vote combined with the taint of the so-called corrupt bargain meant that Adams lacked legitimacy as president. Jackson's supporters, in addition to their anger over the 1824 election, were a new breed of politicians who wanted to oust the elite and aristocratic officeholders represented by Adams and inaugurate a new, more democratic era in American politics. To his opponents, and to many Americans, John Quincy Adams was simply out of touch with the times. He was a member of the educated elite, a patron of the royal courts of Europe, and an advocate of federal power. As Senator Thomas Hart Benton observed, "No President could have commenced his administration under more unfavorable auspices, or with less expectation of a popular career."[65]

Despite the fact that Congress had killed the naval academy proposal, Secretary Southard refused to give up. Repeating his recommendation to establish the school in his annual report for 1827, he contended that, because midshipmen entered the service at such a young age, it was impossible for them to have received sufficient education before starting their naval career. Service on board ships at sea "renders it equally impossible that they should there make much literary or scientific acquisition beyond the practical duties of the seaman." Furthermore, midshipmen's pay did not allow them to attend a civilian college; in any case, the time consumed by their naval duties would prevent them from completing a college course of studies. Southard also revived his argument that education was no less important for the navy than it was for the army: "The science and information requisite for a navy officer are in no respect inferior to those required by army officers and engineers."[66]

Adams, too, was unwilling to let the naval academy matter drop. In his annual message to Congress in December 1827, he argued that, whereas seamanship and navigation could be learned at sea, naval architecture, mathematics, astronomy, literature (which was needed to place U.S. naval officers on the same "level of polished education with the officers of other maritime nations"), law, and ethics could only be studied at an academy. Suggesting that the practice of privateering was beneath the United States, Adams declared that knowledge of the law and the development of moral principles in naval officers were crucial to maintain the distinction between "the warrior-patriot and the licensed robber and pirate."[67]

Both Adams and Southard viewed the navy as an instrument for scientific advancement, which was an important component of national progress. Through scientific endeavors, the United States could contribute to human knowledge, improve the quality of life, and ensure continued economic prosperity by discovering new markets in the Pacific and the Far East. For Adams, the United States had to engage in scientific discovery in order to achieve status as a great nation. Many Americans in the post–War of 1812 era were convinced that their nation was destined to become a world power. Adams believed, correctly, that to secure public support for scientific projects, he would have to portray such endeavors in nationalist terms.[68] In early 1828 his administration made plans to launch a naval exploring expedition to the South Seas. The leading spokesman for this project was Southard's friend Jeremiah N. Reynolds, an Ohio newspaper editor and amateur scientist. Reynolds used nationalist arguments to justify the scientific mission to the American people: "When our naval commanders and hardy tars have achieved a victory on the deep, they have to seek our harbours, and conduct their prizes into port, by tables and charts furnished, perhaps, by the very people whom they have vanquished." He asked rhetorically, "Is it honourable for the United States to use, forever, the knowledge furnished us by others . . . and add nothing to the great mass of information that previous ages and other nations have brought to our hands?"[69]

When Southard began organizing the expedition, he consulted Lieutenant Charles Wilkes about the assignment of officers for the mission. Wilkes boasted an impressive scientific résumé for a naval officer, having attended a Columbia University preparatory school in New York City and completed advanced studies in mathematics, navigation, and natural philosophy. Unfortunately, Wilkes's scientific background was unique in the navy and there were not enough officers with comparable knowledge to conduct the explorations envisioned. The scarcity of officers with a scientific education was further evidence, in Southard's opinion, of the need for a naval academy. Because of the lack of qualified naval officers, Southard decided to employ civilian scientists to staff the expedition, which would remain under naval command. Although it was a logical solution to the navy's personnel problem, some felt this situation would inevitably lead to conflict, with naval officers resenting the presence of civilians on board. Having civilians work with naval officers on scientific expeditions had previously been a problem in European navies.[70] In a letter to Adams, Southard justified the use of civilian scientists on the grounds that naval officers simply were incapable of performing the scientific research necessary for a successful expedition. "They are not profound astronomers," explained Southard, "nor are they skilled naturalists." He admitted that combining naval officers and civilians on the expedition could be problematic and had caused "jealousies" that resulted in "unpleasant consequences" during scientific expeditions by other nations. However, the Navy Department had little choice but to rely on civilians. Assigning only naval officers to a scientific mission for which they lacked the proper education and experience would lead to failure.[71]

Although the use of civilian scientists was necessary, it sparked opposition in the Senate and within the naval officer corps. Senator Hayne proved to be a formidable obstacle to the expedition. Although he and Southard had been friends and had previously worked together to improve the navy, they had a falling out by the end of the Adams administration. Southard had failed to endorse Hayne's proposal for the establishment of a navy yard in Charleston, South Carolina—Hayne's hometown. The fact that Southard had proceeded to organize the exploratory expedition without consulting Hayne, who was chairman of the Naval Affairs Committee, embarrassed the senator. Hayne used the proposed employment of civilian scientists as a way to kill the expedition, arguing that the civilians would exercise too much authority over the naval officers under the plan devised by Southard. He further objected to the fact that Southard would be spending Navy Department funds that Congress had appropriated for other purposes to finance the expedition. Another major player in the proposed mission's demise was naval officer Charles Wilkes, a man in whom overconfidence and self-importance predominated. Perceiving his relatively low profile in the expedition to be an insult to his scientific achievements, he quietly set out to sabotage it.[72] The end result was the cancellation of the mission.

Southard again addressed the naval academy issue in his final report as secretary of the navy. "Our navy . . . has rendered incalculable service to the defence, prosperity, and glory of the nation, and never fails to find its place in our fondest anticipations of the future," he declared. "It deserves to be sustained . . . by wise laws and liberal appropriations." Southard listed the establishment of an academy among the Navy Department's top needs. Although Congress had failed to act on his naval academy recommendation, Southard's tenure as navy secretary would prove to be the highlight of his political career, and he took a great deal of pride in what he was able to accomplish. Southard improved medical care for naval personnel and built the navy's first dry docks for the repair and maintenance of ships. Though denied his wish to organize a naval academy, he initiated a ship library program that provided naval personnel with the opportunity for self-improvement through access to books on mathematics, navigation, gunnery, history, law, geography, naval architecture, travel, and natural philosophy. Southard also increased the American naval presence in the Pacific with missions to Hawaii and Tahiti and ordered the sloop of war USS *Vincennes* to sea on a cruise that would ultimately lead to the first circumnavigation of the world by a U.S. Navy ship.[73]

In the post–War of 1812 era, the establishment of a naval academy became a prominent national issue for the first time. The navy's popularity during and after the war combined with the fact that West Point finally came into its own under the leadership of Sylvanus Thayer gave new impetus to the naval academy issue. Although navy secretaries William Jones and Smith Thompson supported the establishment of an academy, they failed to provide the leadership necessary to guide the required legislation through a reluctant Congress. Their successor, the energetic and capable Samuel Southard, did provide that leadership and found a presidential patron in John Quincy Adams, who included a naval academy recommendation in three out of four of his annual messages to Congress. Establishing a naval academy fit perfectly into Adams's overall vision of improvement for the United States. For Adams and his supporters, a naval academy would have served as an agent of national progress, enabling the United States to join the front rank of world powers. The partisanship of the era, rather than a failure of leadership, prevented Southard from accomplishing his full agenda for naval reform.

Despite the apparent favorable conditions for organizing a naval academy in the period after the War of 1812, the navy's effectiveness during that war led many to question whether naval officers really needed an academy education; they seemed to be doing fine under the existing system. Although West Point was experiencing a renaissance, it was not an appropriate model for the proposed naval academy in one important sense—the U.S. Military Academy also performed an important civilian function. West Point was the only institution in the country that offered a technical education emphasizing mathematics, science, and engineering. Many Americans traveled on roads or through canals built by army engineers, but fewer citizens would benefit directly from the economic opportunities that would result from scientific and diplomatic missions conducted by naval officers. In the end, as for Southard, it was bitter partisanship that prevented the president from achieving his broad agenda for national improvement, including a naval academy. Although some opponents took issue with the idea of using an academy to produce naval officers who were better educated, more cultivated, and in a sense more aristocratic than their peers in the general public, resistance to the establishment of a naval academy was rooted more in personal opposition to John Quincy Adams. The best evidence for this is the fact that the naval academy issue did not fade away during the subsequent Jacksonian era, but instead gained momentum.

CHAPTER 4

Academies and Aristocracy in Andrew Jackson's America

The election of Andrew Jackson to the presidency in 1828 ushered in a new era in American politics and society. Jackson's background as a frontier general and his apparent lack of interest in naval affairs did not bode well for the U.S. Navy. Yet during the 1830s, the navy assumed a much larger role in national life because of America's rapidly growing maritime commerce. No longer responsible only for national defense, naval officers increasingly took on the task of expanding American commerce through diplomacy and scientific exploration. The navy's broadened role seemed to suggest the need for an improved system of education for officers. Some Americans believed the establishment of a West Point–style academy for the navy was the best way to meet this need. Others, especially politicians of the Jacksonian persuasion, looked upon the Military Academy with suspicion and hostility. Although this antagonism had a negative influence on the naval academy movement in the 1830s, the navy's expanded responsibilities meant that naval education continued to be a matter of national prominence.

The spirit of improvement that characterized the United States in the 1820s emphasized the country's developing commerce as the foundation for national progress. U.S. trade grew steadily in the Jackson years, with the country's exports increasing by 94 percent. The transportation revolution combined with continued westward settlement fueled significant growth in agricultural exports such as cotton, tobacco, and food crops. A "gospel of commerce" pervaded American society during this period. Americans could not help but recognize that the most advanced civilizations throughout human history were commercial powers. In the United States, commerce encouraged scientific and intellectual pursuits as well as individual initiative and enterprise. It also served as a vehicle for the spread of American republicanism and civilization to other parts of the world, particularly the Pacific, the Far East, and Latin America. Maritime commerce had a direct connection to territorial expansion across North America. Although the term "Manifest Destiny" was not yet coined, Americans believed it was the destiny of the United States to extend its influence across the continent all the way to the Pacific, improving the new territories it acquired by bringing them American political, economic, social, and moral values. More land meant more agricultural surplus and increased exports. Political and business leaders envisioned the continental United States becoming a base of operations for an American maritime empire that would spread throughout the world. "In every age of the world, there has been a leading nation," declared author Ralph Waldo Emerson, "one of a more generous sentiment, whose eminent citizens were willing to stand for the interests of general justice and humanity. . . . Which should be that nation but these States? . . . Who should be the leaders, but the Young Americans?"[1]

The Navy in the Age of Jackson

In his first annual message to Congress, Andrew Jackson stated: "In time of peace we have need of no more ships of war than are requisite to the protection of our commerce." The new president was signaling his intention to maintain a minimum naval force with a strictly defensive mission. Traditionally, this had been the navy's role—fighting wars at sea and protecting U.S. commerce. From the navy's establishment in the 1790s through the 1820s, this protection had included fighting corsairs, enforcing smuggling laws and the ban on the African slave trade, and maintaining an American presence in major ports and areas of commercial activity such as the Mediterranean, the Atlantic, and the Caribbean. Over the course of Jackson's presidency, however, commercial expansion forced him to broaden the navy's mission. By the time he left office, Jackson had become a proponent of the navy: "The increase of our commerce and our position in regard to the other powers of the world will always make it our policy and interest to cherish the great naval resources of our country." New commercial opportunities in the Pacific and the Far East prompted merchants to lobby the federal government for greater naval exploration and protection to support America's growing economic interests in those regions. Because of the country's expanding commercial interests, the navy's role in national affairs changed dramatically. In fact, the navy took the lead in developing America's burgeoning maritime empire. In addition to fighting wars and protecting merchant shipping, naval officers were now responsible for conducting scientific exploration to locate new areas of economic opportunity and for negotiating treaties and commercial agreements with foreign countries. No longer limited to the Atlantic and the Mediterranean, the navy's activities spread throughout the world. Nationalism was at the heart of America's commercial, diplomatic, and scientific endeavors. The United States had to compete with the European maritime powers, especially Britain, for access to profitable new markets. Its programs and prosperity depended on the navy's ability to produce officers who were effective diplomats and explorers.[2]

By the early 1840s, the U.S. Navy deployed six permanent squadrons throughout the world, each with its own geographic area of operations: the Mediterranean Squadron (Mediterranean Sea, Europe, and North Africa, established 1801), Pacific Squadron (Pacific Ocean between the Americas and Hawaii, 1821), West India Squadron (Atlantic Coast and the Caribbean, 1822; absorbed into the Home Squadron, 1841), Brazil Squadron (South America and the South Atlantic, 1826), East India Squadron (Asia and the Indian Ocean, 1835), and the Africa Squadron (West Africa, 1843).[3] In many ways, the naval officers assigned to these stations were America's principal diplomats within their area of operations. By 1838, the U.S. State Department maintained permanent diplomatic ministers in only thirty-one countries, which meant that naval officers often served as the nation's diplomatic representatives. These officers were tasked with protecting American shipping and American citizens abroad; searching for new markets and economic opportunities to ensure the nation's continued prosperity; conducting combat operations or demonstrations of force when necessary; serving as enforcers against pirates, smugglers, and slave traders; negotiating treaties with foreign countries, interacting with foreign officials, and supporting the diplomatic activities of State Department officials; and performing humanitarian missions such as rescuing shipwrecked sailors or American missionaries facing hostile natives. Naval officers also protected American interests in a symbolic way by "showing the flag" around the world. From the 1790s to 1845, the navy engaged in diplomatic activities in Europe, Latin America, the Caribbean, the Middle East, the Pacific, the Far East, Africa, and the Indian Ocean as well as operations off the coasts of Florida, Oregon, and Texas before those territories became part of the United States. Before the invention of the telegraph, communications between naval officers and Washington were extremely slow. It could take weeks, even months, for messages to reach Washington from foreign stations and vice versa. This enabled naval officers to enjoy a great deal of discretion in the conduct of their duties. It was impossible for the secretary of the navy to maintain direct control over ships at sea. Orders from the president and the navy secretary were usually of a general nature, giving an officer a high degree of independence in carrying out the assigned mission.[4]

Finding new economic opportunities required exploration and, in 1836, Congress finally authorized a naval expedition for that purpose. After two years of delays, the U.S. Exploring Expedition—a squadron of six ships under the command of Lieutenant Charles Wilkes—set sail from Norfolk on August 18, 1838. Over the course of its four-year mission, the expedition sailed 85,000 miles, explored 280 islands, and surveyed the coast of Antarctica as well as the Pacific coast of North America. It made significant scientific contributions to the fields of geography, astronomy, oceanography, meteorology, zoology, botany, geology, anthropology, and navigation in addition to collecting thousands of ethnographic artifacts and plant and animal specimens. These collections would eventually form the foundation of the Smithsonian Institution in Washington, D.C. The geographic and oceanographic information obtained by the Wilkes expedition led to the production of 241 charts, which meant that American mariners no longer had to rely exclusively on charts made by foreign countries. The navy was still using some of these charts during World War II.[5]

The navy also developed facilities to support its scientific activities. In 1830 it established the Depot of Charts and Instruments in Washington, D.C., to house and maintain all of the navy's charts, chronometers, telescopes, nautical instruments, and nautical books. Previously, these items, when not in use on board ship, were scattered in storage facilities at the various navy yards; they were not maintained properly in storage and often became unusable. The depot eventually added an observatory and began making regular astronomical observations. In 1842 Congress authorized the construction of a new building for the depot, and Lieutenant Matthew Fontaine Maury became its superintendent. Maury expanded the depot's scientific activities to include oceanography and meteorology. He used logbooks and navigational, meteorological, and oceanographic data collected by navy ships to analyze the currents and weather patterns along various sea routes. He then used this information to produce charts illustrating the average sailing conditions along these routes during the different seasons. This work continued throughout the 1840s and 1850s and made Maury a pioneer in the field of oceanography. After the new building opened in 1844, the depot was renamed the U.S. Naval Observatory and became the center of naval research in astronomy, oceanography, and meteorology until after the Civil War. By the 1840s, then, two of the country's foremost scientists—Charles Wilkes and Matthew Fontaine Maury—were naval officers.[6]

The navy's wide-ranging economic, diplomatic, and scientific responsibilities suggested the need for an improved system of naval education. The Jacksonians had effectively killed the Adams administration's attempts to establish a naval academy. On the surface, this would seem to indicate their opposition to improving the education of midshipmen. In reality, partisan politics rather than actual hostility to the idea of a naval academy was the basis for their opposition. Andrew Jackson himself, in his first inaugural address, indicated his support for "progressive improvements in the discipline and science of both branches of our military service."[7] Two of his secretaries of the navy, John Branch and Levi Woodbury, recommended improvements to the navy's system of education and endorsed the establishment of a naval academy. This is the best evidence of the partisan nature of the Jacksonian opposition to the naval academy plans of John Quincy Adams, since as U.S. senators both Branch and Woodbury had voted against his proposal in 1827.

John Branch was a North Carolina planter who, though lacking experience in naval affairs, was an accomplished politician with previous service as a state legislator, governor, and senator. In his first annual report as secretary of the navy, Branch recommended that Congress legally recognize the informal schools previously established at the Boston, New York, and Norfolk navy yards. When midshipmen were not at sea, the navy usually assigned them to a navy yard. At the yards, they had few duties and a lot of free time to go into the city. The navy set up informal schools where the younger midshipmen could receive instruction in mathematics and other relevant subjects and senior midshipmen could study for their lieutenant examination. In addition to their educational benefits, the navy hoped the schools would keep the midshipmen out of trouble. Several problems hampered the schools' effectiveness. First, although the Navy Department encouraged midshipmen to attend these schools, attendance was not mandatory. Second, instruction was actually limited to mathematics even though the original plan called for comprehensive instruction in the physical sciences, naval architecture, naval tactics, gunnery, law, history, geography, and English grammar. Third, the schools did not necessarily provide an atmosphere conducive to study. Although the lieutenant examination was intended to weed out young men unfit for naval service, it became little more than a formality over the course of the 1830s. In fact, in 1842 every midshipman passed the exam. Because most midshipmen no longer considered the test to be much of an ordeal, they saw little need to devote serious time and effort to studying for it. Cramming just before the examination date became a common practice. Matthew Fontaine Maury was assigned to the school at the New York Navy Yard to prepare for his exam. When Maury, a serious student, found the antics of his less-dedicated comrades distracting, he received permission to study on his own while residing with relatives in Washington, D.C. A fourth problem with the navy yard schools was the uneven quality of the instructors. Although many were dedicated teachers, other schoolmasters were incompetent and set a poor example for the midshipmen. Legend has it that one individual assigned to the school at the New York yard was an alcoholic who charged the midshipmen twenty dollars for tutoring and evaluated his students according to their drinking ability and how quickly they paid his fee.[8]

In recommending legal recognition of the navy yard schools, Branch specifically pointed out the lack of adequate instruction in modern foreign languages as evidence of the need for improvements in naval education. Naval officers routinely interacted with foreign officials; their inability to understand foreign languages, in either spoken or written form, could have serious consequences for the United States. Branch emphasized that the navy yard schools were "mere temporary arrangements" that offered very limited instruction and had not been formally recognized by Congress through legislation. He believed a good first step toward improving naval education was to recognize the schools by law and expand the instruction provided for midshipmen.[9]

In 1830 Branch moved beyond suggesting improvements to the navy yard schools and recommended the establishment of a true naval academy. Naval officers had important duties: commanding ships at sea, leading squadrons, judging the conduct of their fellow officers at courts-martial, and engaging in diplomatic negotiations with foreign officials. In fact, naval officers had a wider range of responsibilities than almost any other government official. Midshipmen thus required an academic background that prepared them to carry out the various duties they would one day have to perform. Branch argued that the "sons of the wealthy" could acquire an excellent education on their own. "But without the aid of public instruction," he asked rhetorically, "how are the sons of the less affluent to become qualified to command in the naval service?" Branch also favored an academy for moral reasons. Young men needed direction in their lives, whether it be from their parents or from a commanding officer. Those midshipmen not serving at sea lacked a major authority figure and would naturally develop bad habits such as laziness, inattention to detail, insubordination, or intemperance, all of which could undermine the navy's effectiveness in times of emergency. The solution to this problem, according to Branch, was the establishment of an academy similar to West Point.[10]

Branch's successor, Levi Woodbury, was primarily concerned with reducing the Navy Department's expenditures, and he provided at best "cautious leadership" when it came to naval improvements. Woodbury gave rhetorical support to the idea of naval reform but exerted little effort toward achieving that goal beyond making suggestions to Congress. In his annual report for 1831, he stated that he did not believe it was useful to repeat the recommendations made by his predecessors regarding naval personnel, including the establishment of a naval academy, even though he agreed with them. Woodbury did propose increasing the pay of the civilian schoolmasters who instructed midshipmen. The following year, he suggested that the navy provide libraries and instruction for midshipmen serving on smaller vessels such as sloops and schooners (during this period, the navy only assigned schoolmasters to frigates and ships of the line). He believed it was necessary to convert every navy ship into a "floating academy" but implied that this was a temporary measure until Congress approved an alternative system of educating the midshipmen—an indirect reference to a naval academy.[11] In addition to recommending educational improvements, Woodbury ordered that all midshipmen who had previously been to sea but were not actively deployed to "consider it their duty" to report to the New York, Norfolk, or Boston navy yard, attend school there, and perform any duties ordered by the commandant of the yard. He also required the navy yard commandants to provide accommodations for the midshipmen on receiving ships and hired additional schoolmasters. The requirement that midshipmen attend the navy yard schools when not deployed or on furlough appeared in the navy regulations submitted for congressional approval in 1833.[12]

After completing his tenure as navy secretary in 1829, Samuel Southard had returned home to New Jersey; he subsequently served as state attorney general, then as governor. In 1833 the state legislature sent him back to the U.S. Senate, where his colleagues appointed him chairman of the Naval Affairs Committee. Southard used this new position to revive his fight to upgrade the education of midshipmen. In June 1834 Southard reported a bill to establish a naval academy. The measure authorized the president to locate the school on any land already held by the United States for naval or military purposes. It also empowered him to appoint the academy's commandant from among the navy's captains and a faculty consisting of a professor of natural and experimental philosophy, a professor of mathematics and navigation, a teacher of history and geography, a teacher of the French and Spanish languages, and a fencing master. The bill authorized the Navy

Department to provide the proposed academy with all of the books and scientific equipment needed for instruction. Once more, Southard was unable to persuade Congress to act on his proposal.[13]

In the meantime, New Jersey politician Mahlon Dickerson succeeded Levi Woodbury as secretary of the navy in 1834. Dickerson was indecisive and provided little leadership as navy secretary. Although not a proponent of a naval academy, he did recommend sending midshipmen to West Point for one or two years to study science, engineering, and military tactics. This plan never gained much support. The *Army and Navy Chronicle* opposed Dickerson's recommendation because it would be unpopular with the officers of both the army and the navy. Furthermore, the *Chronicle* argued, "If the navy is to be allowed anything beyond the schools, now in operation at the Navy yards, it ought to be on a scale commensurate with its growing importance to the country; not to be tacked as an appendage to the military branch of the service." Though it made no effort to establish an academy, Dickerson's department did introduce some needed improvements to naval education. In 1835 the civilian schoolmasters received a new, more prestigious title—professor of mathematics—and a pay increase. The navy also began requiring its civilian instructors to pass a competency examination administered by a board of "scientific gentlemen."[14]

The Jacksonian Assault on West Point

The navy's expanded responsibilities and corresponding need for broader education notwithstanding, the Jacksonian period proved to be an unfavorable environment for establishing a second federal military academy. By 1828, a revival of political democracy had combined with a growing anti-intellectualism within American society. During the 1828 presidential campaign, pitting John Quincy Adams against Andrew Jackson, it was not difficult for the Jackson camp to portray Adams as an intellectual elitist. Adams was, after all, an accomplished scholar and former Federalist who had spent most of his adult life representing the United States in the royal courts of Europe. Jackson, on the other hand, seemed to reflect the values of America. The frontiersman and war hero had risen from humble origins to achieve wealth, fame, and influence on nothing but his natural abilities. Despite the fact that he was a wealthy lawyer and politician who lived in a mansion on a large plantation maintained by slave labor, Jackson was able to depict himself as a simple American farmer. In the minds of many Americans, Jackson was all-American while Adams seemed more European.[15]

The late 1820s saw a distinct bias against men of intellect. Most Americans considered life experience and practical wisdom to be far more important than academic studies. Intellectual achievements, civility, and cultural pursuits defined the men of Europe; American men were supposed to be different. The American frontier fostered a manhood ideal based on the values of hard work, common sense, simplicity, practical knowledge, and moral and physical toughness. Adams failed to understand that American values were changing, and he consciously cultivated his image as a scholar and an intellectual. What he perceived as his greatest qualifications for the presidency were actually a detriment.[16] In 1828 a group of New York State Jacksonians declared: "We do not claim for General Jackson the distinction of the academy . . . but we do claim for him those higher attributes which an active public life alone can teach, and which can never be acquired in the halls of the university—a knowledge of mankind." In the opinion of many Americans, Jackson's life experiences made him better qualified to lead the nation than Adams's academic achievements.[17] The anti-intellectual and anti-aristocratic attitudes displayed during the 1828 election easily translated to West Point and to the naval academy debate.

In the late 1820s West Point was emerging from a golden age in its history. Sylvanus Thayer had transformed a small mathematical school into a widely respected, prestigious educational institution. John Quincy Adams, a patron of military education, described West Point as "the living armory of the nation" that "enlarges the dominion and expands the capacities of the mind." In 1826 the academy's Board of Visitors observed that "the national spirit and character . . . pervade the institution," and the *North American Review* commented that West Point had "acquired a wide and honorable reputation, and is deservedly in favor both with the people and the government."[18]

In spite of its distinguished reputation, the election of Andrew Jackson and the rise to power of his political disciples posed a potential threat to the academy. To many people, Jackson's victory over British army regulars at New Orleans had almost single-handedly made up for the army's generally poor showing during the War of 1812. Americans remembered the Battle of New Orleans as a victory won by rough and undisciplined frontier militia, specifically Kentucky riflemen. A Jackson campaign song immortalized the role these militiamen played in defeating the highly trained British soldiers commanded by Major General Sir Edward Pakenham. Citizens reveled in the fact that Jackson, the untrained frontier militia officer, had whipped the professional and aristocratic Pakenham. The untrained, undisciplined character of the militia troops seemed to suggest that Americans were natural warriors who did not need formal military education. This theory conflicted with West Point's academic approach to the military profession. Sylvanus Thayer was a college-educated military scholar who made it his goal to produce officers in that mold for the U.S. Army. A clash in philosophies between the Jacksonian Democrats and Thayer's West Pointers was inevitable.[19]

Jacksonian views on military policy and military education were somewhat confusing and contradictory. Jackson himself once declared to his nephew, a West Point graduate, that the U.S. Military Academy was "the best school in the world." Jackson's support for West Point was also evident in his first annual message to Congress when he commended the academy for having "the happiest influence upon the moral and intellectual character of our Army."[20] Even though Jackson himself praised West Point and had no desire to abolish it, many of his followers subjected the academy to withering criticism. The 1830s and early 1840s represented a difficult period for the army in general and West Point in particular. The age of Jackson brought a return to the Jeffersonian policy of scaling back the War Department's budget and relying on the militia (at least in theory) as the foundation of national defense. Because there was no foreign enemy on the horizon, many Americans viewed the army as an expensive, unnecessary, and undesirable institution. During the Jacksonian period, the troop strength of the army was kept at an absolute minimum (under ten thousand men). Army forces were scattered throughout the United States, mostly serving as garrisons for coastal and frontier fortifications. Officers and soldiers suffered from low morale.[21] Although Jacksonian military policy resembled Jeffersonian policy, there was an important difference—military education. Thomas Jefferson was the president who signed the legislation creating the U.S. Military Academy. Jeffersonian Republicans, despite their preference for the militia, did see the need for formal military education, whether it be at West Point, at civilian colleges, or in the form of standardized training for militia troops. Many Jacksonians, in contrast, argued that American fighting men required no formal military education or training to be effective. As Samuel P. Huntington has observed, "Technical competence was required of the good Jeffersonian officer; militant enthusiasm of his Jacksonian counterpart." New Orleans made Jackson the model of American military greatness in the eyes of his followers, and comparisons to George Washington were common. Besides the fact that both men achieved fame as generals, both lacked formal education but possessed the common sense and solid instincts that made them natural military leaders. Washington and Jackson proved that courage and a willingness to fight were all that were necessary in the makeup of a military officer.[22]

Although Jeffersonians and Jacksonians both regarded military professionals with suspicion, they did so for different reasons. The Jeffersonians feared a professional military as a potential threat to liberty, whereas the

Jacksonians were more concerned with the elitism and privilege associated with a professional officer corps. Professional military officers, specifically West Point graduates, were an elite cadre who received a special privilege—a free scientific education. When the Jacksonians looked at American society in the 1820s, they viewed with disdain the emergence of an aristocracy of wealth, an elite group of people who controlled the government and the economy. The wealthy were a privileged minority who used their influence to increase their own wealth and power while ignoring the needs of the common man. Equality of opportunity for all white men was the primary goal of Jacksonians, who denounced any kind of favoritism. Allowing a small segment of the population to enjoy special advantages limited the freedom and equality of nonelite Americans. America could maintain its republican virtue and principles only by placing power with the majority and by ensuring equal opportunity for all. In short, for Jacksonians, the ideal republican society was one that eschewed artificial distinctions, provided equality of opportunity, emphasized practical wisdom, and limited federal power.[23]

Many Jacksonians viewed West Point in the same light as the hated Bank of the United States—an institution that catered to an elite minority. Stephen E. Ambrose has effectively summarized the reasons why many Jacksonians opposed the Military Academy: "[West Point] was obviously aristocratic, with its lily-fingered cadets in their fancy little uniforms who received money for their free education and became upon graduation snobbish officers in a caste-ridden army that was hostile to democracy or, worse, who resigned their commissions in order to cash in on the mathematical and engineering knowledge the government had given them." Jacksonians did not hold that there should be no distinctions at all in American society. People had different intellects, talents, and work ethics, all of which would naturally lead to differences in education, wealth, and influence. "But," Andrew Jackson argued, "when the laws undertake to add to these natural and just advantages artificial distinctions, to grant titles, gratuities, and exclusive privileges, to make the rich richer and the potent more powerful, the humble members of society . . . who have neither the time nor the means of securing like favors to themselves, have a right to complain of the injustice of their Government."[24] In the minds of Jacksonians, this was the essence of aristocracy: a select minority that used the institutions of the federal government to grant themselves special privileges and prevent others from enjoying similar opportunities. Jacksonians were waging "a war on privilege," and West Point became one of their favorite targets.[25]

The democratic atmosphere created by the Jacksonians provided an excellent opportunity for former West Point superintendent Alden Partridge

George Catlin's famous depiction of cadets participating in artillery drill on "The Plain" (parade ground) at West Point in 1828. Courtesy Anne S. K. Brown Military Collection, Brown University Library.

to exact a measure of revenge against the army, the Military Academy, and Sylvanus Thayer. Partridge's tenure (1814–17) was a turbulent period in West Point's history. He was a micromanager who alienated the faculty with his arbitrary and dictatorial style of leadership. Complaints from the faculty and allegations of misconduct against him prompted President James Monroe to relieve Partridge of his duties in 1817, appointing Sylvanus Thayer in his place. Partridge departed briefly after Thayer's arrival but then returned to assume command of West Point on his own authority. The army's chief of engineers, the superintendent's immediate superior, ordered the arrest and court-martial of Partridge. Although the court-martial board found him guilty of disobedience and mutiny and sentenced him to dismissal, the army permitted him to resign because of his previous service to the academy.[26]

After leaving the army, Partridge moved back home to Norwich, Vermont, and in 1819 opened his own private military school—the American Literary, Scientific, and Military Academy—as, he envisioned, an alternative to West Point. In fact, his overall goal was to discredit the idea of federal military education, abolish West Point, and replace it with private military academies on the Norwich model. Just as he had at West Point, Partridge made sure that he was in complete control of every aspect of life at the Norwich academy. The catalog listed him as superintendent and professor of mathematics, philosophy, and military science. In 1825 Partridge moved his school to Middletown, Connecticut, apparently to attract more naval students. Four years later, the institution was back in Vermont and thriving, becoming Norwich University in 1834.[27]

Partridge believed in a comprehensive system of military schooling, one that included naval education. He had been interested in expanding the country's program of military education since his superintendency of West Point. In May 1815 Partridge had submitted a plan for the establishment of two additional military academies, one in Washington, D.C., and one in Pittsburgh, Pennsylvania, to Acting Secretary of War Alexander J. Dallas. West Point and the new academies would each enroll 150 cadets, ages thirteen to eighteen, who had chosen the military as their career in addition to 250 cadets who wanted a military education but did not plan to enter the service. The military-bound cadets would receive their education at government expense, while the other cadets would pay tuition. Partridge intended for all three academies to admit young men intending to pursue a naval career. After completing their studies at one of the academies, the naval cadets would receive practical training on a navy ship. According to Partridge's plan, all three faculties would include professors and assistant professors of natural and experimental philosophy, mathematics, engineering, chemistry and mineralogy, history and geography, natural history, languages, and belles lettres. The superintendents would double as professors of tactics, and the chaplains would serve as professors of ethics. The faculty would also include a drawing teacher, riding master, and sword master. The three academies would report to an inspector general of military academies (a brigadier general), who would supervise the operation of the schools assisted by a Board of Visitors composed of "scientific Military Gentlemen."[28]

Partridge maintained that his plan would be beneficial in several ways. First, military knowledge would be spread throughout the United States and would produce more competent and effective militia officers. Second, the navy would be furnished with scientific officers. "I cannot see why an acquaintance with the theory of his profession, is not as necessary for a naval, as for a land officer," Partridge stated, pointing out that mathematics formed the foundation of both professions. Third, educating army and navy officers together would form a bond of cooperation and friendship between the two services, enhancing military efficiency.[29]

Although his plan never materialized, Partridge was able to apply some of his ideas at Norwich. Overall, the American Literary, Scientific, and Military

Academy was very similar to West Point in its curriculum and organization. The major difference was that Norwich students paid tuition. As at West Point, the course of studies emphasized mathematics, science, and engineering. However, Partridge's academy provided more instruction in the humanities, including history, geography, law, English composition, logic, ethics, metaphysics, the classics, and music. The cadets studied military tactics, drilled regularly, participated in military parades, performed guard duty, and received instruction on the duties of soldiers and officers—all of which was comparable to the training at West Point's summer encampment. The rules and regulations at Norwich closely resembled those in force at West Point. Cadets were required to wear uniforms, follow a highly regimented daily schedule, undergo regular inspections, and attend Sunday worship. They were not permitted to leave the grounds, gamble, drink, visit taverns, be in debt, or engage in disorderly conduct. The students had to pass two major examinations each year, one of which the academy's Board of Visitors attended. According to Partridge, he looked after his cadets with parental "care and attention," maintaining the "strict, but correct" discipline that would facilitate the "full development and due cultivation of all those liberal, manly, noble, and independent sentiments which ought to characterize every American, whether citizen or soldier."[30]

Alden Partridge was one of West Point's most outspoken critics during the Jacksonian period. One can interpret his disapproval in two ways. First, he had devised an alternative system of military education—private academies on the Norwich model—that he believed to be superior to America's reliance on a single federal academy. He therefore wanted to advocate his system in a public forum. Second, Partridge's criticism of West Point was retribution for the institution's rejection of his leadership and his replacement with Sylvanus Thayer, who subsequently achieved national recognition for his administration of the U.S. Military Academy. Partridge had articulated his desire for retribution some years earlier in a letter to Brigadier General Joseph G. Swift, the army's chief of engineers, who had removed Partridge as West Point superintendent. Though insisting he was not motivated by revenge, Partridge vowed: "I am near thirty three years of age and should I live to be seventy, this subject shall never within that time be abandoned, unless justice be done." Partridge informed Swift of his plan to establish his own military academy, which he would be able to run without the interference "of men who, whatever may be their rank or pretensions, are really ignorant of the first rudiments both of military and every other science."[31]

Partridge's anger had not subsided by 1830, when he published a pamphlet that sharply criticized West Point and Thayer. Although Partridge used the pseudonym "Americanus," his authorship was well known in government and military circles. Partridge divided his pamphlet into three parts, one directed to Congress, one to the president, and one to the American people. In the first part, he noted that the U.S. Military Academy had expanded well beyond the small school for engineers that the government had originally intended in 1802. Since then, West Point had grown to such an extent that it violated the Constitution and the nation's republican principles. In his opinion, "there is not on the whole globe an establishment more monarchial, corrupt, and corrupting than [the Military Academy]," the purpose of which was "to introduce and build up a privileged order of the very worst class—a military aristocracy—in the United States." Partridge defined an aristocracy as "an order or class of individuals in a community who claim and exercise privileges and immunities of which the great body of the people are deprived." The virtual monopoly held by West Point graduates over officer commissions in the army violated the principle that federal offices be open to all. The pamphlet also contained a scathing indictment of Superintendent Thayer's leadership, claiming that he was lazy because he did not teach the cadets personally as Partridge had done. Moreover, it accused Thayer of incompetence, excessive punishment of the cadets, convening courts of inquiry without authorization, and in some instances withholding cadet pay.[32]

Partridge argued that West Point was of no benefit to the militia, as many academy supporters often claimed. Its graduates who entered the military joined the regular army and those who returned to civilian life rarely served in their local militia company. Furthermore, militia soldiers did not wish to serve under "the *refuse* of the military academy" because of the level of discipline required. Given its aristocratic nature and the fact that it did little to improve the militia, Partridge recommended that the government abolish West Point as a four-year military college. Instead, the academy should offer a six-month course of practical instruction in mathematics, military engineering, and infantry and artillery tactics for all men who received officer commissions (including deserving noncommissioned officers). West Point should also serve as a school of practice for entire units, which would rotate through the academy on a regular basis for training. This new system, Partridge asserted, would save the government $200,000 a year and eliminate the undemocratic character of the Military Academy.[33]

The second part of the pamphlet, directed at President Andrew Jackson, compared Partridge's own record as superintendent with that of Thayer, a man who had "acquired a fictitious importance and popularity." In Partridge's mind, the innovations credited to Thayer actually originated during his own administration. Thayer did not instruct or drill the cadets personally, delegating those tasks to the faculty and the commandant of cadets. Moreover, there had been cadet mutinies under Thayer, whereas there had been none during his own tenure. Thayer's treatment of the cadets was "tyranical, unjust, and even barbarous"; he had ordered "degrading and unmilitary punishments," including the illegal use of flogging on the West Point grounds.[34]

In the part of his pamphlet directed to the American public, Partridge contended that West Point was unnecessary. The greatest generals in American history—men like George Washington, Nathanael Greene, Andrew Jackson, and William Henry Harrison—never attended a military academy. Civilian colleges could provide almost all of the education officers needed. Private military academies such as Norwich, military courses at civilian colleges, or a school of basic military instruction and practice along the lines of what Partridge had already suggested for West Point could provide the necessary military knowledge for prospective officers at much less expense to the public. The cadets were pampered by the "*effeminate* and *pedantic* system" at West Point—they had relatively comfortable quarters, were provided all of the necessities of life, and were required to drill only in good weather. West Point thus did not prepare them for the rigors and hardships of war. Thayer's request for appropriations to construct a building where the cadets could drill in inclement weather particularly drew Partridge's wrath and the declaration that the cadets could never withstand the privations endured by the Continental army during the Revolutionary War. The officers produced by West Point were "military *dandies*," not soldiers. They were considered elite gentlemen and, as such, were not subjected to the brutality of war, which would "injure their *beauty*." The majority of cadets were the sons of politicians or the wealthy, people who could easily afford to pay for their college education. Partridge concluded his pamphlet by urging the public to tell their representatives in Congress to vote to abolish West Point and to spend the money saved to improve the militia.[35]

The arguments in Partridge's pamphlet formed the basis for an assault on the U.S. Military Academy waged by the Jacksonian Democrats in Congress. The most frequent criticisms were that West Point catered to a privileged class of youth and was "the hot-bed of a military aristocracy." Begun as a small school for the military engineers who would build America's defensive fortifications, the academy had been "perverted" into an expensive school "for the great and the wealthy, where none but the sons or favorites of men possessing power or popularity can be entered." Legendary frontiersman and Tennessee congressman David Crockett denounced higher education generally for fostering aristocracy and social division in the United

States: "This College system went into practice to draw a line of demarcation between the two classes of society—it separated the children of the rich from the children of the poor." Applying Crockett's concept to the army, Jacksonians asserted that the children of the rich went to West Point and the children of the poor served as enlisted soldiers. While the charges of aristocracy were greatly exaggerated, it was true that a number of cadets at West Point came from prominent, influential families—among them, the nephew of President James Monroe, the son of President Martin Van Buren, two grandsons of President William Henry Harrison, two sons of Speaker of the House Henry Clay, the son of Senator John C. Calhoun, the grandson of Alexander Hamilton, the son of future secretary of state William Seward, and two nephews of President Andrew Jackson.[36]

In selecting candidates for West Point, congressmen usually sought young men from "respectable" families. But this did not mean that all cadets came from wealth. The vast majority were of the middle class, though their families usually had political connections. According to a study of over one thousand cadets from the antebellum period, only 4.2 percent described their backgrounds as "affluent." Most—83.2 percent—characterized their status as moderate or middle class, while 10.7 percent and 1.9 percent indicated "reduced" and "indigent" circumstances, respectively.[37]

Although most cadets were of the middle class, there was some truth to the claim that West Point fostered a sense of elitism among its graduates. Several factors contributed to this perception. Cadets understandably felt a great deal of pride in completing the academy's rigorous academic and military program. Because the number of graduates was relatively small, West Pointers who entered the U.S. Army enjoyed an elite status similar to that bestowed upon aristocratic military officers in Europe. Furthermore, the Jacksonian attacks resulted in a defensiveness that tended to alienate West Pointers from civilian society. This feeling of resentment toward civilians represented a form of elitism. Beginning in the 1830s, West Point graduates adopted a symbol of their elite status: the class ring.[38]

The charge that West Point was aristocratic was unfair, despite the political connections of many cadets. First, the academy did not have a say in who received appointments. Politicians—the president, the secretary of war, and members of Congress—made those decisions. Second, appointees from influential families still had to pass the entrance examination before gaining admission. The school's Academic Board, which one cadet described as "the most rigid, cold and merciless looking group of men" he had ever seen, conducted these exams in a strict and impartial manner. Finally, because of the Thayer system, West Point was in many ways the nation's ultimate meritocracy. Once a young man became a cadet, his social background and political connections were irrelevant. No cadet received special privileges based on his family's social standing; the only thing that mattered was academic and military performance. All cadets took the same courses, read the same textbooks, took the same examinations, participated in the same drills, and were subject to the same discipline. Merit was the only factor that determined a cadet's class rank and the branch of the army he would enter upon graduation. As the *American Quarterly Review* observed, "There is no institution in the world whose members are placed on a more perfect, republican basis of equality, than are the cadets of the United States Military Academy. . . . "The rich and the poor . . . are . . . placed in precisely the same situation, receive the same pay, dress in the same uniform, eat at the same table, and in all respects enjoy the same advantages. It remains for talent and merit alone to draw any line of demarkation."[39]

Another major source of opposition to West Point was its supposed bias against young men from the South and the West. This was particularly troubling to the Jacksonian Democrats, who commanded stronger political support in those regions of the country. According to an 1830 report on applications and appointments to West Point, the Academic Board rejected, for academic deficiency, a higher percentage of applicants from southern and western states than from northern states. From 1825 to 1829, an average of 73 percent of rejected applicants were from the South or the West. These figures are not surprising given that those regions offered fewer educational opportunities during the antebellum period. The common school movement of the 1830s—to provide free public elementary schools for all children—did not reach beyond the northern states. In the slaveholding states, elite planters could afford private tutors, while middling white southerners often sent their children to private academies, denominational schools, or schools run by itinerant teachers. The rest of the population had little access to schooling. Educational opportunities in the frontier West were also very limited. According to the *Army and Navy Chronicle*, much of the criticism leveled against West Point originated with former cadets who failed to graduate. These individuals returned home with "tales of injustice and persecution" as a way to save face: "The truth is, that the mass of persons who oppose the Academy, are actuated either by some private pique, or a desire to make it a monster, which they may immortalize themselves in subduing."[40]

In the eyes of many Jacksonians, one of the most troubling aspects of the so-called West Point aristocracy was that academy graduates monopolized the army's officer commissions. In 1836, 71 percent of army officers were West Pointers. This was logical given the small size of the army during this period. West Point graduates usually received the few officer commissions that did become available because they were clearly the most qualified candidates by virtue of their academic background and military training. Nevertheless, it was still possible for civilians and noncommissioned officers to receive commissions. To many Jacksonian Democrats, however, the preference given to academy graduates was just another example of the way in which the wealthy and influential excluded the rest of society from the privileges they enjoyed. Opponents of West Point argued that officer commissions should be open to all, not confined to a select minority.[41]

Jacksonians frequently criticized those West Pointers who resigned from the army after a brief period of service to pursue more lucrative careers in the civilian world. Particularly disturbing to Pennsylvania congressman Charles Brown was the number of West Point graduates who resigned during the Second Seminole War in Florida in the late 1830s and early 1840s. He was appalled that academy graduates felt no obligation to serve their country after receiving a free education. Brown contrasted this attitude with the courage and military prowess shown by Andrew Jackson and the "uneducated officers under him" during the War of 1812 and during conflicts with Indians.[42]

Yet there were legitimate reasons why some West Point gradates chose nonmilitary careers. First, life in the antebellum army was not appealing. Most officers were stationed at remote posts on the frontier, where the army served as a constabulary force against the Indians. Officers received low pay and promotion was extremely slow. The *Army and Navy Chronicle* calculated that a twenty-year-old second lieutenant entering the army in the mid-1830s could not expect to become a captain until approximately age fifty-four. Second, the knowledge and skills resulting from a scientific education at West Point were very marketable in the civilian world. Engineering companies, colleges, and railroads offered higher salaries and greater prestige than the army could provide.[43]

Many cadets viewed the academy as just another college and had no intention of making the military their career. The opportunity to receive a free, scientific education that could lead to a well-paying civilian career was very appealing to middle-class young men and their parents, especially if the family could not afford the tuition at a civilian college. A good example was Ulysses S. Grant, a member of the West Point Class of 1843. Grant's father made his children's schooling a priority because of his own lack of formal education. He could not afford college tuition so he arranged for his son to receive an appointment to the U.S. Military Academy without the boy's knowledge. Young Ulysses enrolled at West Point but hated it for the most part. "A military life had no charms for me," Grant wrote in his memoirs, "and I had not the faintest idea of staying in the army even if I should be graduated, which I did not expect." Never a diligent student, one of Cadet Grant's favorite pastimes was reading newspaper accounts of the debates in Congress, hoping to find that the academy had been abolished.[44]

Cadet behavior was another source of ammunition for opponents, who tried to make the case that West Point was a dismal failure when it came to character development. It was bad enough that the cadets received special privileges, but to engage in delinquent behavior was even worse. In the eyes of critics, the cadets were out of control. Cadet Jefferson Davis, for example, misbehaved throughout his four years at West Point, committing such violations as being absent from quarters after taps, cooking in his barracks room, spitting on the floor, making noise during study hours, and firing a musket from his barracks window. Davis's record stood in stark contrast to his fellow southerner, Cadet Robert E. Lee, who graduated second in his class and never earned a single demerit. Unfortunately for West Point, its critics focused on cadets like Davis rather than those like Lee. Based on the number of demerits and courts-martial at the school, the Military Academy did have its share of disciplinary problems, although they were by no means unique to West Point. The early nineteenth century was a period of student unrest at colleges throughout the United States. Harvard, Princeton, and several other schools experienced major student riots in addition to duels, vandalism, and brawls. Serious offenses plagued the University of Virginia in the 1830s, including the murder of a professor by students.[45]

Some detractors of the Military Academy went so far as to question cadet manliness and fortitude. Speaking on the floor of the House in support of the creation of a corps of dragoons to fight Indians on the frontier, Kentucky congressman Albert Hawes said he did not wish to see West Point graduates leading the proposed unit. In his opinion, they were unprepared for the arduous nature of frontier duty. "A corps of women would be as serviceable against Indians as a corps of West Point graduates," he declared. Representative Francis Smith built on this theme by suggesting that the academy fostered unmanliness among its students and pointing to appropriations for the new building where cadets could drill in inclement weather during the winter as evidence of his assertion. Smith, who was from Maine, deemed the expense unnecessary; the government should not "pamper the effeminacy of these young gentlemen" who apparently lacked the moral and physical toughness to be soldiers. Senator William Allen of Ohio criticized the academy for requiring cadets to take dancing lessons as part of their training.

West Point's purpose was to train young men to fight; taxpayers were not interested in funding a "dancing school."[46]

In the minds of many of its critics, West Point seemed to be undermining the physical and strenuous character of American boyhood by sheltering the cadets and overemphasizing the academic aspects of the military profession. American boys had their own cultural values, which stressed the physical. They judged each other based on their physical strength, endurance, and athleticism, as well as character traits such as courage and loyalty. In addition to playing sports and participating in outdoor activities like hunting and hiking, boys frequently engaged in military pursuits—playing soldier, fighting mock battles as a member of a junior militia company, or even drilling with adult militiamen. To many followers of Andrew Jackson, West Point simply did not instill proper American values. School textbooks are a valuable tool for analyzing the predominant ideals and values of American society at any given time. One of the main purposes of nineteenth-century textbooks was to indoctrinate American children in the principles that defined the nation. The study of history was particularly important to this process. The ideals and values most often found in nineteenth-century history texts were patriotism, heroism, perseverance, and the notion that character was more important than intellect. Accordingly, George Washington was the country's greatest hero, remembered as the finest example of American manhood—a man of action, not an intellectual. As a boy, he always preferred outdoor activities to school, a trait that many nineteenth-century Americans encouraged young boys to emulate.[47] Many people viewed learning as experiential rather than academic. This attitude, prevalent among the Jacksonians, meant that the best way to produce a military officer was to put a young man in the field with an active regiment, not in a classroom at West Point.

Professions in the nineteenth century often had gender notions attached to them. Some professions, such as politics and law, were considered more masculine because they emphasized power, competition, and aggression; other fields, such as teaching and the ministry, were considered less masculine because they emphasized morality and concern for others' well-being.[48] No one could deny the masculine orientation of the military, but there were gender implications involved in how young men entered that profession. Though spartan by civilian standards, West Point was still a nurturing environment when compared to the rigors of army life in the field. Furthermore, its cadets devoted the bulk of their time to study rather than to physical activity—the academy did not introduce a formal athletic program until the late nineteenth century. Based on the rhetoric regularly heard in the halls of

Congress, many Jacksonians were convinced that West Point was an aristocratic, effeminate, and thoroughly un-American institution.

Beyond the Rhetoric:
Military Education and Antebellum Society

Despite the seemingly "imposing character" of congressional opposition, the U.S. Military Academy was never in serious danger of being abolished in the 1830s and early 1840s. Although debates on funding often included denunciations of the aristocratic academy, appropriations bills for West Point always passed in both houses. Representative Edward J. Black of Georgia dismissed the antagonism in Congress "as a mere expenditure of threats, made . . . for home consumption, in particular parts of the country." This assessment seems to capture the essence of the objections to West Point during the Jacksonian period. There is no doubt that West Point was very unpopular in certain parts of the country, especially in the West. As a result, politicians from those areas regularly criticized the Military Academy to pander to the voters back home. Probably the best example of this trend was the approach taken by Tennessee congressman David Dickinson, who delivered a speech against West Point on the floor of the House in June 1834 and then had the speech published as a pamphlet by a Washington printer for distribution to his constituents.[49]

Regardless of their rhetoric, most congressmen had no real desire to see the Military Academy abolished because cadet appointments were a valuable source of patronage. Prior to 1843, the president granted appointments on the recommendation of the secretary of war, who usually endorsed the candidates put forward by members of Congress. Generally, the War Department distributed cadet appointments in proportion to each state's representation in Congress, meaning that each congressman could recommend one individual to the secretary of war. A law passed on March 1, 1843, made this system official. By dispensing cadet appointments to their political allies, congressmen were able to solidify their political standing at home. Therefore, it was ultimately in their best interest to maintain West Point and its valuable cadet appointments. Increased congressional control over appointments was a significant factor in the decline of criticism of the academy in the 1840s.[50]

In addition to its political benefits, the Military Academy was the nation's preeminent technical school during the first half of the nineteenth century. The engineering curriculum of Rensselaer Polytechnic Institute, which was established in 1824 and graduated its first civil engineers in 1835, reflected the strong influence of West Point and used textbooks that had first been published for the cadets. As the number of engineering schools in the United States increased, it was often West Point graduates who dominated the faculties. American higher education experienced a transformation in the first half of the nineteenth century, when the traditional college curriculum based on classical studies came under attack by proponents of practical education that emphasized modern languages, natural history, the physical sciences, and engineering. However, change was gradual and the classical curriculum was still predominant during this period, meaning that West Point's scientific and technical course of studies remained unprecedented.[51] West Point was also unique in that its primary goal was to educate young men for a particular profession. Civilian colleges during this period adhered to the premise that the purpose of higher education was not to prepare students for a certain occupation but rather to develop the mind in a more general sense. According to an 1828 report by Yale College, which maintained its emphasis on classical education, "Our object is not to teach that which is peculiar to any one of the professions, but to lay the foundation which is common to them all." Classical studies disciplined the mind and established an intellectual basis for future learning by developing a student's memory, reasoning, analytical, and communications skills.[52] The classics were practically nonexistent at West Point. This put the academy on the cutting edge of educational reform in the nineteenth century. Brown University president Francis Wayland, a leading proponent of modernizing American higher education through greater emphasis on science, modern languages, and professional studies, specifically looked to West Point as a model for civilian colleges: "The course of study at West Point Academy is very limited, but the sciences pursued are carried much farther than in other institutions in our country; and it is owing to this that the reputation of the institution is so deservedly high."[53] Because the academy was the country's premier engineering school during the first half of the nineteenth century, abolishing it would have hindered the nation's economic development.

Perhaps the best evidence that the Jacksonian opposition to formal military education was rhetorical more than real was the large number of state and private military academies founded beginning in the late 1830s. The most famous of these were the Virginia Military Institute (established in Lexington in 1839) and the Citadel (established in Charleston, South Carolina, in 1842). Even as Jacksonian Democrats criticized West Point, military academies were becoming a prominent feature of American education, especially in the South. Both state and private military academies usually modeled their curriculum, training program, and disciplinary system after West Point's and often hired West Point graduates as faculty members. The cadets at these academies read textbooks that were used at West Point and wore gray uniforms that were nearly identical to those worn by West Point cadets. These "West Points of the South" frequently advertised their similarities to the U.S. Military Academy in an effort to impress parents.[54]

Although much of the criticism of West Point came from southerners, the South clearly did not oppose the idea of military education. Southern criticism of West Point was the result of the region's traditional suspicion of federal institutions, its opposition to any expansion of federal power, the large number of southern appointees dismissed by West Point for academic deficiency, and the apparent West Point bias against the militia. Indeed, military education became a prominent feature of the antebellum South. Despite the opposition of some southern politicians, many southern boys dreamed of going to West Point. For those unable to gain admission, state and private military academies offered a very respectable alternative. Military academies benefited the South because they provided a practical, scientific education that produced teachers, engineers, and physicians. These schools generally offered more scholarships than were available at civilian colleges, thus providing nonelite southerners greater access to education. They also expanded opportunities for acquiring military knowledge and helped to improve the militia. Furthermore, many people believed the system of discipline imposed on academy cadets built strong moral character by fostering diligence, obedience, self-discipline, personal responsibility, and patriotism. Some harried parents hoped that a military education would reform their uncontrollable sons.[55] The fact that West Point was the model for state and private military academies indicated it had achieved a level of respect and prestige that ensured its survival as a national institution.

ULTIMATELY, THE JACKSONIAN PERIOD actually advanced the idea of a naval academy. In fact, during the debates about West Point, some politicians argued that a naval academy would play a more important role than the existing Military Academy. An 1834 congressional report, the main purpose of which was to defend West Point, stated that the lack of a naval academy was a great disadvantage to the navy. When compared to West Point cadets, navy midshipmen received an inferior education. The report recommended the establishment of a naval academy where midshipmen would obtain a "competent knowledge . . . of the art of ship-building, the higher mathematics, and astronomy; the literature which can place our officers on a level of polished education with the officers of other maritime nations; the knowledge of the laws, municipal and national; [and] acquaintance with the principles of honor and justice which constitute the distinction of the warrior patriot."

David Dickinson, one of the most vocal critics of West Point, contended that the few wars in America's future would be fought at sea. For that reason, the navy was the nation's most important defense organization. This meant that the education of naval officers was of greater importance to national security than the education of army officers. The Tennessee congressman stated: "If I could be brought to support any such institution as the West Point Academy, it would be one for the instruction of the young midshipmen in those branches of naval science that would render them accomplished, skilful, and efficient officers." Because a navy did not threaten liberty the way a standing army did, Dickinson expressed surprise that the nation's leaders had not yet authorized the formation of a naval academy.[56]

Many naval officers believed they deserved the same access to higher education as their army counterparts. On June 20, 1835, a group of naval and marine officers on board the frigate *Constitution* met to draft a petition calling on Congress to authorize the establishment of a naval academy. Copies of the document circulated throughout the navy and were sent to the secretary of the navy and the chairmen of the House and Senate Naval Affairs committees. In the preamble, the petitioners expressed their belief that the existing system of naval education was completely inadequate to the needs of the nation and the "heartfelt wishes" of the officer corps for greater educational opportunities. They resolved that a grounding in the arts and sciences was "of peculiar importance to the sea officer" and that the scientific knowledge that was "almost indispensable to the military seaman" in the modern era could only be acquired at a naval academy. By abolishing the position of professor of mathematics, the navy would save enough money to "liberally sustain a scientific institution" for the instruction of its officer candidates. Endorsing the petition, the *Maryland Republican* observed that a naval academy would have the "happy effect" of preventing "youths who are too stupid to receive scholastic instruction, and too vicious to be kept at home" from entering the navy through the political influence of their relatives. Not surprisingly, the newspaper suggested Annapolis as an excellent location for the proposed institution.[57]

In a May 1836 report of the Senate Naval Affairs Committee supporting the *Constitution* petition, Samuel Southard contended that America's involvement in maritime commerce made a naval academy an absolute necessity. Referring to U.S. naval officers, he declared: "They are, indeed, our national representatives in all other countries, and from them much of the estimate of us, as to our manners, intelligence, and character as a nation, must be drawn." The diplomatic responsibilities of naval officers made formal education more significant for midshipmen than for army cadets. Although army officers were involved in America's continental expansion, they had relatively little responsibility in foreign affairs. Despite the important and complex duties the midshipmen would one day perform on behalf of their country, most of them entered the navy before they had the chance to develop into "well-informed and disciplined scholars." Once assigned to a ship, they had few opportunities to improve themselves intellectually. The committee recommended that the navy abolish the existing system of education at sea and establish a naval academy in its place. Yet once again Congress failed to act.[58]

The age of Jackson was in many ways a transitional period in the history of the U.S. Navy and in the development of military education in the United States. The navy's assumption of increasingly complex responsibilities required officers with a stronger academic background, particularly in science, modern languages, and international law. The fact that Congress had not abolished West Point combined with the increasing number of state and private military academies throughout the United States demonstrated that formal military education had gradually become an accepted part of American society. The concern that military education bred aristocracy by creating an elite corps of career officers could not overshadow the benefits of technical education and greater professionalism. In addition to providing practical, scientific knowledge that served the public in numerous ways, military academies offered the discipline that was necessary for character development. Nonetheless, the rhetorical opposition to West Point indicated that some segments of the American citizenry and their political leaders were still uncomfortable with the idea of using government funds to educate a professional officer corps. If members of Congress were condemning the nation's first military academy on a regular basis, they would be unwilling to establish a second academy for the navy. Frustrated with the political process and the continuing resistance of politicians, a growing reform movement within the naval officer corps took its case for improved education directly to the American public.

CHAPTER 5

The Sword and the Pen

After basking in the glory of its outstanding performance in the War of 1812, the U.S. Navy experienced a significant decline in popularity in the 1820s. It also suffered from neglect by the federal government despite performing a wide range of important missions in service to the nation. Public indifference led to a loss of morale within the naval officer corps similar to that experienced by army officers. In the midst of this largely negative atmosphere, however, the navy was able to make strides toward greater professionalism in the 1830s and 1840s. No longer receiving the acclaim they had enjoyed after the War of 1812, naval officers increasingly closed ranks and looked within their own community for professional fulfillment. Led by a group of progressive reformers within the officer corps, more and more naval officers made it their goal to transform the naval service into a true profession through intellectual and moral improvement. The establishment of a naval academy became the central component of this quest for greater professionalism, as well as the status and the respect associated with it. To gain support for educational reform, naval officers put their case before the American public and, by doing so, ensured that naval education remained a prominent national issue.

In the first half of the nineteenth century, several professions began gradually shifting from apprenticeship to academic studies as the primary method for training individuals entering the field. The main reason for this change was the varied quality of the practitioners produced by the apprenticeship system. In the late eighteenth and early nineteenth centuries, a young man wishing to become a physician began his apprenticeship between the ages of fifteen and twenty-five after having already completed a preliminary education that usually included classical studies. The apprentice learned the medical profession under the guidance of a practicing physician who provided instruction, books, and equipment in exchange for a fee and the trainee's labor. Apprenticeships in medicine usually lasted for three years and combined book learning and clinical experience (assisting the doctor in performing medical procedures). At the end of that period, the new physician received a certificate from his mentor and began his own practice. This system worked well if the mentoring physician was a competent practitioner and dedicated teacher. But not every physician who accepted apprentices was competent or dedicated to teaching, and poor physicians were the result. The apprenticeship in law was even more informal. A young man studied with a practicing attorney and learned his profession by reading law books and statutes. He gained some practical experience by copying legal documents and assisting his mentor in preparing cases. After completing the apprenticeship and receiving a certificate from a practicing attorney, the new lawyer was admitted to the bar. As with physicians, the quality of mentoring attorneys varied greatly.[1]

By the 1830s and 1840s physicians and, to a lesser degree, lawyers were gradually turning to formal education as a way to elevate their professions. This trend led to a significant increase in the number of colleges and professional schools nationwide. In 1783 there were 13 colleges in the United States. By 1831 there were 46 colleges, 22 theological seminaries, 16 medical schools, and 7 law schools; by 1850 those numbers had soared to 119 colleges, 44 seminaries, 36 medical schools, and 16 law schools.[2] Although medical schools had been established at Harvard, Columbia, and the University of Pennsylvania by 1800, most early medical schools were for-profit institutions that were not usually affiliated with a college or hospital. These "proprietary" schools started out as adjuncts to medical apprenticeship, but by the mid-nineteenth century they had largely superseded apprenticeship as the primary method of American medical education. Antebellum medical schools offered a lecture-based curriculum that emphasized subjects such as anatomy, physiology, pathology, pharmacy, and surgery; the curriculum included very little laboratory work or clinical training. Despite the growing number of medical schools in the United States, apprenticeship continued well into the nineteenth century and offered students the practical experience that medical schools did not provide. The transition to formal education was slower in the legal profession. Although Harvard offered a course of studies in law by the 1840s, law schools remained supplementary to the office-based apprenticeship until the late nineteenth century. The law schools that did exist during the antebellum period emphasized lectures and readings in contracts, torts, property law, mercantile law, and criminal law. While moot courts and debating clubs did give students some useful practical experience, working with a practicing attorney remained the preferred method of acquiring the procedural knowledge needed to practice law. The movement toward increased professionalism through academic studies continued throughout the nineteenth century and went beyond medicine and law to include such fields as education, engineering, and the military.[3]

The 1830s and 1840s represented a formative era in the development of military professionalism in the United States. Published writing was the most visible sign of the emerging profession of arms. Officers, sometimes using a pseudonym to avoid retribution from their superiors, published articles and letters in newspapers, military journals, and mainstream literary magazines. Topics included problems in the military and possible solutions, the need for improved education and training, civil-military relations, strategy and tactics, and military history. Army officers also published books on professional subjects. Officers assigned as instructors at West Point participated in the Napoleon Club, an intellectual forum on the military art under the leadership of Professor Dennis Hart Mahan. The club's weekly meetings featured the presentation and discussion of scholarly papers analyzing Napoleon's military campaigns and contributed to the professional development of the officers assigned to the academy staff. Several factors led to this increase in military professionalism and scholarship within the U.S. Army. Perhaps most important was the requirement that officers master an increasingly specialized body of knowledge and expertise just like medicine, law, and other fields. A related factor was the growing belief that military officership, because of its specialized body of knowledge, called for a stronger academic background. Furthermore, the almost constant rhetorical attacks against military professionals by the Jacksonian Democrats put army officers on the defensive. This compelled them to embrace greater professionalism in part to justify their role within American society and to prove they were essential to the nation's well-being. Army officers sought to present themselves as true professionals who deserved the same level of respect and prestige enjoyed by practitioners in other fields.[4]

Army officers in the first half of the nineteenth century viewed their profession as "a blend of character and learned skills." In addition to personal traits such as courage, physical strength, honor, and discipline, officers should also possess social respectability and the benefits of a liberal education. Education was crucial not only because it provided knowledge and intellectual discipline, but also because it conferred status. As the *American Quarterly Review* put it, "The true modern soldier ever carries with him the intelligence and the refined feelings of the accomplished scholar, as well as the polished manners and manly spirit of the gentleman." The education provided at West Point was the most significant factor in the elevation of the military profession in the 1830s. West Point provided both an educational standard and a professional model for army officers. The ideal West Point graduate possessed "technical knowledge, mental and military discipline, cosmopolitan gentility, and republican dedication."[5] Naval officers also wanted to enjoy the status of respected professionals and increasingly wrote about the navy's need to move beyond the traditional apprenticeship system and adopt an academic course of studies for midshipmen. West Point increased the army's level of professionalism. A naval academy would do the same for the navy.

The Naval Lyceum

The center of the naval profession in the 1830s and early 1840s was the U.S. Naval Lyceum, established at the New York Navy Yard in Brooklyn in November 1833. The lyceum's mission was "to elevate and adorn the character of our Navy" through the acquisition of professional and general knowledge. In addition to promoting knowledge, the lyceum hoped to develop an esprit de corps that would solidify the professional identity of the naval officer corps.[6] West Point served as the army's professional and cultural center, offering officers and cadets access to a library, museum collections, monuments, and war trophies. In the absence of a naval academy, the Naval Lyceum was the navy's alternative professional and cultural center.[7]

The Naval Lyceum was part of a larger lyceum movement in the United States. The term "lyceum" comes from ancient Greece; the original lyceum was the building in Athens where Aristotle taught. The American lyceums aimed to distribute useful knowledge to the citizenry in order to advance national progress through moral and intellectual development. In addition to general lyceums in local communities, there were also lyceums for particular occupations and trades. Teachers, lawyers, physicians, engineers, farmers, and mechanics formed lyceum associations to foster professionalism and self-improvement. Most lyceums gave their members access to a library, a museum collection, and scientific equipment, and they regularly hosted lectures, debates, and scientific demonstrations on topics of interest to the general public or to members of a specific occupation. Some lyceums published journals and some operated schools for professional training. By the 1830s New York City had supplanted Philadelphia as the commercial, cultural, and intellectual center of the United States. In addition to the Naval Lyceum, New York was home to several other intellectual and cultural institutions including lyceums, historical and literary societies, scientific institutes, colleges, libraries, museums, theaters, concert halls, and publishing houses.[8]

The Naval Lyceum, located in Building No. 1 of the New York Navy Yard, contained a library, reading room, lecture hall, and scientific collection. The library housed over one thousand volumes, hundreds of American and European periodicals, and a collection of maps and charts. Its holdings emphasized books on history, government, law, the sciences, and professional naval subjects as well as travel narratives and the classics of literature. The lyceum's museum-quality scientific collection included shells, minerals, insects, fish and bird specimens, a stuffed leopard, and archaeological artifacts. The lyceum also owned an impressive art collection that featured presidential portraits, naval paintings, and a bust of George Washington. Lyceum members held weekly meetings, usually on Tuesday evenings, most of which included the presentation of a paper followed by a discussion of the topic. The papers covered subjects such as nautical science, sailing and navigation, naval equipment, and the cleanliness and ventilation of navy ships.[9]

The lyceum's membership reflected a wide variety of backgrounds. Active members within the American naval community included Matthew C. Perry, James H. Ward, Samuel F. Du Pont, Alexander Slidell Mackenzie, and Franklin Buchanan. Also on the rolls were U.S. Army and U.S. Marine Corps officers, State Department officials, college professors, British naval officers, and an Italian prince. Among the honorary members were the most prominent and powerful men in the United States: President Andrew Jackson, Vice President Martin Van Buren, Congressman (and former president) John Quincy Adams, authors James Fenimore Cooper and Washington Irving, Commodore John Rodgers, and current and former cabinet secretaries.[10]

The combined mission of the Naval Lyceum's library, scientific collections, and seminars was to enhance the intellectual and moral character of the naval community. Since most naval officers did not have the opportunity to attend college and there was no naval academy, the navy expected them to devote their leisure time to self-improvement. A well-rounded officer did not limit his studies to navigation and mathematics; he also read widely in the sciences and the humanities.[11] Such self-improvement was necessary for officers to maintain their status as gentlemen: "The advantages offered by a free access to an excellent library, and the principal papers and periodicals of the day, to the collections of specimens of nature and art, belonging to the institution, will cooperate to polish and adorn the mind, and render us [naval officers] better able to sustain ourselves in those refined circles of society in which, both at home and abroad, we are, by the peculiar character and standing of our profession, entitled to mix."[12] Society generally considered an officer of the U.S. Navy to be a gentleman regardless of his family's wealth or whether he had received a classical education. However, an officer needed more than the gold braid on his uniform to maintain his social status. As one military journal explained, "A commission is, unquestionably, a letter of introduction to the envied circles of polite society . . . but without polished manners, refined sentiments, elegant conversation, and a cultivated mind," the officer would soon be dismissed by high society.[13]

Intellectual refinement was one of the hallmarks of respectability and gentility. Other than formal education, reading was the primary means of improving one's mental culture. After his promotion to captain in 1804, Stephen Decatur, who intended to marry the daughter of a prominent Norfolk businessman and politician, felt insecure about his level of intellectual refinement. Decatur realized that his father-in-law's social status as well as his own high rank would require him to socialize and converse with well-educated people. Although he had attended Episcopal Academy and the University of Pennsylvania's grammar school in his hometown of Philadelphia before joining the navy, Decatur had not been a serious student. He thus sought help from his family's physician, Dr. Benjamin Rush, a distinguished member of the revolutionary generation who counted John Adams, Thomas Jefferson, and the late Benjamin Franklin among his personal friends. Rush prepared a reading list of books on history and government for Decatur, who embarked on his self-education with enthusiasm. The young captain soon acquired a reputation among contemporaries for his ability to converse intelligently on a variety of topics. Nineteenth-century Americans believed that reading increased one's knowledge, cultivated good manners, improved one's speech and conversational skills, and helped to form good character. As the *United Service Journal*, a British military publication, observed: "We have seldom seen anything mean, or unworthy of an officer, in persons truly sensible of the beauties of Shakespeare." The possession of books was an outward sign of one's refinement—a major reason why so many naval officers maintained personal libraries. The vast increase in the amount of printed material available to Americans in the nineteenth century, in addition to the growth of libraries and lyceums, attested to the social importance of reading.[14]

The most valuable subjects for self-improvement were thought to be history and biography because they provided life examples to emulate or to avoid, philosophy and theology because they disciplined the mind, and science and travel literature because they provided useful information. Fiction, other than the classics or morality tales, was considered to be of little value because it lacked significant intellectual benefits and tended to promote idleness and vice.[15] Benjamin F. Butler, in a speech at West Point, encouraged the cadets to cultivate an appreciation for "letters," especially history. This appreciation was a vital part of their development as professional men of good character. Not only did reading "enlarge and refine the intellect," but it also tended to "promote civility and refinement of manners." Butler observed that George Bancroft's *History of the United States*, James Fenimore Cooper's *History of the Navy*, and Washington Irving's *Voyages of Columbus* were especially valuable for military men. Secretary of the Navy James K. Paulding, in a letter to James Fenimore Cooper, praised the author's history of the American navy and his nautical novels: "I know not where our young officers can find better practical illustrations of Seamanship than they contain." Historical works provided important lessons for young men by examining the lives of heroes like George Washington, who served as role models, and villains like Benedict Arnold, who served as warnings of the dangers associated with a lack of virtue. The Naval Lyceum particularly encouraged midshipmen to make use of its library and scientific collection. Officers had to master self-control before they could command others. Spending time at the lyceum was a way for midshipmen to learn self-discipline because it would keep them away from "the seductions of pleasure and from dissipation." The lyceum was careful to remove any works from its library that might have a negative effect on the naval officer corps. For example, in 1836 it banned *The Liberator* and other abolitionist publications from the reading room in an effort to prevent an internal war within the naval community over the issue of slavery.[16]

To distribute the scientific and professional knowledge accumulated by naval officers, the Naval Lyceum published a journal, the *Naval Magazine*, from 1836 to 1837. Edited by the Reverend Charles S. Stewart, a navy chaplain, each issue included navy news (promotions, resignations, transfers, marriages, obituaries, ship deployments, and port calls), meteorological data, scientific articles, travel narratives, information on foreign navies, articles on naval history, biographical sketches, fictional short stories, and articles on naval subjects such as discipline, education and training, health and medicine, and naval architecture. The *Naval Magazine* also became a vehicle for naval reformers.

James Fenimore Cooper wrote the lead article in the *Naval Magazine*'s first issue. Cooper had a strong interest in naval affairs because of his personal background. Originally bound for the legal profession, Cooper entered

Yale College in 1803 but was expelled in 1805 for fighting with another student and then using gunpowder to blast the door off the student's dormitory room. After returning home to Cooperstown, New York, Cooper became fascinated with the seafaring life and decided to become a naval officer. To strengthen his application, he signed on to a merchant ship to gain some nautical experience and completed a transatlantic voyage from 1806 to 1807. Appointed a midshipman in January 1808, he served in the navy for two uneventful years. Cooper's service as a midshipman sparked a lifelong interest in the navy. In his essay for the *Naval Magazine*'s inaugural issue, he asserted that it was time for the United States to take its place as one of "the foremost nations of Christendom," a goal that required a strong navy. America possessed all of the resources to be a great naval power—abundant timber and naval stores, an established shipbuilding industry, skilled sailors, and the financial means—but needed the vision and the will to make it happen.[17]

In addition to articles in professional and popular periodicals on subjects such as navigation, astronomy, natural history, the physical sciences, geography, naval architecture, and naval technology, naval authors also published memoirs, journals kept at sea, accounts of travel in foreign lands, works of naval history, biographies, and nautical fiction. As one observer noted, "Sailors wash the tar from their hands, and write verses in their logbooks; midshipmen indite their own adventures; and naval commanders, not content with discovering countries and winning battles, steer boldly into the ocean of literature."[18] Besides their literary efforts, naval officers took up their pens in support of the burgeoning naval reform movement.

Going Public with Naval Reform

The Naval Lyceum became the base of operations for a group of progressive, reform-minded officers dedicated to improving the navy. One of the leaders of this emerging naval reform movement was Matthew Calbraith Perry, a founding member of the Naval Lyceum while serving as commander of the recruiting station at the New York Navy Yard. Perry later became commandant of the navy yard and devoted this period of shore duty to modernizing the navy, particularly in the areas of steam engineering and naval education. Born in 1794 in Newport, Rhode Island, Perry was a member of one of America's foremost naval families. His father, Christopher Perry, served on privateers and in the Continental navy during the Revolutionary War. After sailing as a merchant master, Christopher was appointed captain in the U.S. Navy during the Quasi-War and commanded the frigate *General Greene*. Matthew's older brother, Oliver Hazard Perry, became one of the heroes of the War of 1812 after defeating the British on Lake Erie. Three other Perry brothers also served in the navy, and two of Perry's sisters married naval officers.[19]

Matthew C. Perry became a midshipman in January 1809 at the age of fourteen. He served under his brother Oliver on the schooner *Revenge* before the navy transferred him to the frigate *President* under the command of Commodore John Rodgers, who would become his mentor. Perry distinguished himself as a midshipman and became the commodore's personal aide. He saw action in the War of 1812 while serving on board the *President*. After his 1814 marriage to Jane Slidell, the daughter of prominent New York merchant John Slidell, Perry was able to gain command experience during a furlough from the navy as master of a merchant ship owned by his father-in-law's company. On returning to active duty, Perry served as first lieutenant on two ships, and commanded a schooner and a sloop of war.[20]

As naval officers, Perry and his older brother were total opposites in almost every respect and reflected the professional changes occurring within the naval officer corps. Oliver was the quintessential naval hero—daring, tenacious, hot-tempered, and impulsive. Matthew was more studious, thoughtful, scientific, and deliberate. The only similarity between the two was their dedication to the education of their midshipmen. While commanding the sloop of war *Concord*, Matthew Perry employed two instructors, one to teach English and mathematics and one to teach the French, Spanish, and Italian languages. He required his midshipmen to attend classes, opened his private cabin for use as a classroom, and gave the young men access to his personal library. When in port in the Mediterranean, Perry organized sightseeing tours for the midshipmen. He took a great deal of pride in his role as teacher and mentor and often boasted to his fellow officers that his midshipmen studied constantly.[21]

Perry's extensive experience as an officer convinced him that the navy was in need of reform and that one of its top priorities should be the establishment of a naval academy. In 1827 and 1828 he published a series of articles on naval reform in the *National Gazette*, including a piece devoted to naval education. His mentor, John Rodgers, probably encouraged him to publicize the issue since the commodore himself, as a high-ranking officer, could not publicly express such ideas. Perry argued that the best system of naval education was one that combined practical training at sea with a naval academy on shore and pointed to West Point as an appropriate model. A naval academy curriculum, in his opinion, should include navigation, mathematics, astronomy, mechanics, geography, nautical surveying, drawing, history, English, modern languages, maritime and international law, gunnery, and naval science. Before being admitted to the academy, a midshipman should be required to complete at least six months of sea duty to determine his fitness for the service. Perry recommended attaching a sloop and ten or twelve boats to the academy for seamanship training and exercises in tactics and maneuvering. He prophetically suggested Annapolis, Maryland, as the best location for the school. The seaport city provided easy access to Chesapeake Bay; moreover, its placement in the South would balance West Point's location in the North. Perry believed American naval officers should be "distinguished for their correct and gentlemanly deportment—for their professional attainments, for love of country, and a perfect knowledge of arms to defend it." A naval academy was necessary to achieve that ideal.[22]

Perry's articles in 1827 and 1828 served as a preview of a larger trend that would characterize the 1830s and early 1840s: naval officers "going public" with the need for reform, particularly educational reform. Progressive officers made it their goal to educate the public by calling attention to the need for reform and by offering solutions to the most serious problems plaguing the navy. Although they genuinely wanted reform, ambition, the desire for public acclaim, and a sense of self-importance also fueled their efforts. Through petitions and essays published in professional journals and popular magazines, officers brought much-needed reforms to the attention of politicians and the public. Naval officers had grown tired of waiting for Congress to act. Enlisting the public's support might force politicians to pay greater attention to the needs of the navy.[23]

The basic premise of the naval reformers was that the United States required a larger, more efficient force to defend the nation's commerce and its honor on the high seas; the navy needed better-educated, more professional officers to lead this expanded and improved fleet. Attacks on American shipping had resulted in the Quasi-War with France, the Barbary Wars, and the War of 1812. And despite the maritime character of the United States, seven other countries—Britain, France, Russia, Turkey, Holland, Sweden, and Egypt—possessed larger navies. Noting sarcastically that the U.S. Navy was launching ships "that would be a disgrace to the Chinese Navy," Lieutenant Alexander Slidell Mackenzie, Matthew C. Perry's brother-in-law and one of the navy's most prolific authors, asserted that the United States had to keep pace with Britain and France, the world's two strongest naval powers and the nations most frequently encountered by American ships at sea. Mackenzie and others believed the naval officer corps was suffering from "professional stagnation" as a result of the navy's inadequate, ineffective system of education.[24] Naval reform writers presented a strong argument in support of a naval academy by offering two main criticisms of the navy's traditional educational methods. First, naval education at sea was limited to practical instruction in seamanship and navigation. And second, a warship provided a poor environment for learning and, more importantly, for character development.

Midshipmen entered the navy after receiving only a basic education; instruction thereafter focused almost exclusively on seamanship and navigation. While acknowledging the importance of practical instruction, naval reformers argued that an effective officer also required a thorough knowledge of mathematics, international law, modern languages, the sciences, and naval tactics. As Commodore James Barron pointed out, the navy's relatively small size in peacetime gave midshipmen little opportunity to learn fleet tactics through practical instruction; a naval academy was the best alternative. In time of war, the size of the navy would increase substantially, making fleet tactics, which were as different from single ship tactics as individual combat was different from fighting by armies, a necessary part of every naval officer's professional knowledge. Recognizing that the teenage years were the best time for education, the naval reformers lamented that the navy was wasting that window of opportunity by placing midshipmen on warships, where only minimal learning could occur. It would be far preferable to send midshipmen to a West Point–style academy *before* they went to sea. An academy would provide the proper environment for molding their minds and teaching them the theoretical aspects of naval science to facilitate mastery of the practical components of their profession.[25]

The reformers' second criticism involved the learning environment on board ship. There were too many distractions on a warship for any meaningful learning to take place. The daily activities of the crew caused a great deal of noise, making it difficult to find a quiet place to hold classes. Midshipmen were often called away to perform their shipboard duties, which always took precedence over their studies. The civilian instructors did not hold naval rank and, as a result, exercised little authority over their students. On some ships, the professor's quarters were located in the steerage alongside the midshipmen. There was no standard curriculum; instruction varied from ship to ship depending on the interests and educational background of the instructor. Captains had their own views on naval education. Some were supportive of the civilian instructors, while others dismissed the need for classroom instruction. In the words of E. C. Wines, a former schoolmaster on board the frigate *Constellation*, "The difficulty of training the mind to habits of systematic thinking and philosophical reasoning on board a man of war, furnishes one of the strongest arguments that can be urged in favour of the establishment of a Naval Academy."[26]

In the minds of the naval reformers, instruction at sea was useless scholastically and harmful to the moral character of the midshipmen. Placing teenage boys on a navy ship before their character had fully developed was dangerous. Character formation had to take place before a midshipman was exposed to "the bustle, the excitement, the novelties, and the evil examples" associated with life on board ship and in seaport cities. The profanity, gambling, drinking, cruelty, and theft that midshipmen witnessed on a regular basis undermined their moral development. An academy on shore would provide an appropriate learning environment, insulating them from the vices of the seafaring world and fostering "habits of virtue and propriety." An academy would encourage a love of reading, an ennobling leisure activity that would help to steer the young men away from pernicious activities like gambling and drinking. An academy would also efficiently weed out, in Alexander Mackenzie's words, "all the incorrigibly stupid, all the vicious, [and] all the insubordinate" youths who were unfit for a naval career. The informal navy yard schools—little more than glorified study halls where midshipmen crammed for the lieutenant examination—were a poor substitute for a well-organized naval academy. Moreover, their location in large cities and their lax discipline made them less than ideal for character development.[27]

Despite the obvious need for a naval academy for academic, moral, and military reasons, such an institution did not yet exist. In determining who was to blame for this situation, most reformers singled out Congress, whose members had repeatedly asserted that a naval academy was unnecessary and too expensive. The naval heroes of the past had not studied at an academy; what mattered was victory in battle, not academic achievement. Alexander Mackenzie stated that an academy had the support of the Navy Department and the public, but Congress had not created one because of the "intricacies of parliamentary proceedings" or "the clashings of party interests." The lawmakers' inaction was detrimental not only to the navy but also to the nation as a whole. The sea was the "common highway" where America interacted with other nations. These nations would judge the United States "by the worth, by the intelligence, and by the courtesy of [its naval] officers."[28]

"Our army does not appear abroad," navy chaplain George Jones explained. "Its officers are unknown there; foreign nations scarcely know that we have an army; but our Naval officers are everywhere, and everywhere affect most seriously the interests of our country." An academy was, therefore, more necessary for the navy than for the army. Strongly disagreeing with the notion that ignorance was not a problem as long as men performed well in battle, Jones stated that the expansion of American interests around the world demanded educated naval officers:

Look at our land, and mark its interests rising as those of no land ever rose before, and look at those interests, spreading, interweaving themselves with the politics of every nation on the globe, and every day becoming more complicated and important; then look at our young officers, and think, that when they grow up, and become the heads of our Navy, those interests will be committed to their care, requiring in each Captain, not only a well skilled commander but a wise and able statesman, and then tell me is it not pitiful to confine their studies to Bowditch's Navigator.

In foreign ports, naval officers were required to negotiate treaties, settle disputes involving American merchants, deal with scheming foreign officials, and defend the honor of the United States. The method of education developed in the navy's early years was simply no longer adequate given its expanded role in national and international affairs. Jones also repudiated the view that a naval academy was too expensive, demonstrating that an academy would actually cost less than the existing system of education at sea.[29]

Naval reformers published several proposals for the organization and curriculum of a prospective academy. Most of these plans resembled Matthew Perry's earlier design, combining academic studies in the liberal arts, sciences, and professional naval subjects with practical training at sea. The time spent at the academy would serve as a probationary period, both academically and morally; those young men deemed unfit for the service would be "purged from the profession" before they ever made it to the deck of a ship. While most reformers focused on the creation of an "undergraduate" naval academy, George Jones advocated the establishment of a comprehensive naval college that would provide undergraduate studies for midshipmen and continuing education programs for commissioned officers assigned to shore duty between cruises. Most reform writers considered a relatively secluded location on the water to be the ideal place for an academy. In an effort to blunt criticism from tradition-minded officers who clung to the belief that midshipmen could only learn their profession at sea, the academy plans called for practical training in seamanship, navigation, and gunnery on board a training ship attached to the academy. During training cruises, older midshipmen would serve as officers while the younger midshipmen would perform the enlisted crew's duties. These training exercises would give the senior midshipmen leadership experience while enabling the junior midshipmen to learn the nautical skills that would one day be performed by the sailors under their command. Through this improved system, observed Commander Levin M. Powell, "the skill of the thorough-bred seaman would be added to the science of the Mathematician, and the gentleman-like accomplishments which exalt a national character in the eyes of strangers. . . . It is no longer a question whether education . . . will improve a Navy, and through it, the nation to which it belongs. All other [naval] powers are invoking its aid *now* to obtain power on the high seas—for knowledge *is* power, even on the ocean."[30]

Some reformers connected the naval academy issue with another controversy during the Jacksonian era: the use of steam power in naval vessels. The U.S. Navy had been experimenting with steam power since the War of 1812 but still had made little progress by the 1830s. Although there was support for using steam power as an auxiliary to the sailing fleet and for coastal defense (floating artillery batteries and small armed steamships to operate in shallow water), many opposed the construction of steam frigates. Opponents of steam power generally made two arguments against its widespread use by the U.S. Navy: tradition and practicality. Many senior officers viewed steamships as unattractive, dirty, and noisy when compared to majestic sailing ships. Steamships also required less skill in seamanship because they did not rely on wind and current for power. On a more practical level, steamships were more expensive to build and maintain and required large amounts of coal, which took up valuable space on the ship and depended on coaling stations located in areas where the navy operated. Furthermore, early steam engines were often unreliable, while paddle wheels and visible engine machinery made steamships more vulnerable to attack. Congress did authorize the construction of the steam frigates *Mississippi* and *Missouri* in 1839, but progress was slow because of the hostility of senior officers and the indifference of civilian officials. As a result, U.S. Navy ships had undergone little change since the days of John Paul Jones.[31]

Although the more progressive naval officers made a strong case for reform, the political situation in the 1830s discouraged innovation in the navy. While President Andrew Jackson gave rhetorical support to improving the navy and viewed it as an important national institution, he failed to provide any real leadership in naval affairs. His successor, Martin Van Buren, had little interest in naval reform and once proclaimed that the United States "needed no navy at all, much less a steam navy."[32] The navy secretaries during this period, though willing to acknowledge the need for improved naval education, were unwilling to press the issue with Congress. James K. Paulding, secretary of the navy under Van Buren, reflected this trend. Given his background, Paulding seemed to be an excellent candidate to usher in a new era in naval education. An accomplished poet and historian, he had previously served as a navy agent in New York City. Paulding was conservative on many issues, especially steam power. Complaining that he was "steamed to death," the secretary viewed steam engineering as nothing more than a temporary fad. He famously proclaimed, with literary flair, that he would "never consent to let our old ships perish, and transform our Navy into a fleet of sea monsters." Despite his conservatism, Paulding did support the establishment of a naval academy. In his annual report for 1838, he noted that the existing system of educating midshipmen on board ship and at navy yard schools was inadequate and that the naval officer corps strongly favored opening a naval academy. Paulding also pointed out that the cost of an academy would not be prohibitive.[33] The lawmakers still failed to act. During the Jacksonian period, one of Congress's defining characteristics was its parsimony. Salaries of government officials remained low, and requests by cabinet secretaries for additional clerks were denied. Congress was very reluctant to create new federal agencies, even if there was an obvious need, because of the costs involved.[34] Despite the indifference of the country's political leaders, however, the naval reform movement continued to gain momentum in the early 1840s.

Matthew Fontaine Maury's "Scraps from the Lucky Bag"

The most influential voice for naval reform in the early 1840s was Lieutenant Matthew Fontaine Maury. Born in 1806 on his parents' small tobacco plantation in Spotsylvania County, Virginia, Maury joined the navy to follow in the footsteps of his older brother, John, who had entered the service as a midshipman in 1809 and entertained young Matthew with stories of his adventures at sea. When the family moved to Tennessee in 1810, Matthew entered a local private school. A quick learner and a voracious reader, he was particularly interested in mathematics. After learning everything he could at the local school, he expressed the desire to continue his studies at Harpeth Academy in Franklin, Tennessee. His father was reluctant to lose Matthew as a field hand on the family farm but eventually agreed after Matthew suffered a serious back injury and was unable to do farmwork. At Harpeth, Matthew studied Latin, Greek, literature, geography, English, mathematics, natural and moral philosophy, surveying, and logic. Although he excelled at his studies, his father viewed the boy's desire for education to be an annoyance and did not take much interest in his academic achievements.[35]

In July 1823 the family received the devastating news that twenty-eight-year-old Lieutenant John Maury had died of yellow fever a month earlier while at sea, where he was buried according to naval custom. As Matthew approached the end of his studies at Harpeth, his principal encouraged him to go to college. Given Maury's interest in science and mathematics, the principal recommended West Point, which provided the best scientific education in the country for free. The prospect of a military career appealed to Maury, and he set his sights on the U.S. Military Academy. But his father was against the idea. He had already lost one son to the military and was not about to lose another. Although his principal offered to help pay his college tuition, Matthew declined the generous offer out of pride and an "unwillingness to lay myself under such obligations."[36]

Though his father would disapprove, Matthew decided to apply for an appointment as a navy midshipman. If accepted, he would receive a free education that emphasized mathematics, then go on to enjoy an adventurous life at sea like his older brother before him. Tennessee congressman Sam Houston recommended him for the appointment, which he received on February 1, 1825. When Matthew told his father what he had done, the elder Maury was furious. He refused to give his son any travel money, and the two became estranged. Matthew's mother was also upset by his decision and feared for his life, but, understanding his determination, she wished him well.[37]

Maury's midshipman years proved to be disappointing. He had thought the navy would provide him with a solid education, but instead he ended up having "to search for grains of knowledge among bushels of chaff." He lamented "the want of books and proper teachers in the Navy" and learned the naval profession, in his words, through an "accident of education." Maury tried to compensate for the navy's deficiencies by being a diligent student on his own, writing out trigonometry problems with a piece of chalk on cannon shot. When it came time to prepare for his lieutenant examination, Maury's love of science and mathematics led him to study in much greater depth than the test required. Rather than limiting himself to practical knowledge of navigation (which most midshipmen did by memorizing the formulas in Bowditch's navigation textbook), he also studied the mathematical theory behind navigational principles. This diligence actually ended up causing him trouble during the exam in March 1831. While responding to a question on navigation, Maury went into a long demonstration of a spherical trigonometry problem instead of simply repeating the appropriate formula from Bowditch. The examining board was unable to follow his mathematical analysis and said his response was incorrect. Although he passed the test, the board ranked him far lower than warranted (twenty-seventh out of forty midshipmen), which meant that it would take him longer to receive a promotion to lieutenant.[38]

While still a passed midshipman, Maury took his first steps toward becoming one of the navy's preeminent scientists. He published an article on navigation and meteorology in 1834 and decided to write a navigation textbook for midshipmen that he hoped would replace the venerable Bowditch. Maury believed Bowditch's text was inadequate because it provided formulas without discussion or explanation of mathematical theory. The result was that most midshipmen possessed only a superficial knowledge of navigation; they had no real understanding of the underlying mathematical and scientific principles. A text that explained the theory and practice of navigation was vital, in Maury's opinion, because of the lack of a "regular system of education" for midshipmen.[39]

Maury's book, *A New Theoretical and Practical Treatise on Navigation*, was published in 1836, just before his promotion to lieutenant. It provides substantial instruction in algebra, geometry, logarithms, and trigonometry in addition to nautical astronomy and practical navigation. In contrast, Bowditch's is more of a "how to" approach—how to make various calculations, how to measure latitude and longitude, how to use a quadrant and sextant, how to survey a coast or harbor. Maury's volume received praise from his fellow officers and from reviewers, though some senior naval officers dismissed it as the work of a presumptuous passed midshipman. A reviewer in the *Southern Literary Messenger* hoped the book would spark future scientific studies by naval officers: "The spirit of literary improvement has been awakened among the officers of our gallant navy. We are pleased to see that science also is gaining votaries from its ranks." By 1837 every navy ship had a copy of Maury's *Treatise on Navigation*, and in 1844, by order of the secretary of the navy, it replaced Bowditch as the standard navigation textbook for U.S. Navy midshipmen.[40]

Maury's own experience as a midshipman also prompted him to become actively involved in the naval reform movement. Serious injuries from a stagecoach accident in 1839 required a long period of recovery and prevented him from returning to sea duty. After the Navy Department denied his request for an administrative assignment in Washington, D.C., Maury decided to use his abundant free time to improve the navy, which was "in a lamentable condition." He had seen firsthand the onerous challenges that plagued the navy, and he believed some relatively simple reforms could correct these deficiencies.[41] If he could not serve the navy from the deck of a ship or from behind a desk in Washington, he would do so by publicizing the navy's problems and offering reasonable solutions.

Maury's crusade to improve the navy took the form of a series of essays published anonymously in the *Southern Literary Messenger*, a popular periodical. Maury entitled the series "Scraps from the Lucky Bag." The "lucky bag" was a navy ship's lost-and-found bin, whose contents included "a little of everything"—from articles of clothing to cooking utensils. In a similar way, Maury's essays addressed a wide variety of naval reform issues. He wrote the articles under a pseudonym, "Harry Bluff," because he feared that some of what he had to say might be considered insubordination and lead to his dismissal from the navy.[42]

The basic premise of Maury's essays was that the navy needed reform because it had failed to keep pace with America's progress in the nineteenth century. In the republic's early years, when the U.S. Navy was a small force with a relatively limited (albeit important) defensive mission, there was no need for a naval academy or other improvements. Since then, however, the navy's mission had changed as its obligations increased. The navy was now responsible not only for the country's maritime defense, but also for expanding commerce, negotiating treaties, and conducting scientific exploration. The navy's condition in 1840 was simply inadequate given the multiple tasks it performed. Although the service was the country's pride and joy after the War of 1812, efforts to improve the fleet focused only on increasing the number of ships, not on upgrading personnel. Maury agreed that the navy needed more ships, but it also required a more efficient personnel system, the introduction of flag rank, a more effective administrative structure, a better system of naval education, improved coastal and harbor defense, greater use of steam power in naval vessels, and naval justice reform. For Maury, naval reform was a matter of national honor and economic prosperity.[43]

Maury believed education was the key to improving the navy as an institution. He used his own midshipman experience to demonstrate that the existing system was inadequate. On his first cruise, his schoolmaster was George Jones. Though intelligent and a dedicated teacher, Jones had no authority over the midshipmen; he did not even have a real classroom. As a result, despite Jones's best efforts, Maury and his peers "learned nothing." On his next cruise, Maury had a teacher from Spain who limited instruction to the Spanish language. The midshipmen quickly became bored and protested by tossing their grammar books overboard. On a later cruise, Maury's instructor was a young lawyer who knew nothing about navigation and was "not on speaking terms with the reefers [midshipmen]." On still another cruise, there was no instructor at all. Maury's final example was an instructor who spent all of his time writing a book and did not do any actual teaching.[44]

The lack of respect for the civilian instructors was a serious problem. "At our universities, in our colleges, academies, and in every school," Maury explained, "experience has taught us the necessity of clothing the preceptor with authority to enforce obedience and command attention to his precepts. Not so in the man-of-war." To most midshipmen, the professor was a landlubber without rank, unworthy of their respect. In an essay published in

The Madisonian, a navy professor of mathematics suggested that the navy's educational situation was indicative of a larger anti-intellectual trend in the United States: "Among many of our citizens the name of a teacher is a term of contempt," he lamented. "It is a favorite reproach in the mouths of foreigners that notwithstanding our boasts of the universal diffusion of education among our citizens, there is scarcely any country . . . in which learning is so little respected and its labours so vilely rewarded."[45]

In addition to the practical instruction in seamanship and navigation provided by the navy, Maury advocated a liberal education that would consist of more theoretical studies and more science, including advanced mathematics; the physical sciences related to the sea, like oceanography and hydraulics; geology, botany, and mineralogy to enable the midshipmen to conduct scientific surveys; professional subjects like naval architecture, tactics, gunnery, and pyrotechny; and subjects of obvious importance to the navy such as drawing, international and maritime law, and modern languages. Despite the vast amount of knowledge required to perform the duties of a naval officer, Maury was aware of only one officer who had earned a college degree. One consequence of the navy's disinterest in academics was the lack of scholarly works written by naval officers. Although some had published several travel narratives and descriptions of voyages, naval officers had contributed few treatises on professional subjects. Army officers, in contrast, produced several scholarly works on the profession of arms. The main difference between the two services was that the army had West Point, which provided officer candidates a solid academic background.[46]

Although Maury advocated a liberal education for midshipmen over the long term, preferably at an academy on shore, he proposed that the navy implement a transitional measure to improve the situation immediately. That measure would be to use one of the ships "rotting in Norfolk" as a school ship. The ship would remain in port most of the year, serving essentially as a floating classroom, then set sail on an annual two- or three-month training cruise with the midshipmen acting as the crew. On Maury's school ship, education would be the top priority, meaning that the vessel would be a school first and a warship second. West Point's use of its own graduates as instructors confirmed Maury's belief that naval officers were the best teachers for midshipmen. It would make little sense for a lawyer to teach medicine; then why should a landsman teach navigation and naval science? Only naval officers could maintain discipline among the midshipmen. In addition to holding naval rank, which commanded respect, officers would serve as professional role models. This would solve the problems of authority associated with civilian instructors. New midshipmen would attend classes on the school ship for three years before their posting to a warship for an additional three years of active duty in the fleet. After this probationary period, midshipmen would take their lieutenant examination. Those who completed their studies, served at sea in a satisfactory manner, and passed the exam would receive a promotion.[47]

In Maury's mind, a major drawback of the existing system was that a midshipman had no incentive to become familiar with the theoretical aspects of naval science; in fact, the navy seemed to frown on it. As Maury himself found out the hard way, a midshipman moving beyond practical knowledge during the lieutenant examination was likely to be "black-balled" by his examiners: "He who repeats 'by heart' the rules of Bowditch, though he does not understand the mathematical principles involved in one of them, obtains a higher number from the [Examining] Board, than he who, skilled in mathematics, goes up to the black board, and drawing his diagram, can demonstrate every problem in navigation." Maury told the story of his own exam as an example, though he claimed to be describing a friend's experience. The attitude of many politicians "that officers were wanted to *fight*, and that *book* learning was a thing with which a man-of-war's man had nothing to do" was wrong. Because of deficient schooling, naval officers were lacking in inductive reasoning, research skills, and innovation. This put American naval officers "behind the times" in their professional attainments, resulting in inefficiencies on board ship, mismanagement within the Navy Department and at navy yards, and the wasteful expenditure of appropriations.[48]

Maury connected the need for improved education with personnel reform. The government's haphazard appointment of officers had no correlation with the number of ships in commission. The most serious personnel problem was the large number of young men serving as passed midshipmen. Though deemed qualified to be lieutenants, the navy forced them to waste the "early vigor of manhood" until the "tedious process of disease and death shall make room for them in the rank above." This situation had created a "spirit of discontent" within the junior ranks of the naval officer corps. Passed midshipmen often performed tasks usually assigned to midshipmen, making the midshipmen little more than glorified errand boys. This fostered idleness and irresponsibility among the "young gentlemen" and hindered their professional development.[49]

To make his point, Maury compared the plight of the midshipmen to other professions. When newly minted physicians and lawyers finished their training, generally after two or three years, they began to practice their profession. Midshipmen endured a much longer apprenticeship; even after passing the qualifying examination, they had to wait several more years be-

A sailing master, passed midshipman, midshipman, and lieutenant (left to right) wearing their full dress uniforms on the deck of a navy ship. Courtesy Special Collections and Archives Department, Nimitz Library, U.S. Naval Academy.

fore becoming commissioned officers. This situation did not exist prior to 1815. In the early navy, an officer could reasonably expect to make captain within fifteen years. By the early 1840s, a new midshipman had to wait that long before making lieutenant. The *Army and Navy Chronicle* estimated that it took an average of six years to receive a promotion from midshipman to passed midshipman and another ten years to become a lieutenant. The main problem was gridlock at the top of the naval officer pyramid. In the 1830s and 1840s most captains in the U.S. Navy had achieved that rank before or during the War of 1812. Since the navy did not have a retirement system, vacancies occurred only when senior captains died. Despite this logjam in the officer corps, there was no decrease in the number of midshipmen appointed because such appointments were a valuable source of patronage for politicians.[50]

To solve this problem, Maury suggested that all midshipmen who completed the school ship's course of studies and passed the lieutenant examination, but did not receive a promotion to lieutenant, would enter a naval reserve corps and sail with the merchant marine until recalled as lieutenants, subject to the needs of the navy. In peacetime, the merchant employer, not the government, would pay the salaries of these reserve officers. Besides improving the merchant service and providing the navy with a well-trained reserve, this system would help to end the "ancient and barbarous practice of privateering" in time of war. Although earlier in its history the United States had engaged in privateering out of necessity, many Americans by the early 1840s, including Maury, had come to believe that the practice was immoral, undignified, and beneath the character of the republic. Rather than resort to glorified piracy in time of war, the government could arm merchant ships and absorb them into the navy with the corps of reserve officers ready for action.[51]

Maury's essays in the *Southern Literary Messenger* received a great deal of attention among naval officers, government officials, and the American public. Although he had not been officially identified as the author of "Scraps from the Lucky Bag," circulating rumors established his authorship and made him well known. In fact, there was a movement to promote his appointment as secretary of the navy. Maury had no interest in the job and was actually concerned that some might misinterpret his essays as a bid for the secretaryship. Although these articles "whet up the animosity of the old Officers, a portion of them at least," the younger, more progressive officers praised Maury's work. Officers assigned to the navy yards in Washington and Philadelphia had the "Scraps from the Lucky Bag" reprinted and distributed throughout the navy. The officers in Philadelphia petitioned the government to reorganize the navy according to Maury's proposals. Officers assigned to the Mediterranean Squadron praised his "professional capacity, enlarged views, and sterling patriotism."[52]

In the spring of 1841, Maury answered his supporters' call to write a sequel article, publishing a piece entitled "More Scraps from the Lucky Bag." Although he did not discuss naval education, he did advocate that U.S. Marine Corps officers be selected from among the graduates of West Point to ensure that the officers had received a thorough scientific and military education.[53] Maury expressed pride in the interest his writings had generated. In a letter to his cousin, he mentioned having been informed that the officers of the ship of the line *Delaware* were planning on "publishing in pamphlet form & laying on the desk of every member of Congress the last 'Scrap.'" He also won praise from the officers of the ship of the line *Ohio*. Maury concluded that even if some of the older officers were against him, "the majority of the Officers approve of my acts." In July 1841 an anonymous naval officer wrote a biographical sketch of Maury, identifying him as "Harry Bluff" and praising his efforts on behalf of naval reform. This officer hailed the "Scraps from the Lucky Bag" as "masterful productions" that "turned the attention of the whole nation towards the Navy." The author credited Maury with having "produced an enthusiasm throughout the whole extent of the country, which has not subsided, and will not subside until the whole Navy is reorganized."[54]

After his identity became public, Maury decided that it was time for "Harry Bluff" to retire. But he did not abandon his crusade to reform the navy. Maury began a new series of articles entitled "Letters to Mr. Clay"—a reference to Senator Henry Clay of Kentucky—under the pseudonym "Union Jack." In the second essay, he dropped his school ship proposal and instead called for the establishment of a naval academy on shore. He believed the best location for such an academy was on the Mississippi River in Memphis, Tennessee, adjacent to a proposed navy yard he supported. Maury believed that by placing the school in a western state, the navy could introduce itself to that region and avoid the criticism voiced by many western citizens of the U.S. Military Academy. Maury emphasized that the advent of steam power was the main reason why a naval academy was necessary. Because the use of steam would only increase in the future, naval officers needed to acquire an understanding of the scientific principles and machinery associated with steam engineering. Under Maury's plan, midshipmen would study at the naval academy for four years, with three-month training cruises annually, and serve at sea for an additional three years after graduation.[55]

Matthew Fontaine Maury succeeded in bringing the need for naval reform to the public's attention. People read his essays with such interest that the editor of the *Southern Literary Messenger* asked him to write more. Maury addressed a wide range of subjects, including naval education, the creation of admirals, corruption in the shipbuilding industry, naval expansion into the American West, and administrative reorganization of the Navy Department. Although most of these ideas were not original with Maury, he raised public consciousness of problems within the navy and convinced the American people that naval reform was necessary to ensure continued economic prosperity and national progress.[56]

Abel P. Upshur, Conservative Reformer

The naval reform movement found another ally in 1841, when President John Tyler appointed Virginia judge and politician Abel P. Upshur secretary of the navy. At first glance, Upshur would seem to have been an unlikely advocate of progressive reform in the navy. He had no previous experience in naval affairs and was the quintessential conservative southerner—a slaveholder and strong defender of states' rights. Upshur was born in 1790 into an aristocratic Virginia family. He received a classical education from private tutors on his family's plantation, then attended college at Princeton, where he was expelled in 1807 after taking part in a student rebellion. On his return to Virginia, Upshur studied law in Richmond and was admitted to the bar. In addition to his legal practice, Upshur held several political offices including commonwealth attorney for Richmond, member of the Richmond city council, and member of the Virginia state legislature. In 1826 he was elected a judge of the General Court of Virginia, the state's highest court for criminal cases. Over the course of his public career, Upshur earned a reputation as a staunch southern conservative who opposed democratic reform in Virginia, supported the doctrine of nullification, and defended the institution of slavery. In the wake of the nullification crisis, Upshur joined the Whig Party to oppose what he saw as the despotic tendencies of Andrew Jackson.[57]

Unlike some of his predecessors at the Navy Department, Upshur was a diligent administrator who frequently worked in his office until eleven o'clock at night. His main complaint about the job was the amount of tedious paperwork required. Although a trusted adviser to the president on "great matters of public interest and on great questions of international law," he also had "to decide whether or not a drunken midshipman shall be dismissed [from] the service." Perhaps in part due to the department's inefficient administrative structure, he decided to focus on reform, something that, unlike the mundane paperwork, was worthy of his attention. In fact, Upshur said he would prefer to return to the bench unless he could "do good" as secretary of the navy. Another reason for his strong interest in naval reform was the fact that his younger brother, George, was a naval officer.[58]

Abel P. Upshur was determined to improve the navy in a comprehensive manner through administrative, personnel, educational, and legal reform, as well as innovation in shipbuilding and scientific advancement. Unlike his predecessors, he developed his reform program in consultation with all segments of the officer corps. While preparing his annual report for 1841, Upshur discussed naval affairs with numerous officers, both senior and junior, including Captain Charles Stewart, Captain Thomas ap Catesby Jones, Captain Beverley Kennon (a personal friend of Upshur's), members of the Board of Navy Commissioners, the commandant of the Marine Corps, his brother George P. Upshur, and several progressive officers who advocated reform. Upshur was familiar with the most recent commentary on the navy, including the ideas expressed by Matthew Fontaine Maury. Maury's influence on Upshur's thinking was significant, and many of Maury's ideas found their way into Upshur's annual report.[59]

His annual report outlined a broad plan for naval reform, expansion, and modernization. As a former judge, Upshur was particularly interested in reforming the naval justice system, which he believed was too arbitrary. He proposed developing a comprehensive code of laws and regulations for the navy, with clear statements of what actually constituted an offense and standard guidelines for punishment. Upshur also proposed abolishing the Board of Navy Commissioners and replacing it with a bureau system. Separate bureaus, each with its own area of expertise and responsibility, would perform the administrative duties previously carried out by the board. A more efficient administrative structure was critically important because Upshur also called for a massive expansion of the fleet. To protect commerce and maintain economic prosperity, the U.S. Navy had to keep pace with its British and French counterparts. Falling behind the European naval powers, all of which were expanding and modernizing their fleets, would invite hostility toward American interests abroad. Specifically, Upshur recommended that the United States operate a navy half the size of the Royal Navy. A large portion of this expanded fleet would be composed of steamships, which the British were already successfully employing in naval operations. Favoring innovation in shipbuilding, Upshur called for experiments in constructing steam warships made from iron rather than wood. He also recommended that an enlargement of the Marine Corps accompany expansion of the navy.[60]

Regarding personnel reform, Upshur proposed adding more naval officer ranks, including flag rank, which existed in every navy except America's. Introducing more ranks would provide officers with greater professional incentive and would improve morale, discipline, and competency. Flag rank was necessary because there were captains commanding single ships and captains commanding entire squadrons (captains commanding a squadron received the courtesy title of commodore, but were still technically captains). Captains commanding squadrons were at a disadvantage when dealing with foreign admirals, who refused to consider the Americans their professional equals. Parity with the U.S. Army was also a factor that pointed to the need for flag rank. The army had nine officer ranks, including generals, while the navy had less than half that number. In recommending the establishment of naval academies, Upshur emphasized that the rise of steam power required naval officers who possessed greater scientific and technical knowledge.[61]

The press greeted Upshur's report favorably. Some editors who had initially criticized President Tyler's selection of Upshur praised the secretary's leadership and reform agenda. The *Philadelphia North American* declared that Upshur's report "came like thunder on a stagnant sea." Despite the favorable reception in the press, Upshur faced an uphill battle in Congress.

Even members who supported the idea of naval reform were cautious in implementing Upshur's recommendations.[62] Representative Joseph Fornance of Pennsylvania spoke for many of his colleagues when he stated that he was unwilling to support such a massive and costly expansion of the navy when the United States was not at war. He was "opposed to building squadrons to rot in our harbors" in a misguided effort to project an image of naval strength to the rest of the world. The American people did not want a large peacetime army and navy like the British had. Maintaining large military and naval establishments cost too much and would inevitably threaten liberty by involving the country in war.[63]

Upshur's suggestion that the United States should operate a navy half the size of the Royal Navy struck several members of Congress as preposterous. His 1841 report indicated that the U.S. Navy consisted of 11 ships of the line, 17 frigates, 18 sloops of war, 2 brigs, 9 schooners, 4 steamers, 3 storeships, and 3 receiving ships—for a total of 67 vessels. One congressman estimated that the British navy at the time had 578 ships. To reach Upshur's goal, the U.S. Navy would have to build an additional 222 ships. New York congressman Samuel Gordon called Upshur's proposals extravagant and irresponsible. The secretary was recommending that the United States maintain a large, British-style navy complete with admirals, a class of "useless officers to be paid for living in idleness out of the public purse." Gordon suggested that President Tyler replace Upshur with "some practical business-man, who would conduct the affairs of the navy with more prudence."[64]

Although unwilling to give Upshur a blank check for naval expansion, Congress did implement some of his proposals, most notably replacing the Board of Navy Commissioners with five separate administrative bureaus: Navy Yards and Docks; Construction, Equipment, and Repairs; Ordnance and Hydrography; Provisions and Clothing; and Medicine and Surgery. Prior to 1830, the board had been an effective policymaking organization and a valuable component of naval administration. But in the years that followed, extreme conservatism, opposition to innovation and reform, and internal disagreements plagued the board and hampered naval policymaking. The elimination of the board signaled a shift in naval policy leadership from the older, more conservative officers to the younger, more progressive officers. The new system promised much greater efficiency in naval administration since the officers heading each bureau had the individual authority to make decisions formerly made by the board as a collective body.[65]

Upshur's report sparked a new round in the naval academy debate, one that focused on the democratic and sectional issues associated with naval education. Some members of Congress believed that the navy's system for appointing midshipmen was undemocratic; particularly troubling was its practice of discriminating against enlisted seamen in granting midshipman appointments. Regardless of intelligence, skill, experience, or valor, the navy did not permit enlisted sailors to become midshipmen. Representative John Reynolds of Illinois referred to this policy as "slavery before the mast"; enlisted seamen were nothing more than naval slaves because they performed the physical labor necessary to operate a navy ship but were denied the opportunity to improve their station in life. The same situation existed in the army. The army did not permit enlisted soldiers to become officers because the government treated West Point cadets as an elite "nobility" and granted them a monopoly on officer commissions. The Declaration of Independence stated that all men were created equal, yet the army and the navy refused to allow qualified enlisted men to rise through merit to become commissioned officers. Pennsylvania congressman Charles Brown took issue with a statement made by Upshur that the sons of naval officers received preference in midshipman appointments. In Brown's opinion, this represented an aristocracy that was similar to the hereditary class system that existed in European society. The congressman recommended that the government appoint midshipmen from the enlisted ranks because it was the sailors who had experience at sea, which made them more qualified to command.[66]

An article in the *Southern Literary Messenger* praising Upshur's annual report stated that the naval academy issue was "commanding a larger share of the public attention, now, than we have ever before known it to do." The article suggested that "sectional prejudices" had prevented the establishment of a naval academy in the past and implored the country to look beyond such biases and open an academy, which "the public interest, the honor and the welfare of the service" required.[67] The rise of the abolitionist movement beginning in the 1830s pushed the slavery issue to the forefront of national life and heightened the sectional tension between the free labor North and the slaveholding South. As was the case in many policy areas, antagonism over slavery began creeping into naval affairs, including the naval academy debate, by the early 1840s.

Several congressmen criticized the regional bias that existed in the granting of midshipman appointments, a bias that would undoubtedly continue if the navy created an academy. Representative Horace Everett of Vermont argued that midshipman appointments were the best way to secure the whole country's support for the navy, but the government did not distribute appointments equitably among the states. In fact, none of the young men Everett recommended ever received an appointment. He related the story of how he tried to secure one for a deserving orphan in his district. Despite the large number of appointments granted at the time, the boy was rejected. According to Everett, Virginia, Maryland, and the District of Columbia received preferential treatment, to the detriment of young men from other states. New York congressman Christopher Morgan concurred, noting that his applications for appointments were denied because all of the navy's vacancies had been filled. He later discovered that some Virginians received appointments after his New York applicants had already been rejected.[68]

Reports prepared by navy secretaries Samuel Southard and Levi Woodbury proved that Virginia, Maryland, and the District of Columbia did receive more than their fair share of midshipman appointments. Although the most likely explanation for this preferential treatment was geographic proximity to the nation's capital, some northern congressmen suggested that the sinister influence of slavery lurked behind this favoritism. An abolitionist newspaper accused President Tyler of trying to place the navy under the control of officers from the slave states. Representative Brown of Pennsylvania stated that Virginians had always received more than their fair share of government offices. "Why was it supposed all over the world," Brown wondered, "that Virginians are more intelligent, more courageous, and more chivalrous than other citizens of the United States?" Citizens from all of the states should have an equal claim to military commissions. Citizens from states other than Virginia had served with honor in the Revolutionary War and the War of 1812. In Brown's opinion, a poor boy from Philadelphia would probably be denied an appointment as a midshipman despite possessing strong moral character, whereas "a young Virginian, nurtured in idleness, with negroes to wait upon him, and to be kicked and cuffed at his pleasure, could be appointed by some political influence or species of favoritism."[69]

In July 1842 a bill to establish naval schools was introduced in the Senate. If passed, the measure would authorize the secretary of war to transfer up to five forts or other military posts not needed by the army to the Navy Department for use as schools. It would empower the navy secretary to develop a curriculum and a set of rules and regulations for the schools, which would provide instruction for new midshipmen and midshipmen preparing for the lieutenant examination. The secretary could assign naval officers and navy professors of mathematics to the schools as needed and hire foreign language teachers. The bill provided an appropriation of one thousand dollars to purchase a model steam engine for each school.[70]

The Senate debated the naval schools bill in August 1842. While admitting that the schools might be beneficial, Senator William Allen of Ohio feared they would become "a nursery for wealthy young men" who, after receiving a free education, would leave the service for higher-paying civilian jobs. If the schools were intended to educate the "sons of poor widows" or the sons of deceased navy veterans, he would probably support the bill, but these institutions would most likely cater to the sons of politicians and the wealthy as, in his opinion, West Point did. Allen declared that the U.S. Navy had earned the high status of "wonder of the world" without "land-lubber schools." The naval officers who achieved glory during the War of 1812 had learned their profession on the deck of a ship, not in a classroom: "Set a man down in the dark retreat of a college cell, to learn how to manage a ship in a storm! No sir. Send him to sea, and there let him learn how to control the elements." The navy should continue to educate midshipmen on "a martial principle," where "ambition and not the rod of the schoolmaster" served as the primary motivation for diligence.[71]

Senator James Buchanan of Pennsylvania said he would vote to approve one naval school, but not five. The government simply did not have the money. South Carolina senator John C. Calhoun, a former secretary of war and a strong patron of West Point, suggested amending the bill to provide for only one naval school, to be located in the Chesapeake Bay area. After some debate, the Senate voted to accept the amendment authorizing one school instead of five.[72]

New Hampshire senator and former secretary of the navy Levi Woodbury pointed out that determining the fitness of a young man for a naval career was crucial. The only way to find out if he "could bear the exposure and roll of the ocean" was to send him to sea. There was no sense educating a youth for a naval career if he was unfit for life at sea. Woodbury believed the best way to develop a naval officer was to combine instruction at sea with schooling on shore, preferably at a navy yard. But the time at sea was the most important. "The naval officer should be a sailor," Woodbury said, "an informed, intelligent, moral, and intellectual sailor, if you please; but still a son of the ocean, and dedicated, heart and soul, for life, to all its arduous duties . . . and high responsibilities." It made as much sense to keep a midshipman on shore as it did to send a West Point cadet to sea. Woodbury supported the naval school bill since he viewed education during "leisure hours" on shore as an important supplement to instruction at sea. The Senate passed the naval school bill on August 9, but the House failed to enact the legislation before the close of the congressional session.[73]

In October 1842 Secretary Upshur began preparing his second annual report. In response to congressional criticism of the financial cost of his department's agenda, Upshur decided to emphasize the navy's importance to the nation's economy. He believed the amount of money in the treasury was not the measure of a nation's wealth. How much money its citizens possessed was a far more significant indicator. The navy spent 90 percent of its appropriations paying American citizens for labor, materials, and provisions. It pumped money into the economy and fueled prosperity by giving "employment to industry" and "encouragement to enterprise," benefiting the entire nation, not just the Atlantic seaports. Agricultural and manufacturing interests nationwide depended on U.S. trade, which in turn relied on the navy for protection. Upshur repeated his earlier recommendations to create the rank of admiral, to enlarge the Marine Corps, and to embrace innovation in shipbuilding and naval technology. He also called for the establishment of a navy yard on the lower Mississippi River in order to connect the navy with the western states.[74]

Upshur acknowledged that the public had been "occasionally offended with displays of disreputable behavior" by naval personnel, but such behavior was not surprising given that the navy had received "little more than a step-mother's care" from the government. He was convinced that improvements in discipline had to begin with the midshipmen, the navy's future leaders. Only young men suitable for the service should be appointed. Too many youths with disciplinary problems, whose parents and teachers could not control them, entered the navy. To desperate parents, the navy's discipline offered the last hope for reforming their sons. Noting the House's failure to pass the naval school bill during the previous session of Congress, Upshur stated that such a school would go a long way toward improving the behavior of the midshipmen.[75]

Upshur made several recommendations for the organization of a naval school. The best location for the school would be an old army fort on the Atlantic coast. The instructors should be naval officers and professors already employed by the navy. The procedure for admission would be similar to West Point's. Students who successfully completed their studies and demonstrated their intellectual, moral, and physical fitness for a naval career would receive an appointment as midshipman and go to sea. After several years of satisfactory sea duty, the young men would take their examination and, if successful, would serve as passed midshipmen until there was a vacancy in the lieutenant rank. Upshur repeated the familiar argument that education was more important for the navy than for the army because naval officers represented the nation abroad, conducted negotiations with foreign officials, preserved the peace, and, given the geographic location of the United States, would form the front line of defense if war broke out. The naval officer was "the standard by which foreign nations will be most apt to measure [America's] moral and intellectual character." It was the government's responsibility to ensure that every naval officer was professionally competent and possessed good moral character. Preparatory education could accomplish that goal.[76]

Unable to secure congressional approval for a naval academy during his tenure, Upshur left the Navy Department in July 1843 to become secretary of state. Overall, he had proved to be an innovative and visionary navy secretary. Although he did not fully achieve his ambitious agenda, he did enjoy some important victories. He reformed the navy's inefficient administrative structure and made some progress in modernizing the American fleet through advances in steam power and the creation of a naval engineer corps. Upshur clearly articulated a broad vision for the American navy and directed the public's attention to the need for continued reform.[77]

The "New" Naval Officer

Although the various attempts at naval reform had mixed results, a new conception of the naval profession had emerged by the early 1840s. Before 1815, the navy's only concern was to produce daring and tenacious warriors who won battles—men like John Paul Jones, Stephen Decatur, and Oliver Hazard Perry. After 1815, the navy needed a new kind of officer, one who could win battles but who could also negotiate treaties, expand trade, explore new lands, conduct scientific research, command technologically advanced ships, and publish books and articles on professional subjects. Men like Matthew C. Perry and Matthew Fontaine Maury represented the new naval officer corps. "Are animal courage and nautical skill," asked the *Military and Naval Magazine of the United States*, "all the requisites for a commander of a foreign station—the individual who is charged with the power of negotiating treaties, and corresponding on a variety of subjects with foreign governments?" By the early 1840s, the answer to that question was a resounding no.[78]

The navy's commercial, diplomatic, and scientific responsibilities combined with advances in steam engineering signaled the need for a change in how naval officers prepared for their profession. Because of their activities overseas, naval officers were a reflection of the United States. "The representative of his nation abroad, sometimes in critical emergencies," observed the *Naval Magazine*, "the enlightened knowledge of the naval commander becomes, not infrequently, the touchstone of the honor of his flag."[79] The naval profession had advanced to the point where it was no longer possible for a teenage boy to go to sea and learn what he had to know on a ship. Whereas the navy had formerly encouraged furloughed midshipmen to sail with the merchant service, by the early 1840s this was no longer the case. Although seamanship was still very important, it was not the navy's primary concern in the professional development of midshipmen. Formal academic studies, combined with practical training at sea, seemed to be the only way to impart all of the knowledge needed by antebellum naval officers. As navy chaplain George Jones explained, a captain required "an assemblage of qualities seldom found in one man—a mind well disciplined; expanded views of society; thorough knowledge of history, laws and governments; sound judgment; quickness, decision, firmness and intrepidity." Writing about the officers of the Continental navy, James Fenimore Cooper argued that naval officers needed more than just nautical skills: "While many gallant and suitable men were chosen [as Continental officers], some of the corps had little to recommend them besides their practical knowledge of seamanship." Cooper believed that a natural aristocracy, men of intelligence and refinement, should govern the nation and that the masses should defer to the judgment and leadership of these "natural aristocrats." The ideal American naval officer, in his opinion, was a member of this natural aristocracy and must possess gentility and a liberal education as well as the knowledge and skills of an expert mariner. Among the officers of the Revolutionary navy, Cooper explained, "There was no lack of competent navigators, or of brave seamen, but the high moral qualities which are indispensable to the accomplished officer, were hardly to be expected among those who had received all their training in the rude and imperfect schools of the merchant service." All of the officers in the nineteenth-century U.S. Navy should possess the "high moral qualities" that characterized Cooper's ideal of an officer and a gentleman.[80]

Although the naval and merchant services both required knowledge of seamanship, navigation, and naval architecture, they were distinct professions with different purposes. Merchant ships transported cargo, but naval ships protected commerce, fought wars, conducted exploration, and engaged in diplomacy. The system of organization and discipline on board a warship was completely different from that on a merchant ship. The naval officer had a responsibility to the nation that went far beyond that of a merchant captain to his employer. As the *Naval Magazine* observed in 1837, the naval officer "affords to foreigners, in his own person, a standard of national character." He required greater knowledge than a merchant shipmaster, including an understanding of the physical sciences, nautical surveying, geography, international law, diplomacy, gunnery, and naval tactics, all of which made formal education a necessity. "The vulgar notion, that education and nautical skill are incompatible . . . has now few supporters." For the naval officer, "seamanship is a means, and not an end."[81]

The additional knowledge required for naval officers was what separated the navy from the merchant service and what gave naval officers their professional identity. "Theoretical understanding" was the defining characteristic of a profession and the critical factor that separated the professions from other occupations. The professions called for more scientific and theoretical knowledge than the trades, which demanded only practical training and the acquisition of skills through apprenticeship. The theoretical aspect gave professionals social status and a collective sense of pride in their work. Even within a particular occupational field, there were distinctions made between professionals and tradesmen. In the eighteenth and nineteenth centuries, for example, the field of medicine distinguished between physicians and surgeons. A physician had usually received a classical education in addition to medical training through an apprenticeship, whereas a surgeon had completed an apprenticeship to learn the practical skills needed to perform his job. Because there was no theoretical science associated with its practice initially, surgery was considered more of a trade than a profession. A classical education was often the crucial factor in determining who was a professional and who was not.[82]

Naval officers going as far back as John Paul Jones had always considered themselves gentlemen, and society respected them as such. But Americans generally did not think of military officership as a learned profession. That began to change for the army after Sylvanus Thayer's reforms at West Point, which gave the military profession an academic character. The navy, however, lacked an academy and a professional standard of education. The progressive, reform-minded officers of the antebellum navy—men like Matthew C. Perry, Matthew Fontaine Maury, Alexander Slidell Mackenzie, Franklin Buchanan, and Samuel F. Du Pont—viewed themselves not only as gentlemen but also as professionals, and they wanted public recognition for that. They sought to elevate the naval officer corps to a more professional level through formal education.[83] These officers devoted considerable time and effort to self-education through reading and scientific inquiry. They wrote books and articles about history, biography, and naval subjects with the goal of improving their profession. They supported scientific exploration and technological innovation in the navy. They established the Naval Lyceum to provide officers with a forum for professional development and self-improvement. They argued tirelessly for the establishment of a naval academy to provide a standard of professional education for all naval officers. This group of officers embraced a more intellectual, even scholarly, approach to the naval profession that was similar to what Thayer had introduced to the military profession. This was a significant transformation within the navy. Although officers from earlier generations—men like Edward Preble, Oliver Hazard Perry, and Stephen Decatur—were undeniably sophisticated

gentlemen of culture and a credit to the uniform, they based their professional identity almost exclusively on their seamanship skills and their role as
fighting men. The "new" naval officer was both a warrior and, to a degree,
a scholar.

Historical events played a critical role in the development of the professions. The American Revolution, with its emphasis on government and law,
influenced the development of the legal profession. Epidemics of diseases
in the early national period made medicine more scientific and professional.
The Great Awakening and Second Great Awakening forced more traditional
members of the clergy to defend their profession against criticism from less
scholarly evangelical preachers.[84] In a similar way, the nationalism and commercial expansion of the post–War of 1812 era provided the historical context
for the rise of the naval profession.

By the 1840s higher education was the foundation of the emerging middle-
class "culture of professionalism." Middle class was more than an economic
status; it was also a culture that was becoming more prevalent in the United
States in the 1830s and 1840s. A major component of middle-class culture
was a dedication to professionalism. Many middle-class Americans made
their living as professionals and defined themselves according to their education, respectability, refinement, discipline, and moral character. In the eyes of
the middle class, formal education became increasingly necessary to ensure
professional legitimacy, authority, and social status. Professional education
in an academic environment allowed for admission standards and standardized training through courses and textbooks. Objective academic standards
ensured greater professional competence while also maintaining the democratic principle of merit over hereditary privilege. Gradually, over the course
of the nineteenth century, the American people accepted the middle-class
concept that "the regularly trained professional . . . was superior to the
merely experienced operator."[85]

Although the movement to establish a naval academy gained more supporters in the 1830s and early 1840s, tradition and indifference were still
major obstacles to overcome. Captain Charles Stewart represented the power
of tradition. Even though he supported improving and broadening the instruction provided for midshipmen, he opposed creating a West Point–style
academy for the navy. "The *best school*," Stewart maintained, "for teaching
the young officer his profession is the ship itself, kept in active employment."
In the 1840s the U.S. Navy was in transition. The last vestiges of the sailing
navy were disappearing with the War of 1812 generation. When the old "sea
dogs" of the 1812 era complained that the navy was not what it used to be,
they were correct.[86] Growing professionalism within American society and

within the army officer corps provided a favorable environment for the development of the naval profession and advanced the movement to establish a naval academy. A younger, more progressive group of naval officers rose to prominence and went public with the need for naval reform and greater professionalism within the officer corps. In the process, this group of officers introduced a new concept of the naval profession and a new professional model for the American naval officer. By the early 1840s an American naval officer was, simultaneously, a warrior, a mariner, a diplomat, and an explorer. He also had to be a gentleman of intellect and culture who reflected the greatness of the American republic. The naval profession was on the rise, but it still lacked a crucial component—a West Point–style academy that would provide a standard of education for naval officers, serve as a professional and cultural center for the navy, and create an appropriate environment for character development.

CHAPTER 6

Mutiny, Midshipmen,
and the Middle Class

By the early 1840s Americans had debated the naval academy question in the halls of Congress, in the wardrooms of navy ships, and on the pages of newspapers and magazines. Although some politicians, naval officers, and members of the public still did not see the need to replace the navy's traditional on-the-job approach to education, disturbing social problems within the navy pointed to the need for a naval academy. In the antebellum period, life at sea took on a threatening, almost sinister character. The maritime literature of authors such as James Fenimore Cooper, Herman Melville, and Richard Henry Dana moved away from romanticized images of adventure at sea and focused instead on darker, more realistic descriptions of the sailor's life. These writers contrasted the majesty of the sea with its harsh and unforgiving nature. They emphasized the experiences of common sailors—the hardships they endured and the cruelty they suffered at the hands of merciless, dictatorial sea captains. The U.S. Navy was very much a part of this changing view of seafaring life. Politicians, the press, and the general public no longer lavished the navy with praise, as they had during and after the War of 1812; increasingly they questioned the moral character of naval personnel. Secretary of the Navy James K. Paulding best articulated the country's new attitude when he said that "a low, dirty, sordid feeling . . . seems to pervade all ranks of the Navy."[1]

The naval academy debate in the 1830s and 1840s coincided with the gradual emergence of the American middle class, which was becoming more vocal in advocating its values of respectability, morality, education, and professionalism. Concerned with the moral development of America's young men, middle-class reformers gave a great deal of attention to the navy and its midshipmen. The controversial hanging of a midshipman at sea for mutiny on board the navy training ship *Somers* in 1842 directed the public's attention to the need for moral reform in the navy. Believing that formal education was a crucial component of character development, middle-class reformers argued for the establishment of a naval academy to ensure that the young men who would one day command the navy's ships and represent the nation abroad were not only well educated, but also gentlemen of the highest moral caliber.

A Disorderly Corps

A breakdown in discipline was the most obvious symptom of the navy's malaise. One congressman complained that the navy "was composed of the most disorderly corps" of people in any government and required "a court-martial sitting nearly the entire year for their trial." Court-martial offenses included desertion, being absent without leave, insubordination, conduct unbecoming an officer and a gentleman, drunkenness, mutiny, negligence, assault of a superior, fighting, disorderly conduct, embezzlement, misuse of government property, gambling, theft, profanity, cruelty, and oppression. An article in *Niles' Register* commented that "the general impression is that the discipline and character of the navy are at a very low ebb." Although the author believed the sentiment was exaggerated, he did admit that the navy had "deteriorated from the exalted elevation it had attained at the close of the late war [War of 1812]" and warned that the navy's problems "if not speedily eradicated, will not only lose it the affections of the nation, but make it the scorn and contempt of the world." There was too much personal animosity among naval officers and not enough professional pride in the merits and accomplishments of the officer corps as a whole. In addition, the younger officers seemed to lack commitment to their profession, viewing it as just another job rather than a higher calling.[2]

Shipboard conflicts between captains and lieutenants were common by the early 1840s. At the heart of these conflicts was mutual resentment. Junior officers resented the senior captains because they delayed the promotion of younger officers by remaining on active duty well beyond their prime years. Isaac Hull was a case in point. As commodore of the Mediterranean Squadron in 1838, Hull was in no condition for active duty. He was sixty-five years old, nearly deaf, and actually suffered two strokes during the cruise. Hull's ill health ultimately resulted in a rebellion among his lieutenants, who were dislodged from their quarters on the flagship *Ohio* by Hull's wife and sister-in-law, the commodore's caretakers. For their part, senior officers felt anger and resentment over what they perceived to be disrespect from the junior officers. The navy's lack of flag rank and the resulting professional stagnation experienced by senior captains undoubtedly contributed to these feelings. Commander Samuel F. Du Pont believed the main problem was that the senior and junior officers failed to perceive their common professional interests and, instead, viewed each other as adversaries. Such antagonism undermined professional unity and created a rift within the officer corps.[3]

A related problem was that commanding officers exercised a great deal of discretion in bringing disciplinary charges against their subordinates. Many senior officers were quick to take offense at any remark or action that seemed the slightest disrespectful or noncompliant. Senior officers could use such general offenses as conduct unbecoming an officer or scandalous behavior as reasons for prosecuting subordinates. On the arrival in New York of the famous U.S. Exploring Expedition in June 1842, its commander, Lieutenant Charles Wilkes, brought charges against two lieutenants, one passed midshipman, and a navy surgeon for disrespect and disobedience. In turn, one of the lieutenants and the surgeon brought charges against Wilkes for excessive punishment, cruelty to native peoples encountered by the expedition, oppression, violation of enlistment terms, and conduct unbecoming an officer. There was also an accusation that Wilkes falsified a report to the secretary of the navy concerning the discovery of the continent of Antarctica in order to preempt a French claim of discovery around the same time. The subsequent legal proceedings generated more interest than the actual mission and its many scientific accomplishments. In the end, a court-martial found Wilkes guilty of seventeen counts of illegal punishment (involving flogging) and sentenced him to a public reprimand by the navy secretary.[4]

As a former judge, Secretary of the Navy Abel P. Upshur had a special interest in reforming the naval justice system, which he viewed as too arbitrary. It appeared to him that many senior officers had become petty tyrants who abused their authority by disciplining their subordinates for relatively trivial offenses. The navy's captains seemed to place more importance on their own rules than on the navy's official regulations. Although Upshur believed that strict discipline was crucial to carry out the navy's mission, discipline imposed in an arbitrary manner undermined morale and the navy's effectiveness as a fighting force. Charles Wilkes, whom one historian has characterized as a combination of Captain Ahab and Captain Bligh, was exactly the kind of officer Upshur sought to challenge. The secretary ordered a court-martial for Wilkes, one of the most prominent naval officers at the time, to demonstrate to his commanders and to the American public that no officer was above the law. Upshur feared the navy's system of discipline was spinning out of control. The number of courts-martial and courts of inquiry resulting from long deployments was far too high. "It is the rarest thing in the world," he complained, "for an American squadron to return from abroad without bringing with it a long list of disputes and mutual complaints between the superior and inferior officers." Upshur expected all officers to behave in a manner befitting "well-bred gentlemen in society." He continued, "It is true the forms of the drawing room are unsuited to the ship's deck, but authority may be stern without being harsh; respect may be enforced, without exacting servility along with it." While it was the duty of a junior officer to obey his superior, officers must avoid giving orders from the "mere arrogance of power."[5]

The *Army and Navy Chronicle* summarized the situation by stating that "each captain disciplines his ship according to his own ideas; and we have as many systems as we have [pennants] flying." Too many commodores and captains were, to use a modern term, micromanaging their commands. This problem derived from what Upshur described as an "inordinate love of regulating everything, even to minute trifles," a practice that undermined the dignity of their high rank and the authority of their subordinate officers. The constant interference of the captain prevented the lieutenants from exercising the appropriate amount of authority over the crew. For the chain of command to remain intact, senior officers had to show that they respected and trusted their subordinates. Junior officers, though obligated to show respect to their superiors, were not supposed to be subservient. Using the analogy of slavery, Upshur declared: "The relation which the inferior officer holds to his superior is not that of the slave to the master."[6]

To many Americans, the navy's basic problem was its apparent detachment from the rest of society. A basic, though incomplete, egalitarianism had been the foundation of the republic since the American Revolution. Yet the idea of equality was alien to the U.S. Navy, which more closely resembled an aristocracy. A navy ship, in the words of navy schoolmaster and chaplain George Jones, represented "a thorough monarchy, sheltered under the wings of republicanism." In the eyes of critics, it seemed that the officers were an elite social class who ruled the navy through arbitrary justice, oppression, and cruelty. As Harold Langley puts it: "Every warship was like a little kingdom that was ruled with a firm hand by a captain, assisted by junior officers who were analogous to nobles. At the bottom of this social structure were the seamen, who were characterized as serfs, peasants, or unruly rabble, but seldom as freemen." New York congressman Samuel Gordon argued that the navy needed captains who were humane and practical, not would-be aristocrats. He believed that merchant or whaling ship captains were fully capable of commanding naval vessels in time of war and preferable to naval officers, who tended to "lord it over their inferiors" and let their "military vanity" and "high-flown notions" overwhelm their common sense. Gordon suggested that the government could correct the problems within the officer corps by no longer appointing "young men of aristocratical pretensions" as midshipmen, a reference to Virginia's dominance of midshipman appointments at the expense of youths from the Northeast.[7]

To counter the increasingly prevalent image of captains as martinets, the *Naval Magazine* stated that the ideal naval commander was "a benevolent and reflecting officer" who looked after the welfare of his crew, strived to know his men as individuals, helped them avoid ignorance and vice, treated them with respect, rewarded them for competence and good conduct, and imposed just punishments for failure and misbehavior. As a leader of men, the captain had a "great moral responsibility" and should not engage in the "cursing and whipping madness, which some weak and miserable minds have mistaken for greatness." The *Army and Navy Chronicle* concurred, asserting that a naval academy would help to produce a more humane and dignified naval officer, which was crucial in "sustaining our institutions and national power." An academy would provide the knowledge and character development necessary to "make men capable of commanding others; men who will elicit confidence and respect by sound knowledge, by mild, firm, and just conduct, and make them altogether different from the inflated despot, who knows no law but his own will, and a brutal coercion on all occasions by the lash."[8]

Rebellious Youths

If the behavior of the navy's commissioned officers was troubling, the conduct of its midshipmen was of even greater concern. In 1828 Secretary of the Navy Samuel Southard reported that the navy made every effort to ensure that only young men possessing "a sound constitution, correct habits, and good English education" received appointments as midshipmen. Southard further explained that a midshipman's first six months of duty was a probationary period used to weed out those unfit for a naval career. The examination for promotion to lieutenant, taken after several years on board ship, was a "rigid" test that those unsuited to the service could not pass; failing the examination twice meant automatic dismissal from the navy. In Southard's opinion, "It is not very probable, under these arrangements, that improper or incompetent persons will pass the ordeal, and become commissioned officers."[9] Despite his confidence in the officer development system, a growing number of Americans were questioning the fitness of the midshipmen—the navy's future captains—for the crucial duties they would one day perform.

Historically, midshipmen had a reputation for being rowdy and disorderly. In antebellum times, they generally suffered from low morale in large part because there were too many of them. Many were stationed on shore at navy yards, where they received only half pay and were under minimal supervision. They easily found trouble in the city, while their knowledge and skills dissipated. The rank of passed midshipman was a poor substitute for a lieutenant's commission—a kind of professional "purgatory" and a superficial promotion at best. Passed midshipmen at sea still lived in the steerage (the midshipman's traditional home) and continued to wear a midshipman's uniform (the only difference being the addition of a star on the collar). Many passed midshipmen continued performing the same duties as before. Some performed the work of a lieutenant but without the rights and privileges of a commissioned officer. In 1830 a group of passed midshipmen sent a petition to the House Naval Affairs Committee requesting the creation of a new rank, "sub-lieutenant," for those midshipmen who passed their examination but could not receive commissions as lieutenants because of the lack of vacancies in that rank. Sub-lieutenants would perform the duties of a lieutenant and receive the status and privileges of a commissioned officer. The passed midshipmen demonstrated the injustice of their situation by contrasting it with the more favorable position of West Point cadets. The army gave cadets four years of uninterrupted study to prepare for their profession. At graduation, the cadets were awarded a diploma and a commission as brevet second lieutenant. The new officer received the pay and performed the duties of an army second lieutenant until a vacancy in that rank occurred. Navy midshipmen had to go to sea and perform actual duties while preparing for their profession, with little opportunity for "intellectual improvement." After passing their examination for lieutenant, they could expect to spend several more years as passed midshipmen though qualified to serve as lieutenants.[10]

Midshipmen often took out their frustrations on the field of honor. Dueling, considered an honorable way for gentlemen to settle their disputes, was a fairly common occurrence in the U.S. Navy and in the American South in the first half of the nineteenth century. Dueling was less frequent in the U.S. Army because of an 1806 regulation that made the practice illegal (though some army officers occasionally ignored the law). Navy duels, caused by real or perceived slights to an officer's honor, took place between U.S. naval officers, between U.S. naval officers and foreign officers, and between U.S. naval officers and American or foreign civilians. Officially, the navy prohibited quarrels between officers; in reality, naval authorities never enforced this regulation in cases of dueling. According to a tradition that originated in the Royal Navy, officers of different rank did not duel each other because junior officers could then use the duel as a way to speed up their promotion.[11]

Commodores Stephen Decatur and James Barron, both well-known senior officers, fought the most famous duel in American naval history near Bladensburg, Maryland, in 1820. The bad blood between the two men was a result of an incident in 1807, when the British warship HMS *Leopard* had opened fire on the U.S. frigate *Chesapeake*, commanded by Barron, after Barron refused to allow the British to board his ship in search of Royal Navy deserters. Because the *Chesapeake* was not prepared for battle and suffered numerous casualties and severe damage, the U.S. Navy court-martialed Barron. Decatur was a member of the court-martial board that sentenced Barron to a five-year suspension from active duty without pay. Decatur later opposed Barron's reinstatement to active duty. During their duel, Barron's shot killed Decatur, one of the country's greatest naval heroes. Barron was wounded but lived until 1851, eventually rising to the top of the navy's seniority list.[12]

Although senior officers were the combatants in the navy's most famous duel, midshipmen were the most frequent duelers. Generally, older officers were more reluctant to engage in a duel, doing so only when they believed it was absolutely necessary to maintain their authority, professional credibility, or social status as a gentleman. Of the eighty-two duels recorded from 1799 to 1850, midshipmen or passed midshipmen were participants in more than half of them. Usually, midshipmen challenged other midshipmen, but occasionally a midshipman would duel a civilian or, despite naval tradition, a lieutenant. Midshipmen were quick to take offense because of their personal and professional insecurities. A midshipman who had not yet experienced combat might fight a duel to prove his courage and manhood. Some trivial matter often sparked the fight. For example, two midshipmen once fought a duel because one of them had entered the mess wearing a hat, offending his comrade. Rear Admiral Samuel R. Franklin, who served as a midshipman during the antebellum period, noted: "Midshipmen, upon the slightest provocation, would go out and have a crack at each other."[13]

Opinions differed on whether dueling was appropriate behavior for U.S. naval officers. Some officers attempted, with only limited success, to prevent dueling in the navy. A group of officers—among them, Oliver Hazard Perry and James Lawrence—tried unsuccessfully to create a "Court of Honor" to settle disputes in a nonviolent manner. Ironically, Stephen Decatur ordered his midshipmen to come to him to settle their disputes before resorting to a duel. Other senior officers adopted a similar policy. Overall, however, dueling continued because many of the country's political leaders, particularly those from the South, considered it acceptable behavior. Although he frowned upon dueling between officers and civilians, Andrew Jackson (himself no stranger to the field of honor) saw no problem with duels "between officers whose profession was fighting, and who were trained to arms." Vice President John C. Calhoun, a former secretary of war, writing to former navy secretary Southard regarding a midshipman who had participated in a duel, stated: "My impression has ever been, that an officer should not be dismissed for a duel fairly & honorably conducted." In a September 1804 duel at Syracuse, Sicily, Midshipman Frederick C. De Kraft killed Midshipman William R. Nicholson. In an effort to send a message that dueling was unacceptable, the navy convened a court-martial to try De Kraft for murder. The navy dropped the charge and restored De Kraft to duty after one of Nicholson's relatives, Representative John H. Nicholson of Maryland, wrote to the secretary of the navy that the two men had conducted the duel as gentlemen and De Kraft should not be court-martialed for his actions. This case set a precedent, and, subsequently, the victors of fatal duels were not charged with murder.[14]

The participation of midshipmen in duels caught the attention of the press. In 1825 *Niles' Register* reported sarcastically: "Two boys, midshipmen, attached to the Constellation frigate, amused themselves by shooting at one another . . . by which one of them was killed, and the other has the pleasure to say that he has slain a brother!" An 1842 article about recent events in the navy, also appearing in *Niles' Register*, related that two midshipmen "indulged in the pastime of making each other a target for a bullet." One young man "received a ball through his cheek." The report concluded, "A more ridiculous affair has not taken place for six months past." Such accounts contributed to an unflattering image of the navy as a community governed by archaic traditions. This perspective was especially prevalent among middle-class Americans, North and South, who viewed dueling as a barbaric and immoral practice that was incompatible with modern, civilized society.[15]

The unseemly behavior of midshipmen had many causes, but the root of the problem seemed to be that the service was accepting too many immature young men of questionable character. As Samuel Southard observed, "When appointed, [midshipmen] are mere boys, generally without experience or skill, or well established habits and character." Historically, many Americans believed that military service—whether it involved serving on active duty in the army or navy, attending West Point or a state or private military academy, joining a local militia company, or participating in infantry drill at a civilian college—helped to form good moral character by instilling the virtues of discipline and self-restraint. Many parents, especially those from the middle and upper classes, considered the navy to be a good place to send their rebellious, uncontrollable sons to learn discipline and responsibility. Although this was a logical assumption, these parents were often disappointed. Young men expelled from secondary schools or colleges rarely developed into good naval officers; their misbehavior usually continued after they joined the navy. Sometimes the navy accepted youths the army had failed to reform. Lieutenant Matthew F. Maury complained about former cadets, dismissed by West Point for academic deficiency or misconduct, being "palmed off upon the Navy as Midshipmen." Secretary Upshur lamented: "It is a notorious fact, that wayward and incorrigible boys, whom even parental authority cannot control, are often sent to the navy, as a mere school of discipline, or to save them from the reproach to which their conduct exposes them on shore. It is not often that skilful officers or valuable men are made out of such materials."[16] Unfortunately for the navy, Upshur's statement came true in a very public way.

Mutiny on the Somers

Setting sail from New York on September 13, 1842, the training ship *Somers*, though full of promise, was destined to be the setting for one of the darkest, most controversial events in American naval history.[17] The *Somers* was deployed as part of the navy's experimental apprenticeship program that sought to recruit, educate, and train American boys for service as enlisted seamen. The goal of the program was to decrease the number of foreign sailors in the American navy and to offer underprivileged boys the opportunity to learn useful skills that would help them rise out of poverty. A brand-new brig of war, the *Somers* was ideal for this type of service because of its small size (just over one hundred feet long) and easy shiphandling. Featuring two masts and an armament of ten guns, the *Somers* was one of the fastest warships in the U.S. Navy. The training mission assigned to the *Somers* was the delivery of dispatches to the sloop of war *Vandalia* off the coast of Africa. The *Somers* crew included five officers, seven midshipmen, eight petty officers, nineteen seamen, eight cooks and stewards, and seventy-four seaman apprentices. Captain Matthew C. Perry, commandant of the New York Navy Yard and director of the apprenticeship program, handpicked the officers, midshipmen, and senior enlisted men for the cruise. To command the *Somers*, Perry chose his brother-in-law, Alexander Slidell Mackenzie. Among the ship's other commissioned officers were Lieutenant Guert Gansevoort (the first lieutenant and Herman Melville's cousin) and

Lieutenant Matthew C. Perry Jr. (the sailing master and Matthew Perry's son). When the *Somers* set sail, there were 121 crew members on board, well over the ship's intended complement; 70 percent of them were under the age of nineteen.[18]

Commander Mackenzie was thirty-nine years old, of medium height, with thinning auburn hair. His personality was one of studious reserve combined with friendliness and likability. He considered himself a refined gentleman and looked the part. Born Alexander Slidell, he added the surname "Mackenzie" in honor of his mother's brother, a bachelor. The son of a New York merchant, young Alexander had spent many hours on the docks of New York City watching the ships sailing in and out of that busy seaport. Fascinated by the navy's victories in the War of 1812 and prevented from attending college because of his father's reversal of fortune, he entered the navy as a midshipman at the age of eleven. In addition to being a naval officer, Mackenzie was an accomplished author, arguably the best naval writer of his time. He published accounts of his travels in Spain and England, a collection of essays on professional naval subjects, and biographies of naval heroes Oliver Hazard Perry and John Paul Jones. Mackenzie's literary patron and mentor was Washington Irving; his principal literary adversary was James Fenimore Cooper. The rivalry between Mackenzie and Cooper was personal and bitter. It revolved around Cooper's description of the Battle of Lake Erie in his popular *History of the Navy* (1839). Mackenzie felt that Cooper had diminished the greatness of Oliver Hazard Perry, the American commander at Lake Erie and Mackenzie's former captain and personal hero, by giving too much credit to Perry's second in command.[19]

Mackenzie was an experienced captain, having previously commanded the schooner *Dolphin* and the steam frigate *Missouri*. He was relieved of command of the *Missouri* after only five months when the ship ran aground in the Potomac River. Such a mishap was, and still is, a major professional embarrassment for any naval commander, and Mackenzie probably viewed the *Somers* experiment as a chance to redeem himself. His amiable personality, studious demeanor, and impressive literary achievements seemed to make him an ideal officer to lead a ship whose primary mission was educational.[20]

Matthew F. Maury once wrote: "One discontented spirit at sea is enough to destroy the peace and harmony of a whole ship's crew, and sometimes even to threaten the safety of the ship herself." For the *Somers*, that "discontented spirit" was Midshipman Philip Spencer, the tall, pale-skinned, eighteen-year-old son of Secretary of War John C. Spencer, a distinguished New York lawyer and politician. An intelligent young man who did not apply himself, Philip had attended Hobart College and Union College before joining the navy but dropped out of each school because of disciplinary problems and poor grades. Spencer had a problem with authority and a reputation as a troublemaker. But to most people who knew him personally, he seemed more of a "class clown" than truly dangerous even though he did have a well-known obsession with pirates. Spencer signed on to a whaling ship but changed his mind before sailing. The elder Spencer could no longer deal with his troubled son and turned to the navy and its discipline as a last resort. His father's political connections and the fact that his uncle was a navy captain secured Philip Spencer a midshipman's appointment in 1841.[21]

Spencer's troubles followed him into the navy, where he was disciplined for drunkenness and striking a superior officer. While serving on the frigate *John Adams*, he got into a drunken brawl with a group of civilians in Rio de Janeiro. The commander of the U.S. Navy's Brazil Squadron, Commodore Charles Morris, decided to make an example of Spencer and court-martialed him for his misbehavior. Spencer offered to resign instead, and Morris accepted his proposal. On his arrival in the United States, Spencer wrote a letter to Secretary Upshur apologizing for his conduct and asking the secretary to reinstate him. Although Upshur declared that "I am mortified to learn that one more young officer of the Navy and one brought up as you must have been has been guilty of the degrading and disqualifying vice of drunkenness," he gave Spencer another chance because the young man acknowledged his offenses and showed remorse. No doubt the fact that Spencer's father was a fellow cabinet member also was a consideration in Upshur's leniency. The secretary placed Midshipman Spencer on probation and allowed him to rejoin the navy. By the time Spencer reported for duty on the *Somers*, he had already received preferential treatment because of his father's political connections. He had committed serious offenses that would have resulted in a court-martial and dismissal for a midshipman who did not have a powerful father. Spencer was known for issuing thinly veiled threats to his superiors by reminding them of his father's prominent position in the government. After learning about Philip's troubled past and concerned that he would be a bad influence on the impressionable teenage apprentices who made up the bulk of the *Somers* crew, Mackenzie tried to have him transferred to another ship. Perry denied the request, possibly believing that the training cruise might help to reform Spencer. In the end, it was probably the most serious mistake of Perry's otherwise illustrious naval career.[22]

The unique situation on board the *Somers* meant that maintaining discipline would be more difficult than normal. First, because of the ship's training mission, the crew would not receive the customary navy liquor ration.

Captains often used the threat of taking away the sailors' grog as a way to maintain discipline. Second, confinement as punishment was problematic because of the ship's small size and overcrowded condition. Finally, there was only one marine on board, the master-at-arms. Navy ships usually carried a complement of marines who served as a kind of police force afloat in addition to their military duties. Not surprisingly, Philip Spencer challenged navy discipline right from the start of the voyage. As a midshipman and a future commissioned officer, he was prohibited from fraternizing with the enlisted sailors. Preferring the company of enlisted men to that of his fellow midshipmen, Spencer disregarded the rule and quickly became friends with Chief Boatswain's Mate Samuel Cromwell, a veteran sailor in his mid-thirties who had once worked on a slave ship. Cromwell was a malcontent who was easily offended. One of his duties was flogging crew members when so ordered by the captain. He relished the job to the point where Mackenzie demanded that he exercise restraint when disciplining the young seaman apprentices, who were just boys. Cromwell's best friend on the *Somers* was Seaman Elisha Small, an unsavory character who had also worked on a slave ship and claimed to have killed a man. Cromwell and Small were unusual in that they were both capable of navigating the ship (most enlisted men could not).[23]

On the outbound voyage to Africa, some members of the crew took note of the activities of Spencer and Cromwell. Spencer would sometimes throw coins on the deck and watch the apprentice boys scramble for them. He also began sneaking brandy and cigars from the officers' wardroom to Cromwell. Crew members saw Spencer and Cromwell talking quietly on several occasions; one man overheard them discussing how the *Somers* would perform as a pirate ship. These activities might simply have been an attempt by Spencer, a loner, to be popular with the crew, but many people would later see sinister intentions behind his behavior. When the *Somers* arrived at the island of Madeira (roughly three-quarters of the way to Africa), there was a noticeable change in the morale on the ship. Crew members seemed depressed and began neglecting their duties. Spencer and Cromwell especially attracted attention to themselves. Spencer was insubordinate, spoke disrespectfully about Mackenzie, and disobeyed the captain's order to keep a journal (a requirement for all midshipmen). Cromwell also spoke out against Mackenzie, accusing him of overworking the crew. This criticism of Mackenzie was unusual for a couple of reasons. First, it was a serious offense, usually resulting in severe punishment, to speak of the captain in a disrespectful manner. Second, by most accounts Mackenzie was a good captain. Although he had ordered forty-three floggings since the ship left port (for offenses such as skulking, disobeying orders, sleeping on duty, disrespect, fighting, theft, and profanity), he had actually shown leniency in punishing the miscreants, at least by navy standards. Other members of the crew attested to his paternal interest in those under his command—looking after their health, seeing that they received the best food available, and granting liberty whenever possible.[24]

As the *Somers* approached Africa, Spencer's behavior became even more bizarre. He bragged to the master-at-arms (essentially the ship's policeman) that he could take over the ship with only six men. He also made a drawing of a ship that resembled the *Somers* flying a black pirate flag and began studying charts of the West Indies in an attempt to find the location of a famous pirate lair. Most disturbing were his comments that he would soon be commanding his own ship. Given the extremely slow rate of promotion in the navy, Spencer was not talking about an official command. He took to giving enlisted seamen tobacco, then asking them if they would like to serve under his command. Mackenzie began reprimanding Spencer for inattention to his duties. To Mackenzie, this was a routine part of the commanding officer's job; he would do the same when other midshipmen needed correction. But Spencer took it personally, cursing the captain behind his back and threatening to throw him overboard.[25]

After learning that the *Vandalia* had already left Africa for the Caribbean, Mackenzie ordered the *Somers* to follow. During the journey back across the Atlantic, Spencer's suspicious behavior continued. He and Cromwell were still having secret chats, and Spencer was seen jotting down notes in a foreign language and talking quietly to selected members of the crew. After approaching the purser's steward, James Wales, and making him swear an oath of secrecy, Spencer told Wales of his plan to take over the *Somers* and turn it into a pirate ship. The elaborate plot included murdering the officers with Spencer himself killing Mackenzie. Spencer claimed to have twenty men on his side. After seizing control of the ship, he would choose the most useful crew members and toss the rest overboard, including most of the young apprentices. Wales was terrified after hearing this plan but acted as if he were going along with it. He then quietly informed his immediate superior, the ship's purser, about the plot. The purser told Lieutenant Gansevoort, who in turn reported it to Mackenzie. At first, Mackenzie was skeptical. But given the dark mood of the crew and Spencer's reputation for trouble, such a mutiny was not inconceivable. After observing Spencer's behavior inconspicuously, Gansevoort told Mackenzie that the midshipman was acting in a suspicious manner. To be on the safe side, the lieutenant recommended that Spencer be placed under arrest and confined in irons. This put Mackenzie in a very difficult position. If Spencer and his fellow mutineers were successful, they could kill many of the crew members and use the *Somers* to kill innocent people and steal valuable cargo. Though small and lightly armed, the *Somers* could easily overtake and defeat any unarmed merchant vessel. Furthermore, the ship's speed would make it hard for the navy to track it down. On the other hand, what if the plot was a joke? Arresting the son of the secretary of war without a valid reason could have serious consequences for Mackenzie's career. In the end, the commander determined that it was his duty to take action before the mutineers did. He could not risk the safety of his ship, his crew, and the lives of American and foreign citizens.[26]

On November 26 Mackenzie approached Spencer about the alleged plot. Spencer admitted talking about a mutiny but said it was all a joke. Mackenzie did not believe him and placed him under arrest. Spencer's sword was confiscated, and he was put in irons (handcuffs and leg chains fastened to the deck). After the arrest, Mackenzie ordered Gansevoort to search Spencer's locker in the steerage. The search yielded two papers. One was a list of names written in Greek under the headings "Certain," "Doubtful," and "To Be Kept, Willing or Unwilling." The names marked with an "X" were the crew members Spencer thought he had successfully recruited for the mutiny. The second paper described the planned locations of the mutineers during the takeover. Discovery of the plot in writing troubled Mackenzie. At best, Spencer was a mentally disturbed young man; at worst, he was a potential mutineer and murderer. Either way, Mackenzie had a serious problem on his ship. The tense atmosphere on the *Somers* after Spencer's arrest worsened after two strange incidents occurred. The first was an apparent accident involving one of the ship's masts and its sails and rigging. Mackenzie believed the incident could have been an act of sabotage meant to distract the officers as a prelude to the mutiny. Elisha Small's involvement seemed to be the most compelling evidence of sabotage. Mackenzie ordered the arrest of Small and Cromwell. The second incident occurred when, by order of a midshipman, a petty officer began swinging a whip to prod a group of sailors back to work. In an effort to escape the whip, the sailors ran toward the quarterdeck, where Mackenzie and Gansevoort were standing. The two officers thought they were being rushed by mutineers and went for their weapons until the midshipman informed them of what had occurred. All of the officers, on edge from the recent events, armed themselves with swords and pistols.[27]

Disciplinary problems on the ship continued to escalate after the arrests. Stealing, insubordination, and failing to report for duty became frequent. Mackenzie addressed the crew to explain why he had arrested Spencer, Cromwell, and Small, and to warn his young charges about the consequences of mutiny. Spencer admitted to Gansevoort that he had previously plotted mutinies on the *John Adams* and the frigate *Potomac*, the ship that returned Spencer to the United States after Commodore Morris had accepted his resignation. The crew's strange behavior resulted in four more arrests, including the apprehension of one sailor who apparently had an unhealthy interest in knives. With the *Somers* still a week away from port on the island of St. Thomas, Mackenzie felt compelled to take drastic action to prevent losing control of his ship. Mutiny was punishable by death, but only a general court-martial could convict and impose the death penalty, and only the president, secretary of the navy, or commodore of a squadron could convene a court-martial. On November 30, Mackenzie ordered his officers and senior midshipmen to investigate the alleged plot, report their findings, and recommend punishment. The officers met in the wardroom and received testimony from witnesses. After some discussion, they brought their findings and recommendation to Mackenzie on December 1: Spencer, Cromwell, and Small were guilty of conspiracy to commit mutiny and should be executed immediately. This conclusion concurred with Mackenzie's own thoughts on the matter. As long as the three men lived, the ship and crew were in danger. Other than the officers and midshipmen, Cromwell and Small were the only crew members who could navigate the ship, a necessary skill for the plot to succeed.[28]

Mackenzie quickly ordered the executions. Spencer and Small asked for forgiveness from Mackenzie and from God. Cromwell maintained his innocence to the very end. The crew assembled on the deck and, on Mackenzie's order, the three men were hanged from the yardarm, the navy's traditional mode of execution. One hour later, Mackenzie conducted a memorial service for the deceased and the bodies were buried at sea. As Mackenzie had hoped, the crew's morale and discipline improved thereafter.[29]

The *Somers* returned to the New York Navy Yard on December 14. Three days later, the story of what had taken place on board broke "like claps of thunder in a clear sky." The plot to take over the ship and the subsequent hanging of three men on an American naval vessel were certain to attract attention from the press. But the incident received even more interest because one of the executed men was a midshipman and the son of a prominent politician. Sensational headlines about mutiny, murder, and pirates greeted the readers of American newspapers. The day the story broke, the *New York Herald* described an elaborate plot by some members of the *Somers* crew to murder the officers, seize the ship, and become pirates engaging in plunder, murder, and rape on the high seas. The paper pointed out that the *Somers* would make an ideal pirate ship because of its speed. Within a day, according

The U.S. brig-of-war Somers *sailing on December 1, 1842, the day that Midshipman Philip Spencer, Chief Boatswain's Mate Samuel Cromwell, and Seaman Elisha Small were hanged at sea on the charge of mutiny. Note the two men hanging from the ship's yardarm on the ship's starboard side. The other alleged mutineer hangs from the port side of the yardarm. Courtesy U.S. Naval Academy Museum.*

to the *Herald*, the *Somers* affair had generated "unsurpassed interest" among the American people. Rumors substituted for the small number of facts the public received. The *Richmond Whig* and the *New York Express* reported an actual mutiny in which Spencer pointed a pistol at Mackenzie. According to these accounts, the officers overpowered the mutineers after a struggle, placed them under arrest, and conducted a court-martial. The press coverage fueled speculation and debate in coffeehouses, in taverns, and on the streets of America's cities.[30]

The public's initial reaction was that Mackenzie's handling of the situation was necessary and proper (many people erroneously believed that the council of officers Mackenzie had convened to investigate the alleged plot was an official court-martial). There was a great sense of relief that he had thwarted the mutiny. The *New York Herald* proclaimed, "Too much praise cannot be awarded to Commander M'Kenzie and his officers, for so promptly nipping in the bud an enterprize that would have brought misery and destruction upon hundreds of our fellow citizens." If the plot had succeeded, the mutineers-turned-pirates could have sailed for years before the navy captured them because of the ship's speed, allowing "the seas . . . [to] become the scenes of outrage and blood unparalleled in the records of piratical crime." The *New York Courier and Enquirer*, in describing Mackenzie, declared that "a more humane, conscientious and gallant officer does not hold a commission in the navy of the United States." Despite the early praise, New York lawyer George Templeton Strong believed Mackenzie would have to prove the executions were an "absolute necessity," although his action must have been necessary given his reputation as a man who would not "act either in a passion or in a panic."[31]

The press portrayed Philip Spencer as the quintessential troublemaker. To the *New York Herald*, he was "a bad fellow" who "justly met his fate"; the paper praised Mackenzie's decision not to bring Spencer home for trial. If he had been tried in the United States, Spencer almost certainly would have been exonerated because of "the facility with which criminals having wealthy and influential friends, can evade the hands of justice." The *Richmond Whig* stated that Spencer had been a "dare-devil" since boyhood, while the *New York Tribune* hoped that his misdeeds would serve as a warning to young men who wanted to leave their family and go to sea for excitement and adventure. Youths at sea were "surrounded by dangers and temptations," and, as Spencer demonstrated, such a situation could have fatal consequences. Philip Hone, the former mayor of New York City and a friend of Mackenzie's father, seemed to capture the mood of the American public in the pages of his diary: Mackenzie was "a brave, gallant young officer," whereas Spencer was "a worthless fellow" who would have been dismissed from the navy earlier had it not been for "the respectable character and high station of his father."[32]

But the condemnation of Philip Spencer was not universal. On December 20 an anonymous article (signed *S*) appearing in *The Madisonian*, a Washington newspaper, described Spencer as a "mere boy" who was simply "amusing himself" by concocting an imaginary plot. The piece, presented in the form of a legal argument, portrayed Mackenzie's actions as unnecessary—an overreaction resulting from "unmanly fear" or "despotic temper." Furthermore, the executions, without trial by court-martial, were illegal. It was rumored at the time that the anonymous author was Spencer's father, Secretary of War John C. Spencer. Not only was the article written in the forceful, legalistic style of an accomplished attorney, but also the author knew a great deal of personal information about young Spencer and had obviously read Mackenzie's official report to the secretary of the navy.[33]

Even before this scathing indictment, the public's opinion of Mackenzie was beginning to change. Newspapers now reported that there had not been a court-martial on board the *Somers* and that there were serious questions about the necessity and the legality of the hangings. More and more people began to think that Mackenzie and his officers had only imagined the plot to take over the ship. "The officers would seem to have acted under a panic," declared the *New York Herald*. And Philip Hone now believed that unless Mackenzie could fully justify the extreme measures he had taken, he was "ruined past redemption." Naval officers were reflections of the country, and the *Somers* incident had become a matter of national honor because of the extensive press coverage it was receiving on both sides of the Atlantic. As Hone stated, "Not only the character of Captain McKenzie, but that of the flag under which he sails and of the nation which he serves, is deeply concerned in his making out a complete justification."[34]

Secretary of the Navy Upshur ordered a court of inquiry to investigate the incident. Three senior captains composed the court, which convened on December 28 on board the receiving ship *North Carolina* docked at the New York Navy Yard. U.S. Attorney Ogden Hoffman, a navy veteran of the War of 1812, served as the judge advocate (prosecutor). Mackenzie waived his right to legal counsel. According to the *New York Herald*, "There never has been any case whose examination has awakened such universal and pervading interest—such keen and animated discussion—such variety of well-contested opinion. . . . It is the great topic of the day." Reporters were present at the inquiry, and newspapers published transcripts of testimony each day. The inquiry heard testimony from Mackenzie, the officers, and the crew, including the African American stewards (a rarity in antebellum American courts). After hearing testimony and deliberating, the court of inquiry cleared Mackenzie of any wrongdoing and confirmed that Spencer, Cromwell, and Small had been plotting a mutiny. But before the court had even issued its findings, Mackenzie requested trial by court-martial in an effort to clear his name, which by this point the press was dragging through the mud. In a letter to his friend and fellow naval officer Samuel F. Du Pont, Mackenzie stated his belief that the public and the "respectable press" in New York supported him. That was a self-serving and distorted view of the situation. The *Herald* reported on January 8, 1843 that "the evidence thus far, has created a great revolution against McKenzie." By January 19, the *Herald* was reporting that newspapers were ten to one against him. The paper also suggested that Mackenzie and his officers were insane from panic when they executed the alleged mutineers.[35]

In January 1843 the navy brought court-martial charges against Mackenzie for murder, oppression, illegal punishment, conduct unbecoming an officer, and cruelty. The court convened on February 2, 1843, again on board the *North Carolina*; it later moved its proceedings to the navy yard chapel to accommodate the large number of spectators, many of whom viewed the trial as entertainment. Eleven captains and two commanders formed the court. This time, Mackenzie retained the services of two prominent defense attorneys: John Duer, a former federal judge, and George Griffin. The judge advocate was William H. Norris, an unknown and relatively inexperienced lawyer from Baltimore. While admitting that he did order the executions, Mackenzie stated that his action was necessary and entered a plea of not guilty. Far more dramatic than the previous court of inquiry, the court-martial featured some heated exchanges during the examination of witnesses. Norris, despite his lack of experience, poked several holes in Mackenzie's account of the incident. In the end, though, it did not matter. On March 28, the court rendered a "not proved" verdict for each charge, which was somewhat confusing since the court neither found Mackenzie guilty nor completely vindicated him. The verdict was technically only a recommendation to the convening authority, in this case Secretary Upshur, and it was actually the president, as commander in chief, who would have the final say in the matter.[36]

After receiving the court's findings, Upshur carefully reviewed the testimony and evidence before recommending to President John Tyler that he uphold the verdict. Although Upshur was deeply concerned about captains imposing arbitrary discipline, in his judgment the court-martial had been fair and impartial in accordance with the law. Upshur issued his recommendation to Tyler during a cabinet meeting with Secretary of War Spencer in attendance. Spencer was outraged with the verdict and demanded a new court-martial. Upshur refused to convene a second trial, stating that such a course would be illegal on the grounds of double jeopardy. This led to a heated argument between Upshur and Spencer that turned into a brief physical altercation. The president himself had to separate the two men. Although Tyler upheld the court-martial's verdict exonerating Mackenzie, the president had doubts that a mutiny plot ever existed and decided that Mackenzie was unfit for command at sea. He later told Edmund Ruffin, "I determined that as long as my power should last, Captain Mackenzie should never be entrusted with another command." After the trial Mackenzie returned to his home in Tarrytown, New York, to work on a biography of Stephen Decatur.[37]

Opinion within the press, the navy, and the general public regarding the *Somers* affair remained divided. To many people, Mackenzie was a hero who did what was necessary to protect his ship, his loyal crew, and the nation's security; Philip Spencer, on the other hand, was an undisciplined and dangerous troublemaker whose father's influence had always protected him from punishment. Numerous others, however, believed Mackenzie was a tyrant and a murderer who had violated the Constitution and navy regulations by ordering the execution of a young midshipman whose only crime was having an overactive imagination.

In a letter to Mackenzie, Richard Henry Dana, an author, a lawyer, and a former merchant sailor, wrote: "Among the educated people, in the professions, and in what we call in America the upper classes, you were . . . a hero, and not a hero of the sword, but the hero of a moral conflict." Mackenzie's status as an officer combined with his literary accomplishments made him a true gentleman, a member of America's respectable society. The middle and upper classes, which Dana claimed to be speaking for, valued the importance and necessity of order, discipline, respect for authority, and good moral character. Because Mackenzie had acted in defense of these values, his actions were justified. Attorney and future U.S. senator Charles Sumner, another supporter of the *Somers* commander, asserted: "He has done more than gain a battle, and deserves more than the homage of admiration and gratitude with which we greet the victor returning from successful war." A group of three hundred merchants and "respectable citizens" started a fund-raising effort to pay Mackenzie's legal fees, and a group of "ladies and gentlemen" in Baltimore began a subscription drive to raise money to buy him a set of gold epaulettes "as a tribute of respect for his firmness and ability as an officer, and his character as a man."[38]

To many citizens, particularly the middle class, Mackenzie represented the greatness of America. Because of his father's financial problems, he had few opportunities for self-improvement through formal education. Yet he strived to educate himself and spent many hours reading and studying, which enabled him to achieve professional and literary success. Mackenzie was, in the words of the *New York Evening Post*, a "self-made man" and "a thorough democrat." In contrast, Philip Spencer, who had all the advantages of money and privilege and access to a classical education, had wasted these opportunities and made it his goal to become a pirate, a low-class criminal.[39]

If Mackenzie was a great hero to some middle and upper-class Americans, others believed he represented everything that was wrong with the navy. One of them was James Fenimore Cooper, who published a pamphlet sharply criticizing Mackenzie's conduct. Though certainly motivated by personal animosity toward his literary rival, Cooper did speak for many Americans who disapproved of Mackenzie's actions. Cooper also reprinted an article by William Sturgis, a Boston merchant and former shipmaster who warned of the danger in praising Mackenzie as a great naval hero. Fearing that young naval officers and midshipmen might view him as a role model, Sturgis pointed out that "few naval officers have an opportunity to distinguish themselves in battle; but any commander can put to death a part of his officers and crew." William Lloyd Garrison's abolitionist newspaper, *The Liberator*, compared Mackenzie's action to that of a merciless slaveowner. According to Garrison, Mackenzie acted in the same "selfish, cowardly, tyrant spirit" that sustained the institution of slavery. By the end of the court-martial, George Templeton Strong had changed his favorable opinion of Mackenzie, referring to "the *Somers* murder" as "a case of cold-blooded lynching."[40]

Senator Thomas Hart Benton, a prominent Democrat from Missouri, believed that the mutiny plot was the product of Mackenzie's "diseased mind." The commander had illegally ordered the executions after an unofficial "drum-head court-martial" in which the prisoners had no opportunity to defend themselves against the charges. The root cause of the *Somers* tragedy, in Benton's opinion, was the culture of elitism and aristocracy within the naval officer corps, which bred a sense of omnipotence among commanding officers. Even though he did not witness the event, Benton described Mackenzie's appearance at the executions in aristocratic terms: "The full uniform of a commander in the American navy had been put on for the occasion . . . and, in this imposing costume—feathers and chapeau, gold lace and embroidery, sword and epaulettes—the commander proceeded to announce their fate to the men in irons." Benton believed that Mackenzie's acquittal, as well as the large amount of public support he received, was a national disgrace that "brought reproach upon the American name."[41]

The Navy, Middle-Class Morality, and the American Republic

Aside from the sensational headlines it spawned, the *Somers* affair captured the public's attention because it took place at a time when many Americans, especially the middle class, looked upon the nation's youth with anxiety. A product of America's unprecedented economic growth in the period after the War of 1812, the middle class gradually formed a social identity around the ideals of respectability, ambition, diligence, education, moral virtue, discipline, advancement through merit, and upward social mobility. Ministers, lawyers, physicians, educators, writers, and middling merchants and manufacturers, who formed the core of the middle class, attempted to instill their values throughout American society. Embracing a mission of moral improvement, these reformers of the antebellum period led a general movement that sought to elevate American society morally and intellectually by building "a world that replaced force, barbarism, and unrestrained passion with Christian self-control."[42] Avoiding the greed and decadence of the wealthy as well as the degradation and discontent of the poor, middle-class Americans considered themselves to be the most virtuous and stable element within republican America. Viewing itself as the guardian of the republic, the middle class thus made character formation among the country's youth its top priority. As economic and social changes in the early nineteenth century jeopardized the moral development of young men, the need to guide them toward the correct path provided the impetus that helped to form middle-class social values and identity.[43]

Prior to 1815, many Americans believed that the actual survival of their republic was at risk because of the threats to the nation and its commerce posed by the British, the French, the Indians, and the Barbary corsairs. After the War of 1812, when American independence was secure, the citizenry shifted its anxiety to the republic's moral character. No longer concerned about a loss of political independence, Americans feared a loss of republican virtue—the willingness to put the public good above personal gain. The post-1815 economic growth of the United States threatened its moral foundation. America was changing rapidly because of expanding market capitalism, rapid industrialization, unprecedented urban growth, and expanding political democracy. Increased immorality—violence, murder, cruelty, drunkenness, gambling, prostitution, greed, corruption, and student unrest—accompanied these economic and social changes. One of the basic tenets of the antebellum reform movement was the importance of environment in the formation of moral character. An individual with character possessed such noble traits as honesty, integrity, self-restraint, diligence, responsibility, and moral courage. In the minds of nineteenth-century Americans, character was not innate—it had to be formed by creating social environments that imposed discipline, encouraged virtue, limited exposure to evil influences, and fostered habits of intellectual and moral self-improvement. Reformers had to challenge the power of vice and corruption, the social by-products of American industrial and urban development, by forming good character in young men, the nation's future leaders.[44] In a sense, these young men became "moral soldiers" in the fight to preserve republican virtue.

One result of the American Revolution was a weakening of social control over the nation's youth. During the colonial period, authority and deference had characterized American society. It was a time when three social institutions dominated the lives of individuals: the family, the church, and the community. These institutions worked together to enforce a code of morality that emphasized such virtues as diligence, self-restraint, chastity, and respect for authority. After the Revolution, it became more difficult for parents, clergy, and community leaders to control young people. The Revolution's emphasis on democracy and individual liberty led many Americans to believe that strict parental control over teenagers was undemocratic; young people should be allowed to make their own life choices—who to marry, what career to pursue, where to live. After the War of 1812, the power of traditional authority waned even further because of economic expansion, industrial and urban development, and a greater emphasis on political and social democracy. One indicator of this change was the relatively large number of college student rebellions in the early nineteenth century. What the middle class feared most was what would happen to the numerous young men who were leaving the safe, nurturing environment of small-town life to take up residence in wild, unrestrained urban neighborhoods to work or attend school. Experience, surroundings, the people with whom one associated, even the books one read were the determining factors in character formation. Young men were particularly vulnerable to temptation because their character was not yet fully developed. Moral disaster resulted when these youths, without the benefit of strong character, succumbed to the lure of the city's taverns, gambling establishments, and brothels.[45]

By the early 1840s it became clear that character development was more successful in "planned, engineered environments." Although the Christian family within a tight-knit, local community remained the ideal environment for forming character, reality dictated that other institutions step in when the family could not succeed on its own. During the antebellum period, Americans devised an institutional response to the problems of modern society. Schools, lyceums, voluntary associations, asylums, and orphanages were intended to supplement or, in some cases replace, the family and local community. Formal education became the most important agent of character development for America's youth. Creating a proper environment for learning and character development was the top priority of educators.[46]

Horace Mann was the most prominent advocate of using education to instill character and maintain social order in antebellum America. A Massachusetts lawyer and state legislator, Mann became secretary of the Massachusetts State Board of Education in 1837 and was a leader of the common school movement, which sought to provide free public elementary schools throughout the nation. The goals of the common school were to form character, provide the knowledge and skills needed to succeed in America's modernizing society, and integrate students into a national culture of ideals and values. Believing the future of the republic depended on producing intelligent and, most importantly, moral citizens, Mann emphasized school discipline to ensure social order in an unstable, increasingly immoral society. The cultivation of moral character through education was particularly important for the United States. Force could keep order in monarchies, but individual virtue and discipline were necessary to maintain order in a republic.[47]

To have a moral society, a nation had to have moral citizens, and the education of young people was the best way to produce a moral citizenry. In the minds of middle-class reformers, the same was true for the U.S. Navy. To deploy a navy led by men of character who were a credit to the nation, the United States had to provide an educational environment for midshipmen that was conducive to character development. Whether one viewed Philip Spencer or Alexander Slidell Mackenzie as the main villain of the *Somers* affair was irrelevant. That incident proved that the environment on board a navy ship did not contribute to the formation of good character. To those Americans who regarded Mackenzie as a hero, Spencer represented everything that was wrong with the navy's traditional method of officer development. Midshipman Spencer clearly demonstrated that the navy lacked an effective system of identifying and eliminating those young men who were unfit to serve as officers. To the people who viewed Mackenzie as a merciless tyrant who had executed three innocent men without cause, the navy had to provide a new learning environment for midshipmen because they should not learn their profession under the command of petty martinets who ignored the rule of law.[48]

The extensive press coverage of the *Somers* affair and the subsequent legal proceedings prompted many citizens to pay closer attention to how the U.S. Navy was developing its officers. The navy became a target of reformers who dedicated themselves to the creation of a more wholesome and humane environment for the boys just beginning their careers. Few aspects of naval life met with the approval of moral reformers. The practice of flogging was particularly troubling. Flogging was the traditional form of naval punishment throughout the world; its long history dated back to ancient times, when slaves composed the majority of the crew on a galley (an ancient warship). The Royal Navy used flogging to maintain discipline among its sailors, many of whom were ex-convicts or the dregs of society. The American navy, beginning during the Revolutionary War, modeled its code of discipline after the British system and employed flogging as punishment for offenses such as drunkenness, cruelty, profanity, sleeping on duty, negligence, or the catchall "scandalous conduct." According to navy custom, a sailor was flogged with a cat-o'-nine-tails whip on the bare back while tied to part of the ship. When a flogging took place, the entire crew witnessed the event, since flogging was not only a punishment for the offender but also a warning to his crewmates. Although the navy did not flog midshipmen (whipping was considered inappropriate for gentlemen), the midshipmen did witness the disciplinary action countless times. In fact, it was not uncommon for a young midshipman to faint after seeing a flogging for the first time. Eventually, most midshipmen became accustomed to the sight.[49]

Another frequent target of reformers was the navy's practice of serving liquor, or "grog" in navy parlance, to sailors as part of their daily ration. At the time, it was widely believed that men required alcohol to perform physical labor. Many reformers traced the navy's disciplinary problems back to the spirit ration. Drunkenness was one of the most common offenses committed in the navy and often resulted in flogging. In fact, one navy lieutenant estimated that 80 percent of the floggings that took place on warships were for alcohol-related offenses. Reformers believed that if the navy eliminated the spirit ration, discipline would improve and reduce the need for corporal punishment. According to a report by three navy surgeons, the distribution of alcohol to midshipmen was detrimental to their health and character. Besides inebriation, drinking often led to the adoption of other vices as well, which resulted in a steady decline in the intellectual, moral, and military character of the young men. The surgeons favored abolishing the spirit ration for midshipmen. In 1842 the navy reduced the amount of grog for all sailors and eliminated the ration entirely for all midshipmen and sailors under the age of twenty-one.[50]

Early exposure to the naval environment was, traditionally, one of the most important reasons why midshipmen received their education on warships. Sooner or later, they would have to experience life at sea, and the navy (and most politicians and citizens) believed that sooner was the best choice. But by the early 1840s, an increasing number of politicians, reformers, and citizens were of the opinion that the naval environment was corrupting the midshipmen, most of whom were immature, impressionable teenagers. Naval service exposed these youths to drunkenness, gambling, and prostitution in addition to inhumane practices like flogging. It has been said that adolescence is the period of human development when "environment and education have their greatest influence." In the navy, midshipmen spent that crucial time on board ships where they received little education and experienced a great deal of temptation. Some captains tried to place a watchful eye over their midshipmen in an effort to prevent their moral corruption. Commodore John Rodgers, for example, did not like the idea of midshipmen roaming the streets unsupervised while on liberty in a foreign city. Whenever he came across a midshipman on shore, he would order the young man to stay with him until liberty expired. Recalling his midshipman years in the early 1840s, Samuel Franklin described his first assignment after joining the navy—the New York Navy Yard receiving ship *North Carolina*. He was given some instruction in navigation but did not understand most of it. The living conditions were equally disappointing: "I was assigned to the steerage, where we lived like pigs." Looking back on life in the steerage and his experience as a midshipman, Franklin declared: "There was something very cruel . . . in permitting a lot of boys to be huddled together, with no one to look out for their well-being, most of them only sixteen or under."[51]

The life of a midshipman, and the various temptations he faced, was the subject of a short story published by the *Southern Literary Messenger* in late 1841. The main character, Robert Seymour, is a naive midshipman reporting to his first ship in New York City. Just recently "cut loose from his mother's apron-string," Seymour describes the spectacle and excitement of New York's bustling streets. The story contrasts the wide-eyed impressions of a young man on his own for the first time—the glamour and the enchantment of New York—with the vices he eventually witnesses in the city. His "adventures" include getting drunk, being deceived into paying for a night out by a con man posing as a fellow midshipman, being approached by a prostitute, searching New York's "haunts of vice" for a sailor who deserted while under Seymour's command, and having to deal with a tyrannical first lieutenant.[52] Though intended to be entertaining, this tale suggests that midshipmen were not learning the naval profession in the best environment. The moral of the story is that most midshipmen were too young, immature, and naive to be on their own.

Several reformers and writers argued the same point. Navy veteran William McNally, in his 1839 exposé on life in the navy and merchant service, said that sailors brought prostitutes on board the ship of the line *Delaware* twice a week while it was in port on the Mediterranean station. Mc-Nally condemned this practice as dangerous to the morals and health of the sailors. He discussed various examples of cruelty on navy ships—among them, soaking the whip used to flog sailors in the pickle barrel where salt beef was preserved in order to make the whip harder and increase the pain of flogging. McNally also described the misbehavior of the first lieutenant on the receiving ship *Java* at the Norfolk Navy Yard in 1834. The officer was ignorant and abusive as well as being a drunk and a sycophant who regularly used prostitutes. McNally sarcastically pointed out that the lieutenant was a great role model for the young midshipmen attending the navy yard school.[53]

The Reverend Charles Rockwell, a former navy chaplain, advocated the establishment of a naval academy based on his experience on a ship assigned to the Mediterranean Squadron. At an academy on shore, midshipmen would "be under far more correct and efficient moral, social, and religious influence than on shipboard, and . . . they would not, when young and reckless, be exposed to strong and overwhelming temptation to vice." Rockwell also recommended that the government be more selective in granting midshipman appointments, noting that many young men with behavioral problems had found their way into the navy as midshipmen. "Impaired by vicious indulgence," "undermined by disease," and "morally debased and depraved," these undesirables were "a burden to the service." An additional concern involved the "delicate boys" who became midshipmen. They experienced total culture shock when they left the safe, nurturing environment of their homes and schoolhouses and took up residence in the steerage of a warship. Such young men were unlikely to become successful naval officers.[54]

An anonymous pamphlet written by a former navy seaman depicted midshipmen as spoiled, tyrannical, and out-of-control young men. They entered the navy as ignorant and inexperienced youngsters, yet they became angry if they did not receive the same respect given to commissioned officers. They learned to be tyrants by watching how commissioned officers treated enlisted men. Also like the officers, midshipmen learned to disregard navy regulations, especially while on foreign stations. Consequently, few midshipmen behaved themselves and acquired a good education. They were often lazy and usually returned from shore leave drunk, which in turn made them abusive toward the enlisted sailors. The author believed the solution was to send midshipmen to a naval academy, not to learn seamanship (which they could only learn at sea) but to learn "how to behave themselves" and "how to treat and command men who save and protect their nation manfully." The *New York Tribune*, obviously referring to Philip Spencer, published the following scathing portrait of a midshipman: "He has no experience, a boy's judgement, passions and caprices; he is usually the son of some rich or eminent man, and has served a full apprenticeship to doing nothing or doing mischief; he is often put into the Navy because his temper is ungovernable or his vices disgraceful . . . and yet this beardless youth, who as yet knows nothing and is good for nothing in the service, from the moment he steps on board ship is the superior of the oldest and ablest seamen in the Navy."[55]

The Virtues of Military Education

By the early 1840s, there was a growing consensus within and outside the navy that a fully organized naval academy represented the type of engineered learning environment that would facilitate character development among midshipmen. Aside from imparting knowledge to students, colleges were agents of character formation. In the absence of parents, the college played a paternalistic role by caring for students, supervising them, and correcting their conduct. According to an 1828 Yale report, it was the college's duty to establish a learning environment governed by moral principles: "When removed from under the roof of their parents, and exposed to the untried scenes of temptation, it is necessary that some faithful and affectionate guardian take them by the hand, and guide their steps." It was through rules and discipline that the college was able to substitute for parental authority. Though not quite as rigid as the discipline imposed at West Point, civilian colleges did enforce a strict code of conduct. Tutors and unmarried professors living in student dormitories often acted as the civilian version of West Point tactical officers. They were responsible for maintaining discipline by serving as the college's informal police force and spy network.[56]

Mental discipline was an important trait to develop in young men, particularly those bound for careers in the military. Success in battle depended on the clear thinking and sound judgment of the commanding officer. Mental discipline was also necessary for the development of strong moral character. In 1841 the U.S. Military Academy Board of Visitors reported to the secretary of war its concern that some of the texts used in classes at West Point were inappropriate for young men: "The principal text-book in the study of the French language . . . is not of the most moral and useful character. . . . It must be obvious to the Department that the youthful imagination is too delicate and too susceptible of wrong impressions to be safely exposed to the exciting scenes frequently introduced into novels of the class to which this work belongs." Philip Spencer was the most famous example of the dangers associated with an overactive imagination. An important question stemming from the *Somers* affair was whether Spencer was an evil, bloodthirsty pirate or merely an immature, confused teenager who let his imagination get the best of him. Many of Spencer's "suspicious" activities prior to his arrest and execution were childish—drawing a picture of the *Somers* as a pirate ship, writing down his alleged mutiny plan, writing that plan in a foreign language, drawing attention to his written notes but not letting anyone read them. The *New York Herald* went so far as to blame the *Somers* affair on the amount of inappropriate literature available to young people. "How much of the crime of this young man [Philip Spencer]," the *Herald* asked, "may be attributed to the miserable trash that the country is daily deluged with in the shape of romantic adventures of pirates, banditti, [and] exploits of celebrated highwaymen?" The paper warned readers: "Magnifying a thief and a murderer into a hero, and throwing a halo of romance around him, is not the best way to improve the morals of the rising generation."[57]

Someone as troubled as Spencer never should have made it to the deck of a navy ship, regardless of his father's political connections. Just after the *Somers* affair became public, Commander Samuel F. Du Pont stated his hope that the incident would "be a death blow to reinstatements of worthless officers through political influence." Captain Charles Stewart believed it was essential for the navy not to spare "the pruning knife, so essential to the production of good fruit" when it came to midshipmen. This would not only rid the navy of undesirable types, it would also help to speed up the rate of promotion. Although Stewart did not favor establishing a naval academy, many naval officers, politicians, and middle-class reformers believed a West Point–style school would solve many of the navy's problems. Such an institution could identify and reject midshipmen whose character deficiencies made them unfit for naval service before they ever boarded a ship.[58]

West Point demonstrated the value of an academy in eliminating those unfit to serve before they became commissioned officers. As a House Military Affairs Committee report stated in 1844, "While holding the warrant of cadet, the young officer is in a state of probation as well as of improvement; his intellectual and moral characters are there tested as well as developed; and, during this probation, the dull, the stupid, the idle, [and] the vicious, gradually drop off; and those who pass the ordeal, go forth stamped with the unquestioned seal of excellence in all that adorns and constitutes the character of the soldier and the gentleman." West Point and other military academies appealed to the middle class because they provided a useful scientific education and a disciplined learning environment conducive to character development. Claudius Crozet, a former West Point engineering professor and one of the founders of the Virginia Military Institute, argued that military academies enabled young men to learn "the correct deportment of a gentleman and the honorable feelings of a soldier." They developed character in their cadets by fostering the virtues of self-discipline, obedience, temperance, self-reliance, sound judgment, industry, perseverance, and honesty.[59]

Military academies became fortresses in the middle-class crusade for moral reform, respectability, status, and gentility. Although Jacksonian Democrats regularly railed against the elitism and aristocracy of West Point, middle-class citizens welcomed the military gentility fostered at the academy. Since colonial times, Americans had associated certain character traits with gentility—proper manners, a refined style of living, high standards for appearance and dress, regal deportment and bearing, aesthetic appreciation, moral character (especially honor and discipline), the ability to speak in an intelligent and articulate manner, and cultural sophistication. In the eighteenth century, gentility and refinement were the hallmarks of the colonial elite—the wealthy merchants of the North and the great planters of the South. Gradually, gentility and refinement became democratized in the early to mid-nineteenth century and spread to the middle class. Middle-class men sought to project an image of themselves as educated gentlemen worthy of the same respect and status enjoyed by the American elite.[60]

The middle class viewed itself not as a hereditary aristocracy on the European model but as a republican meritocracy, an educated elite possessing talent, knowledge, and virtue that would lead the nation and define its values. The aristocracy of merit was a way for Americans to rival the European elite in education and refinement while preserving America's cultural independence from the Old World and avoiding the corruption that characterized societies based on hereditary distinctions. In a sense, the American middle class was attempting the "capture of aristocratic culture for use in republican society." Once gentility and refinement spread to the middle class, these traits no longer seemed inappropriate for a republic. Rather than appearing European and aristocratic, refinement and gentility became desirable characteristics—signs of education, good manners, and respectability. The popular conception of Whig presidential candidate William Henry Harrison in 1840 illustrated America's unique combination of republicanism and genteel refinement. The Whigs were quick to highlight Harrison's frontier hero image and his famous military exploits while also portraying him as a cultivated gentleman who "thinks well—speaks well—writes well, and fights well." This would also best describe what most Americans wanted in a naval officer by the early 1840s: an educated gentleman of middle-class origins who not only fought battles but also could effectively compete as a diplomat and explorer with his aristocratic foreign counterparts on overseas stations.[61] At West Point, cadets succeeded or failed according to their individual merit or lack thereof. They acquired a strong academic background and learned to behave like gentlemen. The navy could solve some of its most glaring social problems by adopting a similar method of education for midshipmen, thus transforming the naval officer corps into a republican aristocracy of merit.

Producing officers who were refined gentlemen and good role models was vital to the security and well-being of the United States. "Can we safely rely upon a commander," asked former chaplain Charles Rockwell, "who is himself profane, licentious, a swindler, and [who] may be intemperate, to watch over and form the moral character of the younger officers of the navy?" Although most officers in the U.S. Navy were "a credit to the service," there were some who "though wearing swords and epaulettes, and claiming to be gentlemen, are so in dress alone." A naval academy, serving as an academic and moral crucible, would help to prevent such men from receiving officer commissions. An anonymous writer attached to the frigate *Constitution* posed a similar argument in reference to the midshipmen: "Of the effect of such a school in . . . refining and elevating their general character, and in *giving them a higher standing in society on shore*, there cannot be a doubt. . . . The necessities of the service are beginning absolutely to demand such advantages of education. The sciences of the age are all in rapid progression. . . . These sciences are penetrating into everything, . . . and any set of men that will not keep pace with them, must be the sufferers."[62] This passage effectively summarized the reasons for establishing a naval academy: to develop midshipmen into refined gentlemen of character and to produce accomplished scientific officers.

By the early 1840s the naval officer corps' quest for greater professionalism had merged with the moral reform crusade of the American middle class. For the middle class, education served a dual purpose: to impart knowledge and to develop moral character. Military academies—including West Point, state academies like the Virginia Military Institute, or private academies like Norwich University—were inherently middle-class institutions that provided useful scientific knowledge and the strict discipline required for character formation. The vast majority of the young men who attended military academies were from middle-class families. Similarly, the majority of navy midshipmen came from middle-class backgrounds, which made the establishment of a naval academy an important issue for reformers. The disciplinary problems of the midshipmen, highlighted by the *Somers* affair, demonstrated the need for significant changes in the navy's traditional approach to officer development. Midshipmen had to learn self-command before they could command others. In the minds of middle-class moralists, such a process was unlikely to occur in the conventional naval environment of the nineteenth century. Rather, a naval academy on shore would be the ideal place to educate midshipmen because it would provide the controlled environment that was necessary for character development and was most conducive to academic studies.

CHAPTER 7

Annapolis

Although there was a growing consensus that a naval academy was needed, the navy had still not achieved that goal by the mid-1840s. Several navy secretaries had advocated for an academy, but to varying degrees. Samuel Southard and Abel P. Upshur had considered its establishment a priority, whereas John Branch and James K. Paulding were content simply to make the recommendation to Congress. Yet their overall strategy was the same: all of them had attempted to secure an academy by consulting Congress. What the service needed was a civilian leader who was willing to take a more unorthodox approach. The navy had that leader in 1845, when President James K. Polk named George Bancroft secretary of the navy. Bancroft not only made the founding of a naval academy his top priority; he was willing to use his own authority to make that happen without the direct involvement of Congress. In his effort to succeed where his predecessors had failed, Bancroft received crucial assistance from Professor William Chauvenet and Commander Franklin Buchanan. Along with Bancroft, both men played significant roles in organizing a permanent school for the navy.

William Chauvenet's Vision

In 1839 the U.S. Navy opened another "study hall" school at the U.S. Naval Asylum in Philadelphia, a hospital and home for disabled and elderly sailors. At first, the new facility was similar to the schools already operating at the Boston, New York, and Norfolk navy yards. It provided midshipmen nearing their lieutenant examination with some instruction in mathematics and navigation and gave them a place to study. Commodore James Biddle, the governor of the Naval Asylum, devised rules and regulations for the new school, but discipline was not strict and morale among the midshipmen was low. The young men, who derogatorily referred to the school as "Biddle's nursery," were required to attend class from nine o'clock in the morning until two o'clock in the afternoon, when they could leave the asylum grounds until sundown. The few restrictions included mandatory attendance at religious services on Sunday and prohibitions against card playing and verbally abusing the cook and waiter assigned to them. When the midshipmen requested that they not have to attend class on Saturdays, Biddle was acquiescent.[1] Although a retirement home would seem to provide a quiet atmosphere conducive to study, that was not the case at the Naval Asylum. When Commodore James Barron succeeded Biddle as its governor, he faced disciplinary problems not only from the midshipmen but also from the asylum's elderly residents. The old sailors regularly became drunk, fought, were absent without leave, cursed the asylum staff, and engaged in riotous behavior. One elderly resident was cited for running around the asylum naked, which Barron described as "a disgusting exposure of his person." The midshipmen often found trouble in the city, including brawling with civilians and fighting duels. Samuel R. Franklin, who entered the navy as a midshipman in 1841, described the Naval Asylum school as completely lacking in organization and structure: "They [the midshipmen] did as they pleased, studied or idled as suited their whims. . . . There was no discipline."[2]

Until 1842, the Naval Asylum school was little more than a glorified study hall. The midshipmen crammed for their examination but spent most of their time exploring the city, looking for trouble, or amusing themselves by watching the antics of the retired sailors. In 1842 William Chauvenet became the Naval Asylum's professor of mathematics. Chauvenet's arrival was a major event in the history of American naval education. His reforms not only improved the asylum school, enabling it to surpass its navy yard counterparts academically, but they also represented a crucial step toward the establishment of a permanent naval academy. Chauvenet made it his goal to create a fully organized school with a formal curriculum where midshipmen would study for a longer period (beyond the eight months already required). Only twenty-two years old when he arrived at the asylum, Chauvenet had graduated from Yale with high honors in 1840 and then worked as a research assistant for Professor Alexander D. Bache's experiments in magnetism at Girard College in Philadelphia. Chauvenet received an appointment as a navy professor of mathematics in 1841 and served on the steam frigate *Mississippi* before his assignment to the Naval Asylum school.[3]

When Chauvenet arrived at the school, the physical conditions for learning were poor. Instruction took place in a dark room in the asylum's basement, where the only equipment for teaching was a small chalkboard that rested on the floor. Chauvenet set out to improve the situation immediately. Commodore Barron, a willing ally in his efforts, provided a large, well-lit room for recitations and obtained chronometers, sextants, and additional chalkboards. Chauvenet made the mathematics instruction more challenging and required regular recitations by the midshipmen. He also instituted a new grading system. After introducing these early improvements, Chauvenet developed a long-range plan for "a regularly organized school in which all the subjects conceived to be indispensable to the naval officer were to be taught under competent instructors." In short, he intended to transform a study hall into a real school with a faculty and a comprehensive course of studies.[4]

Chauvenet felt that eight months of preparation for the lieutenant examination was insufficient, contending that midshipmen should spend at least two years in Philadelphia after serving at sea. He also saw the need for more instructors, both civilians and naval officers. Chauvenet realized that expanding the school would require additional funds, which in turn would demand congressional approval. The best way to accomplish this goal, he decided, was to initiate his reforms, demonstrate that they worked, and then approach Congress for financial support. During the winter of 1843–44 Chauvenet designed an extensive two-year curriculum for the Philadelphia school. In the first year, midshipmen would study algebra, geometry, trigonometry, French, Spanish, writing, drawing, gunnery, naval tactics, and naval history. In the second year, they would proceed to nautical astronomy, navigation, nautical surveying, mechanics, steam engineering, and maritime law, but continue their studies in French, Spanish, drawing, gunnery, and tactics. Chauvenet proposed a faculty consisting of two professors of mathematics; a professor of mechanics and steam engineering, of gunnery and naval tactics, of modern languages, and of history and maritime law; and a drawing teacher. The academic year would run from October to June. During the summer months, the midshipmen would undertake a training cruise on board a small ship commanded by the professor of gunnery and naval tactics. An examining board would convene in September to test both classes of midshipmen. To be admitted to the school, a midshipman had to complete four years of service in the navy and pass an examination in seamanship, geography, arithmetic, and practical navigation. Secretary of the

Navy David Henshaw approved Chauvenet's plan on January 25, 1844, and ordered that it go into effect in the fall.[5]

Chauvenet's plan never came to fruition, mostly due to politics. Henshaw's position as navy secretary had been a recess appointment by President John Tyler during the summer of 1843 and had not been confirmed by the Senate. When the senators took up the appointment, they rejected it for political reasons. Several senators believed that Henshaw had been nominated to help Tyler build a new political coalition that would back his candidacy in the 1844 presidential election. The new secretary of the navy, John Y. Mason, reversed Henshaw's actions and rejected Chauvenet's plan on the grounds that the navy could not spare the midshipmen from sea duty for as long as two years. Undeterred, Chauvenet continued to make substantial improvements to the eight-month course of instruction and added three new instructors: Lieutenant James H. Ward (ordnance and gunnery), Passed Midshipman Samuel Marcy (navigation), and Professor J. H. Belcher (maritime law).[6]

Lieutenant Ward quickly became a spokesman for a broader, more academic approach to naval education after the *Army and Navy Chronicle* published the address he delivered to the midshipmen on his arrival in Philadelphia. Ward had studied at the college level and believed that naval officers needed a more substantial academic background than they could receive on ships at sea. Besides acquiring a practical knowledge of seamanship and navigation, Ward argued, midshipmen should study ordnance, gunnery, naval tactics, naval architecture, and steam engineering. In his opinion, scientific principles, not merely practical skills, formed the core of the naval profession. Youth was the best time for intellectual growth; the navy was wasting that prime period by sending midshipmen to sea to learn only the practical aspects of sailing a ship instead of enabling them to broaden their education. West Point cadets received four years of uninterrupted study before beginning their profession; midshipmen deserved the same privilege. Under the navy's existing system, a midshipman's most rigorous intellectual activity was memorizing the mathematical formulas used in navigation. Ward added a new dimension to the familiar argument that naval officers required more education than army officers: he pointed out that army officers served in specialized branches—infantry, cavalry, artillery, and engineers— and only had to master the particular knowledge and skills related to that branch. Naval officers had a wider range of duties—commanding a ship or a squadron, conducting diplomatic negotiations, judging legal matters, supervising the construction of ships, and outfitting the vessels. Naval officers required a well-rounded education to carry out all of these assignments.[7]

In addition to the work of Chauvenet and Ward in Philadelphia, citizens in Massachusetts and New York City submitted petitions to Congress in support of a naval academy. The Massachusetts petition called for eliminating the navy's professor of mathematics position, which was little more than a sinecure, and, with the money saved, establishing a naval academy at the Boston Navy Yard in Charlestown. Because midshipmen received little or no benefit from the existing system, the navy should combine practical training at sea with a liberal education at an academy on shore. Invoking a nationalistic argument, the petitioners declared that the proposed academy would enhance the nation's international prestige since the naval officers produced by the school would one day represent American interests abroad. The memorial signed by citizens of New York City was very similar to the Massachusetts petition. It too called for the elimination of the professor of mathematics position and the establishment of a naval academy—but at the New York Navy Yard in Brooklyn. "Experienced naval officers" had told them, the New York petitioners wrote, that replacing the existing system with a naval academy was the best course of action for the navy and the nation.[8]

On February 10, 1845, the Senate Naval Affairs Committee endorsed the establishment of a naval academy at Fort Norfolk, Virginia, on the Elizabeth River. To appease the anti–West Point camp in Congress, the committee stated the proposed school would not be an elaborate, expensive institution like the Military Academy. Rather, the navy would simply be rearranging its existing educational activities in a more efficient manner. No additional funding beyond what the government had already appropriated for naval education would be necessary. Despite the fact that service as a naval officer required "high qualities of physical and intellectual vigor as well as moral worth," midshipmen currently received only the "meager course of instruction" provided at the Naval Asylum school the year before they took their lieutenant examination. This program was insufficient for the young men who would one day become the "armed ambassadors of the country."[9]

The Naval Affairs Committee recommended that the naval academy's faculty include officers and civilians. A navy captain or commander would serve as the academy's superintendent, with commissioned officers instructing the midshipmen in naval tactics, seamanship, and gunnery. The civilian faculty would include two professors of mathematics; French, Spanish, and drawing teachers; a professor of engineering; and four assistant professors. The course of studies would cover mathematics, surveying, navigation, astronomy, French, Spanish, drawing, English grammar, geography, history, basic seamanship, physics, steam engineering, hydrography, gunnery and pyrotechny, naval architecture, naval tactics, international and military law, and ethics. According to the committee, all of this would actually cost less than the existing system of education.[10] Despite this endorsement and a workable, cost-effective plan for implementation, the Senate failed to take action.

"I Will Do Nothing in Secret"

In March 1845 President James K. Polk took office and selected George Bancroft, a prominent historian and Massachusetts politician, as secretary of the navy. The appointment was entirely political—a reward for Bancroft's leading role in securing the Democratic Party's nomination for Polk at the 1844 national convention in Baltimore. Bancroft had hoped to receive a diplomatic post in Europe so he could conduct archival research for his multivolume history of the United States and enjoy the company of European scholars. Although disappointed when Polk offered him the Navy Department instead, Bancroft accepted the position with Polk's private promise of a diplomatic post at some future time. The Senate confirmed Bancroft's appointment on March 10.[11]

Born in 1800 in Worcester, Massachusetts, Bancroft was the son of the Reverend Aaron Bancroft, a Unitarian minister. The younger Bancroft attended Phillips Exeter Academy and Harvard College before pursuing graduate studies at the University of Göttingen in Prussia. He received a doctor of philosophy degree in September 1820, a month before his twentieth birthday. Though expected to follow in his father's footsteps as a minister, Bancroft instead turned to teaching. He cofounded the Round Hill School, an elite boarding school for boys in Northampton, Massachusetts. The regimented lifestyle enforced at Round Hill filled each day—from six o'clock in the morning until nine o'clock at night—with scheduled activities. The school attempted to control, as much as possible, the intellectual and moral environment in which the students developed. Bancroft attempted to merge European and American styles of education by combining a traditional classical curriculum with practical subjects and physical activities. The students were required to wear uniforms to ensure a basic level of democracy at Round Hill. Despite his strong intellect and noble aspirations, Bancroft was a poor teacher. He was also very unpopular with the students, who referred to him as "The Critter," and was unable to maintain discipline in the classroom. He was a frequent target of spitballs and, on one occasion, a student threw a watermelon at him. Disillusioned with teaching and his own lack of success as an instructor, Bancroft left Round Hill and turned his attention to history and politics.[12]

Bancroft was a staunch nationalist who believed the history of America, since the arrival of the first European colonists, represented a great quest for political, intellectual, and moral progress. To glorify America's development as a nation, he set out to write the first comprehensive history of the United States. Little, Brown and Company published the first volume of Bancroft's *History of the United States* in 1834. By 1845, when he became secretary of the navy, Bancroft had published the first three volumes of what would become a ten-volume work. Bancroft's very popular *History*, known for its dramatic literary style and blatant nationalism, became the standard nineteenth-century work on America's early history. Just as Bancroft's literary career was taking off, his political career also began to unfold. He quickly became a leader of the Democratic Party in Massachusetts and served as collector of customs in Boston during the Van Buren administration. In 1844 he received the Democratic nomination for governor of Massachusetts but lost the election.[13]

Because he lacked experience in naval affairs, Bancroft's appointment as navy secretary was amusing to his friends, who joked that the scholarly historian "did not know the bow from the stern of a ship." Nevertheless, Bancroft invested all of his energy into improving the navy. A month after assuming office, he called on Massachusetts congressman and former president John Quincy Adams to discuss naval matters. Adams recorded in his diary that "Mr. Bancroft professes great zeal to make something of his Department. I heartily wish he may. He intends to be a hard-working man." Bancroft's overall goal for the navy was greater efficiency and professionalism. Seeing no reason to expand the fleet, the new secretary focused on making the navy more effective, a need heightened by the threat of war on two fronts. In 1845 tensions with Mexico over the U.S. annexation of Texas and with Great Britain over the boundary between the Oregon Territory and British Canada posed a dual threat to American national security. Bancroft adopted a reform agenda that reflected the influence of one of his naval aides, Lieutenant Matthew Fontaine Maury; the agenda included improved naval education, promotion according to merit rather than seniority, a retirement system for elderly officers, competency examinations for naval engineers, and reforms in navy yard management.[14]

Improving naval education became the new secretary's top priority. Soon after Bancroft's appointment, William Chauvenet had asked his mentor Professor Bache (a West Point graduate) to present Chauvenet's proposal for a two-year course of studies at the Naval Asylum school to Bancroft, emphasizing that the plan could go into effect immediately without any additional appropriations. Bancroft was receptive to Chauvenet's ideas but felt that the facilities at Philadelphia were inadequate for a fully organized naval academy. Given Bancroft's personal background, his decision to focus on educational reform is not surprising. Education had been a strong influence in his own life—Bancroft was the best-educated navy secretary to date and an accomplished scholar. He was also a firm believer in the importance of education for character development. His father's sermons often made the argument that youth was the best time to form moral character. The elder Bancroft taught his congregation and his son that discipline and obedience would lead to success in life. As an educator at Round Hill, Bancroft had adopted a strictly regimented program of studies and activities in an attempt to provide a learning environment that would foster strong character in his students. Moreover, he had learned by experience the importance of discipline in an academic setting.[15]

Bancroft was certainly aware of the various problems the navy was encountering in the 1840s, many of which involved character issues, and believed that better education could solve many of these problems. In April 1845 Dr. Thomas Henderson, an army surgeon, published an essay addressed to Bancroft on the continued practice of dueling in the navy. Henderson argued that West Point was the reason why dueling no longer occurred in the army. The moral, intellectual, and military development of the cadets prevented dueling by instilling a devotion to duty, to one's fellow officers, to the nation, and to God. Henderson believed a naval academy would do the same for the navy; it would teach the midshipmen that they did not have to fight duels to have honor. Most duels were the result of character flaws generated by the "inexperienced, untrained, [and] unadjusted impulses of youth." A "naval West Point" would correct this situation and improve the morale and character of the navy. Appealing to Bancroft personally, Henderson stated: "Intellect enlarged and morality liberalized by education made you what you are." He then appealed to the secretary's ego, declaring: "Be assured that whatever reward be made to the historian of his country, one not less ennobling awaits you as the future historian tells of the zeal you displayed for this essential national institution."[16]

On the day of his confirmation as secretary of the navy, Bancroft wrote: "Duty & publicity will be my watchwords . . . I will do nothing in secret." Ironically, his main strategy for establishing a naval academy was to do so completely on his own without informing Congress. Arthur M. Schlesinger Jr. has called Bancroft a "brilliant and devious man." Bancroft was exactly that. Considering the experiences of his predecessors, he realized that submitting a proposal to Congress was a waste of time and effort. He therefore decided to act on his own authority as navy secretary. Essentially, Bancroft adopted the same approach that Chauvenet had devised at Philadelphia—

establish a working institution before consulting Congress. Chauvenet had failed because he did not have the support of Secretary Mason. That was no longer a problem. While keeping Congress in the dark, Bancroft recognized the need to win the support of all segments of the naval officer corps.[17]

Bancroft began the process in May 1845 by collecting information from experts. He wrote to the faculty at the Naval Asylum school, including Chauvenet, to inquire about their teaching duties during the previous year, including the number of hours they taught each day, the number of students they taught, and any suggestions they had for improvements to the school.[18] He ordered Passed Midshipman Samuel Marcy, an instructor at Philadelphia and the son of Secretary of War William Marcy, to visit West Point, observe its operations, and report back to Bancroft on the academy's curriculum and organization. Bancroft already had some knowledge of West Point as a member of the Military Academy's Board of Visitors twenty years earlier. After attending cadet examinations, viewing disciplinary records, observing the Corps of Cadets drilling, and inspecting the barracks and library, he had been very impressed with the educational and military program established by Sylvanus Thayer. It was only logical for Bancroft to employ a similar system at the new naval academy.[19]

Marcy gave Bancroft a detailed report on the U.S. Military Academy in July. Characterizing its organization as "strictly military," he noted that almost all of the professors, assistant professors, and military instructors were West Point graduates. He described the responsibilities of the superintendent, the Academic Board, and the Board of Visitors as well as the requirements for admission and the course of studies. Most of the military instruction took place during the summer encampment. As for the academic program, within each class the faculty divided the cadets into sections based on ability. All cadets were required to perform daily recitations, which formed the basis for the professors' weekly reports to the superintendent on their academic performance. Marcy went on to explain the procedure for examinations, the merit roll, the demerit system, and the dismissal of cadets for academic deficiency or disciplinary violations. He concluded his report by describing the academy's library, observatory, and laboratory. Most impressive to Marcy was the fact that the annual expense to run West Point was less than the cost of operating one U.S. Navy ship of the line.[20]

Marcy recommended modeling the new naval academy, as much as possible, after West Point. Almost all of the academic subjects taught at the Military Academy had naval applications; a summer training cruise to instruct the midshipmen in seamanship and gunnery would substitute for the West Point summer encampment. He suggested that a navy captain or commander serve as superintendent and that the faculty be appointed from among the civilian professors already employed by the navy. Moreover, all midshipmen should spend three years at the naval academy before going to sea. In addition to providing the necessary scientific background, the academy would serve as a proper learning environment where midshipmen could develop morally, free from the temptations and bad influences of shipboard life. There, midshipmen would learn how to apply themselves and use their leisure time for self-improvement. They would go to sea with greater maturity and judgment and would be better equipped to avoid bad habits. Finally, Marcy connected the need for a naval academy to American nationalism. The "preservation of our nationality" depended on U.S. naval officers advancing the science and technology of the naval profession. The United States could not continue to rely solely on advancements that had originated in other nations.[21]

While collecting information about the Naval Asylum school and West Point, Bancroft went about finding a suitable location for the new academy. Any potential site would have to meet four conditions. First, it must be relatively secluded and on the water. Second, it must have plenty of space for future expansion. Third, it must be conducive to military discipline and character development. And fourth, because the Navy Department could not afford the cost of new construction, it ideally would be situated at an existing military post no longer needed by the army. Bancroft also felt that a site in the South, if it were possible, would balance West Point's location in the North.[22] His desire to place the naval academy in a relatively secluded location was in keeping with the common practice of the time. Many educators and reformers believed colleges should be situated far away from the temptations and distractions of large cities. One danger of a large city was the chance that "the young men will sometimes get their ship launched before the keel is laid." It was common wisdom that college boys had not yet formed their moral character and should not be exposed to city life.[23]

On May 31, 1845, President Polk appointed Bancroft to serve as acting secretary of war during William Marcy's absence from Washington. Like many other politicians, Marcy had decided to escape the excessive heat and humidity of summer in the nation's capital. This temporary appointment gave Bancroft the opportunity to take a major step forward in locating a site for the new academy. He soon settled on Fort Severn in Annapolis, Maryland—apparently recommended by an unknown individual.[24] Annapolis was a logical choice for several reasons. Maryland politicians had actively promoted the city as a suitable place for a naval academy since the 1820s. Matthew C. Perry had also recommended it. Other factors that made Annapolis ideal were its location in a southern state, its maritime character, its access to Chesapeake Bay, and the fact that Maryland had produced many naval officers. Finally, Fort Severn had become obsolete since it no longer performed an important national security function. This meant that the army would probably not object to the fort's transfer to the Navy Department.

Maryland's capital since 1694, the seaport city of Annapolis still retained its colonial appearance in 1845. Its major landmarks were the State House, where General George Washington had voluntarily resigned his commission as commander in chief of the Continental army in 1783, and St. John's College. Once a major colonial seaport, Annapolis had entered a period of decline after the American Revolution, when Baltimore took its place as Maryland's principal commercial seaport. The city had approximately three thousand residents. Though quaint and charming in its own way, Annapolis did not appeal to everyone. Edmund L. DuBarry, Bancroft's first choice for surgeon at the naval academy, visited the city and promptly requested a transfer. In a letter to his son, a West Point cadet, DuBarry declared he was "so disgusted with the place that I immediately wrote a private letter to the Secretary requesting that he would not order me there." Annapolis was "the dullest and most horrible place in the United States—it is very old, and I do not suppose a house has been built there in 40 years." Worst of all, the rent for its "dilapidated" houses immediately increased once rumors began to circulate that Bancroft intended to locate the new naval academy there.[25]

The army had built Fort Severn in 1808 in response to the *Chesapeake-Leopard* incident of the previous year. Located on a peninsula between the Severn River and Annapolis Harbor, the grounds encompassed eight acres. The fort itself had a circular design one hundred feet in diameter and a fourteen-foot-high stone wall. The two brick walls (connected at a ninety-degree angle) that enclosed the grounds would serve a valuable function by "restraining the spirits of the young officer-to-be." The other two sides of the post were bounded by water. Besides the fort, the post included several other buildings.[26]

Although as acting secretary of war Bancroft had the authority to transfer Fort Severn from the War Department to the Navy Department, he did consult Secretary Marcy about his plans. Stating that he wished to establish a naval school at low cost and that Fort Severn had been recommended to him as an ideal location, Bancroft asked for Marcy's cooperation in transferring the fort to the navy if that action would not adversely affect the army. He mentioned that he had already discussed the matter with Major General Winfield Scott, the general in chief of the army, and received a favorable response. Replying on June 12, Marcy confirmed that Scott had endorsed

Bancroft's proposal and indicated his own support for the project if the president gave his approval. On June 13, Bancroft requested President Polk's permission to proceed with the transfer of Fort Severn and the establishment of the new naval academy, noting that Marcy and Scott had agreed to the transfer of property. Polk approved the plan on June 16.[27]

Having found a suitable location, Bancroft began his campaign to obtain the support of the naval officer corps. Although many officers favored the establishment of an academy, there was some opposition within the corps, mostly from the most senior officers. Because of this opposition, Bancroft felt the need to have the endorsement not only of the younger, more progressive officers, but also the navy's senior leadership. His strategy was to have officers from each group participate in developing the organizational and academic plans for the school rather than do it himself or simply revise Chauvenet's Philadelphia proposal. Bancroft realized that even though the officers would have to accept the secretary's plan publicly, they would do everything possible to undermine it privately if he did not consult them about its formation.[28]

In June Bancroft wrote to Commodore George C. Read, the president of the Board of Examiners convened at Philadelphia to administer midshipman examinations, requesting the board's assistance in "maturing a more efficient system of instruction for the young naval officers." Bancroft mentioned that Fort Severn had been recommended to him as a better location for an academy than Philadelphia. He also stated his belief that the eight-month period of instruction offered at Philadelphia was too short for midshipmen to derive much benefit from it and asked the board to recommend a more extensive course of studies. Bancroft was ever the crafty politician in giving these instructions to the board. He asked them to consider specific questions related to an improved naval school. Was Fort Severn a suitable location? What subjects should the midshipmen study? He did not ask the board's opinion about whether there should *be* a new school.[29] Bancroft was also careful to present his proposals as suggestions to improve and relocate the *existing* school at Philadelphia—essentially an evolution in naval education rather than a revolution.

In addition to Read, the Board of Examiners included Matthew C. Perry, Thomas ap Catesby Jones, Elie A. F. Lavallette, and Isaac Mayo—all respected senior naval officers. The board had prepared a comprehensive plan for an improved naval school by the end of June. Although three of the board members were unfamiliar with Fort Severn, Jones and Mayo knew the post and agreed it was a suitable location with adequate space and access to Chesapeake Bay for training exercises. The board suggested the creation of a new rank—naval cadet—for the students attending the school. Naval cadets would rank just below midshipmen. After successfully completing the course of studies at the naval school and thus proving his fitness for the service, a naval cadet would receive a promotion to midshipman and go to sea. "By making this grade the source from which all others shall spring," the board explained, "and by imposing upon it acquirements of a comparatively high character, most of the delinquencies now so common in the Navy would be unknown when the proposed system shall have been thoroughly incorporated into the service."[30]

The Board of Examiners further recommended that the academy staff consist of both military and civilian personnel. The naval staff should include a captain to serve as superintendent, a commander to serve as executive officer (second in command), three lieutenants, a surgeon, an assistant surgeon, a purser, a chaplain, a secretary for the superintendent, a clerk, a purser's clerk, a purser's steward, and a marine company (the marine commanding officer would instruct the naval cadets in infantry drill). On the civilian faculty there should be a professor and an assistant professor of English (who would also teach law), a professor of French, a professor and an assistant professor of mathematics (who would also teach marine surveying), a professor of natural philosophy and chemistry, and an instructor of drawing and mapping. The board also suggested that the navy attach a frigate and a small steamship to the academy for seamanship training, gunnery practice, and hands-on experience with a steam engine. Prospective officers would spend two years at the naval school, three years at sea, and one year assigned to the training frigate at the naval school. After completing this period of education and training, the midshipmen would take the lieutenant examination.[31]

The board proposed that West Point serve as a model for the organization of the naval school at Annapolis, which should adopt the admission qualifications, course of studies, and examination system used at the Military Academy. The board did, however, recommend omitting instruction in calculus in favor of a more practical branch of mathematics. By enforcing strict standards of academic performance, discipline, and morality, the board believed that this new system of educating naval officers would more effectively rid the service of those young men who did not possess the intelligence, character, or physical constitution for a naval career. Moreover, boys should be admitted between the ages of thirteen and fifteen, so those deemed unfit for the navy would still be at an appropriate age to prepare for a different profession. The Board of Examiners had provided Bancroft with a detailed edu-

Secretary of the Navy George Bancroft and Secretary of War William Marcy inspect the site of Fort Severn in Annapolis, Maryland, in July 1845. In this painting, Bancroft (far left) talks to Major John L. Gardner of the U.S. Army as Marcy points out the boundaries of Fort Severn to Commodore Lewis Warrington of the U.S. Navy. Painting by J. W. Schlaikjer. Courtesy U.S. Naval Academy Museum.

cational plan. But more importantly, by obtaining the advice and assistance of some of the navy's most respected senior officers, Bancroft succeeded in heading off opposition to the academy within the officer corps.[32]

On July 19 *Niles' Register* reported that Secretary of the Navy Bancroft, Secretary of War Marcy, and Commodore Lewis Warrington had visited Annapolis to inspect Fort Severn and that it was rumored the government was planning to move the Naval Asylum school to the fort. Also in July, Bancroft began his search for a superintendent to head the new school. Although the Board of Examiners had recommended that the superintendent hold the rank of captain, Bancroft thought that assigning such a high-ranking officer to the position would draw opposition from Congress. He decided instead to appoint a commander with command experience at sea and a reputation as a disciplinarian. Bancroft quickly decided on Commander Franklin Buchanan, an officer with thirty years of experience.[33]

Buchanan was born in 1800 into a prosperous Baltimore family. His father was a physician (who died when Franklin was seven after contracting yellow fever from a patient); his mother was the daughter of a signer of the Declaration of Independence. Such a background ensured that Buchanan met the "respectable" qualification needed to receive a midshipman's appointment. The navy's victories in the War of 1812 inspired him to become a naval officer, and he applied, with his mother's approval, for an appointment as a midshipman. Buchanan received his warrant in January 1815 at the age of fourteen. Over the course of his naval career, Buchanan acquired a reputation for being a strict disciplinarian. He demanded absolute obedience and professional competence from those under his command and was quick to punish subordinates who failed to live up to his expectations. When he served as first lieutenant on board the frigate *Constellation* from 1829 to 1831, the enlisted seamen despised him because of his frequent use of flogging to maintain order and discipline. From 1842 to 1844, Buchanan commanded the sloop of war *Vincennes*, where he waged a personal crusade against drunkenness, which he considered a grievous sin for officers and the root of most of the navy's disciplinary problems. This background made Buchanan an excellent choice to head a school full of rowdy midshipmen. Buchanan was also very familiar with Annapolis—his first home after his marriage was located next to Fort Severn.[34]

Bancroft ordered Buchanan to report to the navy secretary's office in Washington. During the subsequent interview, Bancroft informed the commander about his plans to establish an academy at Annapolis and his desire to have Buchanan lead the school. Although Buchanan accepted the appointment, he had some reservations about his capacity to organize and lead an academic institution. Bancroft asked Buchanan to choose a couple of his fellow officers to assist him in developing a plan for the naval academy. Buchanan selected Commander Samuel F. Du Pont and Commander William McKean, both of whom promptly received orders from Bancroft to report to the Navy Department to assist Buchanan in organizing the new school.[35]

Bancroft articulated his thoughts on the proposed academy in an August 7 letter to Buchanan. Emphasizing the importance of avoiding "all unnecessary expense" and any sinecures since either action would provoke opposition in Congress, Bancroft intended to establish a better system of instruction using only the money that Congress had already appropriated for naval education. Furthermore, he wanted to open the new school without requiring any new legislation. The new academy's twofold purpose was to provide midshipmen with a scientific education and to form strong moral character: "Placed by their profession in connection with the world, visiting in their career of service every climate and every leading people, the officers of the American Navy if they gain but opportunity for scientific instruction, may make themselves as distinguished for culture as they have been for gallant conduct." To achieve these goals, Bancroft outlined a course of studies that included mathematics, nautical astronomy, ethics, international law, gunnery, steam engineering, the French and Spanish languages, and "other branches essential in the present day to the accomplishment of a naval officer."[36]

The naval academy, in Bancroft's mind, was the key to solving many of the problems the navy was experiencing with its midshipmen. "At present," he explained, "they are left when waiting orders on shore, masters of their own motions, without steady occupation, young and exulting in the releif [sic] from the restraints of discipline on ship board." He stressed the importance of maintaining strict discipline, well beyond what was in place at civilian colleges: "In collecting them [the midshipmen] at Annapolis for purposes of instruction, you will begin with the principle that a warrant in the Navy far from being an excuse for licentious freedom, is to be held a pledge for subordination, industry, and regularity, for sobriety and assiduous attention to duty." Indeed, President Polk expected the school's system of discipline to produce "an exemplary body [of midshipmen] of which the country may be proud." Bancroft concluded that the Navy Department had all of the means (funds and personnel) for a good naval school at its disposal; it just had to concentrate its resources at a single location and apply them in a more beneficial manner. Unfortunately the midshipmen, unlike college students and West Point cadets, would be unable to spend consecutive years studying at Annapolis, for at any time they could be detached from the academy and sent to sea. The Navy Department would order midshipmen returning from sea duty to report to the academy, which meant that midshipmen would be coming and going throughout the academic year. Bancroft ended his letter by ordering Buchanan to draft a formal plan for the organization of the school.[37]

Although the Annapolis school would provide midshipmen with a solid scientific education, Bancroft was more concerned about discipline and character development. Around the time he was pursuing the academy project, he had to deal with the court-martial of a senior naval officer, Captain Philip F. Voorhees, who was being tried for "scandalous conduct tending to the destruction of good morals." Voorhees's specific crime was lying to the secretary of the navy. En route to the United States, the captain decided somewhere near the equator that he would dock his ship at Annapolis (where his family was located) instead of Norfolk, as Bancroft had ordered. When Voorhees reported to Bancroft, he stated that wind and weather conditions at Norfolk had prompted his decision to sail to Annapolis. Based on testimony from Voorhees's subordinates, Bancroft believed, correctly, that the decision was premeditated for personal reasons and was not the result of poor weather. The court-martial found Voorhees guilty and sentenced him to an eighteen-month suspension from duty. Bancroft was outraged at the court's leniency. In a letter to James Fenimore Cooper, Bancroft acknowledged that Voorhees's actions and the court's verdict had given him "much concern," since being found guilty of "immoral and dishonorable conduct" should be grounds for dismissal. The court's lenient sentence was a disgrace to the navy. Cooper responded that "it is a wise and safe principle to say that the officer who cannot be depended on, in his reports and statement of matters of public moment, is not worthy of holding a commission." He pointed out that many people lied "because they are incapable of seeing the truth," suggesting that the problem was, at least in part, a lack of intellectual capacity. Bancroft ordered the court-martial to reconvene in early August. This time, the sentence was dismissal from the navy. This incident of officer misconduct might have contributed to Bancroft's emphasis on discipline and character development at the new naval school.[38]

In consultation with Samuel Du Pont and William McKean, Franklin Buchanan quickly produced a plan for the naval school and submitted it to Bancroft in mid-August. The superintendent assured the navy secretary that the plan could be implemented using only "means now at the disposal of the [Navy] Department." But this basic plan represented merely the first step in establishing a working naval academy at Annapolis. As the navy expanded and the nation became "alive to the advantages of a more extended education" for the young men who would one day be responsible for defending the country and its honor, the academy would likewise develop and grow to meet the needs of the fleet and the nation. In his "Plan for a Naval School at Annapolis," Buchanan described the makeup of the staff, the requirements for admission, the course of studies, and the examination process. According to the plan, the superintendent was responsible for devising and enforcing a set of rules and regulations for the school. The Navy Department would select faculty members from among the lieutenants, chaplains, passed midshipmen, and civilian professors already serving in the navy. The professors would constitute an Academic Board that would conduct examinations, evaluate the midshipmen's academic performance, report on the instruction offered at the academy, and offer recommendations for improvements to the school. Candidates for admission should possess good character, be at least thirteen and no more than seventeen years old, be able to read and write, be proficient in geography and arithmetic, and be able to pass the physical examination conducted by the school's surgeon. On receiving an appointment, the new acting midshipman would spend a year studying at the naval school. If his conduct and academic performance were satisfactory in the opinion of the superintendent and the Academic Board, he would go to sea. After six months of sea duty, performed to the satisfaction of his commanding officer, the young man would receive his midshipman's warrant. The midshipman would return to Annapolis after three years at sea to prepare for his lieutenant examination. In addition, all midshipmen on waiting orders ashore would be required to report to Annapolis until they were assigned to a ship.[39]

The course of studies at the naval school would include English grammar and composition, mathematics, geography, history, gunnery, steam engineering, French, and Spanish. Buchanan left the curriculum somewhat flexible so other subjects could be added later. The primary method of instruction would be daily recitation. The faculty would prepare weekly reports for the superintendent on the progress and class rank of each midshipman. The superintendent in turn would issue quarterly reports on the progress of the midshipmen to the secretary of the navy. Future examinations for promotion to lieutenant would cover all of the subjects taught at the school. To introduce a practical component into the program, Buchanan recommended that the navy station a sloop at the school for instruction in seamanship and gunnery.[40]

The War Department officially transferred Fort Severn to the Navy Department on August 15, 1845. Having secured a site and a superintendent, Bancroft turned his attention to financing the new academy and appointing a faculty. The budget for the Navy Department in 1845 included just over $28,200 for education. This sum paid the salaries of the navy's twenty-two civilian professors of mathematics and three foreign language teachers. Instructors only received pay when they were actually teaching, either on a ship or at a navy yard. If not actively employed, they were placed on "waiting orders" without compensation. Because the navy secretary controlled the employment of civilian professors, Bancroft placed half of the professors on waiting orders and used the thousands of dollars the Navy Department saved to set up the new school at Annapolis. Most importantly, Bancroft was able to establish an academy without asking Congress for more money, a request that almost certainly would have killed the school. As Samuel Du

Pont noted, the academy "goes into operation in October without drawing a dollar from the Treasury."[41]

The first faculty at Annapolis consisted of civilians and officers. Bancroft appointed William Chauvenet professor of mathematics. In addition to his tireless advocacy for naval reform, Chauvenet was a gifted educator. In the words of a former student, Chauvenet was a natural teacher who "had the faculty of imparting what he knew to others in a higher degree than any man I have ever known, and he had also the peculiar faculty of discerning whether a man at the blackboard knew what he was talking about or not." Henry H. Lockwood received an appointment as professor of natural philosophy after actively campaigning for the job. A West Point graduate (Class of 1836), Lockwood had served as an artillery officer in the Second Seminole War in Florida. He resigned from the army in 1837 and became a farmer in Delaware. A navy professor of mathematics since 1841, Lockwood had previously taught at sea on board the frigate *United States* and at the U.S. Naval Asylum.[42]

Another faculty member making the move from Philadelphia to Annapolis was Lieutenant James H. Ward, the new school's executive officer and instructor of gunnery and steam engineering. Ward possessed a stronger academic background than most of his fellow officers. He graduated from the American Literary, Scientific, and Military Academy (present-day Norwich University) before entering the navy. After completing a cruise to the Mediterranean on board the frigate *Constitution*, he requested a leave of absence to continue his academic studies and spent a year at Trinity College in Hartford, Connecticut. With a strong interest in science, engineering, gunnery, ordnance, naval tactics, and naval history, he joined the faculty of the Naval Asylum school in 1844 and delivered lectures on ordnance and gunnery. Ward later incorporated his lectures into a textbook for midshipmen. Bancroft appointed chaplain George Jones, a prominent naval academy advocate for almost twenty years, as instructor in English. Jones held bachelor's and master's degrees from Yale and taught in Washington, D.C., for two years before entering the navy as the secretary to Commodore Charles Morris and schoolmaster on board the frigate *Brandywine* (one of his students was Matthew Fontaine Maury). He later served on the *Constitution* during a cruise on the Mediterranean station. These cruises led to the publication of Jones's *Sketches of Naval Life* (1829), which was part travelogue and part social commentary on the navy. After leaving the navy in 1828, Jones taught at Yale for two years. In 1831, he was ordained a deacon in the Episcopal Church and became rector of a parish in Middletown, Connecticut. He returned to the navy as a chaplain in 1832, serving on several ships and at the Norfolk Navy Yard.[43]

Arsene Napoleon Alexandre Girault was hired as instructor in foreign languages. Born in Troyes, France, Girault was the son of an army contractor for Napoleon. Arriving in America in his mid-twenties, Girault became a teacher in Philadelphia. He taught Latin and French at a private school and a military school in addition to giving private language lessons. He was the author of several books on the French language. Girault became a U.S. citizen in 1833 and founded a private school for girls in New Jersey in 1836. After the school closed for financial reasons, Girault taught in Washington and Baltimore before being recommended to Franklin Buchanan. Rounding out the first academic staff were surgeon and chemistry instructor John A. Lockwood, Henry Lockwood's brother and an 1832 graduate of the Dickinson College medical school, and Passed Midshipman Samuel Marcy, a self-taught student of the naval profession, who received an appointment as assistant professor of mathematics.[44]

With classes scheduled to begin in early October, Buchanan had less than two months to transform Fort Severn into a naval academy. He kept Bancroft personally informed of his progress, traveling to Washington by train once a week. The superintendent had to finalize the curriculum in consultation with the faculty and arrange for some needed physical improvements to Fort Severn. He and Chauvenet also supervised the shipment of scientific instruments from Philadelphia to Annapolis. On October 1, Buchanan wrote orders to the faculty forming them into the Academic Board. Lieutenant Ward would preside over the board, which was responsible for organizing the midshipmen into classes and developing a detailed course of studies.[45]

Ward submitted a curriculum report for Buchanan's approval on October 7. Instruction was organized under six professorships—mathematics; natural philosophy; chemistry; ordnance, gunnery, and steam engineering; history, geography, and English grammar; and modern languages. The board recommended that the midshipmen also receive optional instruction in fencing and participate in infantry drill, which would serve as a healthy form of exercise and "elevate the military character of the school." Putting his West Point background to good use, Professor Lockwood volunteered to serve as the drill instructor. The board decided to divide the midshipmen into two classes—junior and senior. New midshipmen who had not yet been to sea would form the junior class. The senior class would include midshipmen who were a year away from their lieutenant examination. The faculty would assign midshipmen who had been to sea but were not yet approaching their examination to either the junior or senior class according to ability. The course of studies for the junior class included mathematics (arithmetic, algebra, and geometry), navigation, geography, English grammar and composition, and either French or Spanish. The junior class would also attend the senior class's lectures in natural philosophy, gunnery, ordnance, and chemistry. Members of the senior class would continue their studies in mathematics (algebra, geometry, and trigonometry), navigation, English composition, and a foreign language in addition to studying natural philosophy (including astronomy, mechanics, optics, magnetism, and electricity), ordnance, gunnery, steam engineering, history, and chemistry (see Appendix, Tables 2 and 3). The Academic Board devised a merit roll to rank midshipmen according to their academic performance. All students would recite daily and receive a grade from the instructor, who would record the grades and issue a weekly report to the superintendent. The board also created a demerit system to discipline anyone who violated navy regulations or the school's rules. At the end of the academic year, the board would determine a midshipman's class rank by combining their merit and demerit marks with the grade received on their final examination before a navy examining board.[46]

Not surprisingly, given Bancroft's respect for the Thayer system, the new naval academy reflected the strong influence of West Point. Its organization was nearly identical to the Military Academy's: a superintendent to administer the school and command its personnel, an Academic Board to assist the superintendent in overseeing academic affairs, and an examining board that convened in June to observe midshipman examinations and the operation of the academy. The method of instruction (daily recitation), the merit roll, and the demerit system all derived from West Point. The course of studies reflected the West Point curriculum's emphasis on scientific and technical subjects.

Secretary Bancroft had the authority to order midshipmen returning to the United States from sea duty to go anywhere he wished. As ships sailed into port in the summer of 1845, Bancroft issued orders for the midshipmen to report to Annapolis, thereby providing the new academy with a student body. By October, fifty-six midshipmen had reported. Thirty-six of them had entered the navy in 1840, thirteen had entered in 1841, and seven had just received their appointments as acting midshipmen and had not yet gone to sea. The rest of the navy's corps of midshipmen were at sea.[47] With the arrival of the midshipmen, the Annapolis school was ready to open. In many ways, its success or failure would depend on Buchanan. His leadership, or lack thereof, would set the tone for the academy.

Getting Under Way

The U.S. Naval School in Annapolis officially opened on October 10, 1845. The superintendent addressed the assembled midshipmen and faculty at eleven o'clock in the morning in one of the classrooms. Buchanan talked about the education the midshipmen were going to receive, a privilege denied previous generations of naval officers. He emphasized the importance of strong moral character in achieving professional success; only those midshipmen who demonstrated good morals would go on to receive officer commissions. Buchanan also warned that it was his duty to enforce the school's and the navy's rules and regulations, just as he would on a ship, and that he would not fail to punish any midshipman for a violation. Buchanan then read Bancroft's letter of August 7 in which the navy secretary outlined his thoughts on the purpose of the school; he concluded the opening exercises by reading the Naval School's set of rules and regulations.[48]

These rules and regulations governed all aspects of life at Annapolis. All navy regulations were in force at the school, and all midshipmen and faculty members were required to obey them as well. As was the case at West Point, Buchanan included the midshipmen in the governance of the school. Each day a midshipman would serve as "officer of the day." Stationed at the school's gate, the officer of the day performed multiple duties: carrying out the superintendent's orders for the day; answering visitors' questions; directing visitors to the appropriate building; recording the names of any visitors or workmen who entered the Yard (campus); keeping a log of the weather and temperature, recording entries at 8:00 A.M., noon, and 8:00 P.M.; patrolling the grounds occasionally to ensure "that no improprieties are committed by any one"; extinguishing the lights and fires in the classrooms, mess hall, and kitchen; and making sure that the lights in the midshipmen's rooms were extinguished at 10:30 P.M. The midshipmen were required to obey the professors and could not leave the classroom without permission. The professors were responsible for maintaining order and discipline in their classes. In an effort to provide an environment conducive to learning and character development, the midshipmen were not permitted to bring liquor onto the Yard; smoke in their rooms, the classrooms, or the mess hall; and cook or "give any entertainment" in their rooms or leave the Yard without the superintendent's permission. All professors and midshipmen were required to report any violations of the regulations, crimes, or neglect of duty to the superintendent. Buchanan expected the midshipmen to "abstain from all vicious, immoral, or irregular conduct" and "to conduct themselves with the propriety and decorum of gentlemen." Professor Henry

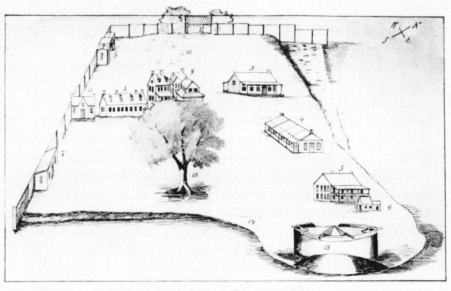

FORT SEVERN IN 1845 (FROM AN OLD MAP).

The numbers refer to the buildings, etc., as named after the Naval School was established.

1. Buchanan Row.	4. Apollo Row.	7. The Gas House.	10. Ring of Poplar Trees.	13. Fort Severn.
2. The Abbey.	5. Rowdy Row.	8. Superintendent's House.	11. Chaplain's House.	14. Site of Practice Battery.
3. Mess- and Recitation-Rooms.	6. Brandywine Cottage.	9. Gate-House.	12. Old Mulberry Tree.	

An early map of the U.S. Naval School's original campus in 1845. Courtesy Special Collections and Archives Department, Nimitz Library, U.S. Naval Academy.

Lockwood hoped the Naval School and its code of rules and regulations would effectively weed out the misfits who had managed to enter the navy. "Before this time, every dismissed cadet from the Military Academy, every third son whose father could do nothing else with him, every hopeless case for civil life, was considered a proper candidate for the navy."[49]

There were no reporters on hand for the Naval School's opening, and the event did not receive much attention in the press. But the academy did receive some coverage in the days and months that followed. As Bancroft intended, most people at the time did not consider Annapolis to be an entirely new institution but rather the new location for the school formerly situated at the Naval Asylum. Newspapers reported that Bancroft had moved the school to Annapolis for three reasons: first, to remove the midshipmen from the temptations and distractions of a large city; second, to collect the best professors already employed by the navy in one location; and third, to improve the "moral discipline and mental culture" of the midshipmen by providing a better environment for learning and discipline. The *National Intelligencer* proclaimed the Naval School to be "indispensable to the welfare" of the navy while also praising Bancroft's selection of Annapolis, a city that was "healthy and secluded, and yet of easy access." The *Maryland Republican* believed the midshipmen added to the city's charm: "About forty 'young gentlemen' have already reported themselves, whose handsome appearance and gentlemanly deportment give a cheerful aspect to the streets of our quiet city, and elicit universal admiration."[50]

Once classes began on Monday, October 13, the Naval School followed the predominant method of instruction in nineteenth-century colleges, including West Point—a combination of lecture and recitation. At most colleges, the professor would lecture to an entire class and then the students would break up into sections headed by a tutor and have their knowledge of the textbook examined through recitation. The main benefit of the recitation method, according to nineteenth-century educators, was that it instilled mental discipline. It fostered obedience to rules, downplayed independent thinking, and encouraged attention to detail. A typical class at the Naval School probably resembled the following description of a mathematics class at West Point. The instructor would start class with a short lecture on the day's topic. He would then answer any questions the cadets might have. Recitations would begin when the instructor called a cadet to the front of the room and assigned him a problem to work out using the principles from the day's lesson, which the cadet presumably had studied the night before. The cadet then went to the chalkboard to work out his problem. After the first cadet started, the instructor called the remaining cadets to the chalkboard to work out problems. When a cadet finished his assigned problem, he faced the instructor and stood at attention. When called on, he explained his solution. The instructor then asked questions and recorded a grade for the cadet. Most classes in other subjects were conducted in a similar fashion.[51]

The purpose of the Naval School was twofold: to provide midshipmen with a scientific education and to develop moral character in the navy's future officers. Buchanan's goal during the first year was to establish a solid foundation upon which to achieve these goals. West Point's emphasis on mathematics, science, and engineering had established a technical character to American military education. By emulating the Military Academy, Annapolis changed the focus of the navy's system of education. Once dominated by seamanship and navigation, the navy began to place more emphasis on scientific and technical subjects. *Niles' Register* declared that the rise of steam power, "which is in [the] future to be the arbiter of naval power," made technical education vital to American national interests. At Annapolis, James Ward taught steam engineering as part of his course on ordnance and gunnery, using the textbook he had published on the subject.[52] The school's technical emphasis actually resulted in a minor controversy in December. The midshipmen requested that Professor Lockwood replace Perschel's *Elements of Physics* textbook with "one of a more elementary character" for his natural philosophy class. According to his students, they were unable to grasp the subject despite "listening with much attention to the Lectures . . . and having devoted as much time and study as possible to the subject." Buchanan supported Lockwood, stating that there was no reason to replace the physics book, which was used at Princeton. In Buchanan's words, "I know not why the standard of education at Princeton should be superior to that at the Naval School."[53]

The Naval School's library, composed of books from navy yard libraries and new purchases by Lieutenant Ward, reflected the school's dual purpose. Books on history and biography, naval and military science, scientific and technical subjects, travel, and law dominated the library's holdings. Although there were only a couple of books on ethics and moral philosophy, history and biography served the character development mission of the school by providing the midshipmen with historical role models to emulate and historical villains whose dishonorable character traits they should avoid. In addition to supporting the academic program, the library was intended to provide midshipmen with a leisure activity that would contribute to their professional and moral development (see Appendix, Table 4).[54]

By necessity, attendance at the Naval School during this early period was irregular. The navy could recall midshipmen to active duty at any moment. This occurred for the first time in November 1845, just one month after the school opened, when seven midshipmen were ordered to sea. Buchanan used discipline as a way to bring some measure of stability to the school and Bancroft supported the superintendent in this effort. Disciplinary problems were to be expected. Most midshipmen at the academy had previous experience at sea and tended to think of themselves as officers on shore duty rather than college students. They were accustomed to relaxed discipline and a great deal of independence when on shore. It would take time for these older midshipmen to adapt to a disciplined academic environment; many of them had already commanded sailors, visited exotic ports of call, toured the great European cities, and maybe even socialized with royalty. Naturally, they resented being treated like schoolboys. Buchanan was strict but fair in enforcing the school's rules and regulations. He wanted to establish a standard of appropriate behavior early on that emphasized obedience, temperance, and devotion to study.[55]

The first major disciplinary problem at Annapolis arose in November, when Professor Girault reported a midshipman for disrespect and insubordination. Buchanan responded swiftly by requesting that Bancroft formally reprimand the offending midshipman. When Bancroft complied, Buchanan read the reprimand in front of the entire school as a warning to the rest of the midshipmen. Despite this incident, Buchanan was generally pleased with the conduct of his young charges. After a Mr. Denison of Baltimore wrote to Bancroft complaining about the ungentlemanly behavior of some of the midshipmen, Buchanan strongly refuted the accusation. Admitting to one "accidental" incident involving a midshipman in October, the superintendent assured Bancroft that the offender had never repeated the improper conduct and had become a "correct gentleman." He also said "the most respectable citizens" of Annapolis had told him they had never witnessed any inappropriate behavior by a midshipman attending the school. Judging by the tone of his letter to Bancroft, Buchanan took Denison's criticism as a personal affront to his leadership of the Naval School.[56]

In the meantime, Bancroft had finally informed Congress of the Naval School's existence. In his annual report, dated December 1, 1845, the secretary explained why and how he had established the new academy while assuring the lawmakers that no new appropriations were necessary to operate it. Although Congress had appropriated money for professors, Bancroft said, "the ship is not friendly to study, and the office of professor rapidly degenerated into a sinecure; . . . the teachers on board the receiving-ships [at the navy yards] gave little instruction, or none whatever, so that the expenditure was fruitless of great results." As he described it, the "idea naturally suggested itself" of concentrating the professors and the midshipmen on shore in one location, Fort Severn, where the young men could receive proper instruction. Most importantly, he was able to set up the school "on an unostentatious and frugal plan." Bancroft then expressed his aspiration for the Naval School: "This institution, by giving some preliminary instruction to the midshipmen before their first cruise, by extending an affectionate but firm supervision over them as they return from sea, by providing for them suitable culture before they pass to a higher grade, by rejecting from the service all who fail in capacity or in good disposition to use their time well, will go far to renovate and improve the American navy." Bancroft concluded his comments by praising Buchanan's leadership, emphasizing that no unnecessary professors or officers were attached to the school, and reiterating that no additional appropriations were necessary.[57]

In January 1846 Buchanan reported to the Navy Department on the operation of the Naval School after its first semester. Eighty-five midshipmen had entered the school since October. Their conduct was satisfactory, and Annapolis residents had praised the midshipmen's "gentlemanly bearing" when they ventured outside the Yard. Buchanan requested that the navy assign a sloop of war to the school for practical training in seamanship and navigation as well as for exercise and recreation.[58] To reward the midshipmen for their generally good conduct and to help develop their social skills, Buchanan organized a "Grand Naval Ball"—also in January. The U.S. Marine Band provided the music, and young women from the Annapolis area were invited. The midshipmen apparently enjoyed the event. On the day after the ball, the officer of the day recorded the following entry in his log: "No recitations today—all hands being employed repairing damages after the Ball."[59]

The new year, however, brought some serious disciplinary problems. In early February, the superintendent reported Midshipman Jefferson H. Nones for leaving the Yard without permission. Nones was a poor student, and Buchanan had ordered him to remain at the school to study. Since this was the first instance of disrespect toward the superintendent himself, Buchanan wanted to make an example of Nones. A couple of weeks later, Buchanan requested a court-martial for Midshipman Augustus McLaughlin. McLaughlin had informed Buchanan that his mother was seriously ill and wished to see her son. Buchanan gave McLaughlin permission to travel to Baltimore and spend the day with his mother. While calling on a friend who was in town and staying at an Annapolis hotel, Buchanan found McLaughlin in the hotel billiard room. As McLaughlin tried to explain that he had missed the train to Baltimore, Buchanan noticed that the young man had been "drinking freely" (McLaughlin had earlier promised Buchanan that he would not drink while under the superintendent's command). Both men returned to the Yard, and Buchanan ordered McLaughlin to go to his room and study. McLaughlin refused, walked out of the gate, and went to Baltimore. After consulting with Buchanan, Bancroft dismissed both Nones and McLaughlin. The secretary had particularly harsh words for McLaughlin: "No drunkard should be tolerated in the navy. The School is not to be a hospital for incurables, but a school for selected young men." Also in February, Bancroft reprimanded two other midshipmen for inebriation. Through their combined efforts, Buchanan and Bancroft were able to reduce alcohol-related disciplinary problems by March. By making the elimination of drunkenness a central feature of Naval School discipline, Bancroft and Buchanan reflected the growing power of the antebellum temperance movement. Temperance reformers condemned the use of alcohol as the root of society's problems, including poverty, crime, violence, laziness, neglect, and worker disobedience.

Similarly, many naval reformers believed the drinking culture that pervaded the navy was the cause of the service's social problems, especially those involving midshipmen. Enforcing temperance at Annapolis was a way to instill discipline and self-restraint.[60] Another problem involved the financial debt incurred by midshipmen. According to a navy proverb, "A sailor earns his money like a horse, and spends it like an ass." This saying apparently applied to the midshipmen at Annapolis. In May, Bancroft introduced a new policy designed to make them more financially responsible: No midshipman would receive a promotion until he had repaid all of his debts to shopkeepers, merchants, tavern owners, and anyone else to whom he owed money.[61]

In April 1846 Buchanan convened the Academic Board to examine the junior class of acting midshipmen (those who had not yet been to sea) in the subjects they had studied over the previous six months. The secretary of the navy would receive the results of the examination and decide the fate of those young men who were "deficient, idle, and not ambitious to improve themselves." After examining the eight acting midshipmen present, the Academic Board deemed three fit for the service, two unfit for the service, and three "indifferent" but capable of improving if they applied themselves more. Bancroft dismissed one of the two acting midshipmen deemed unfit for the navy. In June the Naval School held its first annual examinations. The performance of the midshipmen and the Board of Examiners' opinion of the school's effectiveness would be crucial factors in determining whether the school would remain open. In appointing the examiners, Bancroft essentially "stacked the deck" in the Naval School's favor by naming Commodore Matthew C. Perry and Captain Isaac Mayo, both strong supporters of the academy, to the board. The board examined fifty-two midshipmen and found only three to be deficient; Bancroft subsequently dismissed the three young men from the navy. In its report to Bancroft, the board spoke favorably of the school, suggested improvements to the buildings and library, and recommended that the navy assign a training ship to Annapolis for practical exercises in seamanship and gunnery.[62]

The Naval School had not only survived its first year, it had also demonstrated that a naval academy on shore was a viable solution to many of the navy's social problems. On August 10, 1846, Congress passed an appropriations act that authorized $28,200 "for repairs, improvements, and instruction, at Fort Severn, Annapolis, Maryland." This was the same amount the lawmakers had previously appropriated for naval education. What was significant was that they had officially recognized the Naval School at Annapolis and voted to support it financially. In a letter informing Buchanan about the appropriations, Bancroft ordered the superintendent to use the money to expand the school to accommodate one hundred midshipmen.[63]

GEORGE BANCROFT HAD SUCCEEDED where his predecessors had failed. Several factors explain this achievement. First, Bancroft presented the establishment of the U.S. Naval School as an evolutionary progression in naval education rather than a complete transformation. Many Americans believed the new academy was nothing more than a relocation of the Naval Asylum school from Philadelphia to Annapolis. In several ways, this impression was accurate. Although Bancroft's ultimate goal was to establish a West Point–style military college for the navy, both he and Franklin Buchanan realized that they must do so gradually. The first step was to consolidate and assemble the navy's educational activities at a suitable location that could accommodate future expansion. Bancroft accomplished this first step during his tenure as navy secretary. Despite the new location, the Naval School at Annapolis, like its predecessors at the navy yards and in Philadelphia, continued to teach mostly older, more experienced midshipmen who had already served at sea. Furthermore, the navy could, and did, assign these midshipmen to sea duty at a moment's notice, meaning that the student body at Annapolis, unlike at West Point, lacked stability.[64] Bancroft was unable to establish a true naval college on the West Point model, but by presenting the Annapolis school as an evolutionary rather than a revolutionary development in naval education, he helped to ensure that it would survive and prosper.

The second factor that contributed to Bancroft's success was his ability to convince Congress that the old system was not only ineffective but, more importantly, a waste of money. The Annapolis school demonstrated that it was possible to provide a more effective system of education without requiring additional funds. American foreign relations proved to be a third factor explaining Bancroft's success. By 1845, the United States was facing the threat of war with Britain and Mexico, which provided a political environment conducive to improvements in national defense. The possibility of a two-front war seemed to suggest the need for highly trained and well-educated naval officers.[65] Historically, war or the threat of war has motivated political leaders to improve military education in the United States.

A fourth factor was a law passed by Congress in March 1845 stipulating that the government appoint navy midshipmen from each state and territory in the Union in proportion to the number of congressional representatives and delegates.[66] This law was significant because it more firmly established Congress's authority over midshipman appointments and minimized the executive branch's power. The congressional patronage power associated with cadet appointments had been one factor that prevented West Point's abolishment. Similar power over midshipman appointments might have made Congress more willing to accept the Naval School. Finally, Bancroft's own personality and leadership style were crucial factors in the establishment of the Naval School. Bancroft understood that his predecessors had failed every time they tried to organize a naval academy by going through Congress. Rather than repeat a failed strategy, Bancroft decided to use only the authority of the executive branch—the president, the secretary of war, and himself—to bring an academy into existence. Because of his willingness to work around Congress, the Naval School finally became a reality.

Some politicians were unhappy with Bancroft's novel approach. "By scraps of laws, regulations, and departmental instructions," Senator Thomas Hart Benton complained, "a Naval Academy has grown up, and a naval policy become established for the United States, without the legislative wisdom of the country having passed upon that policy, and contrary to its previous policy, and against its interest and welfare." Benton and others believed Annapolis committed the United States to a more extensive naval establishment than the nation required. With the Naval School producing new officers every year, there would be a constant demand for more ships. Since another naval war would never occur, Benton argued, anything beyond a limited navy was a waste of money for the United States. Even if hostilities broke out, the Royal Navy, America's most likely adversary on the high seas, was too powerful to challenge in large fleet battles. Furthermore, America's previous wars had proved that a small number of naval frigates combined with privateers could disrupt British commerce. A large navy was simply unnecessary, but the government had a responsibility to employ the officers it turned out at Annapolis: "They are the children of the country, and must be provided for—they and their children after them." The senator predicted that none of the "school-house officers" educated at Annapolis would ever reach the level of greatness achieved by the naval heroes of the Revolutionary War and the War of 1812.[67]

In September 1846 George Bancroft resigned as secretary of the navy to become the new U.S. minister to Great Britain. The establishment of the Naval School was the central component of Bancroft's plan to reform and modernize the American navy and his greatest achievement as secretary. In addition to improving naval education, he also called for promotion based on merit rather than seniority and the creation of a retirement system for the navy. Though unsuccessful in realizing these last two goals, Bancroft did eliminate several officer sinecures and introduced competency examinations for naval engineers.[68]

From Naval School to Naval Academy

The outbreak of the Mexican War in 1846 disrupted life at Annapolis. Midshipmen were constantly coming and going. Those who remained generally suffered from low morale and resented having to study while their comrades were seeing action in the war. The war also deprived the Naval School of its superintendent. Franklin Buchanan departed Annapolis in March 1847 to assume command of the sloop of war *Germantown*. His successor as superintendent was Commander George P. Upshur, the brother of former navy secretary Abel P. Upshur. Unlike Buchanan, Upshur was not a disciplinarian. Though he was friendly and popular, his "boys will be boys" approach to discipline left the school in disarray. The midshipmen ran wild, participating in brawls and duels, forming their own social clubs, and drinking to excess. On St. Patrick's Day in 1848, the midshipmen hanged Professor Lockwood in effigy from the school's flagpole. Lockwood was very unpopular because of his role as military drill instructor. The midshipmen resented having to drill like soldiers, which cut into what they perceived to be their free time. In another incident, the midshipmen took advantage of Lockwood's stutter. One day, while drilling them with a battery of artillery, Lockwood stuttered on the command "Halt!" Because he could not complete the word, his charges marched straight into the Severn River with cannons in tow. Unable to maintain discipline, Upshur surrendered, telling the midshipmen: "I cannot govern you, young Gentlemen; so if you will only govern yourselves I should be delighted."[69] Clearly, the navy had to do something to regain control at Annapolis.

The lack of stability at Annapolis also undermined the academic program. Midshipmen who were detached for sea duty often found it difficult to readjust to the academic routine after they returned to Annapolis. The general academic performance of the midshipmen suffered as a result. A related concern was the age range of the student body. The school was responsible for educating older, experienced midshipmen in their early twenties as well as young, newly appointed midshipmen in their teens who had not yet gone to sea. The administration increasingly worried about the influence the older midshipmen exerted over their younger counterparts. These concerns highlighted the fact that Annapolis suffered from "an uncertain educational philosophy" in the years after its establishment. When Bancroft and Buchanan founded the Naval School, the curriculum focused on imparting the theoretical science underlying the naval profession to experienced midshipmen who had already served at sea and (one hoped) had already mastered the practical aspects of the naval profession. In this way, Annapolis was initially a more advanced version of the earlier study hall schools at the navy yards and Naval Asylum. In the late 1840s, a growing number of naval officers, politicians, and moral reformers favored changing the mission of Annapolis—from serving as a professional finishing school to becoming a preparatory military college like West Point, which was designed to transform civilian young men into military officers in a structured environment that facilitated higher learning and character development.[70] The decline in discipline and academics as well as the varied ages of the midshipmen thus suggested the need to transform the Naval School into a military college for teenagers entering the navy directly from civilian life.

In 1849 the Board of Examiners, at the urging of the superintendent and the Academic Board, recommended a major reorganization of the Naval School with the overall goal of making Annapolis more like West Point, particularly concerning discipline. The Mexican War had strengthened West Point's reputation among the American people, effectively silencing the anti–Military Academy rhetoric of the Jacksonian Democrats. West Point graduates had served their country with distinction in Mexico, prompting General Winfield Scott, general in chief and commander of the military campaign against Mexico City, to lavish praise on the academy and its graduates. "But for the science of the Military Academy," Scott declared, "this army, multiplied by four, could not have entered the capital of Mexico." In the opinion of many politicians and military leaders, the Mexican War had conclusively demonstrated the effectiveness of the West Point system of scientific military education and discipline.[71]

In response to the calls for reform at Annapolis, Secretary of the Navy William B. Preston appointed a special board to devise a reorganization plan. The board members included Commander Upshur, Professor Chauvenet, Commodore William Shubrick, Commander Buchanan, Commander Du Pont, navy surgeon William S. W. Ruschenberger, and Captain Henry Brewerton of the U.S. Army Corps of Engineers (the superintendent of West Point). The board recommended several changes, the most important of which was expanding the course of studies to four years. Midshipmen would spend two years at Annapolis before going to sea for three years. After completing the required period of sea duty, they would return to Annapolis for another two years of study. The board called for a revised academic program composed of courses taught by six departments: naval tactics and seamanship, mathematics (including navigation, astronomy, land and nautical surveying, and drawing), natural and experimental philosophy (including mechanics, steam engineering, chemistry, heat, light, electricity, mineralogy, and geology), gunnery and infantry tactics (including fencing), ethics and English (including grammar, rhetoric, history, geography, moral philosophy, and law), and modern languages. The Naval School's executive officer would receive a new title—commandant of midshipmen—to resemble West Point's commandant of cadets.[72]

Under the new regulations recommended by the board, the rules governing the school became stricter; they included prohibitions against dueling, forming social clubs, playing cards, visiting taverns and hotels in town without permission, marrying, and sporting facial hair. Punishments for violating these rules ranged from confinement to the Yard to dismissal. Conduct became a greater factor in determining final class rank, and any midshipman who received more than two hundred demerits in one year was subject to automatic dismissal. Midshipmen were permitted liberty only on Saturday afternoons until eight o'clock in the evening and could no longer wear civilian clothes on the Yard. To further the school's mission to form strong moral values, Sunday chapel attendance became mandatory. Daily inspections of the midshipmen's quarters by the superintendent or commandant became routine at Annapolis. To further enhance the school's military character, the midshipmen were organized into a battalion for infantry drill and leadership training, with midshipman officers, headed by the battalion adjutant and assistant adjutant, responsible for leading the companies. Candidates for admission had to be between the ages of thirteen and fifteen; be proficient in reading, writing, spelling, and arithmetic; be of "good moral character"; and be able to pass an entrance examination and a physical examination by the school's surgeon. Examinations for admission to the school would take place only in October, thus preventing the arrival of new midshipmen at different times during the academic year. The reorganization plan went into effect on July 1, 1850, and the Naval School officially became the United States Naval Academy.[73]

The navy made additional changes to the Naval Academy in 1851. The four years of study became consecutive and were no longer interrupted by a period of sea duty. This enabled the academy to organize classes on the civilian college model with freshmen referred to as fourth classmen or "plebes" (the name given to first-year cadets at West Point); sophomores, as third classmen; juniors, as second classmen; and seniors, as first classmen. From this point forward, midshipmen were identified by their date of graduation from the academy rather than their date of appointment as midshipmen. To appease senior officers who objected to midshipmen spending four years

This view of the U.S. Naval Academy in 1853 prominently features the former Fort Severn battery. Courtesy Special Collections and Archives Department, Nimitz Library, U.S. Naval Academy.

on shore, the navy assigned a training ship, the sloop of war *Preble*, to Annapolis, and the Naval Academy introduced the annual summer training cruise. The summer cruise was a necessary addition to the course of studies because from 1851 on, the academy would be educating young men who had never been to sea. The main benefit of the summer cruise was that it enabled midshipmen to receive practical training in a relatively safe environment, as opposed to an active warship with a military rather than an educational mission. The summer cruise provided the midshipmen with the opportunity to gain practical experience in seamanship, navigation, and gunnery, allowing them to apply the theoretical knowledge they learned in the classroom to actual ship operations. During the summer cruises, the midshipmen performed such functions as trimming, furling, and reefing the sails; serving on gun crews; navigating the ship; manning the helm; performing as quartermasters; and conducting drills for shipboard emergencies such as fire, man overboard, collision, and abandoning ship. First-class midshipmen gained valuable leadership experience by serving as officer of the deck and navigator on a rotational basis. For most midshipmen, the summer cruise represented their first experience dealing with the elements, seasickness, and the navy's less-than-palatable rations. It also offered them the opportunity to interact with other cultures and navies through port calls abroad. The midshipmen toured European naval yards, ships, and arsenals and met with European dignitaries and military officers. These cultural encounters broadened their worldview and taught them how to conduct themselves as officers, gentlemen, and representatives of the United States. In addition to the valuable naval and cultural training they provided, the summer cruises helped to silence critics of the academy's new consecutive four-year curriculum. This new system of education, combining classroom instruction with summer training cruises, offered the theoretical and practical instruction necessary for future naval officers, but in a safer, more structured environment conducive to character development.[74]

The naval academy debate effectively ended in 1845 with George Bancroft's establishment of the U.S. Naval School at Annapolis. Although the school initially resembled the earlier study hall schools operated by the navy, it clearly represented a significant evolution in American naval education. Though certainly not the equivalent of a four-year college, the Naval School at Annapolis was devoted exclusively to education and commanded by an officer whose sole responsibility was to oversee that mission. Though far less extensive than the West Point course of studies, Annapolis offered the standard curriculum that had been lacking at earlier naval schools, together with stricter discipline. Most importantly, Congress legally recognized the Naval School at Annapolis and appropriated funds for its operation. Annapolis provided the navy, for the first time, with a scientific and technical course of studies and a disciplined environment conducive to character development. Bancroft and Buchanan had succeeded in laying the foundation for the U.S. Naval Academy, but their actions were merely a first step. From 1845 to 1851, Annapolis gradually made the transition from Naval School to Naval Academy. The Naval School, like the earlier study hall schools, continued to educate older midshipmen with previous sea experience as well as a smaller number of newly appointed midshipmen who had not yet experienced life at sea. Beginning in 1851, the Naval Academy emerged in its modern form with the mission of introducing teenage young men from civilian life to the naval profession through classroom instruction and summer training cruises. But 1851 did not represent the end of reform at Annapolis. As the United States modernized and extended its influence throughout the world in the second half of the nineteenth century and throughout the twentieth century, the Naval Academy developed as well, adapting to the needs of the navy and the nation it serves.

Homecoming

It had been raining hard all morning in Annapolis on July 24, 1905, but the wet weather did not dampen the day's momentous event. Visible in Annapolis Harbor was the imposing sight of a U.S. Navy squadron of cruisers at anchor. According to an eyewitness, the sun broke through the clouds just as a flag-draped casket was carried slowly off the naval tug *Standish*. With midshipmen standing at attention along the Naval Academy's seawall, an honor guard of American and French sailors and United States Marines escorted the casket in a stately column through the Yard. The Naval Academy band played a funeral dirge as the procession made its way to the academy's new chapel, which was still under construction. The French and American sailors, acting as pallbearers, placed the casket into a brick vault across from the chapel. Marines fired a rifle volley over the vault as a bugler played taps. It was a ceremony befitting a great military hero, and the honored dead was none other than John Paul Jones, America's prodigal sea captain.[1]

Disillusioned with the Continental Congress's lack of interest in developing American naval power after the Revolutionary War, Jones left the United States in search of martial glory elsewhere. Catherine the Great of Russia, in need of a strong naval leader in her war against the Ottoman Turks, made Jones an offer he could not refuse—a rear admiral's flag and a fleet command in the Russian navy. After serving for a relatively brief period as commander of Russia's Black Sea fleet, Jones took up residence in Paris, where he died bitter and alone in 1792. Seemingly forgotten, he was buried in a simple, unmarked grave in a cemetery on the outskirts of the city. Over a century later, in February 1905, General Horace Porter, the U.S. ambassador to France, announced that he had discovered the location of Jones's burial site after a lengthy search. It turned out that the cemetery and Jones's grave had been paved over. Two months after rediscovering the lost graveyard, Porter informed President Theodore Roosevelt that Jones's body had been found and positively identified. Roosevelt was ecstatic. A naval historian and former assistant secretary of the navy, Roosevelt made it his goal as president to build a powerful U.S. Navy composed of modern battleships and led by a highly professional officer corps. Resurrecting the nation's first naval hero would serve that goal by inspiring the patriotism of the American people and providing naval officers with an outstanding professional role model. In June, Roosevelt ordered a naval squadron to France to transport Jones's remains back to the United States. On hearing the news that Jones was returning to his adopted country, several politicians petitioned Roosevelt to have their city become the revolutionary hero's final resting place. But in Roosevelt's mind, there was only one place to bury Jones: on the grounds of the U.S. Naval Academy in Annapolis.[2]

On April 24, 1906, the anniversary of Jones's 1778 victory over HMS *Drake* in the Irish Sea while in command of the *Ranger*, the Naval Academy hosted a special ceremony to honor Jones. The commemoration took place in the armory (present-day Dahlgren Hall) and included speeches by President Roosevelt, the French ambassador to the United States, General Porter, and the governor of Maryland. In attendance were cabinet secretaries, senators, congressmen, diplomats, and high-ranking naval officers—among them, Admiral George Dewey, the great naval hero of the Spanish-American War. The military honor guard for the ceremony included officers and sailors from the American and French navies, Naval Academy midshipmen, and two troops of U.S. Army cavalry. Resting on top of the casket was the gold dress sword presented to Jones by King Louis XVI of France in recognition of Jones's victory over HMS *Serapis*. Roosevelt used the occasion to advance his vision of American naval power. He criticized those politicians who opposed building and maintaining a strong navy. Pointing to the War of 1812 as evidence of the need for naval strength, Roosevelt argued that a strong navy would have prevented the war. He also portrayed John Paul Jones as the prototypical American naval officer, a professional role model for all midshipmen and naval officers. "Every officer in our Navy should know by heart the deeds of John Paul Jones," Roosevelt declared. "Every officer in our Navy should feel in each fiber of his being an eager desire to emulate the energy, the professional capacity, the indomitable determination and the dauntless scorn of death which marked John Paul Jones above all his fellows." After the arrival of Jones's remains at Annapolis, the Naval Academy required midshipmen to memorize a statement about the qualifications of an officer and a gentleman supposedly written by the legendary captain but actually fabricated by a turn-of-the-century Jones biographer.[3]

Following the ceremony, Jones's casket was placed in a temporary tomb under the main staircase in Bancroft Hall, the midshipmen's dormitory. Congress was slow to appropriate the funds needed to complete Jones's intended

President Theodore Roosevelt speaking at the John Paul Jones Commemoration Ceremony in Dahlgren Hall at the U.S. Naval Academy on April 24, 1906. Note Jones's flag-draped coffin below the speaker's dais. Courtesy U.S. Naval History and Heritage Command.

final resting place in the chapel, and the remains of America's first naval hero remained in that somewhat undignified location for almost seven years. The midshipmen, forgetting they were supposed to revere Jones, wrote a song, "Everybody Works but John Paul Jones," poking fun at the deceased hero:

> Everybody works but John Paul Jones!
> He lies around all day,
> Body pickled in alcohol
> On a permanent jag, they say,
> Middies stand around him
> Doing honor to his bones;
> Everybody works in "Crabtown"
> But John Paul Jones!

In 1913 Jones's remains were entombed in a twenty-one-ton marble sarcophagus in the crypt beneath the Naval Academy chapel in a manner reminiscent of the burial of Horatio Nelson, Britain's greatest naval hero, beneath

St. Paul's Cathedral in London. Jones would have reveled in the pomp and circumstance of the martial ceremonies conducted in his honor and in the grandeur of his final resting place at Annapolis. Although his fellow Americans had rejected his vision of American naval power while he was alive, they had finally come around to his line of thinking and given him his just reward.[4]

John Paul Jones's burial at Annapolis was the ultimate sign that the Naval Academy had become the professional and cultural heart of the U.S. Navy, which, by 1906, was well on its way to becoming the modern, powerful, and professional navy Jones had dreamed of commanding after the Revolutionary War. The academy was founded in 1845 for two reasons: first, to provide the academic background, especially in scientific and technical subjects, needed to operate a navy that was gradually becoming more modern and, second, to develop distinguished gentlemen who possessed strong moral character. These goals reflected the values and influence of the American middle class in the nineteenth century. Although many citizens had initially viewed military education as inherently un-American, the middle class embraced military academies because they provided useful knowledge and a structured environment conducive to discipline and character development.[5] By 1906, Annapolis was, like West Point, a prestigious and respected national institution.

No nineteenth-century American would ever have used the term "aristocratic" to describe the ideal U.S. naval officer. Such a statement would have been condemned as scandalous and un-American. Yet many citizens believed, in order to represent and defend the nation's interests abroad, that naval officers must possess the same level of education and gentility as their aristocratic British counterparts. If the United States was going to compete for new economic opportunities, it needed officers who were more sophisticated intellectually and socially—in a sense, more aristocratic. The goal was not to create a European-style hereditary aristocracy, but to adopt some of the characteristics of aristocracy, particularly education and refinement, for the officers of America's republican navy. Ultimately, the Naval Academy did create an exclusive, elite corps of officers, one that Peter Karsten has referred to as the "naval aristocracy." The young men admitted to Annapolis during the period from 1845 to 1925 were largely from the urban middle and upper classes. The majority of their fathers were bankers, merchants, lawyers, judges, politicians, manufacturers, physicians, educators, and military officers. Even if a young man from a relatively humble background had gained admission, he probably would not have lasted long at the academy. Agrarian and working-class boys were far more likely to fail the entrance examination than youths from more elite backgrounds because of the disparity in their preparatory education.[6]

Annapolis soon became the only path to an officer commission in the U.S. Navy. The academy continued to dominate the naval officer corps until the establishment of the U.S. Navy's ROTC program in the early twentieth century. Wars, particularly the Civil War, when enlisted men and civilians received commissions because of the great need for naval officers, created the only exception to this rule. But even during wartime, Naval Academy graduates tended to look down on their non-Annapolis colleagues. The academy forged this naval aristocracy by immersing young men in the professional military culture of the navy, by emphasizing such ideals as service to country and devotion to honor, and by developing in midshipmen the discipline and leadership skills needed to command men in battle. The academy also aimed to mold its midshipmen into gentlemen of character through various social activities, dancing and fencing lessons, and mandatory chapel services. Annapolis became the gateway to another world, a society separate from the rest of the country. The naval officer corps produced by Annapolis was a rigid class society based on obedience, conformity, and subordination. Yet, in creating an elite corps of officers, the Naval Academy was fulfilling one of its main purposes: to weed out those youths unfit for a naval career. Many young men who received appointments as midshipmen did not make it through the academy—some because of academic deficiency, others for disciplinary reasons. Still others simply could not adjust to the navy lifestyle and resigned. Less than half of the young men who received appointments to the academy from 1850 to 1894 actually graduated.[7]

Although the Naval Academy may have fostered a sense of elitism among its graduates, it also represented, like West Point, a system that, at its core, was the ultimate form of republican meritocracy. Once a young man gained admission, his ability and conduct were the only factors that determined whether he would stay. As Midshipman William McCann wrote to his father in 1848, "The boys here are the cream of America." In another letter, McCann told him: "Most of the appointees are Congressmen's sons, or, if not, favorites of those in power, but the professors are the finest set of men I have seen or known, and with them, *there is no partiality*—not its shadow." In 1902 Theodore Roosevelt praised the academy as the highest example of American meritocracy: "Annapolis is, with the sole exception of its sister academy at West Point, the most typically democratic and American school of learning and preparation that there is in the entire country. . . . There each man enters on his merits, stands on his merits, and graduates into a service where only his merit will enable him to be of value."[8]

The Naval Academy was successful in providing a higher-quality education for midshipmen and in improving discipline within the officer corps. One of the side effects of the Annapolis system, however, was that the young men it educated proved to be inferior seamen compared to their pre-1845 counterparts. Annapolis midshipmen studied seamanship and navigation, but in a more theoretical way. The only practical sea experience they acquired was through the annual summer cruises. Alfred Thayer Mahan was the most famous example of this professional trend. A member of the Naval Academy Class of 1859, Mahan was an expert on theory and a brilliant scholar. Yet he was an extremely poor seaman who had more than his share of mishaps at sea, including collisions and groundings. As Peter Karsten has observed, "The academy education made gentlemen of the neophytes, but it did not necessarily make them skilled sailors."[9]

As the United States developed as a nation and expanded its interests throughout the world, the U.S. Navy simultaneously evolved as a professional organization. Although the navy was a highly effective fighting force during the early national period, naval officership was not yet a true profession in the modern sense of the term. Military historian Allan R. Millett has argued that the following criteria make an occupation a true profession:

> (1) the occupation is a full-time and stable job, serving continuing societal needs; (2) the occupation is regarded as a lifelong calling by the practitioners, who identify themselves personally with their job subculture; (3) the occupation is organized to control performance standards and recruitment; (4) the occupation requires formal, theoretical education; (5) the occupation has a service orientation in which loyalty to standards of competence and loyalty to clients' needs are paramount; and (6) the occupation is granted a great deal of collective autonomy by the society it serves, presumably because the practitioners have proven their high ethical standards and trustworthiness.

Naval historian Ronald Spector cites the development of a specialized body of knowledge and the establishment of professional associations and journals as key components of professionalization. Based on these criteria, the navy before the War of 1812 was at best preprofessional or semiprofessional.[10]

There was no standard of education in the pre-1815 navy. Every captain and every civilian instructor had his own views on educating midshipmen. Some captains took the schooling of their midshipmen very seriously; others cared only about developing their nautical skills and assigned little importance to any subjects beyond seamanship and navigation. Civilian instructors taught what they wanted to teach or what they were capable of teaching.

Although the navy had a clear idea about the type [...]
produce, it did not have a standardized educational p[...]
goal. The navy also lacked a professional association and [...]
journal. Furthermore, during the early national period [...]
not possess a professional identity that was completely se[...]
merchant marine. It was common for naval officers to alternat[...]
navy and merchant service; in fact, the Navy Department actu[...]
aged junior officers to sail on a merchant ship to gain valuable e[...]
while on furlough from the navy. During these years, maritime sk[...]
practical knowledge dominated the navy's concept of officer developi[...]
naval officership lacked a theoretical or scientific component.

After the War of 1812, the navy began the gradual process of becoming
more professional by emphasizing the theoretical and academic aspects of
naval officership. For the army, the U.S. Military Academy provided its officer corps with a standard of scientific and technical education, an environment favorable to character development and professional socialization, a
sense of exclusiveness, and a cultural home complete with a military library
and battle monuments.[11] West Point was, and still is, the heart of the American military profession. The navy lacked a similar institution. It tried to
compensate with the Naval Lyceum, but the lyceum's resources and benefits
were limited. The founding of the Naval Academy in 1845 was a crucial step
in the navy's professional development because it established, for the first
time, an educational standard and a permanent cultural center for the naval
service. The Yard remains, to the present day, the physical manifestation
of naval tradition, helping to assimilate young people from civilian life into
the military culture of the navy. Midshipmen walk the same grounds as the
naval heroes of the past and draw inspiration from the numerous monuments
spread throughout the Yard. The Naval Academy also fostered a "spirit of
brotherhood" among naval officers—a critical component of professional socialization—that helped to reduce disputes and factions within the officer
corps. In 1882 the government expanded the Naval Academy's benefits to
the U.S. Marine Corps, and, from that time forward, midshipmen had the
option of becoming marine officers on graduation.[12]

Although the professionalization of the naval officer corps was not complete until the early twentieth century, Annapolis was a catalyst for the further development of the naval profession in the late nineteenth century. In
1873 the U.S. Naval Institute was founded by a group of officers assigned
to the Naval Academy. The institute's purpose was, and still is, to serve as
a forum for the acquisition and distribution of professional knowledge. The
institute soon began publishing a professional journal, *Proceedings*, for the

al War College was established in New-
aduate school for advanced studies in
al tactics, naval and military history,
rue profession, naval officers had to
that was unique to the naval com-
val art," moving beyond the mere
naval operations. The purpose of
iberal education in the arts and
cusing on the art and science
ce, a former Naval Academy
a distinct branch of scientific
n the comparative study of military and
ould discover the basic scientific principles that

nental navy captain, John Paul Jones had been an unfailing
cate of naval power and professionalism. But the infant United States of Jones's era simply was not ready for his ideas. Most Americans were content for their new nation to remain a simple agrarian republic, devoid of the trappings of imperialistic and militaristic Europe. Over time, however, this attitude changed. Throughout history, there has been a close connection between American nationalism and the professional development of the naval officer corps. Over the course of the nineteenth century, the navy's critical role in defending, expanding, and improving the republic led many politicians and citizens to link support for the navy with patriotism. By the time John Paul Jones's remains were returned to the United States in the early twentieth century, professional naval officers were respected symbols of the American nation and Annapolis was a revered American institution. It is fitting that Jones's final resting place is at Annapolis, the professional and cultural center of the modern U.S. Navy he first envisioned during the American Revolution.

APPENDIX

TABLE I. Analysis of the Senate Vote on the Amendment of the U.S. House of Representatives to "A Bill for the Gradual Improvement of the Navy" (March 2, 1827), by Geographic Section, Political Affiliation, and Educational Background. (The amendment would strike the provisions for a naval academy.)

	Number	Yea Votes	Nay Votes
GEOGRAPHIC SECTION			
Northern senators	15	7 (46.7%)	8 (53.3%)
Southern senators	17	9 (52.9%)	8 (47.1%)
Western senators	11	6 (54.5%)	5 (45.5%)
POLITICAL AFFILIATION			
Adams Republicans	19	5 (26.3%)	14 (73.7%)
Jackson Republicans	24	17 (70.8%)	7 (29.2%)
EDUCATIONAL BACKGROUND			
Attended college	23	11 (47.8%)	12 (52.2%)
Did not attend college	20	11 (55.0%)	9 (45.0%)

Sources: U.S. Congress, *Register of Debates in Congress* (Washington, D.C.: Gales and Seaton, 1825–37), 19th Cong., 2nd sess., 501; *Biographical Directory of the United States Congress, 1774–Present*, <http://bioguide.congress.gov>. For detailed voting lists, see William Paul Leeman, "The Long Road to Annapolis: The Naval Academy Debate and Emerging Nationalism in the United States, 1775–1845" (Ph.D. diss., Boston University, 2006), 493–96.

Note: States in the Union, 1827—*Northern states* (9): Connecticut, Maine, Massachusetts, New Hampshire, New Jersey, New York, Pennsylvania, Rhode Island, Vermont; *Southern states* (9): Alabama, Delaware, Georgia, Louisiana, Maryland, Mississippi, North Carolina, South Carolina, Virginia; *Western states* (6): Illinois, Indiana, Kentucky, Missouri, Ohio, Tennessee.

TABLE 2. Senior Class Schedule, U.S. Naval School, 1845

Mathematics (daily)	
First section	8:00–9:00 A.M.
Second section	9:00–10:00 A.M.
Natural philosophy (daily)	
Second section	8:00–9:00 A.M.
First section	9:00–10:00 A.M.
Study (daily)	10:00–11:00 A.M.
Ordnance, gunnery, and steam engineering (Tuesday, Saturday)	11:00 A.M.–12:00 NOON
Chemistry (Thursday)	11:00 A.M.–12:00 NOON
History and English composition (Monday, Wednesday, Friday)	11:00 A.M.–12:00 NOON
Recreation and dinner (daily)	12:00 NOON–1:30 P.M.
French or Spanish (Monday through Friday)	1:30–4:30 P.M.
Recreation and supper (daily)	4:30–6:00 P.M.
Study (daily)	6:00–10:00 P.M.

Source: James H. Ward to Franklin Buchanan, October 7, 1845, entry 25, box 1, folder 9, Letters Received by the Superintendent, 1845–87, Records of the U.S. Naval Academy, Record Group 405, Special Collections and Archives Department, Nimitz Library, U.S. Naval Academy.

Note: Classes met Monday through Friday and on Saturday morning. Exercises in the use of navigational and astronomical instruments were required for senior class midshipmen, but there was no regularly scheduled time for these exercises.

TABLE 3. Junior Class Schedule, U.S. Naval School, 1845

Natural philosophy lecture (daily)	8:00–9:00 A.M.
Study (daily)	9:00–10:00 A.M.
Mathematics (daily)	10:00–11:00 A.M.
Lectures on gunnery, ordnance, and chemistry (daily)	11:00 A.M.–12:00 NOON
Recreation and dinner (daily)	12 NOON–1:30 P.M.
French or Spanish (Monday through Friday)	1:30–2:30 P.M.
Geography, English grammar and composition (Monday through Friday)	2:30–4:30 P.M.
Recreation and supper (daily)	4:30–6:00 P.M.
Study (Daily)	6:00–10:00 P.M.

Source: James H. Ward to Franklin Buchanan, October 7, 1845, entry 25, box 1, folder 9, Letters Received by the Superintendent, 1845–87, Records of the U.S. Naval Academy, Record Group 405, Special Collections and Archives Department, Nimitz Library, U.S. Naval Academy.

Note: Classes met Monday through Friday and on Saturday morning. Exercises in the use of the quadrant were required for junior class midshipmen, but there was no regularly scheduled time for these exercises.

TABLE 4. Original Holdings of the U.S. Naval School Library, by Subject

Subject	Number of Titles	Percent of Total
History and biography	34	21
Naval and military science	26	16
Natural sciences	15	9
Voyages and travels	15	9
Government and law	14	9
Navigation and seamanship	12	7
Literature and languages	11	7
Mathematics	11	7
Geography	10	6
Engineering	9	6
Encyclopedias	3	2
Moral philosophy and theology	2	1
Total	162	100

Source: Franklin Buchanan to George Bancroft, September 3, 1846, including a "Catalogue of the Library of the Naval School" (typescript), Library Original Holdings and Early Textbooks File, Records of the U.S. Naval Academy, Record Group 405, Special Collections and Archives Department, Nimitz Library, U.S. Naval Academy.

Note: The "Engineering" heading includes books on steam engines, naval architecture, civil engineering, and manufacturing. The Naval School library also subscribed to four periodicals: the *Army and Navy Chronicle*, the *Military and Naval Magazine of the United States*, the *Naval Chronicle*, and the *North American Review*.

NOTES

A Note on Quotations from Primary Sources

I have preserved the original spelling, capitalization, and punctuation in all text quoted from eighteenth- or nineteenth-century sources with the following exception: abbreviations have been spelled out.

Abbreviations

ASP:MA   U.S. Congress. *American State Papers: Military Affairs.* 7 vols.
Washington, D.C.: Gales and Seaton, 1832–61.

ASP:NA   U.S. Congress. *American State Papers: Naval Affairs.* 4 vols.
Washington, D.C.: Gales and Seaton, 1834–61.

CG   U.S. Congress. *Congressional Globe.* 44 vols. Washington, D.C.:
Blair and Rives, 1834–73.

CWM   Earl Gregg Swem Library, College of William and Mary,
Williamsburg, Va.

HML   Hagley Museum and Library, Wilmington, Del.

HSP   Historical Society of Pennsylvania, Philadelphia

LC   Library of Congress, Washington, D.C.

MHS   Massachusetts Historical Society, Boston

NA   National Archives, Washington, D.C.

RG   Record Group

USMA   U.S. Military Academy Library, West Point, N.Y.

USNA   Nimitz Library, U.S. Naval Academy, Annapolis, Md.

Introduction

1. George Bancroft to S. A. Allibone, October 11, 1856, Bancroft Papers, MHS.

2. The annual number of visitors is from the U.S. Naval Academy's Armel-Leftwich Visitor Center, e-mail correspondence with the author, July 1, 2004. The distinguished graduate information is from the U.S. Naval Academy website <http://www.usna.edu/Admissions/ notablegrads.htm>. On the integration of minorities and women at the academy, see Gelfand, *Sea Change at Annapolis.*

3. For the most detailed examinations of the academy's origins, see Sweetman, *U.S. Naval Academy,* 3–17; Todorich, *Spirited Years,* 1–18; Soley, *Historical Sketch,* 7–61; Marshall, *History of the United States Naval Academy,* 11–18; Hart, "Founding of the United States Naval Academy"; Paullin, "Beginnings of the United States Naval Academy"; Brown, "Half Century of Frustration"; and Sturdy, "Establishment of the Naval School."

4. My interpretation of nationalism is based primarily on the work of Benedict Anderson (*Imagined Communities*), who defines a nation as "an imagined political community" (p. 6), and Max Savelle (*Seeds of Liberty*), who characterizes nationalism as a "psychological phenomenon" (p. 554). My ideas have also been informed by Hans Kohn, *Idea of Nationalism*; Nagel, *This Sacred Trust*; Royster, *A Revolutionary People at War*; Colley, *Britons*; Waldstreicher, *In the Midst of Perpetual Fetes*; Potter, "The Historian's Use of Nationalism and Vice Versa"; and

Steele, "Thomas Jefferson and the Making of an American Nationalism." The term "armed ambassadors" is from "Report of the Committee on Naval Affairs on the Establishment of a Naval School," February 10, 1845, S. Doc. 92, *Congressional Serial Set*, No. 451, 28th Cong., 2nd sess., 3:2.

5. McCoy, *Elusive Republic*, 5–7; Elkins and McKitrick, *Age of Federalism*, 4, 13; Welter, *Mind of America*, 77; Waldstreicher, *In the Midst of Perpetual Fetes*, 2–3; Steele, "Thomas Jefferson and the Making of an American Nationalism," 10.

6. Richard H. Kohn, *Eagle and Sword*, 296; Skelton, *American Profession of Arms*, 3; Skaggs, *Oliver Hazard Perry*, 212; Cunliffe, *Soldiers and Civilians*, 25–26, 70–75, 392–95, 402–3 (quotation, 68).

7. Cunliffe, *Soldiers and Civilians*, 101, 179; Tocqueville, *Democracy in America*, 2:278.

8. *CG*, 27th Cong., 2nd sess., app., 358.

9. Don Higginbotham, "Military Education before West Point," in Robert M. S. McDonald, *Thomas Jefferson's Military Academy*, 23–29.

10. Ibid., 24–39; Symonds, *Navalists and Antinavalists*, 87–88, 105–33.

11. Cooper, *History of the Navy*, 1:xiii; Nagel, *This Sacred Trust*, 5–7; Skaggs, *Oliver Hazard Perry*, 20, 212. See also Appleby, *Inheriting the Revolution*.

12. McKee, *Gentlemanly and Honorable*, 48–50, 167–70; Soley, *Historical Sketch*, 32.

13. Ekirch, *Idea of Progress*, 26–27, 32–37. The term "crucibles of character" is from Mintz, *Moralists and Modernizers*, xviii.

14. *National Intelligencer*, January 17, 1843; Nagel, *This Sacred Trust*, 61; *Army and Navy Chronicle*, August 20, 1835, 271.

15. Fleming, *West Point*, 15; Cunliffe, *Soldiers and Civilians*, 387–88; Masland and Radway, *Soldiers and Scholars*, 85.

16. Skaggs, *Oliver Hazard Perry*, 18–19.

Prologue

1. The two best biographies of Jones are Morison, *John Paul Jones*, and Thomas, *John Paul Jones*.

2. James C. Bradford, "John Paul Jones: Honor and Professionalism," in Bradford, *Command under Sail*, 39–40.

3. Morison, *John Paul Jones*, 3–11; Thomas, *John Paul Jones*, 13–18.

4. Morison, *John Paul Jones*, 12–17; Thomas, *John Paul Jones*, 17–22.

5. Morison, *John Paul Jones*, 19–21; Thomas, *John Paul Jones*, 23–25.

6. Morison, *John Paul Jones*, 23–24; Thomas, *John Paul Jones*, 30–34.

7. Morison, *John Paul Jones*, 23, 25–27, 31; Fowler, *Rebels under Sail*, 1–2, 4, 8.

8. Butterfield, *Diary and Autobiography of John Adams*, 2:370–71; Morison, *John Paul Jones*, 8, 17, 71–72, 201–2; Barnes, *Fanning's Narrative*, 117. The term "martial equivalency" is from Thomas, *John Paul Jones*, 86.

9. Thomas, *John Paul Jones*, 7–11, 29; Bradford, "John Paul Jones," 40. Abigail Adams quoted in Morison, *John Paul Jones*, 277.

10. Barnes, *Fanning's Narrative*, 70, 106; Thomas, *John Paul Jones*, 37–39 (quotation, 38). For the origins of the term "midshipman," see Lovette, *Naval Customs*, 250–51.

11. Jones to Joseph Hewes, May 19, 1776 (reel 1, 23), Jones to the Marine Board, January 21, 1777 (reel 1, 93), and Jones, "A Plan for the Regulation and Equipment of the Navy," April 7, 1777 (reel 1, 122), all in Bradford, *Papers of John Paul Jones*.

12. Jones to Hector McNeill, May 25, 1782, ibid., reel 7, 1402.

13. Gawalt, *John Paul Jones' Memoir*, 64; Jones to Robert Morris, November 29, 1782 (reel 7, 1439), Morris to Jones, December 5, 1782 (reel 7, 1441), Jones to Morris, February 27, 1783

(reel 7, 1448), and Jones to Hector McNeill, April 26, 1783 (reel 7, 1456), all in Bradford, *Papers of John Paul Jones*. See also Morison, *John Paul Jones*, 331–33.

14. Draft of Jones to Robert Morris, [October 3–4, 1783], in Bradford, *Papers of John Paul Jones*, reel 7, 1480.

15. John Adams to the President of Congress, July 6, 1780, in Wharton, *Revolutionary Diplomatic Correspondence*, 3:833–34; Adams to Jones, August 12, 1782, in Bradford, *Papers of John Paul Jones*, reel 7, 1419.

16. Higginbotham, *War of American Independence*, 8; James C. Bradford, "Navies of the American Revolution," in Hagan, *In Peace and War*, 22; Powers, "Decline and Extinction of American Naval Power," 186.

Chapter 1

1. Stuart, *War and American Thought*, 38, 47–48; Perkins, *Creation of a Republican Empire*, 8–15.

2. J. R. Western, "War on a New Scale: Professionalism in Armies, Navies, and Diplomacy," in Cobban, *The Eighteenth Century*, 182, 209–10.

3. Bailyn, *Ideological Origins*, 34–54, 61–63. For an overview of the British influence on American attitudes toward the military, see Ekirch, *Civilian and the Military*, 3–17.

4. Royster, *A Revolutionary People at War*, 23, 255–57, 327, 329–30, 353–54; Higginbotham, *War of American Independence*, 439.

5. Wood, *Radicalism of the American Revolution*, 240–41; Colley, *Britons*, 186.

6. Colley, *Britons*, 178, 184–85.

7. Cress, *Citizens in Arms*, 75; Royster, *A Revolutionary People at War*, 35–36.

8. Cress, *Citizens in Arms*, 89, 93.

9. Worthington Chauncey Ford, *Journals of the Continental Congress*, 25:953–54; Hamilton to Washington, April 9, 1783, in Syrett, *Papers of Alexander Hamilton*, 3:322.

10. Richard H. Kohn, *Eagle and Sword*, 42–45; Washington to Hamilton, May 2, 1783, in Fitzpatrick, *Writings of George Washington*, 26:374–76.

11. Simons, *Liberal Education*, 31–33; Huntington, *Soldier and the State*, 24–25.

12. Callahan, *Henry Knox*, 20–25, 72 (quotation).

13. Henry Knox, "Hints for the Improvement of the Artillery of the United States," September 27, 1776, Knox Papers, reel 3, MHS; Knox to John Adams, May 16, 1776, Adams Papers, reel 346, MHS; Charles Francis Adams, *Works of John Adams*, 9:384 (quotation from Adams to Knox, June 2, 1776).

14. Butterfield, *Diary and Autobiography of John Adams*, 3:437 (quotations, 445–46); Adams to Knox, October 1, 1776, Adams Papers, reel 89, MHS; Ambrose, *Duty, Honor, Country*, 8–9.

15. Pickering to Washington, April 22, 1783, Pickering Papers, reel 5, MHS; Clinton to Washington, April 17, 1783, Washington Papers, LC.

16. Knox to Washington, April 17, 1783, Knox Papers, reel 12, MHS; Von Steuben to Washington, April 21, 1783, Washington Papers, LC; Von Steuben, "Projet pour L'établissement des academies et manufactures militaires," n.d., Papers of the Continental Congress, roll 45, RG 360, NA.

17. Washington to Hamilton, May 2, 1783, in Fitzpatrick, *Writings of George Washington*, 26:396–97; Ambrose, *Duty, Honor, Country*, 6.

18. Worthington Chauncey Ford, *Journals of the Continental Congress*, 25:722–44; Cress, *Citizens in Arms*, 87–88; Richard H. Kohn, *Eagle and Sword*, 47.

19. Richard H. Kohn, *Eagle and Sword*, 40–41, 50–51; Pappas, *To the Point*, 7–8.

20. Richard H. Kohn, *Eagle and Sword*, 52, 68–70, 277–78, 296; Fowler, *Jack Tars*, 2–4.

21. Cress, *Citizens in Arms*, 95–97; Washington to James Madison, November 5, 1786, in Fitzpatrick, *Writings of George Washington*, 29:52.

22. For the powers of Congress, see U.S. Constitution, Article I, Section 8. For the president's role as commander in chief, see Article II, Section 2. For restrictions on the military authority of the states, see Article I, Section 10. For a discussion of the Constitution and its provisions concerning military authority in the United States, see Ekirch, *Civilian and the Military*, 24–31.

23. Richard H. Kohn, *Eagle and Sword*, 9–13; Cress, *Citizens in Arms*, 112–13.

24. Madison, "A Candid State of Parties," September 26, 1792, in Hunt, *Writings of James Madison*, 6:115–16.

25. Madison, "Letters of Helvidius, No. IV," September 14, 1793, ibid., 6:174.

26. Fowler, *Jack Tars*, 13–14; Washington, [Proposed Address to Congress], April 1789, in Fitzpatrick, *Writings of George Washington*, 30:302; Smelser, *Congress Founds the Navy*, 29–30.

27. U.S. Congress, *Annals of Congress*, 1st Cong., 2nd sess., 1527, 1704–9, 1915 (quotation, 1707).

28. Henry Knox, "Organization of the Militia," January 18, 1790, *ASP:MA*, 1:7–8.

29. Ibid., 8–9 (quotations, 13); Cunliffe, *Soldiers and Civilians*, 183; Smelser, *Congress Founds the Navy*, 29; U.S. Congress, *Annals of Congress*, 2nd Cong., 1st sess., app., 1393.

30. G. Terry Sharrer, "The Search for a Naval Policy, 1783–1812," in Hagan, *In Peace and War*, 29–30; Tucker and Hendrickson, *Empire of Liberty*, vii–viii, 31–32; Perkins, *Creation of a Republican Empire*, 6–8, 91–95, 118–22.

31. Symonds, *Confederate Admiral*, 12; Sharrer, "Search for a Naval Policy," 30–31; Fowler, *Jack Tars*, 6–9, 15–16.

32. Worthington Chauncey Ford, *Journals of the Continental Congress*, 29:842–44; Jefferson to James Monroe, August 11, 1786, in Boyd et al., *Papers of Thomas Jefferson*, 10:225; Fowler, *Jack Tars*, 8–9; Powers, "Decline and Extinction of American Naval Power," 247–49.

33. Sharrer, "Search for a Naval Policy," 30; Fowler, *Jack Tars*, 15–16; Symonds, *Navalists and Antinavalists*, 29; U.S. Congress, *Annals of Congress*, 3rd Cong., 1st sess., 154.

34. Symonds, *Navalists and Antinavalists*, 11–13; Hamilton, Madison, and Jay, *The Federalist*, 64–65.

35. U.S. Congress, *Annals of Congress*, 3rd Cong., 1st sess., 486–90 (quotation, 490).

36. Ibid., 3rd Cong., 1st sess., app., 1426–28.

37. For Truxtun's background, see Ferguson, *Truxtun*, 1–99. Anticipating that his country would once again require a naval force, Morris essentially "privatized" the American navy, which Congress had officially dissolved at the end of the Revolutionary War. He and some of his business partners hired former naval officers to command their merchant ships. This arrangement was beneficial not only for Morris and his partners but also for the nation. Morris's merchant business focused on opening new markets in China, which created new economic opportunities for Americans. At the same time, employment in Morris's merchant fleet helped former Continental naval officers keep their seamanship and navigation skills sharp while also providing practical training at sea for future naval officers. Morris's plan was successful. When the U.S. Navy was established in 1794, several of the men who received officer commissions had sailed in Morris's "private navy" including Truxtun and John Barry, two of the finest captains in the early national navy. See Elizabeth M. Nuxoll, "The Naval Movement of the Confederation Era," in Dudley and Crawford, *Early Republic and the Sea*, 13–14.

38. Truxtun, *Remarks, Instructions, and Examples*, xvi–xviii; Knox, *Naval Documents Related to the Quasi-War*, 1:302 (quotation from Truxtun to William Cowper, August 16, 1798).

39. Truxtun to Thomas Robinson Jr., April 18, 1799, printed in McKee, *Gentlemanly and Honorable*, 166–67; Truxtun to James McHenry, March 3, 1797, in Steiner, *Life and Correspondence of James McHenry*, 251–52.

40. Sharrer, "Search for a Naval Policy," 32–33; Symonds, *Navalists and Antinavalists*, 39–40; Washington to the Senate and House of Representatives, March 15, 1796, in Richardson, *Messages and Papers*, 1:193.

41. U.S. Congress, *Annals of Congress*, 4th Cong., 1st sess., 874, 877, 883–84; Symonds, *Navalists and Antinavalists*, 43–44; Sharrer, "Search for a Naval Policy," 33.

42. Hamilton, Madison, and Jay, *The Federalist*, 65.

43. Fowler, *Jack Tars*, 30–32; Sharrer, "Search for a Naval Policy," 33–34.

44. Symonds, *Navalists and Antinavalists*, 69–70; Fowler, *Jack Tars*, 36; Cress, *Citizens in Arms*, 139.

45. DeConde, *Quasi-War*, 96; Adams to the Boston Marine Society, September 7, 1798, Adams Papers, reel 391, MHS.

46. Fowler, *Jack Tars*, 27–28; Symonds, *Navalists and Antinavalists*, 71–72; DeConde, *Quasi-War*, 90; Smelser, *Congress Founds the Navy*, 158; Elkins and McKitrick, *Age of Federalism*, 628–30 (quotation, 630).

47. U.S. Congress, *Annals of Congress*, 5th Cong., 2nd sess., app., 3724–25; DeConde, *Quasi-War*, 130; Love, *History of the U.S. Navy*, 1:57–71; Fowler, *Jack Tars*, 58.

48. Cress, *Citizens in Arms*, 139; Henrich, "Triumph of Ideology," 84 (quotation).

49. *Philadelphia Aurora*, April 2, 1798; Henrich, "Triumph of Ideology," 86–87.

50. Ambrose, *Duty, Honor, Country*, 10–11.

51. Jefferson, "Anas," in Lipscomb and Bergh, *Writings of Thomas Jefferson*, 1:409–11.

52. Washington, "Eighth Annual Message," December 7, 1796, in Richardson, *Messages and Papers*, 1:202–3.

53. Mitchell, *Alexander Hamilton*, vii–viii; Skelton, *American Profession of Arms*, 96. Adams was never comfortable with Hamilton's position in the expanded army. In fact, he later admitted that one reason he favored the navy over the army was his distrust of Hamilton, whom Adams considered a potential Caesar: "I have always cried, Ships! Ships! Hamilton's hobby horse was Troops! Troops! With all the vanity and timidity of Cicero, all the debauchery of Marc Anthony and all the ambition of Julius Caesar, his object was command of fifty thousand men. My object was the defense of my country, and that alone, which I knew could be affected only by a navy." Quoted in Hagan, *This People's Navy*, 43.

54. Hamilton to Oliver Wolcott Jr., June 5, 1798, in Syrett, *Papers of Alexander Hamilton*, 21:486.

55. Hamilton to James McHenry, November 23, 1799, ibid., 24:69–73; Washington to Hamilton, December 12, 1799, in Fitzpatrick, *Writings of George Washington*, 37:473.

56. U.S. Congress, *Annals of Congress*, 6th Cong., app., 1398–99, 1404.

57. Ibid., 1399–1403.

58. Ibid., 1416, 1420–21 (quotations, 1418).

59. McHenry to Hamilton, February 18, 1800, in Syrett, *Papers of Alexander Hamilton*, 24:236; U.S. Congress, *Annals of Congress*, 6th Cong., 1st sess., 690. According to the index of the 6th Congress, the House did not take up the military academy proposal in the second session.

60. U.S. Congress, *Annals of Congress*, 5th Cong., 2nd sess., app., 3787; Samuel Dexter to John Adams, July 16, 1800, Adams Papers, reel 398, MHS.

61. John Adams to Samuel Dexter, July 25, 1800, in Charles Francis Adams, *Works of John Adams*, 9:65, Adams to Benjamin Stoddert, September 26, 1799, ibid., 9:37, Adams to Stoddert, March 31, 1800, ibid., 9:47.

62. McCullough, *John Adams*, 499; Charles Francis Adams, *Works of John Adams*, 9:586 (quotation from Adams to Thomas Truxtun, November 30, 1802).

63. McCullough, *John Adams*, 177–88.

64. Ibid.; Butterfield, *Diary and Autobiography of John Adams*, 4:17–18 (quotations).

65. Butterfield, *Diary and Autobiography of John Adams*, 4:10.

66. Skelton, *American Profession of Arms*, 7; U.S. Congress, *Annals of Congress*, 6th Cong., 2nd sess., app., 1557–59; Anderson, "John Adams and the Creation of the American Navy," 133–34.

67. For an in-depth study of the Federalists and their military policies, see Richard H. Kohn, *Eagle and Sword*.

68. McCoy, *Elusive Republic*, 175–76; Jefferson to Joseph Priestley, January 18, 1800, in Lipscomb and Bergh, *Writings of Thomas Jefferson*, 10:139.

69. Stagg, *Mr. Madison's War*, 127; Tucker and Hendrickson, *Empire of Liberty*, 16–17.

70. Richard H. Kohn, *Eagle and Sword*, 302–3; Stuart, *Half-way Pacifist*, 3–4.

71. Love, *History of the U.S. Navy*, 1:72–85.

72. U.S. Congress, *Annals of Congress*, 7th Cong., 1st sess., 1306–12 (quotation, 1312); Stagg, *Mr. Madison's War*, 130 n. 30.

73. For the history of West Point prior to the establishment of the Military Academy, see Crackel, *West Point*, 5–28, and Forman, *West Point*, 3–19.

74. Jefferson to Joseph Priestley, January 18, 1800, in Lipscomb and Bergh, *Writings of Thomas Jefferson*, 10:140–41.

75. Huntington, *Soldier and the State*, 198; Molloy, "Technical Education," 175.

76. Jefferson to Monroe, June 18, 1813, in Lipscomb and Bergh, *Writings of Thomas Jefferson*, 13:261; Jefferson to Joseph Cabell, October 24, 1817, including "A Bill for Establishing a System of Public Education" (241), "Report of the Commissioners Appointed to Fix the Site of the University of Virginia," August 4, 1818 (252, 256), and "Organization and Government of the University," April 7, 1824 (275), all in Honeywell, *Educational Work of Thomas Jefferson*.

77. Jefferson to Fulton, August 16, 1807, in Lipscomb and Bergh, *Writings of Thomas Jefferson*, 11:328. Jefferson's personal library included several works on naval and military science covering such topics as naval architecture, steam engines, artillery and infantry tactics, naval and military history, and military organization, in addition to Fulton's pamphlets on torpedoes and submarines and the published memoirs of famous European officers. See Sowerby, *Catalogue of the Library of Thomas Jefferson*, 1:517–28, 547, 550–51.

78. Barlow, *Prospectus of a National Institution*, 34, 36–37; Honeywell, *Educational Work of Thomas Jefferson*, 62–63.

79. Jonathan Williams quoted in Skelton, *American Profession of Arms*, 101.

80. Ambrose, *Duty, Honor, Country*, 24–27; Fleming, *West Point*, 16–17, 19; Pappas, *To the Point*, 32.

81. Jonathan Williams, "Report on the Progress and Present State of the Military Academy," March 14, 1808, U.S. Congress, *Annals of Congress*, 10th Cong., 1st sess., app., 2810.

82. Ibid., 2811–12.

83. Jefferson to the Senate and House of Representatives, March 18, 1808, in Richardson, *Messages and Papers*, 1:445.

84. Molloy, "Technical Education," 286, 325–30; Fleming, *West Point*, 19–20. Theodore J. Crackel (*West Point*, 70) has argued that Eustis's actions toward West Point were the result of incompetence more than actual hostility.

85. Smelser, *Congress Founds the Navy*, 29; McKee, *Gentlemanly and Honorable*, 160–64; Symonds, *Confederate Admiral*, 22; Robert Smith, "Circular to Midshipmen," July 28, 1803, in Knox, *Naval Documents Related to the . . . Barbary Powers*, 2:500–501.

86. Jefferson, *Notes on the State of Virginia*, 175–76; Stagg, *Mr. Madison's War*, 135. Jefferson's policies regarding the navy, specifically his gunboat program, have been sharply criticized by some navalist historians as shortsighted and inadequate. These historians have argued that Jefferson severely undermined the navy's effectiveness. For this line of thinking, see Sprout and Sprout, *Rise of American Naval Power*, and Albion, *Makers of Naval Policy*. For more balanced

viewpoints, see Symonds, *Navalists and Antinavalists*, and Smith, *"For the Purposes of Defense."*

87. Jefferson, "Fourth Annual Message," November 8, 1804, in Richardson, *Messages and Papers*, 1:372; Smith, *"For the Purposes of Defense,"* 1-2, 6-21; Symonds, *Navalists and Antinavalists*, 105-8; Forrest McDonald, *Presidency of Thomas Jefferson*, 44; Jefferson to the Senate and House of Representatives, February 10, 1807, in Richardson, *Messages and Papers*, 1:419-21.

88. Jefferson to Robert Smith, October 24, 1805, Jefferson Papers, LC; Jefferson to Albert Gallatin, [November 1805], including "A Bill for Establishing a Naval Militia," in Henry Adams, *Writings of Albert Gallatin*, 1:272-75. The term "citizen seamen" is from Thomas Jefferson, "Report of the Secretary of State on the Privileges and Restrictions on the Commerce of the United States in Foreign Countries," December 16, 1793, U.S. Congress, *Annals of Congress*, 3rd Cong., app., 1296-97.

89. Smith, *"For the Purposes of Defense,"* 65-72; Robert Smith to Jefferson, [November 14, 1805], Jefferson Papers, LC.

90. Crackel, *Mr. Jefferson's Army*, 34-38, 58-62, 71-73.

91. Prendergast, "Navy and Civil Liberty," 1264-66; Jefferson to James Monroe, August 11, 1786, in Boyd et al., *Papers of Thomas Jefferson*, 10:225.

92. Henrich, "Triumph of Ideology," 331-33; Coxe, *Thoughts on the Subject of Naval Power*, 6-7, 9-10.

93. Jefferson to Adams, November 1, 1822, in Cappon, *Adams-Jefferson Letters*, 2:585.

94. Jefferson to Joel Barlow, December 10, 1807, in Lipscomb and Bergh, *Writings of Thomas Jefferson*, 11:400-401; Joseph J. Ellis, *American Sphinx*, 105 6, 142.

95. Truxtun to Pickering, February 1, 1806, Pickering Papers, reel 27, MHS.

96. Truxtun quoted in Ferguson, *Truxtun*, 128.

Chapter 2

1. Stewart to William Reed, November 26, 1814, *ASP:NA*, 1:356; Skaggs, *Oliver Hazard Perry*, 213.

2. McKee, *Gentlemanly and Honorable*, 210-15.

3. Rodger, *Wooden World*, 263-65; Lewis, *Navy in Transition*, 103; Barnard, *Military Schools*, 628.

4. Cormack, *Revolution and Political Conflict*, 36, 43; Huntington, *Soldier and the State*, 42-43.

5. Jefferson to Elizabeth Chamberlayne, November 24, 1805, Jefferson Papers, LC; Stoddert to Moses Tryon, February 7, 1799, Letters Sent by the Secretary of the Navy to Officers, roll 1, Naval Records Collection, RG 45, NA; McKee, *Gentlemanly and Honorable*, 45-48.

6. McKee, *Gentlemanly and Honorable*, 68-71, 477; Kett, *Rites of Passage*, 31.

7. McKee, *Gentlemanly and Honorable*, 43-45; Smith to Isaac Chauncey, September 16, 1805, Letters Sent by the Secretary of the Navy to Officers, roll 7, NA.

8. McKee, *Gentlemanly and Honorable*, 75-81; Skaggs, *Thomas Macdonough*, 22-27; Merrill, *Du Pont*, 4-5.

9. McKee, *Gentlemanly and Honorable*, 40-43; Smith to Carroll, April 24, 1804, and Smith to Clinton, November 4, 1805, Miscellaneous Letters Sent by the Secretary of the Navy, roll 3, Naval Records Collection, RG 45, NA.

10. U.S. Congress, *Annals of Congress*, 14th Cong., 1st sess., 441.

11. McKee, *Gentlemanly and Honorable*, 81-83; Merrill, *Du Pont*, 5.

12. McKee, *Gentlemanly and Honorable*, 59-67, 474.

13. Ibid., 47-48, 96-103.

14. Barnes, *Fanning's Narrative*, i; McKee, *Gentlemanly and Honorable*, 89-95; Harold D.

Langley, "Robert F. Stockton: Naval Officer and Reformer," in Bradford, *Command under Sail*, 275; Williams, *Maury*, 23.

15. McKee, *Gentlemanly and Honorable*, 109–15.

16. Ibid., 119–23.

17. Williams, *Maury*, 42; Bowditch, *New American Practical Navigator*. The term "midshipman's Bible" is from Philbrick, *Sea of Glory*, 44. The midshipman pay rate is from McKee, *Gentlemanly and Honorable*, 335.

18. For descriptions of life on board a U.S. Navy ship of the early republic, see Fowler, *Jack Tars*, 126–40; McKee, *Gentlemanly and Honorable*, 119–49; and Melville's novel, *White-Jacket*, based on the author's own experience as a seaman on board the frigate *United States* from 1843 to 1844. The crew complement of the *United States* is from Valle, *Rocks and Shoals*, 73.

19. Paullin, *Paullin's History*, 236–37.

20. Fowler, *Jack Tars*, 131; Jones, *Sketches of Naval Life*, 1:94.

21. McKee, *Gentlemanly and Honorable*, 34–35, 122 (quotation); Morison, *"Old Bruin,"* 28; Benjamin, *United States Naval Academy*, 56–60.

22. McKee, *Gentlemanly and Honorable*, 34, 169; Paullin, *Paullin's History*, 136.

23. "U.S. Navy Regulations Issued by Command of President Thomas Jefferson," January 25, 1802, in Knox, *Naval Documents Related to the . . . Barbary Powers*, 2:36.

24. McKee, *Gentlemanly and Honorable*, 127; Symonds, *Confederate Admiral*, 13; Morison, *"Old Bruin"* (quotation, 88).

25. McKee, *Gentlemanly and Honorable*, 153, 167–70 (quotation, 167); Skaggs, *Oliver Hazard Perry*, 18–19. The term "directed doing" is from Burr, "Education in the Early Navy," 213.

26. McKee, *Gentlemanly and Honorable*, 155–56. The view that frigates and ships of the line were the best learning environments for midshipmen was one of the reasons why many naval officers opposed the Jefferson administration's emphasis on gunboats. Since gunboats operated in harbors and coastal areas, they provided no real opportunity for seamanship training. Gunboats were usually commanded by senior midshipmen or sailing masters, so there were no captains or lieutenants on board to serve as proper role models. Lastly, because only one or two officers were assigned to each gunboat, professional socialization was rare.

27. "U.S. Navy Regulations," January 25, 1802, in Knox, *Naval Documents Related to the . . . Barbary Powers*, 2:34; Drury, "Famous Chaplain Teachers of Midshipmen," 681–82, 689; Burr, "Education in the Early Navy," 111; Sweetman, *U.S. Naval Academy*, 8.

28. Burr, "Education in the Early Navy," 129–32, 135–36; Jones, *Sketches of Naval Life*, 1:93–94, 2:261–62; Benjamin, *United States Naval Academy*, 106.

29. Williams, *Maury*, 52; McKee, *Gentlemanly and Honorable*, 194–96, 201–2; Morison, *"Old Bruin,"* 28; Soley, *Historical Sketch*, 9–11; Sweetman, *U.S. Naval Academy*, 8.

30. Burr, "Education in the Early Navy," 141–43; McKee, *Gentlemanly and Honorable*, 168–69, 195; Jones, *Sketches of Naval Life*, 2:272–74; Langley, "Robert F. Stockton," 277.

31. Merrill, *Du Pont*, 11; Skallerup, *Books Afloat and Ashore*, 125; McKee, *Edward Preble*, 219–21; Skaggs, *Oliver Hazard Perry*, 152–53; George C. Read, "Book of Notes and Remarks on Sundry Topics," HSP.

32. Benjamin, *United States Naval Academy*, 107; Alexander Murray to the Midshipmen on Board the *Insurgente*, August 8, 1799, in Knox, *Naval Documents Related to the Quasi-War*, 4:48–49.

33. White, *Jeffersonians*, 285 (quotation); Williams, *Maury*, 44–45.

34. McKee, *Gentlemanly and Honorable*, 223–24; Truxtun, *Remarks, Instructions, and Examples*, xvii; Morison, *"Old Bruin,"* 28.

35. Jones, *Sketches of Naval Life*, 2:276–77; Cady Logbook, LC; Mason Journal, Stockton Journal, and Stockton Logbook, Samuel Eliot Morison Memorial Library, USS *Constitution* Museum.

36. Jones, *Sketches of Naval Life*, 1:19, 45, 212; Wines, *Two Years*, 1:35; Williams, *Maury*, 52–53; Benjamin, *United States Naval Academy*, 66–70; Burr, "Education in the Early Navy," 84–85.

37. Burr, "Education in the Early Navy," 84–87; Symonds, *Confederate Admiral*, 22.

38. McKee, *Gentlemanly and Honorable*, 123–29, 397–411; Schneller, *Farragut*, 13–14; Symonds, *Confederate Admiral*, 10–11, 13–14.

39. Morison, *"Old Bruin"*, 28; Williams, *Maury*, 52; Jones, *Sketches of Naval Life*, 2:261; Wines, *Two Years*, 1:18; McKee, *Gentlemanly and Honorable*, 139–40. Winter later recovered his mental health and was restored to active duty after completing a probationary period in the merchant service.

40. McKee, *Gentlemanly and Honorable*, 289–90, 292; Allison, *Stephen Decatur*, 47–54.

41. Paullin, *Paullin's History*, 150; McKee, *Gentlemanly and Honorable*, 40 (quotation).

42. Samuel Smith [Acting Secretary of the Navy] to Richard Dale, May 20, 1801, Knox, *Naval Documents Related to the . . . Barbary Powers*, 1:465; Robert Smith to Preble, August 2, 1803, in McKee, *Edward Preble*, 131–32.

43. Burr, "Education in the Early Navy," 189; Schroeder, *Commodore John Rodgers*, 8–13, 70–72, 127.

44. Christopher McKee, "Edward Preble and the 'Boys': The Officer Corps of 1812 Revisited," in Bradford, *Command under Sail*, 71–96; Heitzmann, "In-Service Naval Officer Education," 111; Skaggs, *Thomas Macdonough*, 36–47.

45. Allison, *Stephen Decatur*, 29–42; Craig Symonds, "William S. Bainbridge: Bad Luck or Fatal Flaw?" in Bradford, *Command under Sail*, 97–125.

Chapter 3

1. John M. Niles (the contemporary observer) quoted in White, *Jeffersonians*, 272. For relatively brief but useful descriptions of naval operations during the War of 1812, see Fowler, *Jack Tars*, 162–264; Love, *History of the U.S. Navy*, 1:101–29; Howarth, *To Shining Sea*, 88–124; and Hagan, *This People's Navy*, 78–90. The best overall history of the war is Hickey, *War of 1812*.

2. Gholson to the Freeholders of the Congressional District Composed of the Counties of Mecklenburg, Lunenburg, and Brunswick [Va.], August 2, 1813, in Cunningham, *Circular Letters of Congressmen*, 2:853; Hendricks to John K. Graham, April 10, 1820, ibid., 3:1106; Jefferson to Adams, May 27, 1813, in Cappon, *Adams-Jefferson Letters*, 2:324.

3. Fowler, *Jack Tars*, 261–62; White, *Jeffersonians*, 273–76; Eckert, "William Jones," 170–71; Frank L. Owsley Jr., "William Jones," in Coletta, *American Secretaries of the Navy*, 1:101.

4. Symonds, *Navalists and Antinavalists*, 184–89, 199; White, *Jeffersonians*, 273–75; Owsley, "William Jones," 102–3, 105–8.

5. William Jones, "Re-Organization and Extension of the Navy, the Establishment of a Board of Inspectors, and a Naval Academy," November 15, 1814, *ASP:NA*, 1:323.

6. McKee, *Gentlemanly and Honorable*, 203–9; Robert Smith, "Circular to Midshipmen," July 28, 1803, in Knox, *Naval Documents Related to the . . . Barbary Powers*, 2:501; Drury, "Famous Chaplain Teachers of Midshipmen," 683–85; Skallerup, *Books Afloat and Ashore*, 124.

7. Evans to Reed, December 6, 1814 (1:357), Tingey to Reed, December 10, 1814 (1:359), and Stewart to Reed, November 26, 1814 (1:356), all in *ASP:NA*.

8. U.S. Congress, *Annals of Congress*, 13th Cong. 3rd sess., app., 1908; Stagg, *Mr. Madison's War*, 505–6.

9. William Gaston, Circular, April 19, 1814, in Cunningham, *Circular Letters of Congressmen*, 2:894; Stagg, *Mr. Madison's War*, 501–6; Fleming, *West Point*, 21–23.

10. Cress, *Citizens in Arms*, 152–53; Symonds, *Navalists and Antinavalists*, 197–98; Watts, *Republic Reborn*, 240–43.

11. Watts, *Republic Reborn*, 276, 282, 300, 319–20; Stuart, *War and American Thought*, 146,

150–51, 160–62; Buel, *Securing the Revolution*, 242; Henry Adams, *History of the United States*, 9:195; Harry L. Watson, *Liberty and Power*, 59–60.

12. John Kerr to His Fellow Citizens, February 22, 1815, in Cunningham, *Circular Letters of Congressmen*, 2:918.

13. Calhoun, "Speech on the Loan Bill," January 25, 1814, in Meriwether et al., *Papers of John C. Calhoun*, 1:237–38. For Calhoun's views on military professionalism, see Cress, *Citizens in Arms*, 173–77.

14. Kershner, *Sylvanus Thayer*, 1–99; Molloy, "Technical Education," 384–87; Fiebeger, "Sylvanus Thayer"; Ambrose, *Duty, Honor, Country*, 65–66.

15. Ambrose, *Duty, Honor, Country*, 67–69; Molloy, "Technical Education," 393; Pappas, *To the Point*, 213–17.

16. Lovell, *Neither Athens nor Sparta*, 16–20; Molloy, "Technical Education," 388–91; Skelton, *American Profession of Arms*, 123; Pappas, *To the Point*, 100–102, 116–17; Ambrose, *Duty, Honor, Country*, 79; Kershner, *Sylvanus Thayer*, 147.

17. Ambrose, *Duty, Honor, Country*, 71–73; Kershner, *Sylvanus Thayer*, 162–64; Thayer to [Joseph G. Swift], April 14, 1818, in Cindy Adams, *West Point Thayer Papers*, 3:35; Pappas, *To the Point*, 119–20; Crackel, *West Point*, 87.

18. "Rules and Regulations for the Government of the Military Academy at West Point," *ASP:MA*, 2:77–78; Ambrose, *Duty, Honor, Country*, 73–75; Molloy, "Technical Education," 430.

19. Ambrose, *Duty, Honor, Country*, 75–76, 79–80; Pappas, *To the Point*, 102; Forman, *West Point*, 42; Denton, "Formative Years," 184–87.

20. Pappas, *To the Point*, 146–47; Ambrose, *Duty, Honor, Country*, 81–82.

21. U.S. Congress, *Annals of Congress*, 16th Cong., 1st sess., 1603, 1627, 1636.

22. Skelton, *American Profession of Arms*, 138; Hill, *Roads, Rails, and Waterways*, 20–21; Pappas, *To the Point*, 231–32; "Report on the Military Academy," March 4, 1822, *ASP:MA*, 2:350 (Eustis); *Niles' Register*, March 16, 1822.

23. Burr, "Education in the Early Navy," 183; "Memorial of Midshipmen against the Promotion of Sailing Masters," January 16, 1815, *ASP:NA*, 1:360.

24. Paullin, *Commodore John Rodgers*, 20–29, 33; Schroeder, *Commodore John Rodgers*, 1–8; Benton, *Thirty Years' View*, 2:144; Rodgers, "Report of the Navy Commissioners," January 10, 1821, H. Doc. 66, *Congressional Serial Set*, No. 52, 16th Cong., 2nd sess., 8; "Report of the Board of Navy Commissioners upon Subjects Connected with the Naval Establishment of the United States," November 25, 1815, Letters to the Secretary of the Navy, Records of the Board of Navy Commissioners, Naval Records Collection, RG 45, NA.

25. Navy Department, "Order for the Examination of Midshipmen," March 22, 1819, in Bauer, *New American State Papers*, 8:225; Burr, "Education in the Early Navy," 177–82; Jones, *Sketches of Naval Life*, 2:263; Benjamin, *United States Naval Academy*, 115–16; Samuel F. Du Pont to Victor Du Pont, December 26, 1825, Du Pont Papers, W9-179, ser. A, box 1, HML. There was a navy precedent for examining midshipmen. In 1802 Secretary of the Navy Robert Smith issued an order that all midshipmen were required to pass a test of their professional knowledge and moral character before promotion to lieutenant. The practice lasted for only a brief period and was discontinued during the conflict with Tripoli. See Robert Smith, General Order, August 18, 1802, and Smith to John Barry, Richard Dale, and William Bainbridge, August 19, 1802, both in Letters Sent by the Secretary of the Navy to Officers, roll 5, Naval Records Collection, RG 45, NA; McKee, *Gentlemanly and Honorable*, 278–80.

26. Burr, "Education in the Early Navy," 48–49. As early as 1802, Captain George Little of the USS *Boston* had argued for a probationary period. Giving midshipmen their warrants immediately made them "idle and cause[d] them to think so much of themselves that they scarce ever make [good] seamen." Quoted in McKee, *Gentlemanly and Honorable*, 53.

27. Sweetman, *U.S. Naval Academy*, 9; Adams to Jefferson, August 20, 1821 (2:573–74), and Jefferson to Adams, September 12, 1821 (2:575), both in Cappon, *Adams-Jefferson Letters*.

28. Edwin M. Hall, "Smith Thompson," in Coletta, *American Secretaries of the Navy*, 1:123–25.

29. Thompson to Monroe, December 2, 1822, including "Plan of a Peace Establishment for the Navy and Marine Corps" and "A Bill to Fix and Render Permanent the Naval Peace Establishment of the United States," *ASP:NA*, 1:816; U.S. Congress, *Annals of Congress*, 17th Cong., 2nd sess., 348, 645, and 18th Cong., 1st sess., 831.

30. Birkner, *Southard*, 93.

31. Ibid., 15–64, 90 (quotation).

32. Southard, "Report of the Secretary of the Navy," January 24, 1824 (1:908), and "Report on the Condition of the Navy and Marine Corps," December 1, 1824 (1:1005), *ASP:NA*; Unidentified newspaper clipping, [December 1824], Southard Papers, box 134, folder 1, Princeton University Library.

33. Southard, "Opinion of the Secretary of the Navy as to Alterations in the Organization of the Navy," January 1, 1825, *ASP:NA*, 2:44–45.

34. Perkins, *Creation of a Republican Empire*, 147–48, 167–69 (quotations, 148, 159); Paterson, Clifford, and Hagan, *American Foreign Policy*, 1:76, 84–85, 88–91, 94–103; Campbell, *From Revolution to Rapprochement*, 34–44.

35. Lewis, *Navy in Transition*, 21–31.

36. U.S. Congress, *Journal of the Senate*, 18th Cong., 2nd sess., January 10, 1825, 73, and *Register of Debates*, 18th Cong., 2nd sess., 112–13, 127–28.

37. Birkner, *Southard*, 68–71.

38. Hargreaves, *Presidency of John Quincy Adams*, 165–67; Bemis, *John Quincy Adams*, 60–63.

39. *National Intelligencer*, July 7, 1828.

40. John Quincy Adams, "First Annual Message," December 6, 1825, in Richardson, *Messages and Papers*, 2:311–13.

41. Ibid., 316.

42. Charles Francis Adams, *Memoirs of John Quincy Adams*, 7:62–64.

43. John Quincy Adams, "First Annual Message," December 6, 1825 (2:310), and "Second Annual Message," December 5, 1826 (2:362), in Richardson, *Messages and Papers*.

44. Edwin M. Hall, "Samuel Lewis Southard," in Coletta, *American Secretaries of the Navy*, 1:132–34; Hargreaves, *Presidency of John Quincy Adams*, 228–29; Birkner, *Southard*, 109.

45. U.S. Congress, *Bills and Resolutions of the House of Representatives*, H.R. 60, 19th Cong., 1st sess., and *Bills and Resolutions of the Senate*, S. 33, 19th Cong., 1st sess.; Charles Francis Adams, *Memoirs of John Quincy Adams*, 7:90–91.

46. "Application of Maryland for the Establishment of a Naval Academy at Annapolis," January 1826, *ASP:NA*, 2:623; "Memorial of the Citizens of New-London on the Establishment of a Naval Academy or School," February 23, 1826, Records of the Committee on Naval Affairs, File No. HR19A-G13.2, Records of the U.S. House of Representatives, RG 233, NA.

47. U.S. Congress, *Register of Debates*, 19th Cong., 1st sess., 696–97; Adams, "Second Annual Message," in Richardson, *Messages and Papers* 2:362.

48. "A Bill for the Gradual Improvement of the Navy of the United States," U.S. Congress, *Register of Debates*, 19th Cong., 2nd sess., 348–49. Sections 7–11 of the bill dealt with the proposed naval academy and were nearly identical to the naval academy bill that was introduced in the Senate in 1826.

49. Langley, "Robert Y. Hayne," 311–19.

50. U.S. Congress, *Register of Debates*, 19th Cong., 2nd sess., 357.

51. Ibid., 358–59.

52. Ibid., 359.

53. Ibid., 361–62.

54. Ibid., 363–64.

55. Ibid., 364–65, 367.

56. Ibid., 505–8, 510–11 (quotation, 507).

57. Ibid., 509–11; Kimmel, *Manhood in America*, 19, 21; Pugh, *Sons of Liberty*, 18–19.

58. U.S. Congress, *Register of Debates*, 19th Cong., 2nd sess., 512–14.

59. Ibid., 515–16, 519–20.

60. Ibid., 520–22. On Macon and his brand of Republicanism, see Schlesinger, *Age of Jackson*, 20–21, 26–29.

61. U.S. Congress, *Register of Debates*, 19th Cong., 2nd sess., 376, 380.

62. Ibid., 1497–98, 1500.

63. Ibid., 501. The party affiliation of the senators was determined using the *Biographical Directory of the United States Congress, 1774–Present*, <http://bioguide.congress.gov>. The House vote could not be analyzed because the *Biographical Directory*'s information on the representatives' political affiliation is incomplete for the 19th Congress. For detailed Senate voting lists, see Leeman, "Long Road to Annapolis," 493–96. For further analysis of the Senate vote, see Sprout and Sprout, *Rise of American Naval Power*, 103–4.

64. Nagel, *John Quincy Adams*, 297–98, 300–303; Birkner, *Southard*, 72–73.

65. Howe, *Political Culture*, 49–52; Sellers, *Market Revolution*, 271; Bemis, *John Quincy Adams*, 75–76, 126; Benton, *Thirty Years' View*, 1:55.

66. Southard, "Annual Report of the Secretary of the Navy," December 1, 1827, *ASP:NA*, 3:54.

67. John Quincy Adams, "Third Annual Message," December 4, 1827, in Richardson, *Messages and Papers*, 2:390.

68. Stanton, *Exploring Expedition*, 4–7, 16.

69. Quoted in *New York Mirror*, October 4, 1828. For Reynolds's background, see Stanton, *Exploring Expedition*, 13–23.

70. Stanton, *Exploring Expedition*, 19–21; Philbrick, *Sea of Glory*, 7–9, 22–24.

71. Southard to [John Quincy Adams], February 15, 1829, *ASP:NA*, 3:310–11.

72. U.S. Congress, *Register of Debates*, 20th Cong., 2nd sess., 50–52; Langley, "Robert Y. Hayne," 320–25; Stanton, *Exploring Expedition*, 23–25; Birkner, *Southard*, 111–13.

73. Southard, "Annual Report of the Secretary of the Navy," November 27, 1828, *ASP:NA*, 3:215–16; Birkner, *Southard*, 90, 110; Hall, "Samuel Lewis Southard," 134–36, 138; Skallerup, *Books Afloat and Ashore*, 135–37, 230–34; Love, *History of the U.S. Navy*, 1:143–44.

Chapter 4

1. Schroeder, *Shaping a Maritime Empire*, 22–23, 80–82; Perkins, *Creation of a Republican Empire*, 175–78 (quotation, 176–77).

2. Andrew Jackson, "First Annual Message," December 8, 1829, in Richardson, *Messages and Papers*, 2:460; Schroeder, *Shaping a Maritime Empire*, 3–4, 19–23, 25–36; Andrew Jackson, "Eighth Annual Message," December 5, 1836, in Richardson, *Messages and Papers*, 3:257; Geoffrey Sutton Smith, "The Navy before Darwinism," 44–46.

3. On the activities of the various naval squadrons, see David F. Long, *Gold Braid and Foreign Relations* and "The Navy under the Board of Navy Commissioners, 1815–1842," in Hagan, *In Peace and War*, 63–78.

4. Long, "The Navy under the Board of Navy Commissioners," 68–71, 76; Perkins, *Creation of a Republican Empire*, 76; Long, *Gold Braid and Foreign Relations*, xv, 8–9, 11–13, 422–29.

5. Philbrick, *Sea of Glory*, 332–33, 361; Stanton, *Exploring Expedition*, 364–77; White, *Jacksonians*, 497.

6. Weber, *Naval Observatory*, 8–21; Williams, *Maury*, 142–43, 148–51, 158–65; White, *Jacksonians*, 497–98, 505.

7. Andrew Jackson, "First Inaugural Address," March 4, 1829, in Richardson, *Messages and Papers*, 2:437–38.

8. W. Patrick Strauss, "John Branch," in Coletta, *American Secretaries of the Navy*, 1:143; Benjamin, *United States Naval Academy*, 108–10; Burr, "Education in the Early Navy," 149–53, 161, 163–64, 179–81; Williams, *Maury*, 85–87; Thomas G. Ford, "History of the United States Naval Academy," chap. 7, 10. A school was set up in Boston in 1815, but it does not appear that it was in continuous operation. The schools at Norfolk and New York opened in the 1820s.

9. Branch, "Annual Report of the Secretary of the Navy," December 1, 1829, *ASP:NA*, 3:350–51.

10. Branch, "Annual Report of the Secretary of the Navy," December 6, 1830, ibid., 3:758–59.

11. W. Patrick Strauss, "Levi Woodbury," in Coletta, *American Secretaries of the Navy*, 1:151–52; Woodbury, "Annual Report of the Secretary of the Navy," December 3, 1831, *ASP:NA*, 4:8, and "Annual Report of the Secretary of the Navy," December 3, 1832, *ASP:NA*, 4:160.

12. Navy Department, "Order for Midshipmen to Attend Naval Schools at Navy Yards," November 15, 1833, in Bauer, *New American State Papers*, 8:230; Woodbury, "Annual Report of the Secretary of the Navy," November 30, 1833, *ASP:NA*, 4:352; "Rules and Regulations for the Government of the Navy, Prepared by a Board of Officers of the Navy and Submitted for the Sanction of Congress," December 23, 1833, *ASP:NA*, 4:414.

13. Birkner, *Southard*, 118–40, 147; U.S. Congress, *Bills and Resolutions of the Senate*, S. 212, 23rd Cong., 1st sess.

14. W. Patrick Strauss, "Mahlon Dickerson," in Coletta, *American Secretaries of the Navy*, 155, 157; Chisholm, *Waiting for Dead Men's Shoes*, 158; Dickerson, "Annual Report of the Secretary of the Navy," December 5, 1835, *ASP:NA*, 4:732; *Army and Navy Chronicle*, December 17, 1835, 404.

15. Ward, *Andrew Jackson*, 30–31, 42–45, 66–69, 167–79; Harry L. Watson, *Liberty and Power*, 91–93; Kohl, *Politics of Individualism*, 39; Schlesinger, *Age of Jackson*, 36–39.

16. Hofstadter, *Anti-Intellectualism*, 33–34, 48–49, 145–46; Ward, *Andrew Jackson*, 64–66; Howe, *Political Culture*, 44–46.

17. Quoted in Ward, *Andrew Jackson*, 52.

18. John Quincy Adams, "Fourth Annual Message," December 2, 1828, in Richardson, *Messages and Papers*, 2:417; *North American Review* 23 (October 1826): 271–72.

19. Ward, *Andrew Jackson*, 6, 13–29, 46–48; Cunliffe, *Soldiers and Civilians*, 53–54; Fleming, *West Point*, 70.

20. Jackson to Andrew J. Donelson, March 5, 1823, in Bassett, *Correspondence of Andrew Jackson*, 3:191; Jackson, "First Annual Message," 456.

21. White, *Jacksonians*, 187–90.

22. Huntington, *Soldier and the State*, 203–4; Meyers, *Jacksonian Persuasion*, 228.

23. Harry L. Watson, *Liberty and Power*, 10–11; Meyers, *Jacksonian Persuasion*, 31; Kohl, *Politics of Individualism*, 21–22, 26–27, 58–60, 215–20.

24. Cunliffe, *Soldiers and Civilians*, 108–9; Ambrose, *Duty, Honor, Country*, 107; Andrew Jackson, "Veto Message," July 10, 1832, in Richardson, *Messages and Papers*, 2:590.

25. Welter, *Mind of America*, 78; Rudolph, *American College and University*, 202 (quotation).

26. Ambrose, *Duty, Honor, Country*, 38–61; Pappas, *To the Point*, 75–96.

27. Denton, "Formative Years," 239–40; Forman, *West Point*, 62–64; Ambrose, *Duty, Honor, Country*, 113; Cunliffe, *Soldiers and Civilians*, 77.

28. Partridge to Dallas, May 9, 1815, Crawford Papers, Rare Book, Manuscript, and Special Collections Library, Duke University.

29. Ibid.

30. *Catalogue of the Officers and Cadets of the American Literary, Scientific, and Military Academy* (1821), 7–9 (quotations, 8); *Catalogue of the Officers and Cadets* (1826), 23–34. To compare the instruction offered at Partridge's academy with the curriculum and organization of West Point, see "Rules and Regulations for the Government of the Military Academy at West Point," *ASP:MA*, 2:77–78. Although the West Point curriculum did include the humanities, instruction in those subjects was limited.

31. Cunliffe, *Soldiers and Civilians*, 152–53, 260–63; Partridge to Swift, October 20, 1818, Partridge Papers, USMA.

32. [Partridge], *Military Academy, . . . Unmasked*, 3–9 (quotations, 3, 5).

33. Ibid., 10–12 (quotation, 10).

34. Ibid., 12–16 (quotations, 13, 15–16).

35. Ibid., 18–21, 24–25 (quotations, 18, 20).

36. U.S. Congress, *Register of Debates*, 21st Cong., 1st sess., 552–53, and 20th Cong., 2nd sess., 163; Cunliffe, *Soldiers and Civilians*, 162–65.

37. Skelton, *American Profession of Arms*, 140; Morrison, *"Best School in the World,"* 61–62, 159.

38. Skelton, *American Profession of Arms*, 179; Cunliffe, *Soldiers and Civilians*, 166; Pappas, *To the Point*, 227–28. According to the Tiffany Jewelry Company in New York City, West Point was the first American college to have class rings.

39. Morrison, *"Best School in the World,"* 62–63; Skelton, *American Profession of Arms*, 140–42, 177–78 (Cadet Edward L. Hartz quoted on 142); *American Quarterly Review* 16 (December 1834): 374.

40. Pappas, *To the Point*, 192; "Applications and Appointments as Cadets at the Military Academy at West Point from Its Establishment to 1829," March 15, 1830, *ASP:MA*, 4:334–35; Kaestle, *Pillars of the Republic*, 104–35, 192–95; *Army and Navy Chronicle*, December 24, 1835, 413.

41. Morrison, *"Best School in the World,"* 15–16; Pessen, *Jacksonian America*, 92.

42. *CG*, 27th Cong., 3rd sess., 225.

43. Cunliffe, *Soldiers and Civilians*, 109–10; Forman, *West Point*, 65; White, *Jacksonians*, 197–200; *Army and Navy Chronicle*, November 5, 1835, 357.

44. Cunliffe, *Soldiers and Civilians*, 126–28; Grant, *Personal Memoirs*, 10, 14–15, 17–18 (quotation, 17).

45. White, *Jacksonians*, 211; Fleming, *West Point*, 54–56, 79; Rudolph, *American College and University*, 97–98; Demos, *Past, Present, and Personal*, 101–2.

46. U.S. Congress, *Register of Debates*, 24th Cong., 1st sess., 3371, 2nd sess., 2073; *CG*, 27th Cong., 2nd sess., 864.

47. Rotundo, *American Manhood*, 36, 42–43; Elson, "American Schoolbooks in the Nineteenth Century," 412, 417–20.

48. Rotundo, *American Manhood*, 170–72.

49. "Statement of the History and Importance of the Military Academy at West Point, New York, and Reasons Why It Should Not Be Abolished," May 17, 1834, *ASP:MA*, 5:347; *CG*, 28th Cong., 1st sess., 386 (quotation); Dickinson, *West Point Academy*; Ambrose, *Duty, Honor, Country*, 111–12.

50. Forman, *West Point*, 68–69; Skelton, *American Profession of Arms*, 139–40.

51. Hill, *Roads, Rails, and Waterways*, 208–9; Forman, *West Point*, 88; Rudolph, *American College and University*, 110–35, 229–31; Nye, *Cultural Life of the New Nation*, 190.

52. Cremin, *American Education*, 405; "Yale Report of 1828," in Hofstadter and Smith,

American Higher Education, 1:281, 288–90. For the Yale curriculum, see *Catalogue of the Officers and Students in Yale College*.

53. Bledstein, *Culture of Professionalism*, 223–25; Francis Wayland, "Thoughts on the Present Collegiate System" (1842), in Hofstadter and Smith, *American Higher Education*, 1:357.

54. John Hope Franklin, *Militant South*, 167. For Franklin's discussion of southern military academies, see 146–70.

55. Ibid., 140–45; Andrew, *Long Gray Lines*, 11–17.

56. "Statement of the History and Importance of the Military Academy," 353; Dickinson, *West Point Academy*, 1–3 (quotation, 3).

57. *Army and Navy Chronicle*, July 9, 1835, 220; "Proceedings of Certain Officers of the Navy and Marine Corps, Recommending the Establishment of a Naval Academy," *ASP:NA*, 4:884–85; *Maryland Republican*, reprinted in *Army and Navy Chronicle*, July 23, 1835, 236.

58. Southard, "Report on the Expediency and Necessity for the Establishment of a Naval School or Academy," May 14, 1836, *ASP:NA*, 4:969; U.S. Congress, *Bills and Resolutions of the Senate*, S. 262, 24th Cong., 1st sess., *Register of Debates*, 24th Cong., 1st sess., 1453–54, and *Bills and Resolutions of the Senate*, S. 64, 24th Cong., 2nd sess. For an overview of the army and foreign affairs, see Skelton, *American Profession of Arms*, 326–47.

Chapter 5

1. Cremin, *American Education*, 353–54, 357–58.

2. Ibid., 400.

3. Haber, *Quest for Authority*, 104–7; Cremin, *American Education*, 355–60, 364; Bledstein, *Culture of Professionalism*, 185–91; Ludmerer, *Learning to Heal*, 11–16; LaPiana, *Logic and Experience*, 7, 52–53.

4. Huntington, *Soldier and the State*, 217–21; Skelton, *American Profession of Arms*, 247, 257; Crackel, *West Point*, 118; Cunliffe, *Soldiers and Civilians*, 166–67.

5. Skelton, *American Profession of Arms*, 36; *American Quarterly Review* 16 (December 1834): 371; Samuel J. Watson, "Developing 'Republican Machines': West Point and the Struggle to Render the Officer Corps Safe for America, 1802–1833," in Robert M. S. McDonald, *Thomas Jefferson's Military Academy*, 155 (the ideal West Point graduate).

6. *Constitution and By-Laws of the United States Naval Lyceum*, 3; *First Annual Report of the Administration Committee of the U.S. Naval Lyceum*, 3; *Naval Magazine* 1 (January 1836): 5 (quotation).

7. Skallerup, *Books Afloat and Ashore*, 170–71.

8. De Christofaro, "The Naval Lyceum"; Cremin, *American Education*, 312–18, 446–47; Bode, *American Lyceum*, 4–19, 60, 63–64; Skallerup, *Books Afloat and Ashore*, 175.

9. *Naval Magazine* 1 (January 1836): 6–9; Skallerup, *Books Afloat and Ashore*, 173–74, 176; Schroeder, *Perry*, 71; Morison, *"Old Bruin,"* 134–35; *First Annual Report of the Administration Committee of the U.S. Naval Lyceum*, 3–6.

10. The list of members is from the appendix to volume 1 of the *Naval Magazine* (1836): 39–42.

11. *Naval Magazine* 1 (January 1836): 16. Although most naval officers had not attended college, a small number did receive some higher education either before or during their naval career. Two prominent examples from the antebellum navy were David G. Farragut, who attended lectures at Yale, and James H. Ward, who studied at the American Literary, Scientific, and Military Academy (Norwich University) and spent a year at Trinity College in Hartford, Conn. See Burr, "Education in the Early Navy," 165, and Lewis, Sturdy, and Bolander, "First Academic Staff," 1392.

12. *First Annual Report of the Administration Committee of the U.S. Naval Lyceum*, 9.

13. *Military and Naval Magazine of the United States* 4 (December 1834): 255.

14. Allison, *Stephen Decatur*, 11–12, 77–78; *United Service Journal*, reprinted in *Army and Navy Chronicle*, July 25, 1839, 50; Bushman, *Refinement of America*, 280–83.

15. Brown, *Strength of a People*, 131–32; Bushman, *Refinement of America*, 287–88.

16. Butler, *Military Profession*, 32–33, 41–44; Paulding to Cooper, May 20, 1839, in Aderman, *Letters of James Kirke Paulding*, 256; Nagel, *This Sacred Trust*, 61; *Constitution and By-Laws of the United States Naval Lyceum*, 10 (last quotation); *Naval Magazine* 1 (January 1836): 14.–15; Skallerup, *Books Afloat and Ashore*, 178.

17. Taylor, *William Cooper's Town*, 338–45; J[ames] F[enimore] C[ooper], "Comparative Resources of the American Navy," *Naval Magazine* 1 (January 1836): 19–33; Schroeder, *Perry*, 71–73.

18. White, *Jacksonians*, 361; *American Quarterly Review* 5 (June 1829): 344–45.

19. Morison, *"Old Bruin,"* 8–25, 124–26; Schroeder, *Perry*, 5.

20. Morison, *"Old Bruin,"* 26–123; Schroeder, *Perry*, 18–19.

21. Morison, *"Old Bruin,"* 58, 117–18.

22. *National Gazette*, December 24, 1827; Schroeder, *Perry*, 55 (Rodgers's probable encouragement to publicize the need for naval reform).

23. Chisholm, *Waiting for Dead Men's Shoes*, 140–42. The term "going public" is from Samuel Kernell, *Going Public: New Strategies of Presidential Leadership*, 3rd ed. (Washington, D.C.: CQ Press, 1997).

24. A[lexander] S[lidell Mackenzie], "Thoughts on the Navy," *Naval Magazine* 2 (January 1837): 5–14 (quotations, 21, 33). According to Samuel Eliot Morison (*"Old Bruin,"* 127), Matthew C. Perry was a contributor to Mackenzie's essay.

25. [Alexander Slidell Mackenzie], "The Navy," *North American Review* 30 (April 1830): 378–79; Wines, *Two Years*, 2:103–4; [James Barron], "The Navy," *Military and Naval Magazine of the United States* 3 (March 1834): 10. Barron is identified as the author of the latter article in Benjamin Homans to Barron, May 4, 1841, Barron Papers, CWM.

26. Jones, *Sketches of Naval Life*, 2:262–63; Wines, *Two Years*, 1:17, 2:97–100 (quotation, 98).

27. Wines, *Two Years*, 2:97, 102, 111; Jones, *Sketches of Naval Life*, 2:268, 274–75; [Mackenzie], "Thoughts on the Navy," 22; "Naval Academy," *Military and Naval Magazine of the United States* 2 (February 1834): 336–37.

28. [Mackenzie], "The Navy," 379–80.

29. Jones, *Sketches of Naval Life*, 2:264–67, 269–70 (quotations, 264, 267); George Jones, "Naval Education," *Naval Magazine* 1 (May 1836): 213–17. At the time, the navy spent $26,704 annually for professors of mathematics and language instructors. Based on Jones's calculations, a naval academy staffed by a commanding officer, executive officer, seven professors, and two assistants would cost $20,800 if the government had to purchase land for the campus. If the government used land already in its possession, the cost would be only $17,800.

30. [Mackenzie], "The Navy," 380–83; Jones, *Sketches of Naval Life*, 2:268–69; Powell to the Secretary of the Navy [James K. Paulding], February 16, 1840, in *Southern Literary Messenger* 8 (March 1842): 206–7.

31. Bennett, *Steam Navy*, 8–25, 29, 32–36, 39–40; Morison, *"Old Bruin,"* 127–31; Schroeder, *Perry*, 78–84; White, *Jacksonians*, 224–25; Paullin, *Paullin's History*, 178–80; Sprout and Sprout, *Rise of American Naval Power*, 5.

32. Schroeder, *Perry*, 73; Albion, *Makers of Naval Policy*, 190 (quotation).

33. W. Patrick Strauss, "James Kirke Paulding," in Coletta, *American Secretaries of the Navy*, 1:165–67; Paulding to Gouverneur Kemble, June 8, 16, 1839, in Aderman, *Letters of James Kirke Paulding*, 258; Paulding, "Annual Report of the Secretary of the Navy," November 30, 1838, *CG*, 25th Cong., 3rd sess., app., 6.

34. White, *Jacksonians*, 154–56.

35. Williams, *Maury*, 1–28, 30.

36. Ibid., 30–31; Matthew Fontaine Maury to Rutson Maury, August 31, 1840, Maury Papers, box 2, LC (quotation).

37. Williams, *Maury*, 32–34.

38. Matthew Fontaine Maury to Rutson Maury, August 31, 1840, Maury Papers, box 2, LC; Williams, *Maury*, 87–88.

39. Williams, *Maury*, 92–94, 97–98, 103; Maury, *New Theoretical and Practical Treatise*, preface.

40. Maury, *New Theoretical and Practical Treatise*; Bowditch, *New American Practical Navigator*; Williams, *Maury*, 110–11; *Southern Literary Messenger* 2 (June 1836): 454–55.

41. Williams, *Maury*, 121–24, 127–29; Maury to Lucian Minor, December 14, 1840, Maury Papers, box 2, LC (quotation).

42. Williams, *Maury*, 129. Maury published four articles in the "Scraps from the Lucky Bag" series from April 1840 to January 1841 and one sequel article entitled "More Scraps from the Lucky Bag" in May 1841. The quotation is from "Scraps from the Lucky Bag," No. 1, *Southern Literary Messenger* 6 (April 1840): 233. Maury's concern about being disciplined by the navy for what he published is from Maury to Lucian Minor, December 14, 1840, Maury Papers, box 2, LC.

43. [Maury], "Scraps from the Lucky Bag," No. 1, *Southern Literary Messenger* 6 (April 1840): 233–40, No. 2, ibid., 6 (May 1840): 306–11, and No. 4, ibid., 7 (January 1841): 12–25.

44. [Maury], "Scraps from the Lucky Bag," No. 2, ibid., 315.

45. Ibid.; *The Madisonian*, reprinted in *Army and Navy Chronicle*, December 9, 1841, 387. The conditions of navy professors improved significantly in 1842, when they were given the rations of a lieutenant and assigned to the wardroom with the officers instead of the steerage with the midshipmen. See Burr, "Education in the Early Navy," 120.

46. [Maury], "Scraps from the Lucky Bag," No. 2, 316–19.

47. Ibid., 320; [Maury], "Scraps from the Lucky Bag," No. 3, *Southern Literary Messenger* 6 (December 1840): 786–88, 793–95.

48. [Maury], "Scraps from the Lucky Bag," No. 3, 789–90, 793, 795.

49. [Maury], "Scraps from the Lucky Bag," No. 4, 3–12 (quotations, 6).

50. Ibid., 7; Schroeder, *Perry*, 12; Langley, *Social Reform*, 22–23; *Army and Navy Chronicle*, November 5, 1835, 357.

51. [Maury], "Scraps from the Lucky Bag," No. 4, 8–25 (quotation, 9).

52. Matthew Fontaine Maury to Ann Maury, January 10, 1841, Maury Papers, box 65, folder 5, LC; Officers of the Mediterranean Squadron to [Maury], March 2, 1841, Du Pont Papers, W9-655, ser. A, box 2, HML.

53. [Maury], "More Scraps from the Lucky Bag," *Southern Literary Messenger* 7 (May/June 1841): 345–73, 375–79. Maury was not the first person to suggest that U.S. Marine Corps officers be selected from among the graduates of West Point. Samuel Southard proposed the same plan during his tenure as secretary of the navy. See Southard to Calhoun, December 27, 1824, in Meriwether et al., *Papers of John C. Calhoun*, 9:464. Even before Southard's recommendation, a small number of West Point graduates had been commissioned as marine officers. See Solis, "Duty, Honor, Country," 44–45.

54. Matthew Fontaine Maury to Ann Maury, June 21, 1841, Maury Papers, box 65, folder 5, LC; "Lieut. M. F. Maury of the U.S. Navy," *Southern Literary Messenger* 7 (July 1841): 560–63.

55. [Matthew Fontaine Maury], "Letters to Mr. Clay," No. 2, *Southern Literary Messenger* 7 (October 1841): 725–27.

56. Williams, *Maury*, 129–39; Schroeder, *Shaping a Maritime Empire*, 60–61.

57. Geoffrey S. Smith, "An Uncertain Passage: The Bureaus Run the Navy, 1842–1861," in Hagan, *In Peace and War*, 80–82; Paolo E. Coletta, "Abel Parker Upshur," in Coletta, *American Secretaries of the Navy*, 1:177–79. For Upshur's life and career prior to 1841, see Hall, *Upshur*, 7–119.

58. Upshur to Nathaniel Beverley Tucker, October 21, 30, 1841, Tucker-Coleman Papers, CWM. For Upshur's workload as navy secretary, see Hall, *Upshur*, 123, and Upshur to Tucker, December 23, 1841, Tucker-Coleman Papers.

59. Schroeder, *Shaping a Maritime Empire*, 59–60; Coletta, "Abel Parker Upshur," 1:179–80; Hall, *Upshur*, 125, 239 n. 9.

60. Upshur, "Annual Report of the Secretary of the Navy," December 4, 1841, *CG*, 27th Cong., 2nd sess., app., 18–22.

61. Ibid., 21–22.

62. Hall, *Upshur*, 130, 132–33; *Philadelphia North American*, quoted in *Army and Navy Chronicle*, January 29, 1842, 31.

63. *CG*, 27th Cong., 2nd sess., app., 358. According to Senator Thomas Hart Benton (*Thirty Years' View*, 2:452), the U.S. government had a $14 million deficit around the time of the 1842 debates over naval appropriations.

64. Upshur, "Annual Report," 16; *CG*, 27th Cong., 2nd sess., 512, 515, 682.

65. Albion, *Makers of Naval Policy*, 70–71; Paullin, *Paullin's History*, 209–11; White, *Jacksonians*, 216–19; Hall, *Upshur*, 123–24, 145–47.

66. *CG*, 27th Cong., 2nd sess., app., 388–89, and 499, 520, 681.

67. "Our Navy: Judge Abel P. Upshur and His Report," *Southern Literary Messenger* 8 (January 1842): 94.

68. *CG*, 27th Cong., 2nd sess., 498–99.

69. Southard, "Rules Adopted for the Selection of Commissioned and Warrant Officers for the Navy," March 12, 1828, *ASP:NA*, 3:158–62; Woodbury, "Statement of the Principles on Which Midshipmen Are Appointed in the Navy, and the Number Taken from Each State and Territory from 1828 to 1833," February 18, 1833, ibid., 4:295–97; *CG*, 27th Cong., 2nd sess., 499, 520, 681. Representative George Proffit mentioned the newspaper's accusation while speaking on the floor of the House on May 13, 1842.

70. U.S. Congress, *Bills and Resolutions of the Senate*, S. 295, 27th Cong., 2nd sess.

71. *CG*, 27th Cong., 2nd sess., 859.

72. Ibid., 859–60, 864.

73. Ibid., 864, 865–66, 888, 961.

74. Upshur to Nathaniel Beverley Tucker, October 25, 1842, Tucker-Coleman Papers, CWM; Upshur, "Annual Report of the Secretary of the Navy," December 1842, *CG*, 27th Cong., 3rd sess., app., 39–40, 42–43.

75. Upshur, "Annual Report" (1842), 41.

76. Ibid., 41–42.

77. Coletta, "Abel Parker Upshur," 181–84, 193; Hall, *Upshur*, 191–92. On February 28, 1844, Upshur was a guest on the USS *Princeton*, the U.S. Navy's first steam warship powered by a screw propeller. The ship was visiting Washington to show off its innovative features, specifically its twelve-inch "Peacemaker" gun, which could fire a shell a distance of over three miles. During a demonstration, the gun exploded. Upshur, who was standing nearby, was killed instantly along with several other spectators.

78. Schroeder, *Perry*, 24; "Naval Academy," *Military and Naval Magazine of the United States* 2 (February 1834): 336.

79. *Naval Magazine* 1 (January 1836): 14.

80. Chisholm, *Waiting for Dead Men's Shoes*, 158; Jones, *Sketches of Naval Life*, 1:40; Taylor,

William Cooper's Town, 424–27; Madison, "Cooper, Bancroft, and the Voorhees Court-Martial"; Cooper, *History of the Navy*, 1:97–98 (quotations).

81. "Character and Duties of the Naval Profession," *Naval Magazine* 2 (May 1837): 230, 237 (quotations, 239–41).

82. Haber, *Quest for Authority*, 4–6.

83. Calhoun, *Professional Lives*, 16–17; Bledstein, *Culture of Professionalism*, 125. Bledstein argues that the "ego-satisfying pretensions of professionalism" (p. 289) meant more to the middle class than financial gain. The same was true for naval officers.

84. Calhoun, *Professional Lives*, 9–11.

85. Bledstein, *Culture of Professionalism*, 26–31, 121–25 (quotation, 125). This middle-class culture also existed in the antebellum South. In many ways, the southern middle class had a closer cultural connection to the northern middle class than to the elite planter class in the South. See Green, "Books and Bayonets," 7–12, 46–52.

86. Charles Stewart to Abel P. Upshur, March 23, 1842, in *Army and Navy Chronicle*, April 4, 1844, 428; Smith, "An Uncertain Passage," 85.

Chapter 6

1. Egan, "Gentlemen-Sailors," 138; Geoffrey S. Smith, "An Uncertain Passage: The Bureaus Run the Navy, 1842–1861," in Hagan, *In Peace and War*, 90; Hagan, *This People's Navy*, 107 (quotation).

2. *CG*, 27th Cong., 3rd sess., 242; Valle, *Rocks and Shoals*, 95–97; *Niles' Register*, September 8, 1838. Not surprisingly, this criticism struck a nerve with naval officers. A group of officers stationed at the navy yard in Pensacola, Fla., denied the accuracy of statements made about the level of discipline in the navy. See *Niles' Register*, October 6, 1838.

3. Philbrick, *Sea of Glory*, 309–10; Maloney, *Captain from Connecticut*, 446–74; Merrill, *Du Pont*, 97–138; Samuel F. Du Pont to George S. Blake, October 2, 1835, Du Pont Papers, W9–370, ser. A, box 2, HML.

4. Valle, *Rocks and Shoals*, 58; Philbrick, *Sea of Glory*, 308–30; Stanton, *Exploring Expedition*, 281–88. For the controversy regarding the discovery of Antarctica, see Stanton, 170–71.

5. Hall, *Upshur*, 152, 161–62; Philbrick, *Sea of Glory*, 295–304; Geoffrey S. Smith, "An Uncertain Passage," 92 (description of Wilkes as a combination of Ahab and Bligh); Allin, "Abel Parker Upshur," 87, 89, 90 (quotations).

6. *Army and Navy Chronicle*, January 31, 1839, 73; Allin, "Abel Parker Upshur," 87–89 (quotations, 89).

7. Jones, *Sketches of Naval Life*, 1:iii; Valle, *Rocks and Shoals*, 277–78; Langley, *Social Reform*, vii–ix, 274–77 (quotation, vii); *CG*, 27th Cong., 3rd sess., 250. For a discussion of republican equality, see Wood, *Radicalism of the American Revolution*, 229–43.

8. "Character and Duties of the Naval Profession," *Naval Magazine* 2 (May 1837): 238–39; *Army and Navy Chronicle*, November 8, 1838, 302.

9. Southard, "Rules Adopted for the Selection of Commissioned and Warrant Officers for the Navy," March 12, 1828, *ASP:NA*, 3:160.

10. Valle, *Rocks and Shoals*, 90; White, *Jacksonians*, 240–42; Benjamin, *United States Naval Academy*, 104–5 (a kind of professional "purgatory"); "Petition of the Midshipmen of the Navy of the United States," December 11, 1830, Records of the Committee on Naval Affairs, File No. HR21A-G14.3, Records of the U.S. House of Representatives, RG 233, NA.

11. Paullin, "Dueling in the Old Navy," 1155–61; Valle, *Rocks and Shoals*, 88; Paullin, *Paullin's History*, 192–93.

12. Paullin, "Dueling in the Old Navy," 1178–84.

13. Ibid., 1156–58, 1162–97; McKee, *Gentlemanly and Honorable*, 404; S. R. Franklin, *Memories of a Rear-Admiral*, 38.

14. Paullin, "Dueling in the Old Navy," 1159, 1165; Skaggs, *Oliver Hazard Perry*, 38; Paullin, *Paullin's History*, 193 (quotation); Calhoun to Southard, May 2, 1830, in Meriwether et al., *Papers of John C. Calhoun*, 11:154; Valle, *Rocks and Shoals*, 137.

15. *Niles' Register*, October 1, 1825, October 29, 1842; Wells, *Origins of the Southern Middle Class*, 80–87.

16. Southard, "Rules Adopted for the Selection of Commissioned and Warrant Officers," 160; Watts, *Republic Reborn*, 153; [Maury], "Scraps from the Lucky Bag," No. 2, *Southern Literary Messenger* 6 (May 1840): 316; Upshur, "Annual Report of the Secretary of the Navy," December 1842, *CG*, 27th Cong., 3rd sess., app., 41.

17. The *Somers* affair has received a great deal of attention from historians. The best and most detailed accounts are Melton, *A Hanging Offense*, and McFarland, *Sea Dangers*. Hayford, *The Somers Mutiny Affair*, is a collection of primary source documents and related newspaper excerpts. Van de Water, *The Captain Called It Mutiny*, written by a descendant of one of the seamen on board, is somewhat biased against the ship's captain, Alexander Slidell Mackenzie. Shorter, but still useful accounts include Livingston Hunt, "Attempted Mutiny"; Morison, *"Old Bruin,"* 144–62; and Beach, *United States Navy*, 177–95.

18. McFarland, *Sea Dangers*, 48–49; Morison, *"Old Bruin,"* 144–48; Melton, *A Hanging Offense*, 21, 59; Schroeder, *Matthew Calbraith Perry*, 92. See also Matthew C. Perry to [Mahlon Dickerson], October 20, 1834, Perry Letterbook, Rodgers Family Papers, HSP.

19. Melton, *A Hanging Offense*, 44–46, 49–53; McFarland, *Sea Dangers*, 11–12, 15–47; Morison, *"Old Bruin,"* 145; Van de Water, *Captain Called It Mutiny*, 15, 17; Paullin, *Paullin's History*, 200. Mackenzie was the author of *A Year in Spain* (1829), *Popular Essays on Naval Subjects* (1833), *The American in England* (1835), *Spain Revisited* (1836), *The Life of Commodore Oliver Hazard Perry* (1840), and *The Life of Paul Jones* (1841).

20. Melton, *A Hanging Offense*, 54, 56–58.

21. [Maury], "Scraps from the Lucky Bag," No. 4, *Southern Literary Messenger* 7 (January 1841): 8; Melton, *A Hanging Offense*, 25–33; McFarland, *Sea Dangers*, 52, 54–71; Van de Water, *Captain Called It Mutiny*, 26.

22. Melton, *A Hanging Offense*, 34–39; Upshur to Philip Spencer, August 6, 1842, in Hayford, *Somers Mutiny Affair*, 219; McFarland, *Sea Dangers*, 52–53; Morison, *"Old Bruin,"* 148.

23. Melton, *A Hanging Offense*, 59–60, 68, 76–78, 85; McFarland, *Sea Dangers*, 86–91.

24. Melton, *A Hanging Offense*, 78–79, 82–84; Morison, *"Old Bruin,"* 149; McFarland, *Sea Dangers*, 85–86.

25. Melton, *A Hanging Offense*, 86–90.

26. Ibid., 91–98, 100–105; McFarland, *Sea Dangers*, 106–10.

27. Melton, *A Hanging Offense*, 109–15, 119–26; McFarland, *Sea Dangers*, 112–16, 118–22.

28. Melton, *A Hanging Offense*, 126–42; McFarland, *Sea Dangers*, 136–39.

29. Melton, *A Hanging Offense*, 143–53; McFarland, *Sea Dangers*, 139–51.

30. Benton, *Thirty Years' View*, 2:523; *New York Herald*, December 17, 18, 1842; *Richmond Whig*, December 20, 1842; *New York Express*, December 17, 1842, reprinted in Hayford, *Somers Mutiny Affair*, 3.

31. Benton, *Thirty Years' View*, 2:523; *New York Herald*, December 17, 18, 1842; *New York Courier and Enquirer*, December 19, 1842, reprinted in Hayford, *Somers Mutiny Affair*, 6; Nevins and Thomas, *Diary of George Templeton Strong*, 1:194.

32. *New York Herald*, December 18, 20, 1842; *Richmond Whig*, December 20, 1842; *New York Tribune*, December 24, 1842; Tuckerman, *Diary of Philip Hone*, 2:164.

33. *The Madisonian*, December 20, 1842, reprinted in Hayford, *Somers Mutiny Affair*, 7–10. On John C. Spencer's authorship of the article, see Tuckerman, *Diary of Philip Hone*, 2:165; *New York Tribune*, December 24, 1842; and McFarland, *Sea Dangers*, 162–63.

34. *New York Herald*, December 19, 20, 1842; Tuckerman, *Diary of Philip Hone*, 2:165–66, 167.

35. Melton, *A Hanging Offense*, 166–92; *New York Herald*, January 20, 1843; Mackenzie to Du Pont, January 14, 1843, Du Pont Papers, W9–4129, ser. B, box 16, HML; *New York Herald*, January 8, 19, 1843.

36. For detailed accounts of the court-martial, see Melton, *A Hanging Offense*, 192, 200–212, 217–43, and McFarland, *Sea Dangers*, 183–204. John C. Spencer was unwilling to allow the naval justice system to decide Mackenzie's fate. He and the widow of Samuel Cromwell attempted to have Mackenzie indicted for murder in federal court. Judge Samuel Betts of the U.S. District Court in New York ruled that naval officers could only be tried by court-martial for crimes committed at sea and that the federal courts had no jurisdiction in such cases. See Melton, *A Hanging Offense*, 212–17.

37. Hall, *Upshur*, 170–71; Melton, *A Hanging Offense*, 243–44, 254; Ruffin, "Edmund Ruffin's Visit to John Tyler," 210–11; McFarland, *Sea Dangers*, 241, 244. The navy recalled Mackenzie to active duty during the Mexican War. He commanded a ship during that conflict (James K. Polk was the president by then) but never received a promotion to captain. He died in 1848.

38. Richard H. Dana Jr., to Mackenzie, April 16, 1843, in Hayford, *Somers Mutiny Affair*, 159; Livingston Hunt, "Attempted Mutiny," 2088; Egan, "Gentlemen-Sailors," 37–38; [Charles Sumner], "The Mutiny of the Somers," *North American Review* 57 (July 1843): 240; Tuckerman, *Diary of Philip Hone*, 2:183; *Chicago Express*, April 20, 1843, reprinted in Hayford, *Somers Mutiny Affair*, 160.

39. *New York Evening Post*, January 11, 1843; Egan, "Gentlemen-Sailors," 30–31.

40. [Cooper], *Cruise of the Somers*, 5, 114; *The Liberator*, January 20, 1843; Nevins and Thomas, *Diary of George Templeton Strong*, 1:198, 200.

41. Benton, *Thirty Years' View*, 2:522–62 (quotations, 526, 538, 540, 562).

42. Blumin, *Emergence of the Middle Class*, 12–13, 195–99; Halttunen, *Confidence Men*, 29; Hessinger, *Seduced, Abandoned, and Reborn*, 17–20; Sellers, *Market Revolution*, 364; Johnson, *A Shopkeeper's Millennium*, 8 (quotation).

43. Wells, *Origins of the Southern Middle Class*, 86–87; Mintz, *Moralists and Modernizers*, xiv; Hessinger, *Seduced, Abandoned, and Reborn*, 2–4.

44. Halttunen, *Confidence Men*, 9–10; Mintz, *Moralists and Modernizers*, xiii–xiv, 3–6, 13–15; Feller, *Jacksonian Promise*, 106–17.

45. Hessinger, *Seduced, Abandoned, and Reborn*, 2, 4–5, 125–47; Demos, *Past, Present, and Personal*, 99, 102; Halttunen, *Confidence Men*, 1–4, 20–21, 28; Mintz, *Moralists and Modernizers*, 6–11.

46. Kett, *Rites of Passage*, 112, 116, 122–23, 125–26; Feller, *Jacksonian Promise*, 138–53.

47. Cremin, *American Education*, 134, 136–37, 141–42; Nagel, *This Sacred Trust*, 73; Kaestle, *Pillars of the Republic*, 64–69; Mintz, *Moralists and Modernizers*, 10–11, 106–12.

48. Van de Water, *Captain Called It Mutiny*, 221–24.

49. Langley, *Social Reform*, 131–67; Wines, *Two Years*, 1:64; Benjamin, *United States Naval Academy*, 92. The cat-o'-nine tails, or "cat," was an eighteen-inch rope with nine hard twisted cords and a wooden handle. Another type of whip commonly used in the navy was the colt, a three-foot-long twisted rope usually applied through the clothing. The U.S. Army abolished flogging in 1812. However, some army officers, feeling that discipline suffered, went around the law by beating soldiers with a wooden board. Other officers, especially those stationed at remote frontier forts, simply ignored the law and continued to flog their men. The army reinstituted flogging in 1833, but only a court-martial had the authority to order a soldier flogged.

50. Langley, *Social Reform*, 209–38; "Opinions of Naval Surgeons on the Expediency of

Allowing the Spirit Ration to Midshipmen of the Navy," January 14, 1830, *ASP:NA*, 3:468–78.

51. Burr, "Education in the Early Navy" (quotation, 46); Williams, *Maury*, 56; S. R. Franklin, *Memories of a Rear-Admiral*, 16, 29.

52. "Incidents on Ship and Shore in the Life of a Midshipman," *Southern Literary Messenger* 7 (November 1841): 761–70.

53. McNally, *Evils and Abuses*, 23–24, 87, 106, 123–27.

54. Rockwell, *Sketches of Foreign Travel*, 2:422–23.

55. Tiphys Aegyptus [pseud.], *The Navy's Friend*, 9–10, 27–29, 31–32 (quotations, 9); *New York Tribune*, January 28, 1843.

56. "Yale Report of 1828," in Hofstadter and Smith, *American Higher Education*, 1:278, 280; Rudolph, *American College and University*, 103–5; Morrison, *"Best School in the World,"* 104–7.

57. "Report of the Board of Visitors of the United States Military Academy," June 21, 1841, S. Doc. 1, *Congressional Serial Set*, No. 395, 27th Cong., 2nd sess., 1:155; Livingston Hunt, "Attempted Mutiny," 2091–92; *New York Herald*, December 20, 1842.

58. Merrill, *Du Pont* (quotation, 153); Charles Stewart to Abel P. Upshur, March 23, 1842, printed in *Army and Navy Chronicle*, April 4, 1844, 428; "A Plan for a Naval Academy," *National Intelligencer*, January 17, 1843.

59. "Report of the Committee on Military Affairs on the Military Academy," May 15, 1844, House Report No. 476, *Congressional Serial Set*, No. 446, 28th Cong., 1st sess., 2:10, 15–16; John Hope Franklin, *Militant South*, 138 (quotation); Green, "Books and Bayonets," 186–87, 213–23.

60. Cox, *A Proper Sense of Honor*, 25–27; Bushman, *Refinement of America*, xiii, xv; Appleby, *Inheriting the Revolution*, 146.

61. Bushman, *Refinement of America*, 409–25 (quotations, xix, 428); "Character and Duties of the Naval Profession," *Naval Magazine* 2 (May 1837): 240.

62. Rockwell, *Sketches of Foreign Travel*, 2:423; "Moral and Religious Improvement of Our Navy," *Southern Literary Messenger* 9 (February 1843): 75 (emphasis added).

Chapter 7

1. Burr, "Education in the Early Navy," 119, 149, 154–57; Paullin, "Beginnings of the United States Naval Academy," 190–92; Simons, *Liberal Education*, 45.

2. Spencer C. Tucker, *Andrew Foote*, 40–41; James Barron to Abel P. Upshur, September 23, 1842, October 5, 1842, Barron Papers, CWM; S. R. Franklin, *Memories of a Rear-Admiral*, 14. On the history of the Naval Asylum, see Stockton, *Origin, History, Laws, and Regulations*.

3. Benjamin, *United States Naval Academy*, 122–24; Littlehales, "William Chauvenet," 606–7; Lewis, Sturdy, and Bolander, "First Academic Staff," 1393–94.

4. Chauvenet, *History*, 4–5.

5. Ibid., 3, 6–9; K. Jack Bauer, "David Henshaw," in Coletta, *American Secretaries of the Navy*, 1:200–201.

6. Chauvenet, *History*, 9–10; Bauer, "David Henshaw," 201.

7. James H. Ward, "Introductory to a Course of Lectures on Ordnance and Gunnery: Delivered at the Naval School in Philadelphia, before the Class of Midshipmen Examined in 1844," *Army and Navy Chronicle*, 2nd ser., May 30, 1844, 691–95.

8. "A Memorial of the Citizens of the State of Massachusetts Praying for the Establishment of a Naval School at the Navy Yard in Charlestown," January 26, 1844, Records of the Committee on Naval Affairs, File No. HR28A-G14.11, Records of the U.S. House of Representatives, RG 233, NA; "A Memorial of the Citizens of the City of New York Praying for the Establishment of a Naval School," February 13, 1845, ibid.

9. "Report of the Committee on Naval Affairs on the Establishment of a Naval School," February 10, 1845, S. Doc. 92, *Congressional Serial Set*, No. 451, 28th Cong., 2nd sess., 3:1–2.

10. Ibid., 4–5.

11. Nye, *Bancroft*, 134–35; Handlin, *Bancroft*, 198–200.

12. Handlin, *Bancroft*, 18–68, 92–95, 108–9; Nye, *Bancroft*, 12–46, 67–69; Kett, *Rites of Passage*, 122.

13. Handlin, *Bancroft*, xi, 166–69, 193–96.

14. George E. Ellis, "Remarks on the Death of George Bancroft," 298; Charles Francis Adams, *Memoirs of John Quincy Adams*, 12:195; Handlin, *Bancroft*, 204–7. On U.S. tensions with Mexico and Britain, see Paterson, Clifford, and Hagan, *American Foreign Policy*, 1:103–9, and Campbell, *From Revolution to Rapprochement*, 65–73.

15. Chauvenet, *History*, 11; Handlin, *Bancroft*, 19, 21.

16. [Thomas Henderson], "Dueling in the Army and Navy," *National Intelligencer*, April 26, 1845. Henderson signed his essay using the pseudonym "Washington." His authorship is established in Paullin, "Dueling in the Old Navy," 1160.

17. Bancroft to Marcus Morton, March 10, 1845, Bancroft Papers, MHS; Schlesinger, *Age of Jackson*, 162; Handlin, *Bancroft*, 207; Benjamin, *United States Naval Academy*, 125–26.

18. Bancroft to the Faculty of the Philadelphia Naval School, May 1, 1845, typescript, Letters Received by the Superintendent, entry 25, box 3, folder 1, Records of the U.S. Naval Academy, RG 405, Special Collections and Archives Department, USNA.

19. Alexander Macomb to Sylvanus Thayer, April 11, 1825, in Cindy Adams, *West Point Thayer Papers*, 4:34; Bancroft to Thayer, July 2, 1825, ibid., 4:37; Annual Report of the Board of Visitors, 1825, USMA.

20. Samuel Marcy to Bancroft, July 18, 1845, Special Collections and Archives Department, USNA.

21. Ibid.

22. Thomas G. Ford, "History of the United States Naval Academy," chap. 9, 1–2. Ford obtained this information from Bancroft.

23. Rudolph, *American College and University*, 91–93 (quotation, 94).

24. Polk, Memorandum, May 31, 1845, Bancroft Papers (microfilm), USNA; Bancroft to George C. Read, June 13, 1845, Letters Sent by the Secretary of the Navy to Officers, roll 40, Naval Records Collection, RG 45, NA.

25. Norris, *Annapolis*, 214–26; Bushman, *Refinement of America*, 151; Sweetman, *U.S. Naval Academy*, 23; Sturdy, "Establishment of the Naval School," 6 (quotation).

26. Norris, *Annapolis*, 245–47 (quotation, 246); Sweetman, *U.S. Naval Academy*, 25.

27. Bancroft to William L. Marcy, June 6, 1845, typescript, Letters Received by the Superintendent, entry 25, box 3, folder 1, Special Collections and Archives Department, USNA (Scott's endorsement of Bancroft's proposal, dated June 9, was written on the back of Bancroft's letter); Marcy to Bancroft, June 12, 1845, Bancroft Papers, MHS; Bancroft to the President of the United States [James K. Polk], June 13, 1845, typescript, Letters Received by the Superintendent, entry 25, box 3, folder 1, Special Collections and Archives Department, USNA.

28. Chauvenet, *History*, 12; Benjamin, *United States Naval Academy*, 144.

29. Bancroft to Read, June 13, 1845, Letters Sent by the Secretary of the Navy to Officers, roll 40, NA; Benjamin, *United States Naval Academy*, 144–45.

30. George C. Read et al., "Report of the Board of Examiners," June 25, 1845, in Soley, *Historical Sketch*, 44–45.

31. Ibid., 45–47.

32. Ibid., 48–49; Sweetman, *U.S. Naval Academy*, 16.

33. *Niles' Register*, July 19, 1845; Symonds, *Confederate Admiral*, 68.

34. Symonds, *Confederate Admiral*, 8–9, 38–39, 45, 54–57.

35. Ibid., 67; Buchanan to Du Pont, August 4, [1845] (W9-4218, ser. B, box 16), and Bancroft to Du Pont, August 4, 1845 (W9-4462, ser. B, box 17), both in Du Pont Papers, HML; Sweetman, *U.S. Naval Academy*, 16.

36. Bancroft to Buchanan, August 7, 1845, Du Pont Papers, W9-4465, ser. B, box 17, HML. This is a handwritten copy of Bancroft's letter, which was forwarded to Du Pont.

37. Ibid.

38. Madison, "Cooper, Bancroft, and the Voorhees Court-Martial"; Cooper to Bancroft, July 27, 1845, in Beard, *Letters and Journals of James Fenimore Cooper*, 5:48–50 (Bancroft's letter of July 21 is quoted in the footnote to Cooper's letter of July 27); Quaife, *Diary of James K. Polk*, 1:41–43. Although the reconvened court-martial sentenced Voorhees to dismissal from the navy, it unanimously recommended the captain "to the mercy of the Executive." On reviewing the case, President Polk reduced the sentence to suspension from duty without pay for five years. At a cabinet meeting on September 27, 1845, Bancroft expressed his disagreement with Polk's decision and again called for Voorhees's dismissal. Polk asked for the opinions of the remaining cabinet members, and they agreed with the president. Despite his disagreement with the commander in chief, Bancroft faithfully carried out Polk's decision. Voorhees returned to active duty after only two years and received a command in 1849.

39. Buchanan to Bancroft, including "Plan for a Naval School at Annapolis," August 14, 1845, Buchanan Letterbook, Special Collections and Archives Department, USNA.

40. Ibid.

41. War Department, Adjutant General's Office, General Orders, No. 40, August 15, 1845, typescript, Letters Received by the Superintendent, entry 25, box 3, folder 1, Special Collections and Archives Department, USNA; Sweetman, *U.S. Naval Academy*, 16; Sturdy, "Founding of the Naval Academy," 1369–70; Soley, *Historical Sketch*, 41; Du Pont to Garrett Pendergrast, August 26, 1845, Du Pont Papers, W9-933, ser. A, box 3, HML. In 1845 the navy's twenty-two professors of mathematics were distributed as follows: one each at the Boston, New York, and Norfolk navy yards; one at the Naval Observatory in Washington, D.C.; one at the U.S. Coastal Survey; four at the Naval Asylum in Philadelphia; two on special service; nine on ships at sea; and two on waiting orders.

42. S. R. Franklin, *Memories of a Rear-Admiral*, 89; Lewis, Sturdy, and Bolander, "First Academic Staff," 1395–96. For Lockwood actively seeking a job at the naval school, see Lockwood to Du Pont, August 16, 1845, Du Pont Papers, W9-4468, ser. B, box 17, HML.

43. Lewis, Sturdy, and Bolander, "First Academic Staff," 1392–93, 1399–1400; Ward to Samuel F. Du Pont, May 7, 1845, Du Pont Papers, W9-4444, ser. B, box 17, HML.

44. Lewis, Sturdy, and Bolander, "First Academic Staff," 1397–98, 1401–3.

45. Symonds, *Confederate Admiral*, 70–74; Sturdy, "Founding of the Naval Academy," 1372; Buchanan to the Professors Attached to the Naval School, October 1, 1845, Letters Sent by the Superintendent, roll 1, Records of the U.S. Naval Academy, RG 405, USNA.

46. Ward to Buchanan, October 7, 1845, Letters Received by the Superintendent, entry 25, box 1, folder 9, Special Collections and Archives Department, USNA. This folder also contains detailed course plans for instruction in mathematics, natural philosophy (including steam engineering), astronomy, navigation, and surveying.

47. Nye, *Bancroft*, 144; Benjamin, *United States Naval Academy*, 157–58; Sweetman, *U.S. Naval Academy*, 27; *Niles' Register*, January 31, 1846.

48. Buchanan to the Professors and Students Attached to the Naval School, October 10, 1845, Buchanan Letterbook, Special Collections and Archives Department, USNA; Buchanan to Bancroft, October 13, 1845, ibid.

49. Buchanan, "Rules and Regulations for the Internal Government of the Naval School," October 10, 1845, Letters Received by the Superintendent, entry 25, box 1, folder 9, Special Col-

lections and Archives Department, USNA; Henry Hayes Lockwood Notes, typescript, Special Collections and Archives Department, USNA.

50. Thomas G. Ford, "History of the United States Naval Academy," chap. 9, 33; *National Intelligencer* and *Maryland Republican*, both reprinted in *Niles' Register*, October 18, 1845.

51. Cremin, *American Education*, 405; Green, "Books and Bayonets," 101–2; Samuel E. Tillman, "The Academic History of the Military Academy, 1802–1902," in U.S. Military Academy, *Centennial*, 1:253–56.

52. Huntington, *Soldier and the State*, 198–200; *Niles' Register*, November 8, 1845; Bennett, *Steam Navy*, 652–53; Felix Jablonski and John W. Schuman, "The Original Library and Early Textbooks of the United States Naval Academy" (unpublished report, 1966), Library Original Holdings and Early Textbooks File, Records of the U.S. Naval Academy, RG 405, Special Collections and Archives Department, USNA. After Ward's transfer from Annapolis in 1847, steam engineering was neglected at the school.

53. Midshipmen's Petition to Henry H. Lockwood, December 5, 1845, Letters Received by the Superintendent, entry 25, box 1, folder 9, Special Collections and Archives Department, USNA; Buchanan to Lockwood, December 7, 1845, Buchanan Letterbook, Special Collections and Archives Department, USNA.

54. Buchanan to Bancroft, September 3, 1846, including a "Catalogue of the Library of the Naval School," typescript, Library Original Holdings and Early Textbooks File, Special Collections and Archives Department, USNA; Skallerup, *Books Afloat and Ashore*, 162–63.

55. Todorich, *Spirited Years*, 31–32, 37; Soley, *Historical Sketch*, 60–61; Symonds, *Confederate Admiral*, 75–78; Sturdy, "Founding of the Naval Academy," 1374–75.

56. Buchanan to Bancroft, November 26, 1845, Buchanan Letterbook, Special Collections and Archives Department, USNA; Sturdy, "Founding of the Naval Academy," 1374; Buchanan to Bancroft, December 12, 1845, Buchanan Letterbook, Special Collections and Archives Department, USNA.

57. Bancroft, "Annual Report of the Secretary of the Navy," December 1, 1845, *CG*, 29th Cong., 1st sess., app., 17.

58. Buchanan to Bancroft, January 30, 1846, Buchanan Letterbook, Special Collections and Archives Department, USNA.

59. Sturdy, "Founding of the Naval Academy," 1383, 1385.

60. Buchanan to Bancroft, February 1, 17, 1846, Buchanan Letterbook, Special Collections and Archives Department, USNA; Todorich, *Spirited Years*, 38–39 (quotation, 38); Johnson, *A Shopkeeper's Millennium*, 55–61.

61. "Incidents on Ship and Shore in the Life of a Midshipman," *Southern Literary Messenger* 7 (November 1841): 767; Sturdy, "Founding of the Naval Academy," 1380.

62. Buchanan to the Professors Attached to the Naval School, April 10, 1846, Letters Sent by the Superintendent, roll 1, USNA; James H. Ward to Buchanan, April 25, 1846, Letters Received by the Superintendent, entry 25, box 1, folder 9, Special Collections and Archives Department, USNA; Sturdy, "Founding of the Naval Academy," 1379; Symonds, *Confederate Admiral*, 80–81; Todorich, *Spirited Years*, 41–44.

63. "An Act Making Appropriations for the Naval Service for the Year Ending on the Thirtieth June, 1847," August 10, 1846, U.S. Congress, *United States Statutes at Large*, 9:100–101; Bancroft to Buchanan, August 13, 1846, typescript, Letters Received by the Superintendent, entry 25, box 3, folder 1, Special Collections and Archives Department, USNA.

64. Soley, *Historical Sketch*, 60; Hunter, "Propriety and Decorum," 27, 88.

65. Geoffrey S. Smith, "An Uncertain Passage: The Bureaus Run the Navy, 1842–1861," in Hagan, *In Peace and War*, 87; Handlin, *Bancroft*, 204–5.

66. "An Act Making Appropriations for the Naval Service for the Year Ending the Thirtieth June, 1846," March 3, 1845, U.S. Congress, *United States Statutes at Large*, 5:794.

67. Benton, *Thirty Years' View*, 2:571–74.

68. Handlin, *Bancroft*, 206–7; K. Jack Bauer, "George Bancroft," in Coletta, *American Secretaries of the Navy*, 1:221, 226–27.

69. Todorich, *Spirited Years*, 44–45, 47–48, 58–61; Sweetman, *U.S. Naval Academy*, 35–38; Hunter, "Propriety and Decorum," 85–86, 158–83.

70. Hunter, "Propriety and Decorum," 55, 77–78, 85–86, 88; Todorich, *Spirited Years*, 50 (quotation).

71. Hunter, "Propriety and Decorum," 98; Todorich, *Spirited Years*, 67–68; Skelton, *American Profession of Arms*, 345 (quotation).

72. Todorich, *Spirited Years*, 67–70; Soley, *Historical Sketch*, 90–92; "Education in the Navy," *Southern Literary Messenger* 16 (September 1850): 522.

73. Todorich, *Spirited Years*, 68–70; Sweetman, *U.S. Naval Academy*, 38–40; Soley, *Historical Sketch*, 92–93; Hunter, "Propriety and Decorum," 97, 99, 101–2. The Naval Academy raised the age requirement for admission in 1853 (ages 14–16) and 1855 (ages 14–17).

74. William A. Graham, "Annual Report of the Secretary of the Navy," November 29, 1851, *CG*, 32nd Cong., 1st sess., app., 21; Todorich, *Spirited Years*, 165–80; Hunter, "Propriety and Decorum," 26, 226–71; Soley, *Historical Sketch*, 96–97; Sweetman, *U.S. Naval Academy*, 42–43.

Epilogue

1. Stewart, *Jones: Commemoration*, 184, 203–4; Thomas, *John Paul Jones*, 3.

2. Stewart, *Jones: Commemoration*, 15–16, 177–80, 183–84; Callo, *John Paul Jones*, 180–87; Thomas, *John Paul Jones*, 4; Sweetman, *U.S. Naval Academy*, 147.

3. Stewart, *Jones: Commemoration*, 5, 11–12, 15–19, 184 (quotations, 16); Thomas, *John Paul Jones*, 4. On the fabrication of the famous quotation about the qualifications of a naval officer, see Bogle and Holwitt, "Best Quote Jones Never Wrote." The Naval Academy did not officially acknowledge the statement's invention until 2003.

4. Thomas, *John Paul Jones*, 309; Sweetman, *U.S. Naval Academy*, 147–49.

5. For in-depth studies on military education and the middle class in nineteenth-century America, see Hunter, "Propriety and Decorum," and Green, "Books and Bayonets."

6. Karsten, *Naval Aristocracy*, 7–13.

7. Todorich, *Spirited Years*, 79; Karsten, *Naval Aristocracy*, 13, 25–33, 37–43; Janowitz, *Professional Soldier*, 127.

8. William McCann to his father, November 1, 6, 1848, in Drew, *Letters from Annapolis*, 8, 10 (emphasis added); Theodore Roosevelt, "Address at Haverhill, Massachusetts," August 26, 1902, in Roosevelt, *Addresses and Presidential Messages*, 29.

9. Karsten, *Naval Aristocracy*, 33–34.

10. Millett, *Military Professionalism*, 2; Spector, *Professors of War*, 3; Samuel J. Watson, "Professionalism, Social Attitudes," 1414; Todorich, *Spirited Years*, 8.

11. Samuel J. Watson, "Professionalism, Social Attitudes," 1363, 1380.

12. Heitzmann, "In-Service Naval Officer Education," 112; Janowitz, *Professional Soldier*, 127, 131; Valle, *Rocks and Shoals*, 4 (quotation, 6); Sweetman, *U.S. Naval Academy*, 117.

13. Hattendorf, Simpson, and Wadleigh, *Sailors and Scholars*, 5–6, 11–22; Heitzmann, "In-Service Naval Officer Education," 118–19; Spector, *Professors of War*, 3–4, 14–20 (quotation, 11).

BIBLIOGRAPHY

Primary Sources

ARCHIVES AND MANUSCRIPT COLLECTIONS

Earl Gregg Swem Library, College of William and Mary, Williamsburg, Virginia
    James Barron Papers
    Tucker-Coleman Papers
Rare Book, Manuscript, and Special Collections Library, Duke University, Durham,
        North Carolina
    William H. Crawford Papers
Hagley Museum and Library, Wilmington, Delaware
    Samuel Francis Du Pont Papers
Historical Society of Pennsylvania, Philadelphia
    George C. Read, "Book of Notes and Remarks on Sundry Topics"
    Rodgers Family Papers
        Matthew C. Perry Letterbook, 1830–37
Library of Congress, Washington, D.C.
    Horatio Nelson Cady Logbook
    Thomas Jefferson Papers
    Matthew Fontaine Maury Papers
    George Washington Papers
Massachusetts Historical Society, Boston
    Adams Papers (microfilm)
    George Bancroft Papers
    Henry Knox Papers (microfilm; originals at Gilder Lehrman Institute of American
        History, New York City)
    Timothy Pickering Papers (microfilm)
National Archives, Washington, D.C.
    Naval Records Collection (Record Group 45)
        Letters Sent by the Secretary of the Navy to Officers, 1798–1868 (microfilm, M149)
        Miscellaneous Letters Sent by the Secretary of the Navy, 1798–1886 (microfilm,
            M209)
        Records of the Board of Navy Commissioners
    Papers of the Continental Congress (microfilm, M247)
    Records of the U.S. House of Representatives (Record Group 233)
        Records of the Committee on Naval Affairs
Princeton University Library, Princeton, New Jersey
    Samuel L. Southard Papers
U.S. Military Academy Library, West Point, New York
    Alden Partridge Papers
    Annual Report of the Board of Visitors, 1825
Nimitz Library, U.S. Naval Academy, Annapolis, Maryland
    George Bancroft Papers (microfilm)
    Franklin Buchanan Letterbook

Henry Hayes Lockwood Notes on the Founding of the U.S. Naval Academy
Samuel Marcy Letter to George Bancroft, July 18, 1845, Containing a Report on the U.S.
    Military Academy and Recommendations for the Establishment of a Naval School
Records of the U.S. Naval Academy (Record Group 405)
    Letters Received by the Superintendent, 1845–87
    Letters Sent by the Superintendent, 1845–65 (microfilm, M945)
    Library Original Holdings and Early Textbooks File
Samuel Eliot Morison Memorial Library, USS *Constitution* Museum, Boston
    Lucius M. Mason Journal
    Philip A. Stockton Journal
    Philip A. Stockton Logbook

GOVERNMENT DOCUMENTS

Bauer, K. Jack, ed. *The New American State Papers: Naval Affairs.* 10 vols. Wilmington, Del.:
    Scholarly Resources, 1981.
Ford, Worthington Chauncey, ed. *Journals of the Continental Congress, 1774–1789.* 34 vols.
    Washington, D.C.: Government Printing Office, 1904–37.
Knox, Dudley W., ed. *Naval Documents Related to the Quasi-War between the United States
    and France.* 7 vols. Washington, D.C.: Government Printing Office, 1935–38.
———, ed. *Naval Documents Related to the United States Wars with the Barbary Powers.*
    6 vols. Washington, D.C.: Government Printing Office, 1939–44.
Richardson, James D., ed. *A Compilation of the Messages and Papers of the Presidents, 1789–
    1897.* 10 vols. Washington, D.C.: Government Printing Office, 1896–99.
U.S. Congress. *American State Papers: Military Affairs.* 7 vols. Washington, D.C.: Gales and
    Seaton, 1832–61.
———. *American State Papers: Naval Affairs.* 4 vols. Washington, D.C.: Gales and Seaton,
    1834–61.
———. *Annals of the Congress of the United States.* 42 vols. Washington, D.C.: Gales and
    Seaton, 1834–56.
———. *Bills and Resolutions of the House of Representatives.* 19th Congress.
———. *Bills and Resolutions of the Senate.* 19th, 23rd, 24th, and 27th Congresses.
———. *Congressional Globe.* 44 vols. Washington, D.C.: Blair and Rives, 1834–73.
———. *Congressional Serial Set.* 16th, 27th, and 28th Congresses.
———. *Journal of the Senate.* 18th Congress.
———. *Register of Debates in Congress.* 14 vols. Washington, D.C.: Gales and Seaton,
    1825–37.
———. *United States Statutes at Large.* 28th and 29th Congresses.

PUBLISHED CORRESPONDENCE, REPORTS, DIARIES, AND MEMOIRS

Adams, Charles Francis, ed. *Memoirs of John Quincy Adams, Comprising Portions of His
    Diary from 1795 to 1848.* 12 vols. Philadelphia: Lippincott, 1874–77. Reprint, Freeport,
    N.Y.: Books for Libraries Press, 1969.
———. *The Works of John Adams.* 10 vols. Boston: Little, Brown, 1850–56.
Adams, Cindy, ed. *The West Point Thayer Papers, 1808–1872.* 11 vols. West Point: Association
    of Graduates, 1965.
Adams, Henry, ed. *The Writings of Albert Gallatin.* 3 vols. Philadelphia: Lippincott, 1879.
Aderman, Ralph, ed. *The Letters of James Kirke Paulding.* Madison: University of Wisconsin
    Press, 1962.
Barnes, John S., ed. *Fanning's Narrative: Being the Memoirs of Nathaniel Fanning, An Officer
    of the Revolutionary Navy, 1778–1783.* New York: Naval History Society, 1912.

Bassett, John Spencer, ed. *Correspondence of Andrew Jackson*. 7 vols. Washington, D.C.: Carnegie Institution of Washington, 1926–35.

Beard, James Franklin, ed. *The Letters and Journals of James Fenimore Cooper*. 6 vols. Cambridge: Belknap Press of Harvard University Press, 1968.

Benton, Thomas Hart. *Thirty Years' View*. 2 vols. New York: D. Appleton, 1856.

Boyd, Julian P., et al., eds. *The Papers of Thomas Jefferson*. 34 vols. to date. Princeton: Princeton University Press, 1950–.

Bradford, James C., ed. *The Papers of John Paul Jones*. Microfilm ed. Alexandria, Va.: Chadwyck-Healey, 1986.

Butterfield, L. H., ed. *Diary and Autobiography of John Adams*. 4 vols. Cambridge: Belknap Press of Harvard University Press, 1961.

Cappon, Lester J., ed. *The Adams-Jefferson Letters: The Complete Correspondence between Thomas Jefferson and Abigail and John Adams*. 2 vols. Chapel Hill: University of North Carolina Press, 1959.

Chauvenet, William. *History of the Origin of the United States Naval Academy: A Letter from Prof. William Chauvenet to Mr. T. G. Ford, October 1860*. St. Louis: Nixon-Jones, [1910].

Cunningham, Noble E., Jr., ed. *Circular Letters of Congressmen to Their Constituents, 1789–1829*. 3 vols. Chapel Hill: University of North Carolina Press, 1978.

Drew, Anne Marie, ed. *Letters from Annapolis: Midshipmen Write Home*. Annapolis: Naval Institute Press, 1998.

Fitzpatrick, John C., ed. *The Writings of George Washington from the Original Manuscript Sources, 1745–1799*. 39 vols. Washington, D.C.: Government Printing Office, 1931–44.

Franklin, S. R. *Memories of a Rear-Admiral*. New York: Harper and Brothers, 1898.

Gawalt, Gerard W., trans. and ed. *John Paul Jones' Memoir of the American Revolution, Presented to King Louis XVI of France*. Washington, D.C.: Library of Congress, 1979.

Grant, Ulysses S. *Personal Memoirs of U. S. Grant*. Edited by James M. McPherson. New York: Penguin, 1999. First published, 1885.

Hayford, Harrison, ed. *The Somers Mutiny Affair*. Englewood Cliffs, N.J.: Prentice-Hall, 1959.

Hofstadter, Richard, and Wilson Smith, eds. *American Higher Education: A Documentary History*. 2 vols. Chicago: University of Chicago Press, 1961.

Hunt, Gaillard, ed. *The Writings of James Madison*. 9 vols. New York: G. P. Putnam's Sons, 1900–1910.

Lipscomb, Andrew A., and Albert Ellery Bergh, eds. *The Writings of Thomas Jefferson*. 20 vols. Washington, D.C.: Thomas Jefferson Memorial Association, 1903.

Meriwether, Robert L., et al., eds. *The Papers of John C. Calhoun*. 28 vols. Columbia: University of South Carolina Press, 1959–2003.

Nevins, Allan, and Milton Halsey Thomas, eds. *The Diary of George Templeton Strong*. 4 vols. New York: Macmillan, 1952.

Quaife, Milo Milton, ed. *The Diary of James K. Polk during His Presidency, 1845 to 1849*. 4 vols. Chicago: A. C. McClurg and Co., 1910. Reprint, New York: Kraus Reprint Co., 1970.

Roosevelt, Theodore. *Addresses and Presidential Messages of Theodore Roosevelt, 1902–1904*. New York: G. P. Putnam's Sons, 1904.

Ruffin, Edmund. "Edmund Ruffin's Visit to John Tyler." *William and Mary Quarterly*, 1st ser., 14 (January 1906): 193–211.

Steiner, Bernard C. *The Life and Correspondence of James McHenry*. Cleveland: Burrows Brothers, 1907. Reprint, New York: Arno Press, 1979.

Syrett, Harold C., ed. *The Papers of Alexander Hamilton*. 27 vols. New York: Columbia University Press, 1961–87.

Tuckerman, Bayard, ed. *The Diary of Philip Hone, 1828–1851*. 2 vols. New York: Dodd, Mead, 1889.

Wharton, Francis, ed. *The Revolutionary Diplomatic Correspondence of the United States*. 6 vols. Washington, D.C.: Government Printing Office, 1889.

CONTEMPORARY BOOKS AND PAMPHLETS

Aegyptus, Tiphys [pseud.]. *The Navy's Friend, or Reminiscences of the Navy: Containing Memoirs of a Cruise, in the U.S. Schooner Enterprise*. Baltimore, 1843.

Barlow, Joel. *Prospectus of a National Institution, to Be Established in the United States*. Washington, D.C.: Samuel H. Smith, 1806.

Bowditch, Nathaniel. *The New American Practical Navigator*. 5th ed. New York: Edmund M. Blunt, 1821.

Butler, Benjamin F. *The Military Profession in the United States, and the Means of Promoting Its Usefulness and Honour*. New York: Samuel Colman, 1839.

Catalogue of the Officers and Cadets of the American Literary, Scientific, and Military Academy. Woodstock, Vt.: David Watson, 1821.

Catalogue of the Officers and Cadets, Together with the Prospectus and Internal Regulations of the American Literary, Scientific, and Military Academy at Middletown, Connecticut. Middletown, Conn.: Starr and Niles, 1826.

Catalogue of the Officers and Students in Yale College, 1828–9. New Haven, 1828.

Constitution and By-Laws of the United States Naval Lyceum, Established at the Navy Yard, New York. New York: J. Post, 1834.

[Cooper, James Fenimore]. *The Cruise of the Somers: Illustrative of the Despotism of the Quarter Deck; and of the Unmanly Conduct of Commander Mackenzie*. 3rd ed. New York: J. Winchester, 1844.

Cooper, James Fenimore. *The History of the Navy of the United States of America*. 2 vols. Philadelphia: Lea and Blanchard, 1839.

Coxe, Tench. *Thoughts on the Subject of Naval Power in the United States of America; and on Certain Means of Encouraging and Protecting Their Commerce and Manufactures*. Philadelphia, 1806.

Dickinson, David. *West Point Academy: Speech of the Hon. David Dickinson (of Tennessee), In Opposition to the Military Academy, Delivered in the House of Representatives, on Saturday, June 14th, 1834*. Washington, D.C.: James B. Carlisle, 1834.

The First Annual Report of the Administration Committee of the U.S. Naval Lyceum. New York: J. Post, 1835.

Hamilton, Alexander, James Madison, and John Jay. *The Federalist*. Edited by Robert Scigliano. New York: Modern Library, 2000. First published, 1788.

Jefferson, Thomas. *Notes on the State of Virginia*. Edited by William Peden. Chapel Hill: University of North Carolina Press, 1954. First published, 1787.

Jones, George. *Sketches of Naval Life, with Notices of Men, Manners and Scenery, on the Shores of the Mediterranean, in a Series of Letters from the Brandywine and Constitution Frigates*. 2 vols. New Haven: Hezekiah Howe, 1829.

Maury, Matthew F. *A New Theoretical and Practical Treatise on Navigation*. Philadelphia: Key and Biddle, 1836.

McNally, William. *Evils and Abuses in the Naval and Merchant Service, Exposed; with Proposals for Their Remedy and Redress*. Boston: Cassady and March, 1839.

Melville, Herman. *White-Jacket, or The World in a Man-of-War*. Evanston, Ill.: Northwestern University Press and the Newberry Library, 1970. First published, 1850.

[Partridge, Alden]. *The Military Academy, at West Point, Unmasked, or Corruption and Military Despotism Exposed*. Washington, D.C., 1830.

Rockwell, Charles. *Sketches of Foreign Travel and Life at Sea.* 2 vols. Boston: Tappan and Dennet, 1842.

Tocqueville, Alexis de. *Democracy in America.* 2 vols. Edited by Phillips Bradley. New York: Alfred A. Knopf, 1945. First published, 1835, 1840.

Truxtun, Thomas. *Remarks, Instructions, and Examples Relating to the Latitude & Longitude* ... Philadelphia: T. Dobson, 1794.

Wines, E. C. *Two Years and a Half in the Navy, or Journal of a Cruise in the Mediterranean and Levant, On Board of the U.S. Frigate Constellation, in the Years 1829, 1830, and 1831.* 2 vols. Philadelphia: Carey and Lea, 1832.

NEWSPAPERS AND PERIODICALS

American Quarterly Review
Army and Navy Chronicle
The Liberator
Military and Naval Magazine of
   the United States
National Gazette
National Intelligencer
Naval Magazine
New York Evening Post

New York Herald
New York Mirror
New York Tribune
Niles' Register
North American Review
Philadelphia Aurora
Richmond Whig
Southern Literary Messenger

Secondary Sources

BOOKS

Adams, Henry. *History of the United States of America during the Administrations of Thomas Jefferson and James Madison.* 9 vols. New York: Charles Scribner's Sons, 1891–96. Reprint, Antiquarian Press, 1962.

Albion, Robert Greenhalgh. *Makers of Naval Policy, 1798–1947.* Annapolis: Naval Institute Press, 1980.

Allison, Robert J. *Stephen Decatur: American Naval Hero, 1779–1820.* Amherst: University of Massachusetts Press, 2005.

Ambrose, Stephen E. *Duty, Honor, Country: A History of West Point.* Baltimore: Johns Hopkins University Press, 1966. Reprint, 1999.

Anderson, Benedict. *Imagined Communities: Reflections on the Origin and Spread of Nationalism.* Rev. ed. London: Verso, 1991.

Andrew, Rod, Jr. *Long Gray Lines: The Southern Military School Tradition, 1839–1915.* Chapel Hill: University of North Carolina Press, 2001.

Appleby, Joyce. *Inheriting the Revolution: The First Generation of Americans.* Cambridge: Belknap Press of Harvard University Press, 2000.

Bailyn, Bernard. *The Ideological Origins of the American Revolution.* Cambridge: Belknap Press of Harvard University Press, 1967.

Barnard, Henry. *Military Schools and Courses of Instruction in the Science and Art of War.* New York: E. Steiger, 1872. Reprint, Greenwood Press, 1969.

Beach, Edward L. *The United States Navy: 200 Years.* New York: Henry Holt, 1986.

Bemis, Samuel Flagg. *John Quincy Adams and the Union.* New York: Alfred A. Knopf, 1956.

Benjamin, Park. *The United States Naval Academy.* New York: G. P. Putnam's Sons, 1900.

Bennett, Frank M. *The Steam Navy of the United States: A History of the Growth of the Steam Vessel of War in the U.S. Navy, and of the Naval Engineer Corps.* Pittsburgh: W. T. Nicholson Press, 1896. Reprint, Westport, Conn.: Greenwood Press, 1972.

Birkner, Michael. *Samuel L. Southard: Jeffersonian Whig*. Rutherford, N.J.: Fairleigh Dickinson University Press, 1984.

Bledstein, Burton J. *The Culture of Professionalism: The Middle Class and the Development of Higher Education in America*. New York: W. W. Norton, 1976.

Blumin, Stuart M. *The Emergence of the Middle Class: Social Experience in the American City, 1760-1900*. New York: Cambridge University Press, 1989.

Bode, Carl. *The American Lyceum: Town Meeting of the Mind*. New York: Oxford University Press, 1956.

Bradford, James C., ed. *Command under Sail: Makers of the American Naval Tradition, 1775-1850*. Annapolis: Naval Institute Press, 1985.

Brown, Richard D. *The Strength of a People: The Idea of an Informed Citizenry in America, 1650-1870*. Chapel Hill: University of North Carolina Press, 1996.

Buel, Richard, Jr. *Securing the Revolution: Ideology in American Politics, 1789-1815*. Ithaca: Cornell University Press, 1972.

Bushman, Richard L. *The Refinement of America: Persons, Houses, Cities*. New York: Alfred A. Knopf, 1992.

Calhoun, Daniel H. *Professional Lives in America: Structure and Aspiration, 1750-1850*. Cambridge: Harvard University Press, 1965.

Callahan, North. *Henry Knox: General Washington's General*. New York: Rinehart, 1958.

Callo, Joseph. *John Paul Jones: America's First Sea Warrior*. Annapolis: Naval Institute Press, 2006.

Campbell, Charles S. *From Revolution to Rapprochement: The United States and Great Britain, 1783-1900*. New York: John Wiley and Sons, 1974.

Chisholm, Donald. *Waiting for Dead Men's Shoes: Origins and Development of the U.S. Navy's Officer Personnel System, 1793-1941*. Stanford, Calif.: Stanford University Press, 2001.

Cobban, Alfred, ed. *The Eighteenth Century: Europe in the Age of Enlightenment*. New York: McGraw-Hill, 1969.

Coletta, Paolo E., ed. *American Secretaries of the Navy*. 2 vols. Annapolis: Naval Institute Press, 1980.

Colley, Linda. *Britons: Forging the Nation, 1707-1837*. New Haven: Yale University Press, 1992.

Cormack, William S. *Revolution and Political Conflict in the French Navy, 1789-1794*. Cambridge: Cambridge University Press, 1995.

Cox, Caroline. *A Proper Sense of Honor: Service and Sacrifice in George Washington's Army*. Chapel Hill: University of North Carolina Press, 2004.

Crackel, Theodore J. *Mr. Jefferson's Army: Political and Social Reform of the Military Establishment, 1801-1809*. New York: New York University Press, 1987.

———. *West Point: A Bicentennial History*. Lawrence: University Press of Kansas, 2002.

Cremin, Lawrence A. *American Education: The National Experience, 1783-1876*. New York: Harper and Row, 1980.

Cress, Lawrence Delbert. *Citizens in Arms: The Army and the Militia in American Society to the War of 1812*. Chapel Hill: University of North Carolina Press, 1982.

Cunliffe, Marcus. *Soldiers and Civilians: The Martial Spirit in America, 1775-1865*. Boston: Little, Brown, 1968.

DeConde, Alexander. *The Quasi-War: The Politics and Diplomacy of the Undeclared War with France, 1797-1801*. New York: Charles Scribner's Sons, 1966.

Demos, John. *Past, Present, and Personal: The Family and the Life Course in American History*. New York: Oxford University Press, 1986.

Dudley, William S., and Michael J. Crawford, eds. *The Early Republic and the Sea: Essays on the Naval and Maritime History of the Early United States. Washington, D.C.: Brassey's, 2001.

Ekirch, Arthur A., Jr. *The Civilian and the Military*. New York: Oxford University Press, 1956.

————. *The Idea of Progress in America, 1815–1860*. New York: AMS Press, 1969.

Elkins, Stanley, and Eric McKitrick. *The Age of Federalism*. New York: Oxford University Press, 1993.

Ellis, Joseph J. *American Sphinx: The Character of Thomas Jefferson*. New York: Alfred A. Knopf, 1996. Reprint, Vintage Books, 1998.

Feller, Daniel. *The Jacksonian Promise: America, 1815–1840*. Baltimore: Johns Hopkins University Press, 1995.

Ferguson, Eugene S. *Truxtun of the Constellation: The Life of Commodore Thomas Truxtun, U.S. Navy, 1755–1822*. Baltimore: Johns Hopkins Press, 1956.

Fleming, Thomas J. *West Point: The Men and Times of the United States Military Academy*. New York: William Morrow, 1969.

Forman, Sidney. *West Point: A History of the United States Military Academy*. New York: Columbia University Press, 1950.

Fowler, William M., Jr. *Jack Tars and Commodores: The American Navy, 1783–1815*. Boston: Houghton Mifflin, 1984.

————. *Rebels under Sail: The American Navy during the Revolution*. New York: Charles Scribner's Sons, 1976.

Franklin, John Hope. *The Militant South, 1800–1861*. Cambridge: Belknap Press of Harvard University Press, 1956.

Gelfand, H. Michael. *Sea Change at Annapolis: The United States Naval Academy, 1949–2000*. Chapel Hill: University of North Carolina Press, 2006.

Haber, Samuel. *The Quest for Authority and Honor in the American Professions, 1750–1900*. Chicago: University of Chicago Press, 1991.

Hagan, Kenneth J., ed. *In Peace and War: Interpretations of American Naval History, 1775–1984*. 2nd ed. Westport, Conn.: Greenwood Press, 1984.

————. *This People's Navy: The Making of American Sea Power*. New York: Free Press, 1991.

Hall, Claude H. *Abel Parker Upshur: Conservative Virginian, 1790–1844*. Madison: State Historical Society of Wisconsin, 1963.

Halttunen, Karen. *Confidence Men and Painted Women: A Study of Middle-Class Culture in America, 1830–1870*. New Haven: Yale University Press, 1982.

Handlin, Lilian. *George Bancroft: The Intellectual as Democrat*. New York: Harper and Row, 1984.

Hargreaves, Mary W. M. *The Presidency of John Quincy Adams*. Lawrence: University Press of Kansas, 1985.

Hattendorf, John B., B. Mitchell Simpson III, and John R. Wadleigh. *Sailors and Scholars: The Centennial History of the U.S. Naval War College*. Newport, R.I.: Naval War College Press, 1984.

Hessinger, Rodney. *Seduced, Abandoned, and Reborn: Visions of Youth in Middle-Class America, 1780–1850*. Philadelphia: University of Pennsylvania Press, 2005.

Hickey, Donald R. *The War of 1812: A Forgotten Conflict*. Urbana: University of Illinois Press, 1989.

Higginbotham, Don. *The War of American Independence: Military Attitudes, Policies, and Practice, 1763–1789*. New York: Macmillan, 1971.

Hill, Forest G. *Roads, Rails, and Waterways: The Army Engineers and Early Transportation*. Norman: University of Oklahoma Press, 1957.

Hofstadter, Richard. *Anti-Intellectualism in American Life*. New York: Alfred A. Knopf, 1963. Reprint, 1974.

Honeywell, Roy J. *The Educational Work of Thomas Jefferson*. Cambridge: Harvard University Press, 1931.

Howarth, Stephen. *To Shining Sea: A History of the United States Navy, 1775-1991*. New York: Random House, 1991.

Howe, Daniel Walker. *The Political Culture of the American Whigs*. Chicago: University of Chicago Press, 1979.

Huntington, Samuel P. *The Soldier and the State: The Theory and Politics of Civil-Military Relations*. Cambridge: Belknap Press of Harvard University Press, 1959.

Janowitz, Morris. *The Professional Soldier: A Social and Political Portrait*. New York: Free Press, 1960.

Johnson, Paul E. *A Shopkeeper's Millennium: Society and Revivals in Rochester, New York, 1815-1837*. New York: Hill and Wang, 1978.

Kaestle, Carl F. *Pillars of the Republic: Common Schools and American Society, 1780-1860*. New York: Hill and Wang, 1983.

Karsten, Peter. *The Naval Aristocracy: The Golden Age of Annapolis and the Emergence of Modern American Navalism*. New York: Free Press, 1972.

Kershner, James William. *Sylvanus Thayer: A Biography*. New York: Arno Press, 1982.

Kett, Joseph F. *Rites of Passage: Adolescence in America, 1790 to the Present*. New York: Basic Books, 1977.

Kimmel, Michael. *Manhood in America: A Cultural History*. New York: Free Press, 1996.

Kohl, Lawrence Frederick. *The Politics of Individualism: Parties and the American Character in the Jacksonian Era*. New York: Oxford University Press, 1989.

Kohn, Hans. *The Idea of Nationalism: A Study of Its Origins and Background*. New York: Macmillan, 1944.

Kohn, Richard H. *Eagle and Sword: The Federalists and the Creation of the Military Establishment in America, 1783-1802*. New York: Free Press, 1975.

Langley, Harold D. *Social Reform in the United States Navy, 1798-1862*. Urbana: University of Illinois Press, 1967.

LaPiana, William P. *Logic and Experience: The Origin of Modern American Legal Education*. New York: Oxford University Press, 1994.

Lewis, Michael. *The Navy in Transition, 1814-1864: A Social History*. London: Hodder and Stoughton, 1965.

Long, David F. *Gold Braid and Foreign Relations: Diplomatic Activities of American Naval Officers, 1798-1883*. Annapolis: Naval Institute Press, 1988.

Love, Robert W., Jr. *History of the U.S. Navy*. 2 vols. Harrisburg: Stackpole Books, 1992.

Lovell, John P. *Neither Athens nor Sparta? The American Service Academies in Transition*. Bloomington: Indiana University Press, 1979.

Lovette, Leland P. *Naval Customs, Traditions, and Usage*. 3rd ed. Annapolis: U.S. Naval Institute, 1939.

Ludmerer, Kenneth M. *Learning to Heal: The Development of Modern American Medical Education*. New York: Basic Books, 1985.

Maloney, Linda M. *The Captain from Connecticut: The Life and Naval Times of Isaac Hull*. Boston: Northeastern University Press, 1986.

Marshall, Edward Chauncey. *History of the United States Naval Academy*. New York: D. Van Nostrand, 1862.

Masland, John W., and Laurence I. Radway. *Soldiers and Scholars: Military Education and National Policy*. Princeton: Princeton University Press, 1957.

McCoy, Drew R. *The Elusive Republic: Political Economy in Jeffersonian America*. Chapel Hill: University of North Carolina Press, 1980.

McCullough, David. *John Adams*. New York: Simon and Schuster, 2001.

McDonald, Forrest. *The Presidency of Thomas Jefferson*. Lawrence: University Press of Kansas, 1976.

McDonald, Robert M. S., ed. *Thomas Jefferson's Military Academy: Founding West Point*. Charlottesville: University of Virginia Press, 2004.

McFarland, Philip. *Sea Dangers: The Affair of the Somers*. New York: Schocken Books, 1985.

McKee, Christopher. *Edward Preble: A Naval Biography*. Annapolis: Naval Institute Press, 1972.

———. *A Gentlemanly and Honorable Profession: The Creation of the U.S. Naval Officer Corps, 1794–1815*. Annapolis: Naval Institute Press, 1991.

Melton, Buckner F., Jr. *A Hanging Offense: The Strange Affair of the Warship Somers*. New York: Free Press, 2003.

Merrill, James M. *Du Pont: The Making of an Admiral: A Biography of Samuel Francis Du Pont*. New York: Dodd, Mead, 1986.

Meyers, Marvin. *The Jacksonian Persuasion: Politics and Belief*. Stanford, Calif.: Stanford University Press, 1960.

Millett, Allan R. *Military Professionalism and Officership in America*. Columbus: Mershon Center of Ohio State University, 1977.

Mintz, Steven. *Moralists and Modernizers: America's Pre-Civil War Reformers*. Baltimore: Johns Hopkins University Press, 1995.

Mitchell, Broadus. *Alexander Hamilton: The National Adventure, 1788–1804*. New York: Macmillan, 1962.

Morison, Samuel Eliot. *John Paul Jones: A Sailor's Biography*. Boston: Little, Brown, 1959.

———. *"Old Bruin": Commodore Matthew C. Perry, 1794–1858*. Boston: Little, Brown, 1967.

Morrison, James L., Jr. *"The Best School in the World": West Point, the Pre-Civil War Years, 1833–1866*. Kent, Ohio: Kent State University Press, 1986.

Nagel, Paul C. *John Quincy Adams: A Public Life, a Private Life*. New York: Alfred A. Knopf, 1998.

———. *This Sacred Trust: American Nationality, 1798–1898*. New York: Oxford University Press, 1971.

Norris, Walter B. *Annapolis: Its Colonial and Naval Story*. New York: Thomas Y. Crowell, 1925.

Nye, Russel Blaine. *The Cultural Life of the New Nation, 1776–1830*. New York: Harper and Brothers, 1960.

———. *George Bancroft: Brahmin Rebel*. New York: Alfred A. Knopf, 1945.

Pappas, George S. *To the Point: The United States Military Academy, 1802–1902*. Westport, Conn.: Praeger, 1993.

Paterson, Thomas G., J. Garry Clifford, and Kenneth J. Hagan. *American Foreign Policy: A History*, 3rd ed., 2 vols. Lexington, Mass.: D. C. Heath, 1988.

Paullin, Charles Oscar. *Commodore John Rodgers: Captain, Commodore, and Senior Officer of the American Navy, 1773–1838*. Cleveland: Arthur H. Clark, 1910.

———. *Paullin's History of Naval Administration, 1775–1911*. Annapolis: U.S. Naval Institute, 1968.

Perkins, Bradford. *The Creation of a Republican Empire, 1776–1865*. Vol. 1 of *The Cambridge History of American Foreign Relations*. New York: Cambridge University Press, 1993.

Pessen, Edward. *Jacksonian America: Society, Personality, and Politics*. Rev. ed. Homewood, Ill.: Dorsey Press, 1978.

Philbrick, Nathaniel. *Sea of Glory: America's Voyage of Discovery: The U.S. Exploring Expedition, 1838-1842*. New York: Viking, 2003.

Pugh, David G. *Sons of Liberty: The Masculine Mind in Nineteenth-Century America*. Westport, Conn.: Greenwood Press, 1983.

Rodger, N. A. M. *The Wooden World: An Anatomy of the Georgian Navy*. Annapolis: Naval Institute Press, 1986.

Rotundo, E. Anthony. *American Manhood: Transformations in Masculinity from the Revolution to the Modern Era*. New York: Basic Books, 1993.

Royster, Charles. *A Revolutionary People at War: The Continental Army and American Character, 1775-1783*. Chapel Hill: University of North Carolina Press, 1979.

Rudolph, Frederick. *The American College and University: A History*. New York: Alfred A. Knopf, 1962. Reprint, Athens: University of Georgia Press, 1990.

Savelle, Max. *Seeds of Liberty: The Genesis of the American Mind*. Seattle: University of Washington Press, 1965.

Schlesinger, Arthur M., Jr. *The Age of Jackson*. Boston: Little, Brown, 1945.

Schneller, Robert J., Jr. *Farragut: America's First Admiral*. Washington, D.C.: Brassey's, 2002.

Schroeder, John H. *Commodore John Rodgers: Paragon of the Early American Navy*. Gainesville: University Press of Florida, 2006.

———. *Matthew Calbraith Perry: Antebellum Sailor and Diplomat*. Annapolis: Naval Institute Press, 2001.

———. *Shaping a Maritime Empire: The Commercial and Diplomatic Role of the American Navy, 1829-1861*. Westport, Conn.: Greenwood Press, 1985.

Sellers, Charles. *The Market Revolution: Jacksonian America, 1815-1846*. New York: Oxford University Press, 1991.

Simons, William E. *Liberal Education in the Service Academies*. New York: Institute of Higher Education, 1965.

Skaggs, David Curtis. *Oliver Hazard Perry: Honor, Courage, and Patriotism in the Early U.S. Navy*. Annapolis: Naval Institute Press, 2006.

———. *Thomas Macdonough: Master of Command in the Early U.S. Navy*. Annapolis: Naval Institute Press, 2003.

Skallerup, Harry R. *Books Afloat and Ashore: A History of Books, Libraries, and Reading among Seamen during the Age of Sail*. Hamden, Conn.: Archon Books, 1974.

Skelton, William B. *An American Profession of Arms: The Army Officer Corps, 1784-1861*. Lawrence: University Press of Kansas, 1992.

Smelser, Marshall. *The Congress Founds the Navy, 1787-1798*. Notre Dame, Ind.: University of Notre Dame Press, 1959.

Smith, Gene A. *"For the Purposes of Defense": The Politics of the Jeffersonian Gunboat Program*. Newark: University of Delaware Press, 1995.

Soley, James Russell. *Historical Sketch of the United States Naval Academy*. Washington, D.C.: Government Printing Office, 1876.

Sowerby, E. Millicent, comp. *Catalogue of the Library of Thomas Jefferson*. 5 vols. Washington, D.C.: Library of Congress, 1952-59.

Spector, Ronald. *Professors of War: The Naval War College and the Development of the Naval Profession*. Newport, R.I.: Naval War College Press, 1977.

Sprout, Harold, and Margaret Sprout. *The Rise of American Naval Power, 1776-1918*. Princeton: Princeton University Press, 1946.

Stagg, J. C. A. *Mr. Madison's War: Politics, Diplomacy, and Warfare in the Early American Republic, 1783-1830*. Princeton: Princeton University Press, 1983.

Stanton, William. *The Great United States Exploring Expedition of 1838-1842.* Berkeley: University of California Press, 1975.

Stewart, Charles W., comp. *John Paul Jones: Commemoration at Annapolis, April 24, 1906.* Washington, D.C.: Government Printing Office, 1907.

Stockton, Charles H. *Origin, History, Laws, and Regulations of the United States Naval Asylum, Philadelphia, Pennsylvania.* Washington, D.C.: Government Printing Office, 1886.

Stuart, Reginald C. *The Half-way Pacifist: Thomas Jefferson's View of War.* Toronto: University of Toronto Press, 1978.

———. *War and American Thought: From the Revolution to the Monroe Doctrine.* Kent, Ohio: Kent State University Press, 1982.

Sweetman, Jack. *The U.S. Naval Academy: An Illustrated History.* 2nd ed. Annapolis: Naval Institute Press, 1995.

Symonds, Craig L. *Confederate Admiral: The Life and Wars of Franklin Buchanan.* Annapolis: Naval Institute Press, 1999.

———. *Navalists and Antinavalists: The Naval Policy Debate in the United States, 1785-1827.* Newark: University of Delaware Press, 1980.

Taylor, Alan. *William Cooper's Town: Power and Persuasion on the Frontier of the Early American Republic.* New York: Alfred A. Knopf, 1995.

Thomas, Evan. *John Paul Jones: Sailor, Hero, Father of the American Navy.* New York: Simon and Schuster, 2003.

Todorich, Charles. *The Spirited Years: A History of the Antebellum Naval Academy.* Annapolis: Naval Institute Press, 1984.

Tucker, Robert W., and David C. Hendrickson. *Empire of Liberty: The Statecraft of Thomas Jefferson.* New York: Oxford University Press, 1990.

Tucker, Spencer C. *Andrew Foote: Civil War Admiral on Western Waters.* Annapolis: Naval Institute Press, 2000.

U.S. Military Academy. *The Centennial of the United States Military Academy at West Point, New York, 1802-1902.* 2 vols. Washington, D.C.: Government Printing Office, 1904.

Valle, James E. *Rocks and Shoals: Order and Discipline in the Old Navy, 1800-1861.* Annapolis: Naval Institute Press, 1980.

Van de Water, Frederic F. *The Captain Called It Mutiny.* New York: Ives Washburn, 1954.

Waldstreicher, David. *In the Midst of Perpetual Fetes: The Making of American Nationalism, 1776-1820.* Chapel Hill: University of North Carolina Press, 1997.

Ward, John William. *Andrew Jackson: Symbol for an Age.* New York: Oxford University Press, 1955.

Watson, Harry L. *Liberty and Power: The Politics of Jacksonian America.* New York: Hill and Wang, 1990.

Watts, Steven. *The Republic Reborn: War and the Making of Liberal America, 1790-1820.* Baltimore: Johns Hopkins University Press, 1987.

Weber, Gustavus A. *The Naval Observatory: Its History, Activities, and Organization.* Baltimore: Johns Hopkins Press, 1926. Reprint, New York: AMS Press, 1974.

Wells, Jonathan Daniel. *The Origins of the Southern Middle Class, 1800-1861.* Chapel Hill: University of North Carolina Press, 2004.

Welter, Rush. *The Mind of America, 1820-1860.* New York: Columbia University Press, 1975.

White, Leonard D. *The Jacksonians: A Study in Administrative History, 1829-1861.* New York: Macmillan, 1963.

———. *The Jeffersonians: A Study in Administrative History, 1801-1829.* New York: Macmillan, 1951.

Williams, Frances Leigh. *Matthew Fontaine Maury: Scientist of the Sea*. New Brunswick, N.J.: Rutgers University Press, 1963.

Wood, Gordon S. *The Radicalism of the American Revolution*. New York: Alfred A. Knopf, 1992.

ARTICLES

Allin, Lawrence C. "Abel Parker Upshur and the Dignity of Discipline." *Naval War College Review* 22 (June 1970): 85–91.

Bogle, Lori Lyn, and Joel I. Holwitt. "The Best Quote Jones Never Wrote." *Naval History* 18 (April 2004): 18–23.

Brown, F. M. "A Half Century of Frustration: A Study of the Failure of Naval Academy Legislation between 1800 and 1845." *U.S. Naval Institute Proceedings* 80 (June 1954): 631–35.

De Christofaro, S. "The Naval Lyceum." *U.S. Naval Institute Proceedings* 77 (August 1951): 869–73.

Drury, C. M. "Famous Chaplain Teachers of Midshipmen, 1800–1845." *U.S. Naval Institute Proceedings* 72 (May 1946): 681–89.

Eckert, Edward K. "William Jones: Mr. Madison's Secretary of the Navy." *Pennsylvania Magazine of History and Biography* 96 (April 1972): 167–82.

Ellis, George E. "Remarks on the Death of George Bancroft." *Proceedings of the Massachusetts Historical Society*, 2nd ser., 6 (February 1891): 295–300.

Elson, Ruth Miller. "American Schoolbooks and 'Culture' in the Nineteenth Century." *Mississippi Valley Historical Review* 46 (December 1959): 411–34.

Fiebeger, Gustav Joseph. "Sylvanus Thayer." In *Dictionary of American Biography*, ed. Dumas Malone, 18:410–11. New York: Charles Scribner's Sons, 1936.

Heitzmann, Wm. Ray. "In-Service Naval Officer Education in the Nineteenth Century: Voluntary Commitment to Reform." *American Neptune* 39 (April 1979): 109–25.

Hunt, Livingston. "The Attempted Mutiny on the U.S. Brig *Somers*." *U.S. Naval Institute Proceedings* 51 (November 1925): 2062–2100.

Langley, Harold D. "Robert Y. Hayne and the Navy." *South Carolina Historical Magazine* 82 (October 1981): 311–20.

Lewis, Charles Lee, Henry Francis Sturdy, and Louis Harrison Bolander. "The First Academic Staff." *U.S. Naval Institute Proceedings* 61 (October 1935): 1389–1403.

Littlehales, G. W. "William Chauvenet and the United States Naval Academy." *U.S. Naval Institute Proceedings* 31 (September 1905): 605–12.

Paullin, Charles O. "Beginnings of the United States Naval Academy." *U.S. Naval Institute Proceedings* 50 (February 1924): 173–94.

———. "Dueling in the Old Navy." *U.S. Naval Institute Proceedings* 35 (December 1909): 1155–97.

Potter, David M. "The Historian's Use of Nationalism and Vice Versa." *American Historical Review* 67 (July 1962): 924–50.

Prendergast, William B. "The Navy and Civil Liberty." *U.S. Naval Institute Proceedings* 74 (October 1948): 1263–67.

Smith, Geoffrey Sutton. "The Navy before Darwinism: Science, Exploration, and Diplomacy in Antebellum America." *American Quarterly* 28 (Spring 1976): 41–55.

Solis, Gary. "Duty, Honor, Country and *Semper Fidelis*." *Naval History* 17 (October 2003): 44–47.

Sturdy, Henry Francis. "The Establishment of the Naval School at Annapolis." *U.S. Naval Institute Proceedings* 72 (April 1946, Part II): 1–17.

———. "The Founding of the Naval Academy by Bancroft and Buchanan." *U.S. Naval Institute Proceedings* 61 (October 1935): 1367–85.

DISSERTATIONS AND OTHER UNPUBLISHED MATERIALS

Anderson, William Gary. "John Adams and the Creation of the American Navy." Ph.D. diss., State University of New York at Stony Brook, 1975.

Burr, Henry L. "Education in the Early Navy." Ed.D. diss., Temple University, 1939.

Denton, Edgar, III. "The Formative Years of the United States Military Academy, 1775–1833." Ph.D. diss., Syracuse University, 1964.

Egan, Hugh McKeever. "Gentlemen-Sailors: The First-Person Sea Narratives of Dana, Cooper, and Melville." Ph.D. diss., University of Iowa, 1983.

Ford, Thomas G. "History of the United States Naval Academy." Manuscript, Nimitz Library, U.S. Naval Academy, [1887].

Green, Jennifer R. "Books and Bayonets: Class and Culture in Antebellum Military Academies." Ph.D. diss., Boston University, 2002.

Hart, Casper P. "Founding of the United States Naval Academy." M.A. thesis, Columbia University, [1937].

Henrich, Joseph G. "The Triumph of Ideology: The Jeffersonians and the Navy, 1779–1807." Ph.D. diss., Duke University, 1971.

Hunter, Mark C. "With the Propriety and Decorum Which Characterize the Society of Gentlemen: The United States Naval Academy and Its Youth, 1845–1861." M.A. thesis, Memorial University of Newfoundland, 1999.

Leeman, William Paul. "The Long Road to Annapolis: The Naval Academy Debate and Emerging Nationalism in the United States, 1775–1845." Ph.D. diss., Boston University, 2006.

Madison, Robert D. "Cooper, Bancroft, and the Voorhees Court-Martial." Conference paper, 1995.

Molloy, Peter Michael. "Technical Education and the Young Republic: West Point as America's École Polytechnique, 1802–1833." Ph.D. diss., Brown University, 1975.

Powers, Stephen T. "The Decline and Extinction of American Naval Power, 1781–1787." Ph.D. diss., University of Notre Dame, 1965.

Steele, Brian Douglas. "Thomas Jefferson and the Making of an American Nationalism." Ph.D. diss., University of North Carolina at Chapel Hill, 2003.

Watson, Samuel J. "Professionalism, Social Attitudes, and Civil-Military Accountability in the United States Army Officer Corps, 1815–1846." Ph.D. diss., Rice University, 1996.

INDEX

Spencer, John C., 172–73, 179, 181, 263 (n. 36)

Spencer, Philip: troubled past of, 172–73; as discipline problem on *Somers*, 174; alleged mutiny plot by, 174–77, 180; execution of, 177; discussion of, 178–79, 181–82, 186, 189, 190–91

Springfield, Mass., 25, 79

Standish (naval tug), 231

State Department, U.S., 8, 103

Steam engineering, 7, 71, 140–41, 149, 151, 157, 218

Steerage, 56

Steuben, Baron von, 22, 24

Stewart, Charles (naval officer), 49, 66, 72, 150, 160, 191

Stewart, Charles S. (chaplain), 133

Stockton, Robert F., 54, 60, 62, 65

Stoddert, Benjamin, 38, 51

Storrs, Henry, 88

Strong, George Templeton, 179, 183

Sturgis, William, 182–83

Sumner, Charles, 182

Swift, Joseph G., 114

Temperance movement, 221–22

Thayer, Sylvanus: as superintendent of U.S. Military Academy, 9, 74–80, 99, 109–10, 114, 159, 203; views on education, 9, 75–76; background of, 74–75; character traits of, 75; criticism of, 112, 114–16

Thompson, Robert, 71

Thompson, Smith, 82–83, 99

Tingey, Thomas, 57, 72

Tocqueville, Alexis de, 4

Tripoli, 29, 41, 66–67, 72

Truxtun, Thomas, 31, 34, 45, 48, 52, 61, 65, 70, 246 (n. 37)

Tucker, Samuel, 39

Tyler, John, 149, 151–52, 154, 181, 198

United Service Journal, 132

United States (frigate), 32, 33, 56, 213

U.S. Army: and military education, 5, 69; expansion during Quasi-War, 33, 34, 36; Federalist influence in, 47; in War of 1812, 69, 72–73, 94, 109; during age of Jackson, 110, 119; general officers in, 151; dueling in, 168, 202

U.S. Exploring Expedition, 104, 165–66

U.S. Marine Band, 221

U.S. Marine Corps: creation of, 34; duties on board U.S. Navy ships, 34, 174; proposed expansion of, 151, 156; and U.S. Naval Academy, 237

U.S. Military Academy (West Point): rivalry with U.S. Naval Academy, 1; establishment of, 5, 41–42, 47; and American acceptance of professional officers, 9; reforms under Sylvanus Thayer, 9, 74–79, 99, 159; opposition to, 9, 79–80, 92, 101, 110–22, 149, 155, 199, 226; as model for U.S. Naval Academy, 9, 203–4, 207, 215, 216, 218, 223, 226–27; proposed expansion and relocation of, 43–45; proposed enrollment of midshipmen at, 44, 82–83, 108; and War of 1812, 69; method of instruction at, 75–76, 78, 218; as commissioning source for U.S. Army, 79; as engineering school, 79–80, 99, 119, 122–23; monopoly over army officer commissions, 79, 115, 118–19; influence on naval academy debate, 80, 84, 88, 91, 92, 94–95, 101, 106–7, 135–36, 156, 160–61, 191; Andrew Jackson's opinion of, 110; elitism at, 111, 115–19, 153, 155; as model for state and private military academies, 113–14, 123–24, 256 (n. 30); middle-class origins of cadets, 117; selection of cadets, 117–18, 122; as meritocracy, 117–18, 235; early resignations of graduates from army, 119; and manhood ideal, 120–22; and character development of cadets, 120–22, 190–91, 192, 193; as professional and cultural center for U.S. Army, 129–30, 237; and increased professionalism in U.S. Army, 130, 145, 159; and education of U.S. Marine Corps officers, 148, 259 (n. 53); and Mexican War, 226

U.S. Naval Academy (Annapolis): portrayal by Hollywood, 1; establishment of, 1, 203–15, 223–24, 229; alumni of, 1–2, 236; as reflection of American society, 2; purpose of, 8–9, 10, 209–11, 218–19, 220, 234; character development at, 8–9, 210–11, 218, 219, 226, 235; selection of site for, 204–6; curriculum of, 212, 214–15, 226–27, 240; first faculty of, 213–14; midshipmen at, 215, 216–29, 234–36; method of